Seamanship

Alfred Henry Alston

RCH."

ver.

and other
Illu... n the con-

CAPTAIN ALSTON'S

SEAMANSHIP.

NEW EDITION,

REVISED AND ENLARGED BY

COMMANDER R. H. HARRIS, R.N.;

WITH A TREATISE ON

NAUTICAL SURVEYING,

BY

STAFF-COMMANDER MAY,

F.R.G.S;

ALSO,

INSTRUCTIONS FOR OFFICERS OF THE MERCHANT SERVICE,

By W. H. ROSSER.

𝕬ith 𝕿wo 𝕳undred 𝕴llustrations.

Portsmouth.
GRIFFIN & Co., 2, THE HARD,

London.
SIMPKIN MARSHALL & Co.
POTTER, POULTRY.   IMRAY & SON, MINORIES.
NEW YORK—WILEY & SON.
1871.

GRIFFIN & Co., PRINTERS AND PUBLISHERS, THE HARD, PORTSEA.

TO

THE JUNIOR OFFICER'S OF THE NAVY,

This Work,

WRITTEN FOR THEIR GUIDANCE,

IS INSCRIBED BY

THE AUTHOR.

CONTENTS.

SECTION II.—AT SEA.

SECTION III.—ON GENERAL SERVICE.

PART III.

PREFACE TO SECOND EDITION.

BY COMMANDER R. H. HARRIS, R.N.

IT will, I believe, be generally acknowledged that the few years which have elapsed since the first publication of this book have seen not only greater, but far more distinct changes in the build and rig of Her Majesty's ships than at any previous time in the history of the service since Alfred the Great organized his fleet : and, indeed, now are these changes going on with such rapidity, that the fighting ship of the day (with her many inches of armour and powerful battery) is hardly commissioned, before a ship of so much the greater offensive and defensive power is designed, which would, according to all reasonable calculations, take or sink the former in half-an-hour.

In like manner, though perhaps in a less degree, are continual and ever varying changes being made in the rigging and ordinary fittings of the *hull*, to suit the peculiar form and distinctive features of each new description of vessel. Having this difficulty to deal with, it will be seen that I have found it impossible to notice all the novel

b

fittings which are to be seen in individual vessels, though I have endeavoured to select the more important of them and those most likely to be permanently adopted.

In the revision of this work—while introducing much that is new,—I have of necessity been obliged to omit many things that have become obsolete, and to modify other things to meet the custom or requirements of the present day. I have adhered as closely as possible to the original plan of publication adopted by my friend, and old instructor the Author; but I regard *steam* as the motive power, and *sail* as the useful auxilliary only, for a man-of-war.

The subjects now required to be attained before an embryo can hope to be a proficient naval officer are so multifarious, and the general and steadily increasing use of steam power is rendering opportunities of acquiring a practical knowledge of Seamanship so scarce, that it is very certain books will become of more importance than ever as vehicles of instruction, to assist officers in obtaining that sound knowledge of their profession, which, combined with valour, under God's providence, has made the British Navy renowned in the annals of the world.

R. H. HARRIS, COMMANDER, R.N.

January, 1871.

INTRODUCTION TO FIRST EDITION.

BY CAPTAIN ALSTON, R.N.

———◆◆———

ALTHOUGH we are living in what may be called the Steam era, and our Navy is a Steam Navy, I have in this work wholly excluded the consideration of Steam power, as, owing to the great cost of coal, and the impossibility of providing stowage for it except to a limited extent, the application of Steam power for ordinary purposes must be strictly auxilliary and subordinate, and its employment on general service the exception and not the rule. In bad weather the old order of things will re-assert its supremacy, and any lengthened absence from port, or derangement of machinery, must always render the use of canvas imperative.

Thus, then, the study and practice of seamanship are happily not yet a work of supererogation. If Britannia be destined still " to rule the waves," it must be by the help of seamen as well qualified as those who won that supremacy for her; and we trust that the day is far distant, when her trident shall be delivered into the keeping of mere artillerists and mechanical precisians.

The chapter on nautical surveying is intended for the use of those officers, who not having had any experience in surveying operations may unexpectedly find themselves in a situation where such work is expected from them ; and will be found to embrace every useful application of the subject that can possibly be required for common purposes.

The interrogatory form has been adopted in order to bring prominently into view such particulars as might escape the notice of the student in a continuous composition, and the questions being separated from the explanatory part of the work will enable those who feel desirous of improving themselves to *write out* their own methods and solutions, without having mine thrust before their eyes, and thus to think and judge for themselves. It has not been my object to enter into the whole details of a ship's equipment—to state how *all* the ropes are led, nor how *everything* is fitted, as such I conceive would have a mischievous tendency by becoming subservient to the wants of the indolent and unobserving ; my endeavours have been thus purposely limited by an earnest desire to give a helping hand to such as are willing to assist themselves, and to render the various subjects treated of clear to those who are anxious to learn, and who will take the necessary trouble to understand them. Probably my treatment of some matters will prove to be faulty, and, as I am very desirous to remedy such inaccuracy by correction in a future edition, I shall be grateful to any one who will take the trouble of pointing out any errors they may detect, by communicating with me on the subject, through the publishers.

I may indulge the hope that, by the presence of this volume in the gun-room, useful discussion will be promoted, and consequently an increased interest be taken by young officers in their professional duties, and I trust, moreover, that none of my readers will be influenced by the silly outcry against "talking shop," which, of late years, it has been the fashion of young gentlemen to denounce. For such, I do not write ; but, on the other hand, the more forcibly would I urge upon those who are desirous of excelling in their profession, the duty of giving to it a hearty acceptance, and a resolute attention, for it is a service that may worthily claim the exercise of the most vigorous qualities, both physical and intellectual. Therefore, I would say to young officers individually,—master your duties as soon as you are able ; be up to your work on all points within your reach, so that you may be relieved from all those doubts and anxieties which ignorance and hesitation are sure to produce. If true to your calling you cannot be too hopeful, and sooner or later you will meet with opportunities which, if you have the talent to take advantage of them, will lead to the realization of every reasonable desire. Very admirable and worthy of attention is the advice of Sir Walter Scott upon this point :—" I have rarely seen," he says, "that a man who conscientiously devoted himself to the studies and duties of *any* profession, and did not omit to take fair and honourable opportunities of offering himself to notice, when such presented themselves, has not at length got forward. The mischance of those who fall behind, though flung upon fortune, more frequently arises from want of skill and perseverance. Life is like a game at cards ; our hands are alternately good or bad, and the whole seems at first glance to depend on mere chance. But it is not so, for in the long run the skill of the player predominates over the casualties of the game. Therefore, do not be discouraged with the prospect before you, but ply your studies hard, and qualify yourself to receive fortune when she comes your way."

Lord Dundonald, the equal of Nelson in valour and in genius, when commander-in-chief of the Chilian navy, had to take off his coat, and with his own hands mend the pumps, on an occasion when the water was gaining on the ship, and his carpenter was incompetent to repair them. And as I hold that "a good mariner ought to have all knowledge of carnal and worldly cunning, even to tailoring and shoe-making, that he may be able to turn his hand to whatsoever may hap," so I have explained how scrubbing-brushes and sennit hats are made, and many other things which no officer should consider it above his duty to be well acquainted with. They who have seen seamen and soldiers thrown together upon their own resources, and have contrasted the working of their respective systems, will be able to appreciate the importance of this principle in the education of officers.

Forebodings of great wars, every now and then, fill with anxiety the minds of all thinking men.   We feel convinced of the terrible necessity which exists for preparing for the worst, and intimately as this important question affects us, I would say something to my young readers upon it, in order to direct them to the only true principles upon which their efforts, should they be called for, can successfully be based.   More particularly am I desirous of doing so here, as the majority of works of a preceptive character that are put into their hands seem to overlook the fact that, to develop the military faculty, and to render them supreme in *War* is the most immediate object of their training.   Let gentlemen of the Navy bear in mind that the ship in which they sail is called a man-of-war ; that they and the crew are continually exercised in cutlass, gun, and rifle practice, and all other modes of fighting—and for this one purpose surely, that they may be able to fight.   The maintenance of peace, which should be the ultimate object of our efforts, can only be ensured, as all experience proves, by our being in constant readiness in war.   Keeping this in view, we may then, and only then, turn our thoughts to the duties required of us in time of peace ; which, to our men, consist in doing as we would be done by ; cordially recognizing and providing for those capacities for enjoyment which find expression in such common things as " beer and skittles," but which nature will resist every attempt to repress ; treating every man as honest until he prove himself a rogue ; and in all things ruling ourselves and them as becometh good, wise, and temperate Christian gentlemen ; to become which should satisfy the ambition, and be honour enough for any man.—Furthermore, by our influence and example to promote the cause of law, order, commerce—and last, but not least, of Christianity on foreign stations ; all of which is just as noble as fighting— and nobler if you will think, because it obtains the ends of fighting without the ugly means.

Meanwhile, until this responsibility of government falls upon you, be content to learn obedience 'chiefly ; for the powers that be are ordained of God.   Do your daily work, as unto God, and not unto man only ; and remember with George Herbert—

> " Who sweeps a room, but for Thy sake,
>   Makes it, and the sweeper, fine."

If we should be called upon to resort to war in order to keep the peace, or "keep the seas" as it was called, God send you the ancient righteous spirit which animated pre-eminently the old Judæan warriors. No thought for their life took they, nor for aught but the stern work before them : all that concerned them to do or to think was comprised in two short sentences : " Let us behave ourselves valiantly for our people, and for the cities of our God : and let the Lord do that which is good in His sight." This was the pith of their sturdy creed in the days of their glory, when all invincible, they were led to battle by David, "the anointed of God." Those long lists of "mighty" and "most honorable" men, who won their cross of valour three thousand years ago, were written for our learning, and have been preserved as incentives to us when the chivalrous feeling waxes cold within us ; and you cannot, indeed, as a man bred to arms, read the simple record which brings those old-world heroes before us, without feeling the stronger and the better for it ; bewaring, though, lest we should cherish cruelty, ferocity, or pride thereby, to end as those very Jews did, in being hateful and haters of all mankind, believing that God hated every one but them, till the heathen Roman empire had to rise and crush them, as a dehumanized nuisance to the world.

In the quiet time of peace you will not feel the full force of this admonition, nor appreciate the need for storing your mind with such examples against a darker day ; but rely upon it that the hour comes in every man's experience, when he feels the deep want of some precedent which he can unhesitatingly follow and trust to : and you, when you come to face death in the dread work of war (in which we know not how soon we may be involved), will feel your heart lightened, your reason strengthened, and your arm guided by unseen hands, if as an amulet you carrry with you the unchangeable truth, taught in these ancient chronicles. These scriptures if they have any meaning at all for us, are meant to furnish the examples needed to form the character of a man whose occupation in life it is in the present day to fight the Queen's enemies ; and the same Spirit of God, who so strengthened their hearts, and "taught their hands to war and their fingers to fight," caused their histories to be written as a pledge and an assurance of His mighty aid to men who, in His strength, go forth, fulfilling a noble duty, to fight for their country, Queen, religion, and honour, against the enemy, be he who he may.

Though distorted, this teaching was not forgotten in the age of chivalry, at the time when,—

> "Our stout crusading fathers
> Fought and died for God, and not for gold."

Above all, it was not forgotten by the sea-captains of the Elizabethan era, and the scarcely less glorious one of the Commonwealth, who fought and conquered, and wrought deeds of daring beyond belief, with the "praises of God in their mouth, and a two-edged sword in their hands." "Men of heroic courage, marine worthies, beyond all names of worthinesse," teach this faithless age the secret of your greatness! Of him whose motto was, "multare vel timere sperno," we have but a glimpse,—the raging storm, the puny vessel, the open book, and the cheering cry, when the sea was "breaking short and pyramid-wise,"—"We are as near to heaven by sea as by land." "We cannot doubt the book which Sir Humphrey Gilbert, "giving forth signs of joy," read that afternoon before they foundered, on the deck of his ten-ton "frigate." There lay the secret, the "secret of the Lord," which all the noble-hearted men of that day knew; and they were no lachrymose devotees, but bold, uncompromising, resolute men, who feared God, but who feared neither man nor devil besides. Read Barrow's "Life of Drake," young gentlemen, and that of Blake, by Hepworth Dixon; and if you have any worthy longings in your hearts, you will there find abundant encouragement to sustain them, and a high-souled example to direct them.

To give you an insight into the character of men of this stamp, I cannot do better than epitomize the life of Drake :—

This renowned Englishman first distinguished himself in Hawkins's expedition to the West Indies in 1567, when they took Rio de Hacha by storm, on the Spaniards refusing to trade; and then, sailing on to San Juan d'Ulloa, entered the port, in which lay twelve ships, having on board £200,000 in gold and silver, but which Hawkins forbore to touch, as we were then at peace with Spain. The extraordinary sequel is well known, and it shows the dread in which the English name must have then been held. A Spanish fleet of thirteen great ships appeared off the port ; Hawkins, who had only four ships with him, lying at the time, be it remembered, in a Spanish harbour, protected by a battery of brass guns, with the twelve ships of the enemy before mentioned, had the boldness to refuse an entrance to the Spanish fleet until they had promised to maintain peace, and allow him, during his stay, to keep possession of the island on which the battery was placed. Hostages were exchanged, and, we are told, "at the end of three days the Spanish fleete entered the port, the ships saluting one another, as the manner of the sea doth require." While thus "promising great amitie on all sides, the faithlesse Spanyards presentli brought a great hulk,' moored her alongside the "Minion," and in the night filled her with men ; and when everything was prepared, surprised the English. At a given signal, 300 men were poured into the "Minion ;" " whereat our generall (Hawkins) with a loude and fierce voyce called unto us saying, 'God and Saint George! upon those traiterous villaines, and rescue the " Minion," on which he, with his men, leaped on board and drove out the Spaniards. The fight then became general, and continued until night. The "Jesus of Lubeck," Hawkins's ship, having her masts shot away, and being "wonderfully pierced with shotte," they were obliged to abandon ; and the Spanish admiral being supposed to be sunk, the vice-admiral burnt, and some other ships destroyed, they made their escape with their only two remaining ships, one of which was Drake's fifty-ton bark, the "Judith ;" and after undergoing great hardships, returned to England.

Having fitted out *two small ships*, Drake, on Whitsun eve, 1572, "set saile from out of the Sound of Plymouth with intent to land at Nombre de Dios"—then the great storehouse and shipping place for all the gold and silver collected in Mexico and Peru. Before sailing, he had provided himself with "three daintie pinnaces, made in Plimouth, taken asonder all in pieces and stowed aboard." These he set up at Santa Martha, where he left the ships, and with seventy-three men started for the Spanish settlement. Stealing upon Nombre de Dois at night, he surprised the town, marched to the governor's house, the door of which was open, and a light burning on the stairs ; by the light they saw a vast heap of silver piled against the wall, as nearly as they could guess, seventy feet in length, ten in breadth, and twelve in height. Soon after landing, Drake had received a severe wound, but which he concealed for some time, "knowing, if the general's heart stoops, the men's will fail ; and that if so bright an opportunity once setteth, it seldom riseth again." However, he fainted from loss of blood, and was carried down to the boats. " Divers of his men, besides himself, were wounded, though but one, and be a trumpeter, slain. Many of them got good booty before they left the place. But the wines in a Spanish ship, which they found in the harbour, they took along with them for the relief of their captain and themselves. They carried off their prize to an island, which they called the Island of Victuals, where they stayed two days to cure their wounded men, and refresh themselves in the gardens they found there, abounding with all sorts of roots, fruits, poultry, and other fowls no less strange than delicate." Having taken several prizes, he took with him eighteen English and thirty Indians, and set out by land for Panama. On his way he ascended a "goolie and great high tree," and clearly discerned the great Pacific Ocean, whereupon, falling down there upon his knees, he besought God " to give him life, and leave, once to sail an English ship in those seas," and, adds the historian, "he was heard in what he asked, as will hereafter appear." After some daring attempts with a mere handful of men to intercept the gold trains in their route to the coast, he resolved to return, and arrived at Plymouth on Sunday, the 9th of August, 1573. The news of Drake's arrival being taken into church, all ran out "to see the evidence of God's love and blessing towards our gracious Queene and countrey, by the fruite of our captaine's labour and successe. SOLI DEO GLORIA."

The next voyage was that in which he, the first of Englishmen, "ploughed a furrow round the world." With five vessels, the largest of which was his own—the " Pelican" of 100 tons, he sailed out of Plymouth Sound, December 13, 1577. On their arrival at Port St. Julian, Patagonia, Mr. Doughty, one of the gentlemen volunteers, was, as Camden, the oldest and most respectable of all Drake's historians, relates, "called to his trial for raising a mutiny in the fleet, found guilty by twelve men, after the English manner, and condemned to death, which he suffered undauntedly, being beheaded, having first received the holy communion with Drake." Hakluyt, Drake's contemporary, gives a similar account, and tells how, after the execution, Drake "made divers speeches to the whole company, persuading us to unity, obedience, love, and regard of our voyage ; and for the better confirmation thereof, willed every man the next Sunday following to prepare himself to receive the communion, as Christian brethren and friends ought to do, which was done in very reverent sort, and so with good contentment every man went about his business." Thus, with solemn ordinances, and in Christian charity, this man, who is now spoken of by some as a ferocious buccaneer, "organized on that wild shore, a judgment-hall more grand and awful than any most elaborate law court, with its ermine and black cap, and robes of ceremony for mind as well as body ; but which is not to be reconciled with the pirate theory, which we may as well henceforth put away from us."

After getting through the straits of Magelhuns, he parted from all his squadron in various gales, and coasting along, reaching Callao alone, where he found thirty ships of the enemy lying : all of which he deliberately searched. Out of one they took 1,500 bars of silver. He there received intelligence, and went in chase of the " Cacafuego," termed " the great glory of the South Sea " —boarding a brigantine on his way, out of which he took eighty pounds weight of gold, and some emeralds. On coming up with the " Cacafuego," he boarded and carried her. Besides a large quantity of pearls and precious stones, they took out of her eighty pounds weight of gold, thirteen chests of coined silver, and rough silver enough to ballast a ship. He at last sailed away westward, passed the Celebes without accident, but shortly afterwards struck on a rocky shoal. The water was so deep on either side as to render it impossible to lay an anchor out to heave off by, so the ship's company were summoned to prayers—"commending ourselves into the merciful hands of our most gracious God; for this purpose we presently fell prostrate, and with joined prayers sent up to the throne of grace, humbly besought Almighty God to extend his mercy unto us in his son Christ Jesus." This done, they set to work to lighten the ship, and at low water she slid off the ledge of the rock, " and it pleased God that the wind, formerly their mortal enemy, became their friend."

On the 26th of September, 1580, "we safely," says the narrative, "with joyful minds and thankful hearts to God, arrived at Plimouth, the place of our first setting forth, after we had spent two years, ten months, and some odd days beside, in seeing the wonders of the Lord in the deep, in discerning so many admirable things, in going through with so many strange adventures, in escaping out of so many dangers, aud overcoming so many difficulties, in this our encompassing of this nether globe, and passing round about the world.

> Soli rerum maximarum Effectori,
> Soli totius mundi Gubernatori,
> Soli suorum Conservatori,
> Soli Deo sit semper gloria."

Of Drake's raid on the West Indies, and the taking of St. Domingo and Carthagena; of his expedition to Cadiz, which he termed " singeing the king of Spain's beard ;"—of his services in the defeat of the " Invincible Armada," against which he was second in command ;—and, of his expeditions to Corunna, and to the Spanish colonies, you must read for yourselves; but, as an example of how he, whose "name was a terror to the French, Spanyard, Portugall, and Indians," was wont on all occasions to speak of his dependence upon God, I must take leave to quote a passage from one of his letters to Sir Francis Walsingham, Secretary of State, during the Cadiz expedition. After reporting the successful result of " dyvers combatts with the Spanyards and Portyugalls," he says, "God mak us all thanckfull agayne and agayne that we have, althowghe it be littell, mad a begennyng upon the cost of Spayne. If we can thorowghly beleve that this which we dow is in the defence of our relygyon and contrye, no doubt but our mercyfull God for his Christ, our Savyour's sake, is abell, and will geve us victory, althowghe our sennes be reed. God geve us grace we may feare hym, and daylly to call upon hym, so shall nether Sattan, nor his menesters prevayell agaynst us."

This living faith in a living, personal God, and belief in an actual personal devil, shows itself everywhere in him, equally with the other men of that period. Their fuller acquaintance you may cultivate at your leisure in Barrow's " Naval Worthies," and in the publications of the Hakluyt Society, where their imperishable actions lie recorded "for the stirring up of heroick spirits to benefit their countrie, and eternize their names by like noble attempts."

Concerning lion-hearted Sir Richard Grenville you will find something hereafter. Of Sir Martin Frobisher, judge by the following articles in the regulations drawn up by him for his third voyage in 1578 :—

"Art. 1.—*Imprimis.* To banishe swearing, dice, cards-playing, and all filthie talk, and to serve God twice a daie with the ordinarie service, usuall in the Church of England ; and to clear the glasse everie nighte, according to the oulde order of England.

"Art. 8.—If any man in the fleete come upon another in the nighte, and haile his fellowe, knowinge him not, he shall give him this watche worde, 'Before the world was God ;' the other shall answer, if he be one of our fleete, 'After God came Christ, his sonne.' Soe that if any be found amongst us, not of our own companie, he that firste descrieth any such saile or sailer shall give warning to the Admyrall."

Pause as you read these instructions of Sir John Hawkins to one of his little squadrons ; mark the shrewd wisdom, and rare tenderness withal, that these few words display ; and the contrast they present to the hard materialism of this our intellectual age. "Keep good company ; beware of fire ; serve God daily ; and love one another."

The regulations for Luke Fox's voyage commence thus : "For as much as the good success and prosperity of every action doth consist in the due service and glorifying of God, knowing that not only our being and preservation, but the prosperity of all our actions and enterprises do immediately depend on his Almighty goodness and mercy, it is provided—

"First. That all the company, as well as officers and others, shall duly repair every day twice at the call of the bell to hear public prayers to be read, such as are authorized by the Church, and that in a godly and devout manner, as good Christians ought."

Without citing any further instances, it will be seen what a wholeness there was in the character of our warlike ancestors ; and, notwithstanding their manifold temptations, how near to the gates of heaven they really lived. Their greatness we may rest assured we shall never reach, until we condescend to walk in the same relation to God as they did, and have grace to understand, and sense to turn to practical use the fact of all facts, that the Son of God died for all, that they which live should not henceforth live unto themselves, but unto Him who died for them, and rose again. The rejection or neglect of this is at the root of all the failures and misfortunes of men and nations ; and the reception of, and conformity to it must form the basis of all our attempts to do our work in life well, and the ground of all our hopes of being kept from going wrong, and of having the wit to do the right thing, on every occasion, of every day.'

When we listen to the experiences of men of action ; such as Drake, Davis, and others of that stamp, who speak with knowledge, *of* a thing, instead of with knowledge *about* it, they come with an impressiveness such as is attached to no other utterances ; so that, if what they are meant to teach us fall dead upon our ears, neither should we believe if—any greater testimony were conceivable or possible. By their trust in God, and omission of no prudent means for insuring success, they made their age the heroic age of England, and endued it with imperishable life and beauty. They trusted in God, and God fought for them, and, to their minds, as palpably as on that day when He hearkened to the voice of a man : "Sun, stand thou still upon Gibeon ; and thou, moon, in the valley of Ajalon." In more than mortal strength Grenville and his hundred Englishmen, in a single ship, deliberately waited for, and fought for fifteen hours a fleet of fifty sail, manned by above ten thousand Spaniards. "As thy days, so shall thy strength be,"—this he believed who, careful for nothing, performed that desperate act of valour, which, even in those days, filled the world with wonder and astonishment. And when, shot through and through, dying among Spaniards, he cried out,—"Here die I, Richard Grenville, with a joyful and quiet mind," he found God's grace to be, even in his last extremity, sufficient for him.

"Of such stuff," writes Froude, the historian of the Tudors, "were the early English navigators ; we are reaping the magnificent harvest of their great heroism ; and we may see once more in their history, and in what has arisen out of it, that on these deep moral foundations, and on none others, enduring prosperities, of what kind soever, politic or religious, material or spiritual, are alone in this divinely-governed world permitted to base themselves and grow. Wherever we find them they are still the same,—in the courts of Japan or of China, fighting Spaniards in the Pacific or prisoners among the Algerines, founding colonies which by-and-by were to grow into enormous trans-atlantic republics, or exploring in crazy pinnaces the fierce latitudes of the polar seas, they are the same indomitable, God-fearing men, whose life was one great liturgy. 'The ice was strong, but God was stronger,' says one of Frobisher's men, after grinding a night and a day among the icebergs, not waiting for God to come down and split them, but toiling through the long hours, himself and the rest fending off the vessel with poles and planks, with death glaring at them out of the ice rocks, and so saving themselves and it. Icebergs were strong, Spaniards were strong, and storms, and corsairs, and rocks, and reefs, which no chart had then noted—they were all strong, but God was stronger, and that was all which they cared to know.* * * They were of a race which has ceased to be. We look round for them and we can hardly believe that the same blood is flowing in our veins. Brave we may still be, and strong, perhaps, as they, but the high moral grace which made bravery and strength so beautiful is departed from us for ever." Let us pray not !

We all hold in a certain loose way that God's favour is—not indispensable exactly, but still at least a furtherance to success. But, weak and stunted as such a faith is, we do not even act up to it, but by force of habit and the devil's influence, attach more importance to gunnery than ever we do to godliness. We have not been so uniformly successful in our late campaigns as to be induced to rely, altogether confidently, upon our own efforts ; and, as Englishmen, we may ask ourselves what place we should hold among the nations, ever eager for our overthrow, if God were to forsake us. We trust to the inherent bravery of our race, forgetting from whom we derive it ; and, because we have hitherto been spared the humiliation to which every other country in Europe has been subjected, we cling to the conceit that with our wealth and our resources, we can continue, unsupported, to brave the world in arms. These extraneous advantages are but contingent on our allegiance to Him from whom we derive them. He who overthrew the ancient empires of the world, and humbled the godless kingdoms and republics of modern times, will, despite our fleets and armies, bring sorrow upon us if we seek not his guidance in all we do. Let us then, as Cromwell bade his Ironsides, "Trust in God, and keep our powder dry;" make trust in God our first consideration, and then gunnery and seamanship, skill to acquire them, courage to apply them, and all needful things will be added thereto.

The fear of *risk*, and the dread of *responsibility*, paralyzing scruples of modern introduction, will vanish before that faith through which the holy men of old "out of weakness were made strong, waxed valiant in fight, turned to flight the armies of the aliens." Under the influence of this manful spirit (which developed itself in no mere mild amiabilities, but in daring enterprises among icy solitudes, where, as the Arabs say of the desert, "There is nothing but He;" upon unknown seas which led they knew not where, and in constant fight, at all risks, and wherever they could meet with their hated foes), the men of Elizabeth's reign were saved from these appalling bugbears, which are now so terrible to all weak souls. Such *rash* things, too, did they without thinking of the consequences, as would horrify our ancient ladies now-a-days. Overleaping the exact boundaries of duty, their ardent energies admitted no doubts, brooked no hesitation ; and utterly contemning the charge of rashness, which cold unsympathizing minds are ever ready to bring against men whom they cannot understand, went straight to their quest, conscious of right, with a determined, unswerving purpose. They taught the world that valour was the better part of discretion, and the sequel proved that no foe could withstand their *rashness*, nor any hazard prove too formidable for their patriotism. Like a cold shadow, that word "rashness" has fallen on many a noble impulse, and darkened the road to fame. Judged by the common standard, it is a rash thing to take up a burning shell and to hurl it, at the point of explosion, away from the men who lie around it. A supreme and petrifying act of rashness, in this sense, was that committed on the 6th of May, 1801, when Lord Cochrane, in the "Speedy," of fourteen 4-pounders (giving a total broadside of 28 lbs.), attacked the spanish frigate "El Gamo," armed with 32 heavy guns, and, after an hour's cannonade, had the temerity, out of all rule, to board and take her with 50 men against 320 ! The truth is (though I am not attemping to defend the converse), all great actions are open to this charge of rashness. Nothing great is lightly won, or wherein would lie its greatness ? What is termed "the safe course" is so much the easier to follow, that it becomes ungenerous to the last degree to apply the common test of success or failure to a notable, daring, and independent course of action ; yet an exception to these *ex post facto* judgments is rare. If a man succeeds in a perilous enterprise, the world calls it consummate daring, and proclaims him a hero ; but if, whatever be his talents, he meets with unforeseen disaster, his misfortunes are aggravated by the specious charge of inconsiderate rashness, and ever after he is looked upon as little better than a madman. Very frequently emergencies arise, when the discreet precepts of a cautious policy are the most dangerous that can be followed, and when nothing but a bold disregard to mere prudential motives will serve to avert disaster or disgrace. In an energetic warfare great risks must be run, or great things cannot be accomplished. If a line-of-battle ship in a land attack is gallantly and successfully brought into action, with only a few inches water under her keel, all the world is open-mouthed in admiration. But if from the effect of an unseen shot-hole between wind and water, she were to ground, and things to take an ugly turn, what would be the verdict ? Why, that her captain had paid the penalty of his headstrong rashness, and that such men ought not to be intrusted with command. Now this is as mischievous as it is unjust, for men, who would dare anything if assured of being impartially judged upon absolute premises, let slip golden opportunities while balancing between the chances of a doubtful success on the one hand, and of obliquy and censure on the other. Be then prepared for this contingency whenever in after-life you rise to a command. If untrammelled, your natural impulse will probably be the right one. Solicitude for one's own interests is so apt to generate an undue amount of *caution*, that a leaning towards *rashness*, or a contempt of danger, which is its natural equipoise, is indeed little to be dreaded.

Look at Blake, Cromwell's sturdy envoy to the great European powers, who threatened the independence, and provoked the resentment of the young Commonwealth of England. Conspicuous for his godliness, he failed in nothing that he undertook. Though worsted by overwhelming numbers in his second action with Van Tromp, he in two months returned to the charge, and in a desperate engagement, which continued through three long days, gained a great and glorious victory, which broke for ever the dangerous supremacy of Holland.

The prelude to the bombardment of Porto Ferino, which he was compelled to undertake, in order to enforce the restitution of English captives, was a signal made for the performance of divine service in the fleet ; and the result of this God-seeking was that in six months he made the name of Englishmen feared and respected from one end of the Mediterranean to the other.

" Our only comfort is that we have a God to lean upon, although we walk in darkness and see no light," is what he writes in an official letter to the Lord Protector, after describing the wretched condition of his squadron. And in his last letter written in England, addressed to Secretary Thurloe, and dated " aboard the ' Naseby' in St. Helen's Road, March 15th, 1656," after some allusions to certain sudden political transactions, there occurs this passage :—" But we know that God is the Supreme Disposer of all the councils, designs, and confederations in the world ; and we know He is able to order them all for the greater good of His people ; and our trust is that He will do so even for our good also, if we can believe in Him. The Lord help our unbelief, and subdue our hearts to the obedience of His holy will in all things." And so all things worked together for his good, and for the dear old land that sent him forth.

In the Yarmouth church books of 1652, there occur entries which afford an insight into the inner life of Puritan England, and indicate the source from which sprung all the glory and grandeur of her outer life. "This day was spent in seeking God," is an entry that frequently

c

occurs ; and after Blake's temporary defeat by Van Tromp, "on the 7th of December they agreed that on the Thursday following, at ten of the clock, the church should meet to seek God for the navy at sea." How their prayers were answered, let the Dutch admiral, De Witt, tell. "Why," said he in the Assembly of the States, "why should I keep silence any longer? I am here before my sovereigns. I am free to speak ;—and I must say that the English are at present masters both of us and of the seas." Thus the men of England prevailed, because they relied upon the Lord God of their fathers, and the eternal truth was manifested that "blessed is the nation whose God is the Lord."

Against the ports of Santa Crux, where lay moored in a double line the royal galleons of Spain, and against that spiritual despotism which claimed universal dominion over the bodies and souls of men, Blake, in one crowning action, finished the work which God had given him to do. On the morning of that eventful day, April 20, 1657, every man in the English fleet, kneeling down in humble prayer, committed themselves and their cause into God's keeping, in the deadly strife that was awaiting them. Undeterred by the terrific fire that opened upon his ships as they passed, Blake forced the entrance to the harbour, and in six hours silenced the batteries and either sunk or burnt every Spanish ship.

Slowly dying, Blake, after a last visit to Salee, to compel the Moorish corsairs to free their Christian captives, turned his head homewards, and at length arrived off Plymouth. Thousands were assembled to welcome the conqueror home ; but ere the "St. George" had anchored in the Sound, he, in his silent cabin, in the midst of his lion-hearted comrades, had yielded up his soul to God. Precious should be his memory from whatever point we view it, and very serviceable it may also be, if we will only copy him in this, that Lord Clarendon tells us of him ;—that "he despised those rules which had been long in practice, to keep his ships and men out of danger, which had been held in former times a point of great ability and circumspection, as if the principal art in the captain of a ship had been to be sure to come home safe again."

I have thus endeavoured to set before you, at the outset of your career, the examples most worthy of your imitation. To unite the spiritual with the actual is the great problem of life, and they who have acomplished it have performed that for which they were born into the world. The men you have read of solved this problem under circumstances similar to those in which we ourselves may be placed, and the record of their lives must consequently be to us of supreme importance. These remarks you will not therefore consider an inappropriate introduction, I trust, to the study of the work before you ; for until you become ingrained with these principles, as your forefathers were, all the seamanship and science that experience and books can bestow will never make a seaman such as they were, of you or of any British lad. Remember then, that your life's vocation, deliberately chosen, is WAR—War, as I have said, as the means of peace : but still War ; and in singleness of purpose, for England's fame, prepare for the time when the welfare and honour of the service may come to be in your keeping ; that by your skill and valour when that time arrives, and "fortune comes your way," you may revive the spirit, and perpetuate the glory of days that tingle in our hearts, and fill our memories.

December, 1859.

SEAMANSHIP.

SEAMANSHIP,

PART 1.

SECTION 1.

NOTE.—*All Ships before being commissioned are fully rigged by the Dock-yard riggers ; but, Is there not good reason to suppose that in a case of emergency, officers and crew may have to fit out their own ship?——To meet this it is selected as the first subject.*

FITTING OUT.

1. Your sheers are in the water alongside :—get them in, and raise them.

2. Get in, and step the lower masts and bowsprit.

3. Send a whole top over.

4 Send a half-top up.

5. Get a top off.

6. What are used for gantlines?

7. Only one gantline has been rove ; if it unfortunately unreeves, leaving a man at the masthead :—how will you reeve it again ?

8. Cut, and fit a gang of lower rigging.

9. Rig the foremast.

10. Set up the fore rigging.

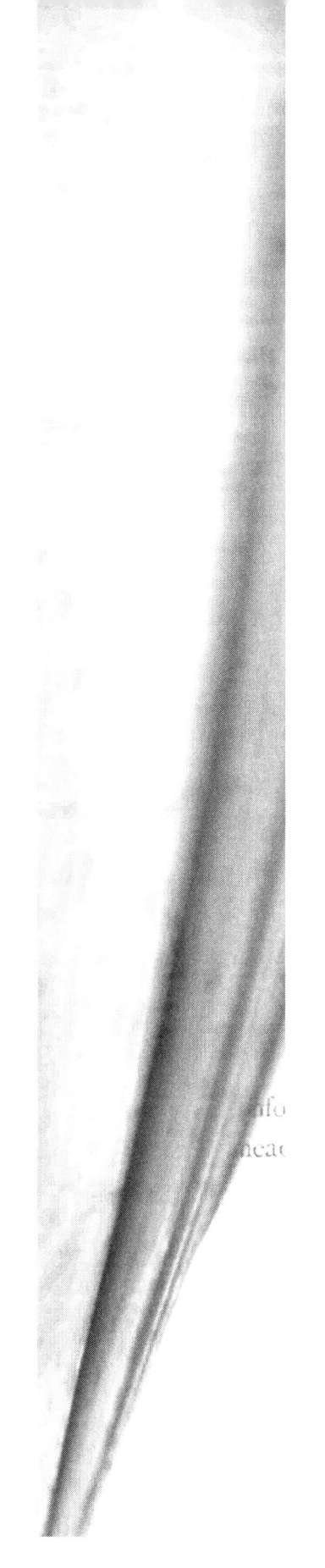

11. Explain the use of battens.

12. What is the object of raking masts?

13. The mainmast of a ship 192 feet long is 64 feet from the deck to the trestle trees. How far abaft the mast will a line from the trestle trees plumb the deck, when the ship is trimmed two feet by the stern;—the mast having been stayed upright when the ship was on an even keel?

14. Your ship is in dock, and on an even keel; and you require to stay your mainmast so that, when she is brought down to her proper trim, say three feet by the stern, the mast may incline from the perpendicular half an inch to a foot. What rake will you therefore give it in the first instance, that such may be the result,—the length of the ship being 200 feet?

15 What is the use of the long batten on the fore side of the lower masts?

16. What are the small triangular pieces of wood nailed on either side of the hoops of a bowsprit; and why are there none outside the housing?

17 State the reason why the legs of the lower pendants are not of the same length, and which are the longest.

18. Which are the standing and which the spring stays (starb. or port) on lower and topmasts; which go on first; and on which side are the outer fore and foretopmast stays?

2

19. How are the standing parts of the lanyards of fore and main stays, and bobstays secured?

20. What is the reason that the mizen stays are smaller than the rigging (fore and main stays being the reverse)?

21. With the rigging properly turned in, cutter's-stay fashion, does the nip lie on the fore or after side of the shroud? and why?

22. When rigging is turned in with the end up, how does the end lie?

23. Give the lead of all the stays.

24. Of the three ways of turning in rigging, which is the strongest,—end up—dead-eye spliced in;—or cutter's stay?

25. In turning in rigging, after forming the knot of the throat seizeing, what is done with the end? and should the lie outside, or underneath?

26. How are the lanyards rove? and why?

27. In setting up lower rigging, how is the lanyard brought to the luff?

28. After the rigging is set up, are the rackings kept on or taken off? and why?

29. Having seen the effect of the different purchases, explain how their power is calculated.

30. Describe single and double Spanish burtons, and state the power gained by them.

3

31. In a tackle of two double blocks, where is the standing part? and why?

32. What size rope would you reeve as a three-fold purchase to raise a weight of 40 tons? and what weight will a rope bear, whose strength is equal to 8·9 tons, when rove as a three-fold purchase?

33. What is the comparative strength of wire with hemp rope?

34. If a schooner's main-stay, of 6-inch rope, to the fore-mast head, were at right angles to the mainmast, it would resist a strain equal to the full strength of the rope, or about 9 tons. What support would it give to the mast, if, when brought down to the deck, it formed with the mainmast an angle of 40°?

We will now proceed to rattle down. Small spars are lashed at equal distances across the rigging; the ratline-stuff of well-stretched 1¾ inch, is handed up:—

35. Give the distance for the ratlines apart.

36. State how they are seized on, and whether the clove-hitch is inside or outside the shroud, with the reason.

37. On subsequently squaring ratlines, you find one about half an inch too long? you would not draw the splice, because that would make it considerably shorter; what will you do?

BOWSPRIT.

38. Gammon and rig it.

39. Which bobstay would you set up first? and why?

40. Then set up one.

4

41. Describe the fitting of a running in bowsprit?

LOWER YARDS, TOPMASTS, &c.

42. Get your main yard in from alongside the jetty.

43. If in the water.

44. Rig a main-yard.

45. Which is the upper side of a lower brace block?

46. What is the difference between lower and topsail brace block strops?

47. Through which sheeve in a lower-lift block should the hauling part reeve?

48. Being sent to the mast-house for your topmasts, you find that only one is ready :—not being marked, how do you know whether it is a fore or a main?

49. Why are additional heel-pieces nailed on a topmast and top-gallant-mast, instead of having a solid heel of the proper dimensions cut at once from the spar?

50. There is no shoulder for the cap on the fore side of lower and topmasts, and on the upper side of bow-sprits :—what is the reason?

51. Describe the topmast and top gallant fids.

52. Main topmast on deck, get it on end ;—the lower mast having been got in by dockyard sheers, with the cap on.

53. Get a lower cap over, after the masts are stepped.

54. Get topmast crosstrees over, and send them down.

55. Rig fore topmast, and set up the rigging.

56. How are the sister-blocks seized into topmast rigging?

57. What objection is there to the usual lead of topsail lifts and reef-tackles; and how would you obviate it?

58. Rig a topsail yard.

59. Rig jib and flying-jib booms, whiskers, and dolphin-striker.

60. What are the advantages of a jib traveller.

61. Rig fore top-gallant and royal masts.

62. What is the reason that a top-gallant stay goes on before the rigging?

63. What are jacks and jack blocks?

64. Send the studding-sail booms aloft.

SAILS.

65. Draw the linings of a topsail.

66. Of a course.

67. Fit a topsail.

68. Fit a course.

69. How are the reef-points of fore-and-aft sails put in?

70. What is the difference between bowline and reef cringles?

71. What is the difference between the fore, main, fore-top, and main top-bowline bridles?

72. Is there any difference in the number of cringles in the leech of a fore and main topsail?

6

73. What is the difference between topsails and courses in the make of their clews?

74. How is the head-rope of a sail spliced into the leech?

75. How are the leech and foot ropes of a topsail spliced together?

76. How is a *sailmaker's*, or *rat-tail* splice formed, and when is it required?

77. Why have topsails a hollow leech?

78. Is there any roach in topsails and courses?

79. You see a square-sail marked on the head as follows— 19½, 29, 12. What information is afforded you thereby?

80. A topsail becoming stretched, has too much hoist :— how will you reduce it?

81. What is the *principal* object in serving the foot of a topsail or course?

82. How many sized ropings are there in a jib, trysail, and topmast-studding-sail?

83. What are the different sizes of canvas; and what sail is each used for?

84. What is the breadth of canvas?

85. What is 18-inch canvas used for?

86. How are the seams of sails sewn?

87. What is herring-boning?

88. How are the eyelet holes in the foot of a topsail or course formed

89. What is the breadth of the seams of sails?

7

90. Are they the same width from head to foot?

91. Are all sails middle-seamed?

92. What are "sick seams"?

93. Having drawn at a foreign yard a topsail of a ship of a smaller rate, which requires an additional cloth in the spread, and having cut the sail up amidships for the insertion of the new cloth, state how you would add to the roping of the head and foot.

94. A similar sail requires a slight reduction in the foot. By cutting it, and bringing it together again with an ordinary long splice, too much will be taken up however careful you may be. What contrivance is there for meeting such a case?

REEVING ROPES ; FITTING GEAR, &c.

95. What part of a ship's rigging is fitted by the dockyard?

96. How will you strop the lower blocks of the *yards, stays,* and *up-and-downs?*

97. What is the best method of fitting a boom-sheet?

98. How do you reeve one rope by another?

99. You are going to reeve a new coil of rope. What do you do after cutting the stop?

100. What is the length of a coil of rope?

101. What is hawser-laid, and what cable-laid rope?

102. Wherein does three-stranded rope differ from four-stranded, besides in the number of strands?

103. What is a rumbowline?

104. Do you reeve the lacing of a jib or staysail with, or against the lay? and why?

105. Fit fore and main staysail stays.

106. Fit and reeve the gear attached to the different staysails.

107. Why are topsail-ties cut so much longer than is necessary for securing the standing part?

108. Do the topmast studding-sail halyards from the masthead to the jewel-block, lead before or abaft the top-sail yard? and why?

109. Do the jib sheets reeve inside, or outside the foretacks and bowlines?

110. How is the lacing rove, on the lower part of the luff of a spanker?

111. What is the advantage, and the disadvantage of the standing part of the peak halyards being secured to the topmast-head?

112. Is there any peculiarity in the make of lower tacks and sheets?

113. How should the sheets of all fore-and-aft sails lead?

114. Through which sheeve in the quarter block do you reeve the sheet?

115. Which is the swivel block of a top tackle?

116. Is a topsail-sheet secured with an inside or an outside clinch?

117. How are top-gallant and royal sheets secured?

9

118. Is the bill of the hook, in the standing part of fore and main sheets, up or down ?

119. What is the advantage of main buntlines leading aft ?

120. Reeve cat and fish falls.

121. What is a cat chain ?

122. What sized hemp cables and hawsers have you on board ?

123. What are the names of reef tackle and clewline, and fore tack blocks ?

124. There are two kinds of toggles in general use : what are they called ?

125. What is a gab-rope ?

126. What is *hiding* a rope ? and how is it done ?

127. What is a spider hoop ?

128. How are the reef-pendants of a boom-mainsail fitted ?

129. What is a triatic stay ?

130. What are the three most usual ways of building boats ?

131. When does a buoy require *bleeding* ? When is it said to *watch* ; a cable said to *grow* ; and a ship to *sew* ? and what is stowing a cask "a-burton" ?

132. How should the spare compass cards be stowed ?

133. What is the principal disadvantage of wide chains ?

134. What is the longest rope ? and what are the three strongest pieces of rigging ?

10

135. What are the two largest blocks supplied?

136. Splice a three and four stranded rope together.

137. Splice a hawser.

138. In splicing a thimble into a large rope, after putting the ends in once and a-half, how do you finish it off ready for serving?

139. In making large strops for general use, how do you splice them?

140. The ends of the lower rigging require cutting;—how do you do it?

141. What colour is the " Rogue's yarn " of the different dockyards?

142. What do you suppose is the strength of a rope-yarn?

143. A collar, of 8-inch rope, requires replacing, but you have nothing larger than 4½-inch on board. A double strop of the 4½-inch is therefore fitted, and considered equivalent to the single collar of 8-inch. Is it so?

144. How do you ascertain the strength of a rope of a given size? and how do you calculate its weight?

145. Which is the stronger,—hawser, or cable-laid rope?

146. What is the object of rope being cable-laid?

147. In round numbers, for practical purposes, state the proportion that hemp rope of a given size bears to its chain equivalent. For instance, if your topsail sheets of 5-inch rope were worn out, and you had nothing hempen to replace them with, would ½-in. chain be a sufficient substitute?

B   II

148. What is the strongest description of hemp rope?

149. You are in a ship without a ropemaker:—describe the gear employed, and show your men how to lay up spunyarn, nettle-stuff, six-thread, hammock-lashings, and nippers; out of a piece of junk.

150. Is three or four stranded rope the stronger?

151. Does a splice weaken a rope?

152. What is a ropemaker's eye used for?

153. How is bunting supplied by the Dockyard, marked?

154. What is the mark on canvas?

155. How is the Elliott's eye in a hemp cable made?

KNOTTING AND SPLICING.

156. Make a sheet bend.

157. A Carrick bend.

158. A Studding-sail bend.

159. A Rolling hitch.

160. A Timber hitch.

161. A Blackwall hitch.

162. A Clove hitch.

163. Hitch a ring-bolt over.

164. Make a common Marling hitch; and show how you would hitch the parts of a large strop over, such as the double strop of a 30-inch purchase block.

165. How is the eye of your stream cable keckled?

166—169. Pass a round, throat, racking, and flat seizing.

170. Form a Shroud knot.

171. A Single wall.

172. Wall and crown

173. Double wall and crown.

174. A French Shroud knot.

175. A Matthew Walker.

176. A Turk's head on one end.

177. The same on a Jacob's ladder.

178. A Reef knot.

179. A Stopper knot.

180—182. A bowline, a running bowline, and a bowline on a bight.

183. A Flemish eye.

184. A fox, and Spanish fox.

185. Point, and graft a rope.

186. Point a 9-inch hawser.

187. What is cross pointing?

188. Show how hitching is done.

189. Pass a rose lashing.

190. Lay up a nettle, and thumb-line.

191. Whip a rope the several ways, and show what is a rough substitute for whipping.

192. Make a Grummet.

193. A Selvagee strop.

194. Common sennit.

195. French sennit.

196. Round sennit.

197. Square sennit.

198. A sword mat.

199. Splice a sword mat, and join two together lengthways.

200. Make a paunch mat, and show how it is repaired.

201. Draw and knot yarns.

202. Show how the two parts of a large strop are hove together before clapping on the seizing.

203. Worm, parcel, and serve? back the worming; and show how worming is hove on taut.

204. What is a marling-spike hitch?

205—210. Make a short, long, eye, cut, horse-shoe, and Grecian splice.

211. Splice a chain and hemp cable together.

212. Splice a deep-sea lead-line.

213. Make a cat's-paw.

214. A sheepshank.

215. Sling a cask with butt, and bale slings,—with a rope's end, and with the head knocked in.

216. Sling a wounded man for sending down from aloft.

217. Bend a couple of hawsers together.

218. Bend a hawser to the ring of an anchor.

14

219. In seizing two legs of a strop together, with an eye in each, you find great difficulty in passing a sufficient number of turns owing to the smallness of the eyes; though they will, at the same time take the requisite number of turns if you can only put the ends through. How will you do it?

220. Work a cringle into a rope or sail.

221. Show how to make a mat, and repair the same when cut.

222. How are boats' fenders usually made?

223. Form a clinch.

224. Make a set of hammock clews.

225. Grass sennit.

226. A Coir brush.

227. What do you understand by a 14-inch spar, a 10-inch block, a 6-inch rope, an inch chain, a 9-inch dead-eye, and a 12-hand mast?

BERTHING, STOWAGE, &c.

228. Berth your ships company.

229. Divide the men into messes.

230. What do you understand by the terms, wet and day provisions?

231. What tackle would you use for hoisting in provisions?

232. Your provisions are nearly expended, you are about to complete, what should be done with those left?

233. How, and where are the different provisions stowed?

234. How will you ascertain the contents of a cask?

235. What are slops?

236. Give the size and capacity of the water tanks usually supplied.

237. Explain how tanks are stowed?

238. How do you start the water from a tank?

239. What is the weight of a pig of ballast?

READY FOR SEA.

240. You are ready for sea, hoist the steam launch in, and give the words of command.

241. The same, ship rolling heavily.

242. State whether you top up, or brace up first, with the reason.

243. Up rigging mats.

244. Weigh a bower anchor.

245. How is it secured for sea?

SECTION II.

AT SEA.

RULE OF THE ROAD.

246. What is the rule of the road, in the event of ships under sail only, meeting on opposite tacks?

16

247. Is a ship on the port tack expected to give way to a ship ahead, which is standing towards her with the wind on the starboard quarter?

248. Two ships, each with the wind a point abaft the beam, are standing towards each other, and will inevitably come into collision if they continue their course. One is steering E. by S., and the other W. by S., with the wind at north;—what is the duty of each?

249. How should two steamers, meeting nearly end on, put their helms, to avoid collision?

250. How should a steamer act, when meeting a sailing vessel, to avoid collision?

251. What lights do vessels carry at night?

252. What measures are taken to prevent collisions during a fog?

253. Make all plain sail, on a wind, giving the orders.

254. Put the ship about.

255. Why do you let go the top-gallant bowlines when you raise tacks and sheets?

256. What would be the effect of shortening in the lee fore, like the lee main tack?

257. In light winds, with a head swell, what precautions would you take to ensure staying?

258. After hauling the main yard, you find the ship falling off again. (Port tack before going round.)

17

259. If, while in stays, you discovered, either just before or after hauling the main yard, that there was danger close upon (what would become) your lee beam, what would you do?

260. The wind freshens considerably; top-gallant sails and royals are taken in:—as officer of the watch, what precautionary directions will you give before hauling the head yards?

261. You observe, since the breeze freshened, that the ship has carried more weather helm;—what is the reason?

262. You want to haul the mainsail up while tacking, what difference does it make in the orders you give, in the evolution?

263. In a dead beat, what proportion does the whole distance run bear to the direct distance gained to windward in a good breeze with no leeway?

264. When the helm is put up or down, does the bow or stern alone move, or does the ship turn on her centre?

265. What is the reason, that when the sails first fill after stays, a ship heels more than after she has gathered way?

266. Wishing to fore-reach as much as possible in stays, what will you be particular about?

267. A vessel close to, renders it necessary that you should fore-reach as little as possible:—what will you do?

268. Working under steam and sail, go about with the watch.

18

269. Your ship is close-hauled on the port tack, with the wind at north; another ship on the same tack bears E. by N ;—which is the weathermost

270. Your course is N.E. but you cannot lay it, and are heading N.W. on the starboard tack :—being taken aback, with the wind ahead, what will you do?

271. Wear under all plain sail.

272. Wear in as short a space as possible.

273. Wear ship in a strong gale.

274. It is absolutely necessary to wear a broken down steamer as she is drawing on shore, it is blowing so hard no canvas could stand for an instant, you endeavour to effect it with a couple of tarpaulins in the fore-rigging, but without success; can you think of any other expedient likely to succeed?

275. Wearing, blowing hard :—how do you shift the fore and main staysail sheets over?

276. Wear under staysails in a gale of wind.

277. Set studding-sails both sides, giving the words of command.

278. Take them in.

279. What is the first thing to be done after setting a top-mast studding sail?

280. What, after taking it in?

281. The ship is before the wind with studding-sails both sides, rolling heavily; you are unable to keep the lower booms out of the water (though they are

19

well topped up), and are thereby endangering the topmast studding-sail booms :—what would you recommend ?

282. In rigging out a fore-topmast studding-sail boom (setting studding-sails), owing to the quarter iron not being clamped, the heel flies up and the boom nearly slips through the outer iron ; you cannot rig it in by the boom-jigger, from the great weight of the outer part :—what will you do?

283.—How is the heel lashing of a topmast and top-gallant studding-sail boom secured?

284. What is the advantage of a studding-sail bend?

285. How will you dip a top-mast studding-sail before all?

286. In setting a weather topmast studding-sail, it gets before all :—what will you do?

287. On the sail being set, *blowing fresh*, you find that there is a hitch with the down-haul round the outer clue ; you cannot take the sail in, for the down-haul will not render : how will you clear it?

288. What do you use for the gear tricing-line forward?

289. You are pitching uneasily in a heavy swell, the sails surging forward and aft with great force : wishing to set studding sails, what precautions will you take on sending the men aloft?

290. Fore-topmast studding-sail set :—reef topsails.

291. You have made all plain sail again, and are going about ten or twelve knots, with the wind on the quarter :—haul up four points.

20

292. You are ordered to get the main-topsail sheets close home ; which sheet will you clap the luff on first ?

293. Would you haul taut the lee-boom sheet in a sea way to steady the spanker boom ?

294. On setting the mizen top-gallant sail, the weather lift and brace come off.

295. Under all plain sail, the breeze increases gradually to a gale :—shorten sail by degrees!

296. Take the second reef in the topsails, giving the necessary orders.

297. While reefing, the weather reef tackle carries away and unreeves : what will you do ?

298. Pass an Earing.

299. How are the third and fourth reef earings of a topsail fitted to the sail, and how are the first and second fitted to the yard

300. What is the first thing to be done after taking in a third reef?

301. Take in a close reef, on a wind.

302. Reef courses.

303. Blowing hard, take in a course.

304. Set a storm staysail.

305. Ship knocking about a great deal, send top-gallant masts on deck.

306. Under close-reefed main-topsail and reefed foresail, take in the latter.

21

307. Stowing a jib, blowing hard, what precautions are to be taken?

308. On a wind, the weather main-topsail brace goes.

309. The same,—wind on the quarter.

310. What do you use for preventer braces?

311. Blowing hard, the weather main-topsail sheet goes, and in clewing up, the clewline carries away.

312. Before the wind, parral of main-topsail yard carries away.

313. Parral goes on a wind.

314. You are officer of the watch, when a topmast stay carries away.

315. On a wind, under double-reefed topsails and top-gallant sails, a bobstay parts.

316. Under the same circumstances, jib-boom carries away, and is hanging at the bows.

317. Jib-sheet carries away, blowing fresh.

318. Main-tack goes, and in clewing up, the clew-garnet goes.

319. What is to be done on a tiller-rope carrying away?

320. A shroud of the lower rigging carries away, and not end enough for knotting and turning it in afresh.

321. Jib downhaul carries away.

322. In a strong breeze, ship rolling heavily, you *spring* your main-yard badly on the weather quarter : send it down and fish it.

22

323. Some time afterwards, the fore-yard *carries away*, in the same place ; fish it, and send it up again.

324. Your rigging has become very slack :—being unable to set it up, what will you do ?

325. Lying-to, in a storm, the mainmast goes over the side, what will you do?

326. What would you propose doing on discovering your bowsprit badly sprung on the under quarter, just outside the gammoning ? the port you are working for being several weeks' sail ahead of you.

327. Running with a gale on the quarter, under close-reefed fore and main topsails and fore-staysail, you are brought by the lee.

328. Scudding in a gale under close-reefed main-topsail, reefed foresail, and fore-staysail : lay the ship to.

329. What is broaching to, to what is it usually owing, and what is the remedy ?

330. Prepare for a hurricane.

331. You are thrown on your beam ends.

332. In a broken-down steamer, dismasted and quite unmanageable :—what will you do to keep the ship from foundering by the sea striking her astern or amidships.

333. The ship is much strained, leaky, and labouring heavily, with the water gaining on the pumps :— what should be done ?

334. A friend of yours, Sub-Lieutenant one of Her Majesty's vessels, cruizing in the Mozambique, is put in

23

charge of a large slaver captured off Quilimane, and
leaves for the Cape on the 12th February, 18—.
A four days' run places her in lat. 27° S., long.
40° E., when the weather becomes unsettled, and
an easterly swell is noticed. On the afternoon of
the 16th, the wind chops round to the S.E., and
the ship is brought to the wind on the port tack.
The sun sets wild and fiery, hollow gusts come up
and rapidly succeed each other as the day wears
on, until 8 P.M., when the ship heels over to a
steady freshening breeze from the southward, and
a reef is taken in, in the topsails. Your friend
goes below, and glancing at the barometer, sees
no cause for apprehension in the not very extraordinary fall from 29·98 at noon, when it was
last taken, to 29·70 in the subsequent eight hours.
The wind continues much the same during the
night, until 6 A.M. of the 17th, when it draws ahead
a little, and at 10 A.M., having made about W.S.W.
80 miles, they tack. At 4 P.M., the breeze having
freshened considerably, the topsails are double-
reefed, the wind being S. by W.; and before 10
P.M., close reefs are taken in, courses and mizen-
topsail furled, it then blowing a gale from the
S.S.W. with a heavy cross sea. The barometer
is referred to, and found to have fallen half-an-
inch, (to 29·15); on which the fore-topsail is with
difficulty taken in, and all made as snug as
possible. At midnight, the wind is round to S.W.,
blowing a terrific gale, and the barometer rapidly

falling. Shortly afterwards, the main-topsail is blown to ribbons, and an attempt is made to lay her to, under tarpaulins in the main rigging, it being impossible to show any canvas to it. The wind by this time is round to W.S.W. About two hours afterwards, the main-topmast goes by the cap, and the mizen-mast a few feet above the deck; the fore-topmast is then cut away to save the foremast, the S. B. anchor cut adrift, and a whole cable veered to endeavour to keep her head to wind. The ship labours on, making a great deal of water, till near four in the morning, it then blowing a hurricane from the westward, when she is thrown on her beam ends, the sea making a clean breach over her, and but for a solitary survivor picked up on a spar, nothing more would have been known of the fate of the lost ship, but that which is contained in the mournful, but, alas! too common epitaph—" Foundered at sea ! "

Point out the error committed, and state what you would have done, had you been placed in a similar position ?

335. As a further illustration of this subject, we will suppose the following case :—

A vessel launched at Bombay, sails for England on the 1st of June, 18—, in charge of a lieutenant from the Commodore's ship, with the necessary subordinate officers, and forty men; and after a tedious passage down the coast, against a strong S.W. monsoon, arrives in lat.

25

6° N., long. 77° E., at noon on the 20th; the monsoon then blowing from the westward, and the course steered E.S.E.

During the day, they ran into a northerly breeze, and the course was altered to S.E., it being their intention to cross the line about the meridian of 86°. At 3 A.M., 21st, the wind logged was N.N.E, 6, *q. u. r.*, bar. 29·90 (the barometer at midnight having stood at 30·01), the brig bowling along under port topmast studding-sails, which they were reluctantly obliged to take in at 6 A.M. (bar. 29·78). At 9 A.M., barometer had fallen to 29·64; and, anticipating a gale, the mainsail was furled, top-gallant-masts sent on deck, and three reefs taken in the topsails, which they had reason to congratulate themselves on having done, for scarcely had they completed these pre-cautionary measures at 11 A.M., when the gale *overtook them*, as they considered, (bar. 29·38), and before noon, sail was reduced to close-reefed main-topsail and reefed foresail, under which they hoped to run out of it, flattering themselves in the mean time that, while flying before the gale, they were making upon their course a good 14 knots an hour. (Bar. at noon, 29·00.)

By 1 P.M., the wind had drawn forward a point, (N.E. by N.), blowing a furious gale, and they were at last com-pelled to round to under the main-topsail and fore-stayail, getting their decks swept in the operation, and the pinnace stove in upon the booms; and, being unable to furl the foresail, the men were called down, and it was allowed to blow away. The log then is as follows:—

26

"2 P.M., blowing a storm (bar. 29·84), weather main-topsail sheet went, and the sail with it, on which the storm main-trysail was loosed and set. 3 P.M., wind N.E., blowing a most terrific hurricane, and ship in great danger; stationed hands for cutting away masts. About three-quarters of an hour afterwards, taken aback by a shift of wind; the vessel went over and lay with her yard-arms in the water, at which awful moment, Mr. ——, midshipman, and five seamen, were washed overboard. By great exertions, Lieut. ——, and several men, suc-ceeded in securing themselves on the weather broadside, and in cutting away some of the weather rigging, when the masts and bowsprit went by the board, and Her Majesty's sloop righted with seven feet of water in the hold."

During the night she nearly foundered, and three more men were swept away while heaving the guns overboard, but by the morning, the weather having moderated con-siderably, and veered to the southward, they were enabled to set about rigging a jury-foremast, and a jigger-mast abaft; under which, having picked up the monsoon again, they arrived without further incident in Trincomalee harbour.

State how this danger and loss of life might have been averted, and what principles are illustrated thereby.

336. Two ships are drifting towards each other in a calm : they lower their boats, and endeavour to tow each other in contrary directions, but they still close :— what should they do ?

337. How do you find the angle your yards brace up to?

338. What is the reason that the upper yards, on a wind, bear bracing in *nearer* than the lower ones?

339. The after-yards brace up sharper than the head-yards: —why then do they *touch* together?

340. Why is there more strain on the weather, than on the lee yard-arm?

341. The capability of a ship to work to windward results from her ability to make headway with the wind before the beam :—explain this property in a ship, and why, when the wind is forward, the ship is not driven astern.

342. You run into a ship and carry away your fore-chains, damaging the chain plates :—as you have no stores on board to build new chains, what will you do?

343. Get stern and quarter-boats inboard.

344. You are in hourly expectation of engaging a steamer of equal force with yourself, state what preparations you will make.

345. What do you consider the most advantageous way of engaging an enemy?

346. The chase is to windward :—when do you tack, and why?

347. If you stand on the same tack as the chase, till you can fetch her on the opposite tack, should she tack also, or stand on?

28

348. The chase is to leeward, on a steamer :—what course will you pursue, and what is her best chance of escape ?

349. How will you fight your ship?

WITH A SQUADRON.

350. In "open" and "close orders," at what distances will you keep from your next ahead ?

351. What is the rule for the distance apart of columns?

352. Explain what is meant by the term " Fleet Numbers?"

353. What are "Columns of Divisions" and "Subdivisions?"

354. What is "Line Abreast ?"

355. "Quarter line," "Two Quarter" or "Two Bow Lines ?"

356. What is the "Direction of a Column ?"

357. On the Signal being made "Tack in Succession," when does the leading ship of the lee line put her helm down, and when do the other ships ?

358. What is a line of bearing ?

359. What precautions will you take as officers of the watch when wearing in line ?

360. Overtaken suddenly by a fog at night, what precautions would you think necessary ?

361. If the Admiral should, without a signal, or hoisting the disregard flag, commence any evolution :— what would you do ?

362. How do you ascertain the results of a trial of sailing?

363. A topsail-yard is sprung in the quarter, in a sailing trial.

364. Your main-topsail splits right across the head.

365. The leech of a topsail is carried away in a fresh breeze you might deem it advisable to repair it :— how would you effect it?

366. Main-stays carried away.

367. Rudder disabled.

368. What are the rudder-chains for?

369. How is a rigging-stopper fitted, and how put on?

370. Away in a prize, your binnacle is washed away ; with no spare compass on board, what will you steer the ship by?

371. The necklace on foremast head carries away ; you cannot stand long on the opposite tack if you go round, so secure the topmast as soon as possible.

372. Take in a brigs boom-mainsail in a squall.

373. How is a boom-mainsail stowed?

374. In a small vessel close hauled, the wind shifts aft :— will you trim the head or after yards first?

375. In your own ship again, reef topsails in stays.

376. " Man overboard !"

   (a) All plain sail set, on a wind; and state whether you haul the mainsail up before or after squaring the main-yard?

30

(b) Plain sail, before the wind.

(c) Studding-sails one side.

(d) Studding-sails both sides.

377. The man is picked up, apparently lifeless :—what steps will you take to restore animation ?

378. On which side is the trigger for firing, and which for letting go the life-buoy ?

379. A topmast is shattered by lightning, you are afraid to start the rigging without taking some precautions:— how will you send it down ?

380. A topsail is on fire by lightning.

381. How is a topsail made up for bending ?

382. A course ?

383. A jib ?

385. Shift mainsail.

386. Shift jib.

387. How would you tell the head of the jib from the tack in the dark ?

388. Shift jib-boom.

389. A top-gallant mast.

390. A topsail-yard.

391. Running in a gale, you spring your main-top-sail-yard : replace it.

392. What do you do with a sail tackle after using it ?

393. The upper block of the sail tackle comes out of the strop, the sail having been swayed up thirty feet from the deck :—what order will you give ?

394. How is a spanker made up ?

395. A topmast studding-sail, for setting ?

396. A lower studding-sail ?

397. How are your topsails and courses stowed away?

398. Is the standing or hauling part of a top-gallant mast rope rove through the lizard, and why ?

399. To which bolt in the cap is the standing part secured ?

400. Under top-gallant sails, the main top-gallant-mast carries away, and falls before the topsail :—how will you send the wreck down ?

401. When stowing a jib in cloth, what part of the sail forms the skin and explain the stowage of this sail.

402. Mark a lead-line.

403. Mark a deep-sea lead-line, and get a cast.

404. What is the best way of taking very deep soundings from a steamer ?

405. Mark a log-line.

406. You are officer of the watch ; the ship is under top-sails and courses, and you see a very heavy squall coming down to windward, the sea white with foam :—what will you do ?

407. Taken unprepared, what is your first order ?

408. Set the fore-topmast studding-sail, blowing hard.

32

409. Take it in.

410. One vessel in tow of another; the headmost one puts her helm down to go round :—how does the other proceed?

411. Prepare to be taken in tow by a steamer, and announce when you are ready.

412. Prepare your ship, for rounding the Horn in the winter months.

413. What is club-hauling and how is it effected ?

414. On a wind, you run ashore.

415. At a quarter ebb, you get on shore, where the rise and fall is very great, and so rapid, that the water lessens quicker than you can lighten the ship :— what will you do?

416. You are taking your ship up a river, and are forced by an ebb tide on a reef of rocks. All attempts to get spars over, as shores, are rendered futile by the rapidity of the current, and, in defiance of all efforts to the contrary, the ship falls over 22°. The usual preparations are made by battening down the hatchways; but, owing to a defect in the pumps, the water gains upon the ship, and she falls over and remains at an angle of 45°:—how will you endeavour to raise her ?

417. Under double-reefed topsails, courses, top-gallant sails, and fore-topmast staysail, you spread a surface of 4,800 yards of canvas, and are going in

33

a fresh breeze 8 knots on a wind; but anxious to get on, you are tempted, though at considerable hazard to the spars, to make sail to whole topsails, jib, and spanker, which gives an increase of 1,600 yards, or *one-third* more canvas than at first :— under these circumstances, what will be the increased rate of speed?

418: Raise a screw propeller.

419. You are making a passage under sail, and find the drag of the screw retards your speed very much; and it cannot be raised what will you do to lessen its dragging?

420. What effect does backing astern, have on the ship's head, if there is any wind?

421. State what advantages and disadvantages twin screws possess, when compared with a sinlge screw?

422. You are coming in from a long cruize, and wish to make a good figure in the squadron; you are to make a running moor,—bring your ship to, and state what you would do that she might look well a few hours after anchoring.

423. A prize is captured off a foreign port, and you are sent in to refit and provision her, preparatory to putting to sea again in three weeks' time. Finding that her three chronometers have been allowed to run down, and that there is no other ship in harbour with whose chronometer of known rate

34

you can compare your own :—state how you would rate them by observation, and how you would avail yourself of the results in the ensuing voyage.

SECTION III.

ON GENERAL SERVICE.

424. In a storm on a lee shore you are riding in a sailing vessel with four anchors ahead, from which you are beginning to drive :—what will you immediately do?

425. Having parted from all your anchors, are your resources, therefore, exhausted?

426. In the port that you are bound for, heavy gales from the N.W. are prevalent, and you are consequently recommended in the local Sailing Directions to moor with open hawse in that direction. How will you lay your anchors out, and with what cable will you moor in 10 fathoms water?

427. Anchor in fine weather with a spring on.

428. What will you look out for on coming to with a weather-tide?

429. When coming to, at the order "Stand clear of the B.B. (or S. B.) cable," what takes place?

430. Name the parts of an anchor.

431. You are in charge of a prize, a sailing vessel, explain how you will get her up or down a river too narrow to admit of her tacking.

432. Rig a nun-boy.

433. Bitt a hemp and a chain cable.

434. Pass a nipper.

435. Heaving in you drag through all.

436. Describe a deck tackle, and state how it is used.

437. How is the cable, BROUGHT TO, with a patent capstan?

438. How many swivels are there in a cable?

439. What is the length between the shackles of chain cables, and how are they marked?

440. What are the uses of the stay-pin in the links of a chain cable?

441. What is a ganger

442. What advantage have hemp over chain cables?

443. How are the hemp cables coiled away, and how are the ends secured?

444. How do you stopper a hemp cable?

445. Pass a hemp messenger.

446. After heaving taut and unbitting, what do you do before heaving round?

447. When and how are hemp cables stoppered when coiled away below?

448. Prepare a hemp cable for coming to with.

36

449. Which end of a chain cable is shackled to the anchor?

450. After putting the slip on, what is done with the cable, before surging?

451. Describe and put on a swivel.

452. Take it off.

453. Ought the cup of the swivel to be kept up or down?

454. You are ordered to Spithead for the winter, and intend to moor with a swivel on, in 11 fathoms water with four shackles on each cable; you therefore, on coming to, run eight shackles taut out on the first anchor, let go the second, veer away, and heave in on the first:—do you by these means ensure mooring as you wish?

455. You are slackly moored, with a swivel on, and are required to take it off, both cables being up and down:—how do you tell the starboard from the port cable, to avoid shackling the wrong cables together?

456. When a ship is moored with an equal strain on both cables, are the two cables, under any circumstances, weaker than a single one ahead would be?

457. How do you keep your hawse clear in a tide-way?

458. Clear hawse.

459. At single anchor in a tide-way, what means will you take to keep a clear anchor

460. Being officer of the watch, you are ordered to see all clear for letting go a sheet-anchor at a moment's notice:—do so.

37

461. Veer cable, blowing a gale.

462. Why do you veer cable in heavy weather?

463. Messenger carries away.

464. The anchor is at the bows with the stock gone:—stock it afresh.

465. It comes up to the bows flukes uppermost.

466. How are the cat and fish hooked

467. The cat-block is found defective: what will you replace it with?

468. You want to let go the anchor again, having just hove it up to the bows :—what is to be done before letting go?

469. Having slipped your cable, return and pick the anchor up again, the buoy having sunk during your absence.

470. You foul another ship as you are getting under weigh, and carry away your boomkin and cat-head flush with the bows :—how will you secure the anchor for sea, and work the foresail?

471. Having hove a sheet anchor up to the bows, get it into its place.

472. Having lost an anchor, take a waist anchor for the bower, and cat and fish it.

473. You have lost all your anchors but one, and that has but one arm :—on coming into an anchorage, how will you let it go to ensure its taking the ground

38

474. Weigh, under sail, in a fresh breeze, making as little stern-way as possible, as there is a ship in your wake, but without laying a kedge out.

475. Lying at anchor close to and parallel with the shore, with a heavy swell setting in on port bow, and no room to cast to starboard :—get under weigh, under sail, and ensure casting to port.

476. How will you pick up your anchor in a strong weather tide, but with a breeze so fresh that the ship is forced taut ahead of her anchor?

477. You are anchored close to a long line of ships on your port beam, with a shoal astern of the leeward-most ship, running at right angles to the line :—weigh under canvas.

478. In weighing, under sail, what is the proper moment for tripping the anchor?

479. You are lying close to a lee shore in a sailing vessel, it is blowing too heavily to warp off, and you are too near the shore to weigh and make sail in the usual manner :—how will you leave the anchorage?

480. Back an anchor.

481. How will you make a kedge which is rather small more effective?

482. Lay a bower anchor out by the launch under ordinary circumstances.

483. In a ship without a launch, lay out a sheet anchor, which it is necessary to back with the stream, for heaving the ship off shore in half a gale of wind.

39

484. Having no available boats, calculate the number of water-casks (butts) requisite to carry out a 95-cwt. anchor.

485. In the event of your not knowing the capacity of the casks to be employed, how would you ascertain it?

486. What number of 4-feet tanks, weighing 7 cwt. each, would you take to perform the same operation? (Internal capacity not given.)

487. What spare spars would you select, in default of other means, for laying out the anchor; and what weight would such spars sustain when used as a raft?

488. Send a stream anchor and cable to a ship's assistance.

489. Seeing, from the way a ship is coming in, that there is a strong probability of her fouling you :—what preparations will you make for the event?

490. As midshipman of a boat, you are sent away with orders to anchor off a certain place, and on arriving there, you find a rocky, irregular bottom; there being great probability of the anchor becoming jambed among the rocks :—what will you do to ensure getting it up again?

491. Sent away in charge of a seining party of raw hands, show them how to shoot it.

492. Your boat stows 14 butts and 12 puncheons :—what quantity of water does she carry in tuns and in gallons?

40

493. In warping your ship out of harbour, it has been necessary to coil a hawser away on deck as it was run in ; and, on a boat coming alongside to receive it again, the end has been taken in the hurry through one of the bights ; consequently, on coiling it in the boat, an overhand knot is found in the hawser, when about half coiled away :—how will you clear it ?

494. What is the usual plan of watering ship, by means of launches ?

495. Get your boat ready for bringing off water in a bulk.

496. How will you get your water through a heavy surf?

497. How will you fit the rain-awnings to your boats ?

498. You see a boat standing for the ship in very bad weather; it is as much as she will do to fetch— if she misses she will be driven to seaward, as she cannot make headway under oars against the sea :— what will you do ?

499. In command of boats you have been employed towing a ship out of harbour ; but, before you part company, a thick fog comes on :—how will you find your way back, having no compass?

500. Ordered to shove off and set fire to an enemy's vessel or buildings, what will you take with you ?

501. In a boat out of sight of your ship, and to leeward of any anchorage, a gale of wind and heavy sea springs up :—what will you do for the safety of the

41

boat, as she is beginning to take water in faster than you can bale it out?

502. On the following day the weather moderates; you pull till nightfall without sighting land; you have no fresh water in the boat, and you are parched with thirst :—what expedient will you resort to for relief?

503. In a heavy surf, land and get off.

504. You are pulling along shore, but, owing to an adverse wind and tide, are not making headway, and it is useless to attempt to beat up :—to what expedient will you resort?

505. You are caught in a squall in charge of a ship's cutter.

506. Having been away in your boat, and had occasion to load your rifles, what will you be particular to do before returning on board?

507. Bullocks are brought off, hoist them in.

508. Hoist in a restive horse.

509. You have a water cask on deck which you wish to up-end :—how will you set about it? Its weight would be about half-a-ton.

510. In what length is condemned rope returned into store?

511. A 64-pounder gun, is on shore dismounted, it would render important service could it be brought into play; you are therefore sent to see what can be done. A party of men are sent after you, but they are unable to bring anything with them that could

42

assist in raising it. Not a spar is to be had any-where, and all you possess, besides the carriage with its sea-service equipment, is the ammunition and usual stores :—with these means are you sufficient to mount and fight her ?

512. It is subsequently required on the summit of a precipitous hill ; you have lately received along with some casks of provisions, two good hawsers :—how will you transport it ?

513. How will you stow a couple of similar guns in your launch, having to take them ashore, and land them on a beach ?

514. Having rigged a triangle ashore, explain the way you would mount them.

515. What are the two ways of working a parbuckle, in transporting dismounted guns for instance ?

516. Having a gun ashore without a carriage, how will you fight her ?

517. Place a field-piece and limber in one of the boom-boats and land it for the purpose of exercise.

518. Land a boat's gun as a field-gun, in the face of an enemy.

519. Describe the purchases you would use to hoist in an 8-inch rifled gun, weighing nine tons ; also how lighter guns are usually got in ?

520. In 1857, a brass gun was captured in one of the forts in the Canton river, which measured from base-ring to muzzle 19 ft. 10 in. Its circumference between

D   43

base and trunnions (a distance of 8 ft. 6 in.), was 7 ft. 1½ in., uniform throughout, but from the trunnions its circumference decreased to 5 ft. 2 in. at the muzzle. The metal in the rear of the base-ring, moulded in the form of rings terminating in a button, weighed about 5 cwt., and its bore was 9 in. :—what was its weight ?

521. What would be the weight of her shot, of 8·7 inches in diameter ?

522. You discover your mainmast to be decayed, dispose of the old one, and get a new one in, having no spars on board suitable for sheers, and being unable to procure any.

523. Get your main yard fore and aft in harbour.

524. Give the words of command for " unbending sails."

525. Get the bowsprit cap off and on.

526. Shift bowsprit with your own means.

527. Will your own spars form sheers capable of getting out a lower mast ?

528. Hoist a paddle sloop's pinnace out.

529. Hoist in a long spar.

530. Hog ship.

531. As mate of the upper deck, state your ideas on the subject of hammocks ?

532. See all ready for dressing ship.

533. With what ceremonies do you celebrate Her Majesty's

44

birthday ; and what is the etiquette on arriving in a foreign port where an Admiral's flag is flying ?

534. Hoist in a gun or mortar, weighing 30 tons. Calculate the strain on the gear employed—the centre of the main hatchway down which it is to be lowered being 15 feet before the mainmast, the hold of the lighter in which it is to be brought off, 10 feet from the ship's side, and the beam of the upper deck, say 50 feet.

535. It is your object to enter a French port, of which you have only a French chart, which states that *les sondes sont exprimées en mètres*, and *la mer marne d'un mètre environ;* your ship draws 19 feet and the shoalest part of the channel is marked 6 ; supposing, then, that to be the actual depth of water at the time, is it sufficient for you ? state also whether you would be able to make use of a Russian, Dutch, Danish, or Spanish chart in the original.

536. Before sailing in charge of an iron steamer, a prize, swing ship to ascertain local attraction.

537. You take a prize upon the stocks,—a ship of 800 tons, nearly completed. No spars have been prepared for her, but as there are plenty at hand of various dimensions, it is decided that she shall be launched and got ready for sea. You are given command of her, and directed to furnish a scale of masts and yards suitable for a ship of her size, and to ascertain the position the masts should occupy.

D 2

Her length on the upper deck, is 152 feet, and extreme beam 35 feet.

Data are also required for masting cutters, schooners, and boats of various rigs.

538. Explain the operation of heaving down.

539. How would you sling a sunken vessel, for the purpose of raising her?

540. How do you ascertain a ship's tonnage?

541. How are your booms stowed?

542. On a fire breaking out on shore, you are sent in charge of a party to aid in extinguishing it :—what will you take with you, and what course will you pursue on landing?

543. How is a rudder attached to the sternpost, and kept from unshipping?

544. What is a balanced rudder, and what are its advantages and disadvantages?

545. Explain the action of the rudder of a screw ship with regard to speed, and a large or small angle of rudder.

546. What causes weather helm?

547. Having sprung your rudder, send it ashore and replace it with a new one.

548. How will you construct a temporary rudder from the ship's stores?

549. What is the object of a false keel?

550. How will you permanently guard yourself, in an

46

enemy's river, against the approach of fire-vessels, torpedo-boats, and explosive machines?

551. Engaged in operations against the enemy, you meet in your boats with a boom and chain, which it is necessary to force :—what is the readiest method?

552. Moor head and stern, in a ship with no appliances for securing stern-chains.

553. How will you replace a sheet of copper on a ship's bottom, several feet below water, without docking, heaving her down, or having the aid of a diving apparatus?

554. On a foreign station, it becomes necessary to dock your ship. The dock not being adapted for the reception of ships of large draught, you clear the ship, and get the masts out. By so doing, she is lightened sufficiently forward, but still draws considerably too much water abaft :—how would you propose to lift her stern over the sole of the dock?

555. In a ship's pinnace, manned and armed, towing astern of a steamer going at full speed, with a sea getting up :—take the necessary precautions for the safety of your boat.

556. Your mizen-mast is discovered to be very unsound from dry-rot; and in your rambles ashore, in a country but little known, you come upon some tall, branchless trees of hard wood whose height, therefore, you are desirous of obtaining :—how will you

47

ascertain it without any appliances but such simple ones as will always be found on the spot?

557. How do you ascertain distance by sound?

558. Your hawse-pipes on each side are broken and cut down by the cables, which you are obliged to work in the spare hawse-holes :—how will you repair the injury?

559. Which rides the easier, a light ship or a deep one?

560. Which end of a spar would you tow foremost, the bluff end, or the small one ; and whereabouts in your boat will you make the tow-line fast?

561. Describe the system of making Flashing Signals?

562. As signal midshipman of the flagship, find the time for making it daylight and sunset at a given place and day, say at Hong Kong, May 1st, 1856.

EXPLANATIONS.

EXPLANATIONS.

PART I.

FITTING OUT.

1. RIGGING SHEERS.—The sheers having been towed alongside, with their heads aft, take two stout hawsers, middle them, pass the bights over the ends of the spar, and secure the underneath ends inboard, the hammock berthing having been previously removed. Reeve the hauling parts of the hawsers through leading-blocks on the opposite side of the deck. Hang small spars from the chains, to keep the sheers clear in coming in. Man the hawsers,—tackles having been clapped on if necessary; parbuckle the spar up to the upper works, and take a turn with the hawsers. Secure three or four small spars in a slanting direction, inboard from the upper works, to ease the sheers down on, and pass the bight of a small hawser from the main-deck ports over each end of the spar for the same purpose, making one end fast and taking a turn with the other; then haul away on the parbuckle, and ease away on the main-deck hawsers till the spar is landed. Proceed with the other in the same manner.

51

However, instead of parbuckle, I should, in preference, get sheers in over the stern, by rigging small sheers over the taffrail, and by them lifting the end of the spar up to the stern port on the upper deck ; then clap on a tackle led along the deck, and rouse it in. By clearing away the head berthing, they may also be advantageously got in forward ; in which case, the lighter end of the sheers would come first.

When in, rig a small pair of sheers ; with them raise the sheer-heads on the poop, cross them by placing the sheer-head of the side on which the mast is coming in upper-most, and lash them with a round lashing of 4 in., passed on the bight with six or seven turns *on each end*, then back again with riding turns,—making 23 or 27 turns in all, and knot.

Protect the sheer-head lashing carefully with old canvas where the purchase-strop takes, and take a four-fold block, double stropped, for the upper block of the main pur-chase ; place the bight of the starboard end over the starboard sheer-head, and the bight of the port end over the port sheer-head, then reeve the ends contrary ways through the bights of the strop, pass bight and bight as before, and knot the ends when the lashing is expended.

The upper block of the small purchase (an upper jeer-block), is placed on the underneath, or after part of the sheers, lashed as the other, but hanging below it, the bights lying on the fore side, and across the turns of the main purchase strop.

Then lash the topping-lift, for which the fish-tackle will do.

52

For sheer-head guys, which are placed next, take the three 9-in. and a 7½-in. hawser, which reeve through four top-blocks lashed at the sheer-heads, those for the fore-guys being uppermost.

For the belly-guys, on the fore and after side of each sheer leg, use the fore and main runners and tackles, and reeve sheer-head gantlines.

Reeve the purchase, using a three-fold purchase-block, and another upper jeer-block for the lower blocks, overhaul the fore-guys and main purchase forward, the former to the cat-heads, and the latter toggled through the hole for the bowsprit. Open the sheers out, place the shoe, lash the heels securely, but slackly, to a fish-davit, or other spar, laid outside the nearest port abaft the heels, and shore all decks well up underneath. Hook up-and-downs forward and aft on each side, as heel-tackles. Bring the purchase to the capstan, man well the fore-guys, and attend the after-guys and heel-tackles. Raise the heads by the small sheers, heaving round and hauling on the purchase; unrig the small sheers when they are of no further use, and heave away. When on end, hook a couple of luffs from one heel to the other, which bowse well taut and frap; transport the sheers aft to the break of the poop,— wetting the deck, and keeping the heels in advance, lash the heels taut between the ports, over cleats on the sheer-legs, looking out that they are stepped over a beam, bowse taut the heel-tackles, set all the guys well up (the sheer-head guys with luffs), and come up the purchase forward.

2. GETTING IN LOWER-MASTS AND BOWSPRIT.—The masts should have the gant-line-blocks and strops for the purchases to toggle to, lashed before launching. The height of the sheers, the length of the mast, and the depth of the housing, must regulate the position of the strops; but supposing the sheers are as taunt as you desire, lash the strop for the main purchase just above the upper-deck partners, the strop for the small purchase above the centre of the mast, and the topping-lift at the mast-head. Canvas must be placed round the mast under the lashings, and cleats nailed above to prevent them slipping.

The mizen-mast being alongside, with the head aft, overhaul the small purchase down, and hook the topping-lift to a strop below the trestle-trees. Lead the fall down the after hatchway, through a leading-block, and bring it to the capstan. Sway away, and when up to the main-deck ports, pass a couple of hawsers out, which bend to the head and heel, ready to ease away as you sway inboard. Reeve the mast-head gantlines, clap a tackle on the heel to bowse it over the mast-hole, pull up on the topping-lift and point the mast, walk back, heave it on the right slue, and lower it into the step; drive four or five wedges in, and come up the purchase.

Transport the sheers before the main partners, and get the mainmast in, in the same manner. Lead the main purchase down the main hatchway, through a leading-block, and bring it to the main capstan; and the small purchase, with the same lead, bring to the fore capstan. The topping-lift work on deck.

54

Having similarly got the foremast in, keep fast the belly-guys to steady the sheers, unreeve the fore sheer-head guys, and shift the blocks to the hounds of the fore-mast. Come up the after sheer-head guys, and secure one part of each to the foremast-head close down, and reeve the other ends through the blocks, and so down on deck, thus converting them into sheer-head topping-lifts.

Haul down on the purchase, ease away the topping-lifts and droop the sheers; then the belly-guys being of no further use, take them off, and shift the fore runners and tackles to the after part of the foremast-head, lashing the blocks where the standing parts of the topping-lifts are secured, then take them aft, and set them up for the support of the mast.

As for the mizen-mast, the small purchase and topping-lift, the latter, slued round, will bring the bowsprit in, which should be slung midway between the housing and the centre. Send the purchase down abaft the boomkin, for, if before, you would jamb the bowsprit between it and the cutwater, and be thereby prevented from swaying it higher; toggle on, hook the masting topping-lift to a strop through the cap, where also hitch a couple of guys rove through blocks at the cat-heads. Sway away, topping on the cap purchase when necessary; when clear of the boomkin, drop the sheers to the required angle, and sway away; point the heel, ease up the main purchase, and, if the partners are well greased, the mast will come down into its place as you pull up on the cap purchase, without the aid of bedding-tackles.

55

The heels of the sheers are then fleeted aft, the sheers lowered down by the topping-lifts, unrigged, and hoisted out.

3. GETTING WHOLE TOPS OVER.—Up-end the top on its after-edge, abaft the mast, underneath side of the top, forward. Lash the gantline blocks on each side of the masthead, as close up as possible, frapping them over the head of the mast to keep them well up. Take the after end of each gantline under the top, up through the after (or next to after) futtock hole, down through lubbers' hole ; and after this, reeving up through the foremost futtock hole ; hitch the end of each gantline to its own part at lubbers' hole. Then get a guy from aft, bend it to the after part of the top, and stop it with the two gantlines already bent to the holes in the fore part of the top. Steady taut the after guy, sway away the gantlines, keep the top clear of the trestle trees with the after guy ; when close up cut the stops, sway the top over, ease it down, place it, cast off the gantlines, get up the sleepers, and bolt the top down to the crosstrees. A mizen-top is nearly always sent up before the mast, that you may have the assistance of a gantline from the mainmast ; if this is done, place the top before the mast, as it would lie when over ; bend the mizen gantlines to the foremost futtock holes, and the main gantline to the fore part of the top : stop all three gantlines to the after part of the top, and sway as before.

4. GET HALF-TOPS OVER.—Place the half-tops on the deck each side of the mast, as if in their place ; lash two planks across the trestle-trees, with a bolt lashed on the

56

top of each, exactly between the trestle-trees. Take the after end of the gantlines abaft all, each on its own side ; bend to the half-tops with a round-turn as near the centre as possible, and hitch each to its own part ; stop the bight to the futtock hole abreast the hitch ; bend a gantline from abaft to the after part of the half-top, to keep it clear as it goes up ; sway until above the crosstrees, rest the midship parts on the planks against the bolts, lower the gantline, remove the planks, place the sleepers and bolt down.

5. SENDING TOPS DOWN.—Bend each gantline with a round turn through lubbers' hole and one of the futtock holes, so slinging the top that the after part will be slightly heavier ; bend a gantline or guy to the fore-part of the top, from abaft, to bring the top aft when swayed off ; unbolt and send down the sleepers, bend a rope's end from the deck to the fore-part of the top, to keep it square while swaying. When this has been done, sway till the fore-part clears the mast-head, haul on the after gantlines, guy clear of the trestle trees ; unbend the rope's end and lower away.

Half-Tops.—Commencing with port half.—Bend the port gantline round the half-top at fore part of lubbers' hole, and stop it to the fore part of the top. Bend a fore and aft gantline to the after part of the top ; sway the upper gantline, haul on the fore and aft gantline, and when clear of the trestle trees, lower away, and proceed in the same manner with the other half.

6. GANTLINES.—For the fore and mainmast, the top

tackle-falls are drawn; peak and throat halyards for the mizen-mast.

7. GANTLINE UNROVE.—Direct the man at the mast-head to draw the splice of the block-strop, unlay the strands and knot the yarns, then send them down as a hauling-line.*

8. CUTTING OUT RIGGING.—Hemp rigging is now almost unknown in Her Majesty's Service; but as the question of how it was fitted, may still be asked, I have thought it as well to insert the answer. Measure the distance with spunyarn, from the bolster on one side of the mast, to the foremost dead-eye in the chains on the other; or take the length of the mast from the wedges to the bolsters, as one side of a right-angled triangle, and the distance from the centre of the mast-hole to the crown of the foremost lower dead-eye as the other, find the third side?

---

* This is a standard *catch question*, and is inserted as a specimen of the nautical enigma known as such. Many midshipmen labour under the delusion that elaborate improbabilities of this description form the staple of the final examination for lieutenant. I have heard a captain under whom I served some years ago, gravely accused of turning a midshipman back for not knowing how to *stow a hold in a gale of wind*. And there is a tradition afloat of an unfortunate candidate having *missed stays*, in consequence of being puzzled how to get a bower anchor out, which was lying inboard;—there being no masts or spars in the ship wherewith to raise it. Considerable erudition has been displayed in discussing this question; and I believe that in such a dilemma the correct thing is to hoist it out with a derrick, formed of its own stock!

At this distance place two posts : take the shroud hawser and lay its end at either post, warp round and round both, laying each turn carefully outside the other, one complete turn for each pair of shrouds, and half-a-turn for the pendants.

Take once-and-a-quarter round the mast above the bolsters, and half this distance measured from the crown of the shrouds, will be the point for commencing the first turn of each serving, which mark with chalk, cut through the centre of the bights at the end you commenced warping ; and on the crown of the other bights, marked with knotted spunyarn, the number of the shroud, commencing with one knot on the inside bight for the purpose of distinguishing them. Run a chalk mark across the upper bights, distant from the post a third of the distance from the deck to the bolsters, which, when you fit the rigging will mark the termination of the service.

Get each length on the stretch separately, ready for fitting. New rope before fitting should be stretched one inch to the foot.

Worm, parcel, and serve the eyes of each pair of shrouds to the chalk mark, but continue the foremost shroud on each side, the whole way down. Parcel the shrouds in the wake of the serving, to keep it from sinking between the parts of the service.

Wire rigging should not be warped off, but the length of the foremost and after shrouds having been measured from the foremost and after dead-eyes, in the chains to

E

the bolster on the opposite side ; divide the difference in length between the intermediate shrouds, adding the diameter of the rope to each pair in succession.

A wire shroud is completely served over ; the pendants are fitted with an eye of the same size, and in the same manner as the shrouds ; one leg being one-third longer than the other, with thimbles spliced into each end.

If it is necessary to have an odd number of shrouds, it will be found a good plan instead of connecting them with a horse-shoe splice, to fit an eye splice in each, and put them on first.

Measure the drift for the stays, and form a collar the length of the masthead, by splicing a fork into the upper end. Form a Flemish eye at each end of the fork, and worm, parcel, and serve, a fathom below the crutch.

In parcelling rigging, the canvas should always be worked up, to prevent water getting between the parts of the parcelling.

9. Rig the Foremast.—Get up, lash, and steady taut the runners and tackles, the uppermost just under the necklace, and the lowermost two-thirds up from the deck. Shift the two mast-head gantlines down to the after cross-tree on each side of the mast, and lash a block on the after side of the mast-head for a short gantline, to reach into, and be worked in the top.

A shroud is sent over, by seizing both parts of a pair together about a quarter down, the gantline bent to a toggle and slipped under the seizing, a rope's end being also bent to it to round down again. The gantline is stopped to the shroud below the eye-seizing, and at the crown of the eye, which is kept open with a piece of spunyarn from the crown to the seizing. Sway away, and when it comes up to the top, bend on the short gantline under the seizing, stop it up to the crown, on the upper side of the shroud, cut the stops of the long gantline, and sway over the mast-head. A short gantline is used, to avoid the trouble of hauling up and dipping the long gantline as you sway each pair of shrouds over, which would be the case were they kept at the mast-head.

Then, first tarring and parcelling the bolsters, place the rigging as follows :—starboard and port pendants, starboard and port pair of shrouds, and so on; beat each shroud well down with commanders; then the after shroud on each side, fitted with an eye splice or horse-shoe. After each pair of pendants and shrouds are roused down separately into their places with up-and-downs on each side, and a luff on each shroud of a pair (both brought to the up-and-downs), the fore stays are sent up by the gantlines, and lashed with a rose lashing abaft the mast.* Then lying close down on the stays, having been passed up between the collars, the jeer-block strop is lashed abaft the mast. Over all, close down to the trestle-trees, is the strop for the fore stay tackle or tackles, fitted with one or two thimbles, as the case may be, and hanging down

* The collars of lower stays are sometimes taken over the cross-trees and cleated down on the mast-head, to allow the yards to brace up the sharper.

E 2

abaft the mast-head.   If a chain strop is used instead it
should be placed on the bolsters before the rigging.   After
the pendants, a strop with a large thimble seized into the
after part is usually placed for the spring main-topmast
stay to set up to,—the strop itself set up with two lashing-
eyes before the mast ; but this is inconvenient for setting
up.   A better plan is, to bring the stay down on deck
after reeving it through the block abaft the mast, and
there setting it up.

The rigging is next set up temporarily, being turned in
with spunyarn, and both shrouds of a pair pulled up together ; previously setting taut the fore stays if the bowsprit is secured.   After the stays and rigging have had a
second good pull, each shroud being equally taut, looking
out for the mast all the time, mark the rigging off and turn
in for a full due.

This is done by seizing a sheer-batten along the rigging,
parallel to the chains, and about three feet from the top of
the lower dead-eye, which, if it is well stretched, is a good
drift for turning in new rigging.   Mark the shrouds and
take the batten off.   Then measure down a couple of feet
on each shroud for half the round of the dead-eye, which
mark off for the crown of the bend for turning in, and, by
strictly adhering to this, you will ensure your rigging being
turned in square, and leave the required drift of about
three feet from dead-eye to dead-eye.

Everything being come up, bring to and steady taut
the foremost swifters : then knock out all the wedges,
hook a tackle (luff upon luff), from forward to a strop

round the mast close down to the deck, and with it and the runners and tackles (steadied forward against a stay-tackle from the mast-head, aft,) bring the mast to its intended rake.   Supposing the mast then to be in all particulars well stayed, drive the wedges in, keeping fast the tackles till you have done so, taking care not to alter the position of the mast ; and the wedges ought never to be started again except to alter the rake.   You may then set up the fore stays, making a small allowance for the mast coming aft as the rigging is pulled up ; then set up the after swifters against the stays, and the rest of the shrouds in succession, commencing with the foremost pair.

10. SET UP FORE RIGGING.—The purchase used for setting up lower rigging is an "up-and-down," and a luff.   The double block of the up-and-down is lashed or toggled to the lower pendant, and the single block hooked to a cat's paw in the hauling part of the luff; the single block of the luff being hooked to a selvagee strop round the shroud, parcelled in the nip, and the double block brought to the lanyard,—the end of the luff being used to round down.

The fore-stays are set up in the same manner as the shrouds, but the lanyard is middled and set up on both ends ; necessitating the use of one luff, and one "up and down" for each end of the lanyard, the falls must be taken through leading blocks, and kept in a line with the stays.

On refitting, when in a long summer's day the rigging should be turned in afresh, fore and aft, if it requires it,

63

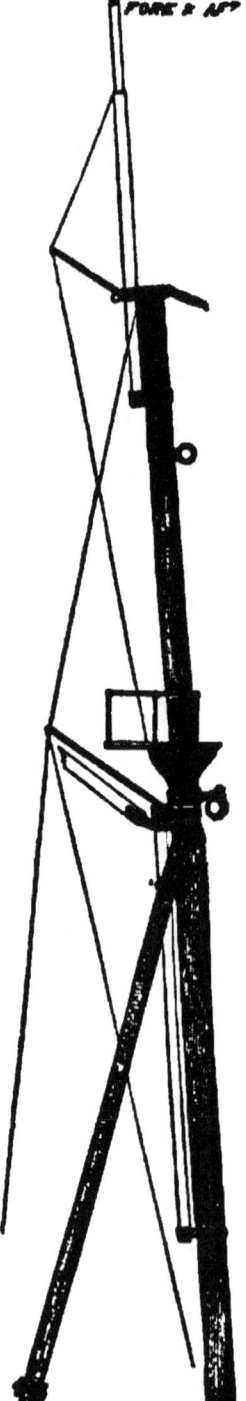

FORE & AFT

and set up, rattled and blacked down before sunset, the loss of time consequent on waiting for the up-and-downs till the stays are secured is of importance : therefore, make use of the stay tackles, the spans being fitted to unhook, and the pendants taken round the mast-head ; so that directly they have got enough of the stays, without waiting for securing, start with the rigging. The ends of stays and rigging are whipped and capped with canvas.

TRIPOD MASTS are of great advantage in turret ships dispensing with lower rigging, while allowing great range of training to the turret guns.

The centre leg of the tripod corresponds with an ordinary iron lower mast, standing nearly upright : the two after legs which take the place of rigging, are fixed to its head below the trestletrees, having about the same angle that the after swifter would have had, and the lower ends bolt to an iron plate in the deck; three or four small wire shrouds are necessary on each side for sending men aloft, which being fitted with slips, are easily cleared away.

The legs of the tripod may be placed before the mast if necessary.

11. STAYING MASTS AND THE USE OF BATTENS.——Conjointly with marks on the deck and masts, battens are used in setting up rigging to show whether the mast requires going to starboard or to port, forward or aft. To cut them, in the first instance, draw a line from the centre of the mast hole across the deck, measure off two equal distances

on each side of the mast, and mark the extremities. Take two long battens of equal length, place one end of each on the marks on each side of the deck, and rest the other ends against the mast. Pull the rigging up on either side, till the two ends come abreast of each other, and the mast must, necessarily, be upright. Drive a nail on each side of

65

the mast and deck for permanent marks, but one batten
only need now be retained.

The rake being determined, say half-an-inch to a foot, a
plumb-line is dropped from the centre of the mast, from
any distance up, and the mast raked till a corresponding
is plumbed. If, for instance, the plumb-line is dropped
from the trestle-trees at 60 feet, the line must plumb at
30 inches abaft the mast.

"The rake of the masts has reference to the keel; but
as the deck and the keel are not parallel, the angle between
their planes must be considered, when determining the
angle the batten should have to the deck, in order that
it may have the assigned angle to the keel."—(*Admiralty
Circular, April, 1858.*)

Draw a fore-and-aft line from the centre of the mast,
place the end of the batten on it, either before or abaft
the mast as most convenient ; mark where the ends take
the mast and deck with a couple of nails, which, with the
side marks and this batten, are for future guidance, it being
needed merely to place the batten afterwards against the
mast, to show how the latter requires to be moved.*

---

* The circular, above quoted, states, that, " in consequence
of the injudicious manner in which the masts have been stayed, and
the lower rigging set up," they are frequently crippled ; and provides
that "to regulate the setting up of rigging, and to determine if a
lower mast is straight, a middle line should be cut on each of its sides
and upon the after part. These lines should be painted a different
colour from the rest of the mast, and extend from the trestle-tree to
the heel. At the upper part of each line a small eyebolt should be

12. OBJECT OF RAKING MASTS.—As the pressure of the wind is perpendicular to the plane of the sail, raking masts produce lifting sails, though the direct propelling power is somewhat lessened thereby ; the loss varying in square sails, as versine of angle of rake.

By the mizen-mast raking considerably, it the more effectually resists the forward strain brought upon it by its own braces and those from the mainmast, and at the same time increases the space between it and the mainmast.

Fincham says, that " the whole of the masts should rake, so that, when the ship is inclined to her most common angle, the plane of the sails should be perpendicular to the longitudinal axis of the ship, or else part of the force of the wind that acts on the sails must depress the ship."

13. DETERMINING RAKE OF MASTS.—Presuming that the angle between the deck and keel is so small as not to be noticeable in a small distance,—

$$192 : 2 :: 64 : x$$
$$x = 8 \text{ inches.}$$

14. STAYING MASTS IN DOCK.—This of course is

placed, and on the line near the deck another such eyebolt. A rope line fastened to the upper one, and rove through the lower, and pulled tight, will, if the mast be straight, coincide with the middle line cut upon it ; or, if not straight, the fact will be evident by the cut line and the rope not being parallel. The amount by which parallelism is departed from, will represent any curve the mast has taken."

67

preparatory to cutting a batten, which could always be used irrespective of the ship's trim. Supposing, then, that you drop the plumb-line from 60 ft. up the mast,—

$$200 : 3 :: 60\ x; \therefore x = 10\cdot8 \text{ in.}$$

½-in. in a foot = 30 in. in 60 feet; so 30 in. − 10·8 in. = 19·2 in., the rake in 60 feet, to be given in the first instance—angle between deck and keel as before.

15. USE OF THE RUBBING PAUNCH ON THE FORE SIDE OF LOWER MASTS.—To protect the mast when striking the yard, and to prevent the yard catching the hoops. The mizen-mast has only a small piece of hard wood in the wake of the yard when up.

16. SMALL PIECES OF WOOD ROUND THE HOOPS OF A BOWSPRIT.—They are wedged-shaped, and nailed on before the bowsprit is got in, to prevent the hoops catching; consequently there is no necessity for them outside the partners.

17. LENGTH OF LOWER PENDANTS.—In the first place, to stay the mast, the runner-blocks must be lashed some way down, to keep the mast from buckling: this determines the length of one pendant. Another pendant is required to lash the tackle to, for setting up the stays, and, to bring it in a line with them, must be dipped over the lower yard. This must necessarily be the foremost one, but as it is unnecessary to cut it longer than is required to keep the tackle clear of the yard, it is therefore the shorter of the two. One-third of the length of the mast from deck to trestle-trees is sufficient for the long pendant, and one-third less for the short one.

18. PLACEMENT OF STAYS.—The starboard stays are the standing, and the port the spring stays; for the port go on first, and consequently, being the lowermost, are the proper ones for setting a sail on (if set on the upper stay, the sail would chafe across the lower one). The starboard fore and fore-topmast stays are therefore the upper and outer ones.

19. STANDING PARTS OF STAY LANYARDS.—The standing part of the lanyard of a bobstay is rove with a running eye round the collar above the heart, and acts as a preventer seizing. The lanyard of a lower stay, being worked on both ends, has no standing part, and, when rove full, the ends are seized to the other parts of the lanyard.

20. COMPARATIVE SMALL SIZE OF MIZEN STAYS.—Because the braces on the mizen-mast, by leading forward, assist the stays.

21. TURNING IN RIGGING CUTTER'S STAY FASHION.—On the starboard with the nip aft—port side, forward; ends, on both sides, inboard. The reason of this is, that rigging should be turned in as the rope would be coiled down, so that it at once accommodates itself to the bend it would naturally take, and no turns are taken out of the lay of the rope. With left-handed rope the same principle holds good, and the result is necessarily

reversed. However, with wire rigging, for the sake of uniformity in appearance, both sides are generally turned in alike, with the nip forward, and the end inside and aft.

70

22. TURNING IN WITH THE END UP.—With the right-handed rope the end will be, on the starboard side, aft ; and, on the port side, forward ; crossing inside, this was the old plan, but wire rigging is now often turned in end up, without crossing, with the end inside.

23. LEAD OF THE STAYS :—

Fore stays, from foremast-head to bowsprit, or knightheads.

— topmast stays, from topmast-head to bees, then in along bowsprit.

— top-gallant stay, from top-gallant mast-head to jib-boom end, and dolphin-striker.

— royal stay, from royal mast-head, to flying-boom end and dolphin-striker.

Main stays, from mainmast-head to a cross-piece before foremast, or to bolts in the deck on each side of the foremast.

— topmast stay, standing, from topmast-head over a chock between fore trestle-trees, then down on

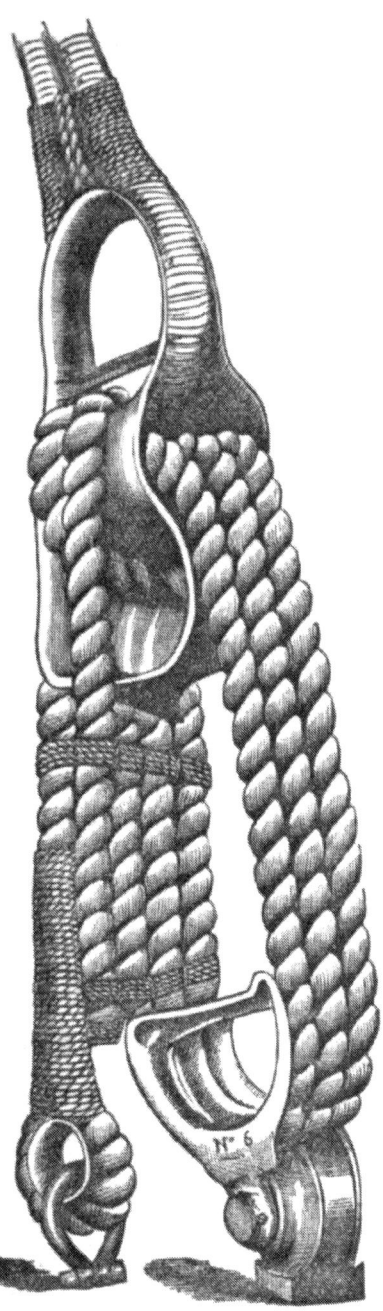

deck, or set up to a strop under the eyes of fore rigging.

Main spring, from topmast-head through iron stropped clump-block on foremast, and down on deck.

—— top-gallant stay, from top-gallant mast-head, through hole in fore cap, and set up in top.

——— royal stay, from royal mast-head, through sheeve-hole in chock of fore topmast cross-trees, down through hole in fore cap, and sets up in top.

—— stays, from mast-head, over rollers ten or twelve feet up mainmast, and set up to bolts in partners.

—— topmast stay, from top-mast-head, to strop between eyes of main rigging.

Mizen top-gallant stay, from top-gallant mast-head, through hole in main cap, and sets up in top.

—— royal stay, from royal mast-head, through hole in chock of main topmast cross-trees, down through hole in main cap, and sets up in top.

24. STRONGEST PLAN OF TURNING IN RIGGING.—By experiments on the three different plans it was found that, under the pressure of a breaking strain, a shroud first gives way at the splice. The next weak point was found, in the cutter's-stay plan, at the nip. The old plan broke at the main part of the rope, at the maximum strain, which, when the seizings are carefully put on, is therefore the strongest; but, by the working of the ship the seizings are

72

liable to slip, and more strain is brought on one part than another, which is the reason that the cutter's-stay plan has been so generally adopted.*

25. THROAT SEIZING.—The end of a throat-seizing is not cut off after the knot is formed, but two or three feet are left and expended round the shroud below the seizing; for, if cut off, there would be no end to work with on turning the rigging in afresh. The knot of the seizing is underneath.

26. LANYARDS OF LOWER RIGGING.—Are spliced round a thimble in an eye-bolt in the chains, inside the dead-eye; before the dead-eye on the starboard side, and abaft on the port side; then through the foremost hole in the dead-eye (starboard side), from in—out, and when rove full, the hauling part will be found under the standing part of the shroud; for there it is that the first and greatest strain comes when setting up, which, if the lanyard were rove any other way, would be brought on the seizing, and would moreover cause the dead-eye to slew. By bringing the standing part to the chains, the purchase is increased; and the tendency to capsize, which dead-eyes in new rigging are liable to, is counteracted. Lanyards are half the size of the shroud, supposing the latter to be hemp.

27. TO BRING TO.—A couple of turns of the lanyard are taken round a large toggle; a strop is then middled, and a turn taken with it round both parts of the lanyard under the toggle, and the luff hooked to the bights.

*Tinmouth.

73

28. RACKINGS ON THE LANYARD.—Are taken off, at first, to bring an equal strain on all parts ; and, when everything has settled well into its place, two or three seizings are put on every two parts, that when the ship, working heavily, slackens the lee rigging and brings up again with a jerk, the strain may come at once on all parts of the lanyard, and not on each part in succession.

29. TACKLES.—The power gained by them is as the space travelled over as you walk the weight up, to the space travelled by the weight at the same time, which, in simple tackles is as the number of parts at the movable block.　For instance, in a single whip no power is gained, the direction only being altered for convenience in working.　In a double whip the power is doubled ; in a gun-tackle purchase, with the standing part at the movable block, the power is trebled ; and the same with a luff or burton, with the double block stationary ; in a side tackle with two double blocks, the power applied is increased fourfold ; and so on.　In a port-tackle fall, a, it is first of all doubled by the runner, then trebled by the tackle, which gives $2 \times 3 = 6$, the whole power gained.　In a runner and tackle, b, $2 \times 4 = 8$; that is, five men on this purchase will lift as much as forty men on a single rope.　Luff upon luff gives an increase of 16 times ; another luff added, 64 times ; and so on.　But this is purely theoretical, and, for practical purposes one-fourth should be subtracted for ordinary tackles, and one-third for a three-fold purchase, as an allowance for friction ; and when the hauling part, coming from the movable block of

74

a tackle, is not parallel to the tackle, there is a further loss
of power = tension on hauling part × cosine of the angle.

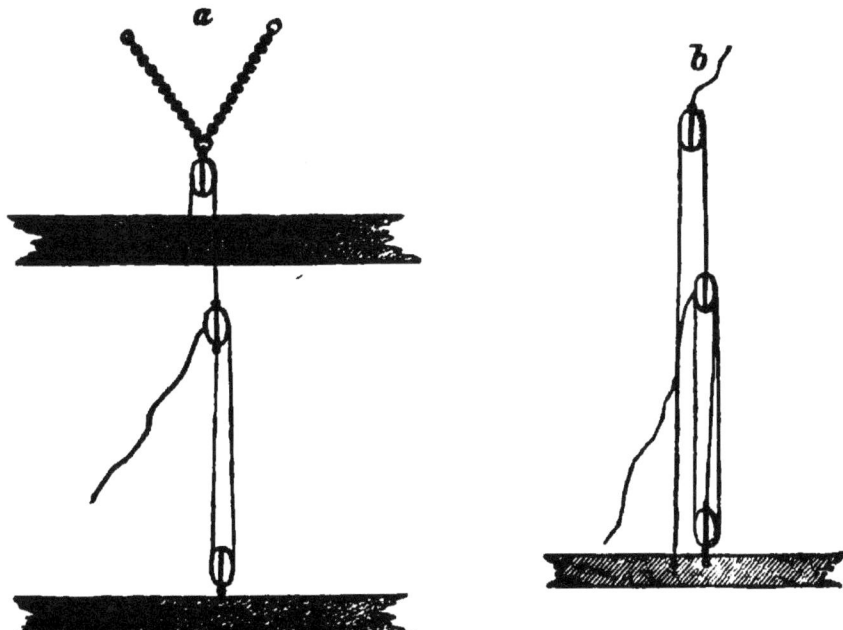

One great advantage of a tackle on board ship, which
renders its application of constant occurrence when mere
power is not wanting, must not be overlooked ; as, for
example, when sudden hoisting or jerking is to be avoided,
and a steady, gradual strain is required, as in staying a
mast. Another advantage of a purchase, when fitted to
any part of a ship's rigging, is that on *coming up*, when
some little must necessarily be given back, only a mere
fractional part is lost on the rope itself ; as in the lanyard
of a dead-eye, the purchase fitted to an after main
brace, &c.*

* From " Tate's Mechanics " is taken the following clear explanation :—

"*Ex.* 1. In the annexed system of pulleys if W = 2 lbs., required
P, when equilibrium takes place.

F

30. SPANISH BURTONS.—A single Spanish burton, a, has two single blocks, the standing part spliced into the strop of the movable block, and the bight seized or bent to the hook.   This increases the power three times.

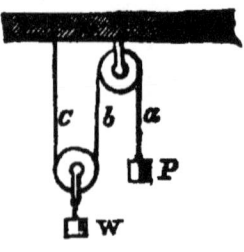

Here, as W is suspended by two cords, c and b, each cord will carry 1 lb., but as the cord is supposed to have a free motion over the wheels, the portions a, b, and c, will have the same stretch or tension; therefore P must be 1 lb.

Let us now consider the equilibrium on the principle of the equality of work.

If W ascend 1 foot, the cords c and b will each be shortened 1 foot, and therefore P must descend 2 feet; hence we have,—

    Work of P = P × 2, and work of W = 2 × 1,
        ∴ P × 2 = 2 × 1, and P = 1 lb."

"Ex. 2.   In the annexed system of pulleys, if W = 9 lb., required P, when equilibrium takes place.

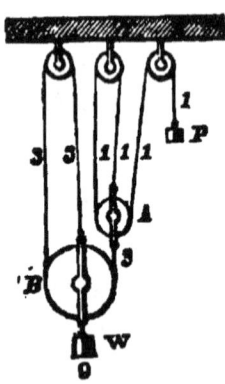

Here the three cords marked 3, form a continuous cord, hence they will each sustain the same stretch; and in like manner the four cords marked 1, will each sustain the same stretch. The weight W, with its pulley B, is supported by three cords, therefore each cord will carry 3 lbs.; there are therefore 3 lbs. suspended from the pully A.   Now the pully A with this weight is supported by three cords, therefore each cord will carry 1 lb., hence it follows that P must be 1 lb.

Or thus on the principle of work :—

If W ascend 1 foot, the pulley A will ascend 3 feet, because each of the three cords marked 3, will give off 1 foot of cord; in like

76

The double burton, *b*, has one double and two single blocks; the standing part spliced into the strop of a single block, then rove through the double or fixed block, and the bight seized to the strop of the lower block, to which the weight to be lifted is hooked. The end is then rove up through the double block, through the lower, and lastly through the single block to which the standing part is

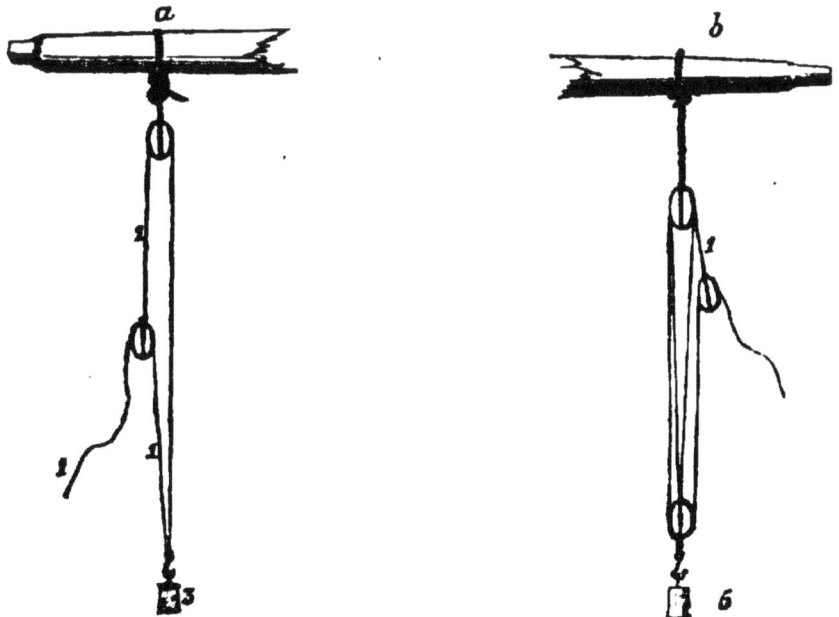

secured. This purchase gives an increase of five times the power applied.

---

manner, if the pully A ascend 3 feet, the weight P must descend 9 feet, because each of the three cords marked 1 will give off 3 feet of cord. Thus it appears that while W ascends 1 foot, P descends 9 feet; hence we have by the principle of work,—

Work of $P = P \times 9$; work of $W = W \times 1$,

$$\therefore P \times 9 = W;$$

and if W be 9 lbs., then P = 1 lb.

In precisely the same manner the equation of equilibrium may be determined for any other system of pulleys."

Other Spanish burtons, *c d*, are formed of single blocks which quadruple and quintuple the power respectively.

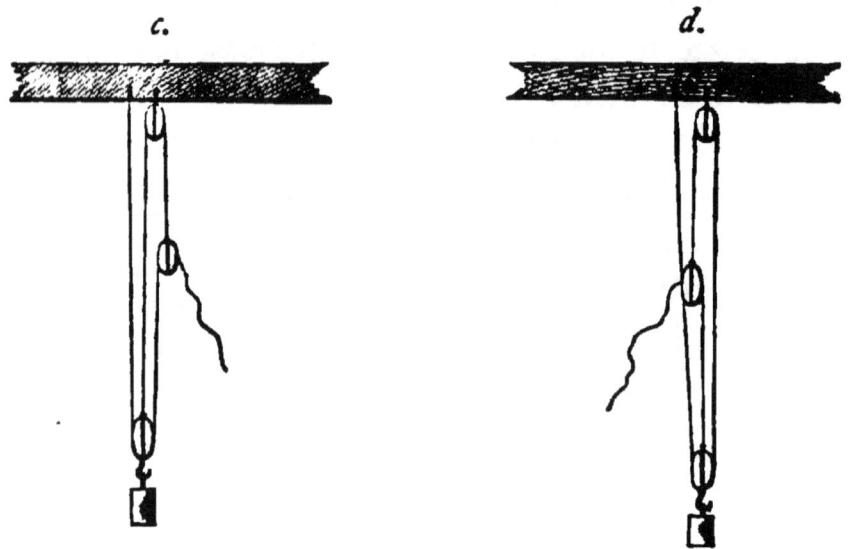

c.   *d.*

31. STANDING PART OF A TACKLE—Should be on the side of the block, opposite to the hauling part, as it thus leads fair, and counteracts the tendency of the hauling part to slue the block.

32. TO FIND WHAT SIZED ROPE YOU REQUIRE, WHEN ROVE AS A TACKLE, TO LIFT A GIVEN WEIGHT.—Divide the weight to be raised by the number of parts at the movable block, to obtain the strain on a single part; add one-third of this for the increased strain brought by friction, and reeve the rope of corresponding strength.*

One-sixth of 40 tons is 6⅔ tons, which, with one-third added, is 9 tons nearly; for which you should reeve a 6-inch or 6½-inch rope

* Table III.

Conversely :—To find what weight a given rope will lift, when rove as a tackle ;—multiply the weight that the rope is capable of suspending by the number of parts at the movable block, and subtract one-fourth of this for resistance.

8.9 tons, the strength of the rope, multiplied by 6, the number of parts at the movable block, minus 13.3 or one-fourth, gives 40.1 tons as the weight required.

33. WIRE ROPE is more than twice the strength of hemp rope of the same circumference ; splicing a rope is supposed to weaken it one-eighth.

34. TO FIND THE LOSS OF SUPPORT CAUSED BY THE ANGLING OF A STAY.—Sine of angle × tension = effective force,* which, in this case, will be found to be 5·8 tons, showing a loss of nearly one-third.

35. DISTANCE OF RATLINES APART—Is fifteen inches : catch-ratlines every fifth.

36. HOW SEIZED ON.—Splice the seizing of two-yarn nettle-stuff into the eye of the ratline ; pass it round the shroud, through the eye, *back* round the shroud, and so on ; the eye lying athwartships.

The hitch crosses outside, for, when you stand on the ratline, it remains firmer, bearing against the shroud, than if hitched inside.

* Tinmouth.

79

37. SQUARING RATLINES.—In this case take two or three turns in the lay.

38. GAMMON AND RIG A BOWSPRIT.—If there are two gammonings to be passed, which is the case in large ships, not fitted with running in bowsprits, the outer must be passed first, or, from its greater leverage, it would slacken the inner.

The gammoning is chain, and the standing part is shackled round the bowsprit, close down to the after part of the saddle; which, with the hole in the cutwater should be well greased. A turn is then passed through the hole in the cutwater at its foremost part and hove taut, as many thoroughfoot turns as can be taken are passed; each turn as it is passed is hove as taut as possible with a pendant, and strong purchase brought to a capstan, and racked by driving nails through the links into the bowsprit. The end is expended in racking turns passed up towards the bowsprit, and the whole is covered with lead.

If thoroughfoot turns were not passed, the outer turns would first feel the effect of the bowsprit working with the pitching of the ship; but, by the inner turns on the bowsprit becoming the outer ones in the cutwater, the strain is equalized: also with a bowsprit of much steeve, the turns would have a tendency to slip down, if passed round and round.

Iron bands screwed down over the bowsprit to the knight-heads, take the place of gammoning in many ships.

Few ships have their bowsprits clothed exactly alike, but

80

the following is the general plan :—At one-third in from the cap, the rigging cleats are nailed round the bowsprit ; and the rigging is placed in the following order :—Inner bobstay collar, inner bowsprit shroud collars, inner fore-stay collar, middle bobstay collar, outer bowsprit shroud collars, outer fore-stay collar, outer bobstay collar.

At nearly the end of the bowsprit the iron stropped heart for the cap bobstay shackles on.

The Bobstay Collars are wire, with an eye spliced into each end ; a heart seized into the centre, and the eyes lashed together, with a rose lashing on the top of the bowsprit.

Bowsprit Shroud Collars are fitted like the bobstay collars, but with a long and short leg lashing on the top of the bowsprit. A fore-stay collar is a wire strop with a heart seized into one end ; the other bight is taken round under the bowsprit and lashed to its own part below the heart, which is chocked to keep it at the side of the bowsprit.

Bobstays are wire strops, spliced after being rove through the cutwater ; the heart is seized in with the splice on its top, and both parts of the bobstay seized together at the cutwater.

Bowsprit shrouds are single wire, with a heart spliced into the outer end, and fitted with a slip to a bolt in the bows at the other.

Chain is now rapidly taking the place of wire rope, for bowsprit shrouds and bobstays

39. BOBSTAYS.—The inner bobstays are set up before

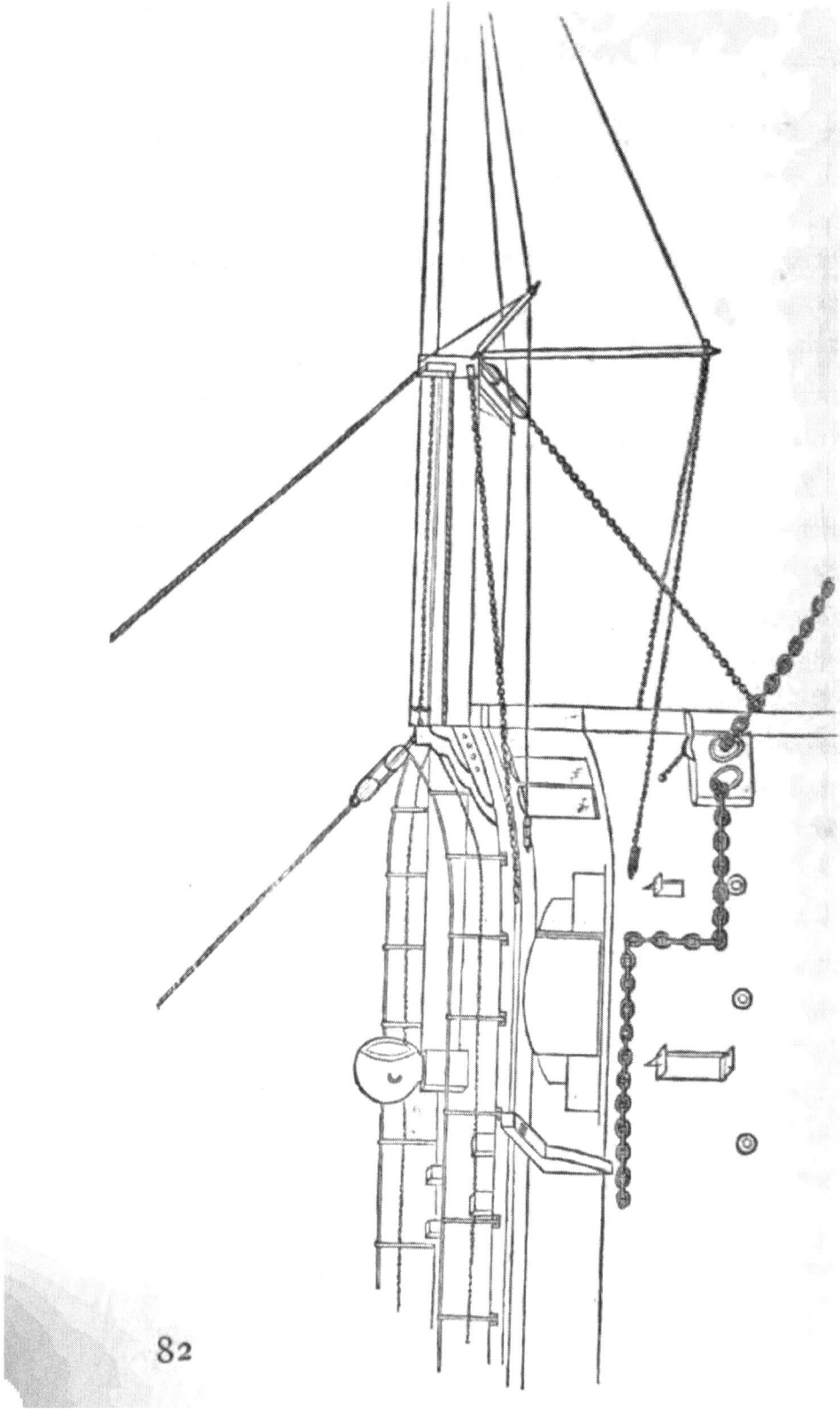

A RUNNING-IN BOWSPRIT.

82

those further out, otherwise you would he unable to work at the inner ones.

40. SETTING UP A BOBSTAY.—The single block of a luff is hooked to a cat's-paw in the lanyard, the double block to a selvagee round the bobstay, the hauling part through a leading part on the bowsprit—led inboard, on to which another luff, or up-and-down, is capped along the bowsprit.

41. RUNNING IN BOWSPRITS.—Ships intended to be used as rams, are usually fitted with running in bowsprits, which are of wood, and four-sided, the heel is kept in place between bitts fitted on the forecastle and with a slip fid; chocks are bolted to the knightheads, and the bowsprit runs out between them over a roller let into the stem head, and is kept down by an irou band which goes over it, screwing down to the chocks.

The bowsprit cap is iron, with bolts for the whiskers, and dolphin striker on it; also two snatches, or iron-bound sheaves for the top-mast stays; inside the cap are iron-bound hearts for the bowsprit shrouds and bobstay to set up to.

Bobstay and bowsprit shrouds are chain, and the standing parts secure with slips to the bows, setting up to the bowsprit with a lanyard in large ships, but in some small vessels it is simply fitted with a screw, which can be tautened up at pleasure with a lever.

42. GETTING IN MAIN YARD FROM THE JETTY.—Ship lying starboard side to the wharf. Reeve the jeers with the standing part aloft, leaving a sheave out of the upper

block, and take them to the capstan, or, if more convenient, through a block at the edge of the wharf, and take them to one of the capstans at hand. Hook up-and-downs to strops out on the quarters of the yard; and to the slings hook a sail-tackle, taken to a bollard ashore and hauled taut. Bend a single guy to each yard-arm, take a turn with them, and heave round the jeers. Pull upon the port up-and-down, to clear the fore rigging, and ease away the port guy, holding on the starboard guy and sail-tackle. When clear, sway the yard across the nettings with the jeers and starboard tackle, easing and working the guys as necessary.

43. MAIN-YARD IN THE WATER ALONGSIDE.—Coming in on the starboard side, haul the yard up with the port yard-arm forward ; lash the jeer blocks to it, and reeve the jeers in the foremost or port block, and secure the standing part round the yard, making three parts.

A jib-boom, mizen topmast, or fish davit may be used as a derrick, the former will, I think be found the most convenient. Get up the largest hawser your jeer and top blocks will reeve ; use an up-and-down for a derrick topping lift, with its double block lashed to one of the masthead pendants ; hook a top block to the other pendant, reeve the end of the hawser through it, through a top block lashed to the derrick head, through the starboard jeer block on the yard, and secure the end outside all, at the head of the jib-boom.

Raise the derrick with the up-and-down, lash the heel, and put a luff on as a martingale.

84

Get a sail tackle on the foremost yard-arm as a guy, a rope's end will be sufficient for the after arm. When already, sway the yard clear of the netting, with the hawser, taking down the slack of the jeers, then haul away foremost guy and jeers, ease the hawser, and when the yard is athwartships, land it on the netting. If necessary, use top burtons as preventer lifts in placing the yard. Reverse the operation in getting the yard out.

44. RIGGING MAIN YARD.—Centre the yard and place the slings, and, on either side, jeer blocks and topsail sheet blocks; truss strops. The clew-garnet block on the quarter, and further out the quarter strop for the rolling tackle.

Yard-arms.—Foot rope, jack-stay, head-earing strop, dog strop for yard tackle pendant, dog strop for preventer brace, dog strop for the after main brace, lift block, standing part of lift, sheet stopper, and standing part of topsail sheet.

The Slings—Consist of two pieces of chain, the foremost ends connected to a large ring, through which the after ends reeve; these join in a long link, to which the slip is attached.

Jeer Blocks—Are single blocks fitted with two single strops of different lengths, to allow the sheeves to lie fore and aft; the foremost strop is the shortest, and the strops are lashed together with a rose lashing on the upper forequarter of the yard. The short jeers are generally kept rove as preventer slings.

Truss Stops—Are chain, with their ends lashed on the

85

top of the yard, one of them on each side has a fair-leader for the hauling part of the truss ; the standing parts shackling to the other, on opposite sides.

Topsail Sheet Blocks—Are fitted with a double strop, which lashes on the top of the yard ; a lashing being passed between them below the yard, to prevent the blocks slipping outwards.

Clewgarnet Blocks—Are best fitted if stropped, with sennit tails to nail round the yard, the block lying well up on the quarter, the standing part of the clew-garnet is secured with a timber hitch outside the block. The quarter strop is a grummet strop with a thimble seized into it.

Yard-arm rigging—foot-ropes are fitted with an eye over the yard-arm, and a small eye in the other end at convenient distances; the foot-rope is kept up by stirrups, through which it is rove ; their upper ends going over the jackstay bolts. The jackstay is wire, and goes with an eye over the yard-arm, reeves through the jack-stay, bolts on the yard, and lashes to the end of the opposite jack-stay in the bunt.

The dog-strop for the yard tackle pendant is a single wire strop ; the pendant is wire, and one-quarter the length of the yard ; is spliced into the dog-strop, with a fiddle-block in the lower end.

Brace Blocks.—Take two coupling thimbles, into one splice the single wire dog-strop ; to the other splice a double strop, into which seize the brace block, so that it will tie with the sheave horizontal.

Lift Block.—A single block, single stropped, with an

86

eye to go over the yard-arm ; the standing part of the lift is fitted with a running eye.

The leech-line blocks—two on each side before the sail, are tailed and hitched to the jackstay ; from these the leech-lines reeve through a double block toggled under the top, and thence down on deck—abaft. The slab-line blocks—two on each side abaft the sail, are secured like the leech-line blocks ; and the slab-lines when rove through them, lead down before the mast through small double blocks. At the length of the yard-tackle pendant in from the yard-arm there is a cheek for the quarter tricing-line and the bill-tricing line is rove through a block on the slings.

45. LOWER BRACE BLOCK.—The side which has the square head of the bolt in it is the uppermost, to prevent the bolt working out.

46. DIFFERENCE BETWEEN LOWER AND TOPSAIL BRACE-BLOCK STROPS.—A lower brace block is fitted with a double strop, topsail brace block with two single strops. The former—to make the block lie horizontal, the latter—vertical.

47. LOWER LIFT-BLOCK.—The hauling part of the lift should reeve through the foremast sheeve, for, if through the after one, it would, on bracing up, bind against the lee rigging and prevent its being overhauled.

48. DIFFERENCE BETWEEN FORE AND MAIN-TOPMASTS. —In a fore topmast, the live sheeve is cut from the port after quarter to the starboard fore quarter, and in a main-

87

topmast, from the starboard after to the port fore quarter.

49. HEELS OF TOPMAST AND TOP-GALLANT MASTS.— If a spar were used large enough to allow the heel to be cut out of the solid, the most important part of the mast would be formed of the core ; thus, a mast of this description would be considerably weaker than one formed of a smaller spar : and moreover, as the younger a spar is, the greater is its comparative strength, owing to its greater compactness (which may be seen by comparing the specific gravities of large and small timber), so the greater is the inducement to employ small spars when applicable for this purpose.

50. SHOULDER FOR THE CAP, ON THREE SIDES OF A MAST-HEAD.—This allows you to make the after side more wedge-like, by giving more to cut away on ; and this form prevents the cap from drooping forward and also from jambing.

51. FIDS.—A topmast fid is of solid iron, with a hole in the end through which is spliced a strop for a jigger to hook to for unfidding—assisted by the top maul.

A top-gallant fid is composed of *a*, the fid, and *b*, the shoe. An iron band *c*, with a pin through the fid, keeps the shoe in its place. The upper part of the fid-hole in the mast is cut so as to

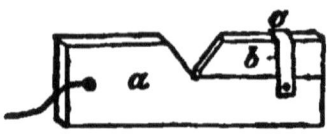

dovetail in between the fid and the shoe. By the working of the mast it is, therefore, impossible for the fid to work out.

88

52. GETTING MAIN-TOPMAST ON END.—Lying on the starboard booms, with head aft. Hook the top blocks, reeve a 7-inch hawser through the starboard block, overhaul it down and hitch it through the live sheeve round the heel of the mast, and pass a lashing round the head of the mast and hawser about a third down, which drift is necessary to allow the mast-head to be swayed up outside the top (being hauled forward by a main top-bowline); should it be requisite to lower it down the main hatchway previous to pointing its head between the trestle-trees. Get up and lash the starboard fore up-and down, and hook it to a strop through the fid-hole. Brace the main yard sharp up on the starboard tack, bring the hawser to the capstan and run it round, easing away the fore tackle. When the topmast is up and down the mast, land it on the deck, unhook the fore tackle, steady the head, slack up the lashing, double the hawser, and sway up high enough to reeve the port top-tackle pendant over the dumb sheeve—well smothered in grease, the upper block being rounded close up to the futtock rigging. You are now ready to sway away and fid.

It may be swayed up from alongside in the same manner.

53. GETTING A LOWER CAP OVER.—Main. Sway a top block up by one of the gantlines, and lash it on the starboard side of the mast-head; reeve a 7-inch hawser through it, overhaul it down, bend on, and sway the cap into the top—(outside all, guying it clear by a fore-and-after, for it will not come up through lubbers'-hole),

89

and place it fair for receiving the head of the topmast. Then overhaul the hawser down again, get the topmast up and down, double the hawser—rove through the live sheeve, and, if high enough, lash the cap, by middling the lashing, clove-hitching it round the mast-head over the cap, reeving each end through the foremost bolt in the cap, its own side—round the mast-head, through the after bolt in the cap, back round the mast-head, and so on till enough turns are passed. 'Place a capstan bar in the fid-hole, with a slue-rope bent to it; sway away, slue the topmast, and lower until the cap is on, when place the capshore.

The same means are employed for sending the cap down, but a capstan bar, slung by one of the gantlines abaft the mast-head, is used for a bumper; the gantline worked on deck.

54. SENDING TOPMAST CROSS-TREES OVER.—Main. Sway the topmast six or seven feet above the cap, and lash the gantline blocks on each side of the topmast-head well up. Up-end the cross-trees abaft the mast, as in sending a top over, bend the gantlines, led underneath, to the after horns, close to the trestle-trees, and stop them up to the foremast horns. Bend a guy from the mizen-mast-head to the fore part, to keep them clear of the top, sway away, and land them on the cap. Bend a couple of bell-ropes to the foremast horns from the top, to steady them, cut the stops, lower the topmast, haul over on the bell-ropes;—keeping a strain on the gantlines, and the cross-trees will fall over the mast-head; then unlash the

90

gantline blocks, and let the cross-trees come down into their place.

SENDING TOPMAST CROSS-TREES DOWN.—Strip the mast, sending down the cap and hanging blocks, unfid and lower it until the cross-trees are one fathom from the cap. Stopper the hawser, and belay it with two fathoms slack— (the distance of the cross-trees above the cap being measured and sent down from aloft to guide you). Off stopper, and bump the cross-trees to start them. Lower the mast and land them on the cap. Pass the ends of the lower mast-head gantlines over the lower lift blocks :— from aft, forward (main topmast cross-trees), and bend them to the cross-trees. Bend one of the fore gantlines or a main-top bowline, to the fore part ; haul taut the gantlines and take a turn with them. Ease the cross-trees down off the cap—(the gantlines lying over the lift blocks preventing them falling far), haul forward on the bowline, and when clear, lower away. Lower the fore topmast cross-trees down abaft, with one of the main gantlines for a fore-and-after.

55. RIGGING AND STAYING FORE TOPMAST.—After the cross-trees are on, the topmast is rigged in the following order :—necklace, bolsters, grummet, mast-head pendants, shrouds, backstays, topmast stays, jibstay.

The Necklace—Is a chain strop round the mast-head under the bolsters, with two short legs on each side ; the hanging blocks shackle to the two after legs, and the jib and fore-topmast staysail halyards to the foremost legs. To send the rigging over, shift the gantlines to the after

G

cross-tree, and put the rigging over in the same manner as lower rigging, only in the order given above.

The pendants are wire, have but one leg, and fitted with a cut splice; the rigging is also wire. The sister blocks should be seized in between the foremost shrouds, below the seizing, before sending them over.

The rigging being over, the topmast cap on, and hanging blocks shackled, fid the mast, get up and steady taut the sail tackle, hook the top burton to the pendants, stay the mast and proceed to set up the rigging. For which use a runner and top burton; the runner fitted with a selvagee tail on one end, and a thimble on the other, rove through a block stopped with a thimble, the lanyard is bent to the thimble, the tail of the runner clapped on the shroud, and the single block of the burton hooked to the thimble of the pendant; pull up and beat down the shrouds successively, fleeting the runner as required to each shroud, and then to the backstays. The topmast cap may either be sent over by gantlines on the topmast head, bent to the foremost bolts, and stopped up to the after, going up before all, or else, the mast lowered after the rigging is sent over, and the cap placed on the top of the rigging, fair for swaying through.

56. SISTER BLOCKS IN TOPMAST RIGGING.—The foremost pair of shrouds are seized together with a stout seizing; the block is then put in, and secured in its place by slighter seizings round it and the rigging.

57. LEAD OF TOPSAIL LIFTS AND REEF-TACKLES.— When the yard is braced forward, these ropes lie right

across the cheek of the block,—a most injurious lead when hauling out the reef-tackles in a gale of wind, and the yard is obliged to be braced by, or at all forward. So instead of the sister block in the rigging, fit a fiddle block to a short pendant spliced into a bolt driven into the trestle-trees; or, if you use a sister block, let it be a swivel one in an iron frame.

58. RIGGING A TOPSAIL-YARD.—The yard in the centre has two iron bands, with eyes on the top of the yard, to which the halliard blocks shackle.

Parrall.—Measure five and a half times round the mast; take once and a half for the short legs, and the remainder for the long legs, splice an eye in each of the ends; seize the legs with their centres together, pudding, marl, and cover with leather. The long legs are passed under the yard, and the eyes are lashed to the eyes of the short legs on the upper after quarter.

The Slings—Are fitted with a running eye round the yard, (outside the tye block on the side the yard comes down), and a standing eye in the end for the sail-tackle, to hook to; then taken over to the other quarter, and secured by a lizard (through the thimble of which the slings are rove), brought through the quarter-strop, and passed with half-a-dozen turns round the yard and slings.

Quarter-strop.—A single strop spliced round the quarter of the yard, with a thimble seized into it.

Quarter Blocks—Are double blocks, with single strops, having an eye in each end, and lashing on the top of the yard with a rose lashing.

G 2

93

Yard-arms—Are rigged in the following order :—Foot-rope ; head-earing strop ; jackstay ; dog-strop for the brace ; lift block strop ; flemish horse ; jewel block; and boom iron.

Foot-ropes—Go with an eye over the yard-arm, rove through the stirrups, and seized to the yard on the opposite quarter ; turks-heads should be worked on each side of the stirrup, as they prevent the foot-ropes falling into long bights ; and if the latter carry away, they will not unreeve to the hazard of men's lives.

Jackstays—Are wire—go with an eye over the yard-arm, and lash together in the bunt of the yard. Dog and lift block strops are single wire-rope, with a thimble seized into them.

Flemish horse.—Thimble over the goose neck seized round the yard, three or four feet inside the foot-rope. Jewel block is stropped with a thimble, which goes over the goose neck.

The foregoing is the ordinary plan of fitting topsail yard-arms, but a much better and far more simple fashion has been adopted lately ; viz., have an iron band to fit the yard-arm, with bolts for the lift and brace block (which must be fitted with clip hooks) to hook to ; the jackstay may be fitted with a small eye splice to go over the eye on the band for the lift block, and the foot-rope goes over the goose neck ; doing away with the flemish horse.

Reef tackles instead of reeving through the sheeve in the yard-arm, being rove through a snatch. There can be

94

no comparison in point of time between this plan and the first mentioned, in shifting topsail yards.

59. RIGGING OF JIB, AND FLYING JIB-BOOMS, WHISKERS, AND DOLPHIN-STRIKER.—*Jib-boom :*—Heel secured by a heel chain shackled to a bolt in the cap, placed in the score, and secured with a slip shackle to a bolt in the other side of the cap : it rests in a saddle, and is kept down by a chain crupper, also fitted with a slip shackle. A funnel goes over the head of the boom (generally), on which the rigging is placed in the following order :—Foot-ropes, martingale, guys, jackstay, flying boom-iron, fore top-gallant stay.

Foot-ropes—Go over the funnel with a cut splice, then stopped out to the guys, and the after ends lashed to bolts in the cap.

The Martingale—Is fitted with an eye over the boom and dolphin striker ends, and is either wire-rope or chain.

Jib-guys—Are fitted with an eye over the boom, and whisker-ends, and are set up by hauling on the whisker-guys. The jackstay is wire, goes with an eye over the rigging, and sets up to the cap. The jib-guys and martingale—if of chain—shackle to bolts in iron bands, at the jib-boom, and dolphin striker ends.

Flying-boom.—Foot-ropes, guys, martingale, and fore royal stay in the score. These are fitted as in a jib-boom ; a hide funnel may be used with advantage, the rigging being sewed to it.

Whiskers.—Jib guy, whisker guy, jumper, lift, flying guy

95

through a hole in the whisker-end; and half-way in, there is a block for the flying jib-sheet. The jumper is fitted with an eye over the whisker end, and sets up with a thimble and lanyard to a bolt in the cutwater. Whisker guy, as the jumper, but sets up to the bows. Lift, the same, and sets up to a bolt in the cap. Flying guy, with a thimble and lanyard to the bows. The fore guy (of lower boom) sometimes reeves through a block on the whisker end.

Dolphin-striker.—Jaw-ropes, jibstay through a sheeve-hole a few feet below the bowsprit. At the end, grummet; back-ropes, middled, crossed, and seized; jib-martingale, fore top-gallant stay, flying martingale, and royal stay—through sheeve-holes.

60. JIB-TRAVELLER.—When shifting the jib in bad weather with the ship pitching heavily, you can lash the tack, &c., on the bowsprit, the traveller being run in to the cap, and afterwards hauled out; or, if the boom complains, you can set the jib half-way out, but in this case you should be prepared with a shifting martingale (a burton, or one regularly fitted). In a small vessel a traveller is very handy, when in rough weather, on a dark night, laying out on the boom to stow the jib is no very enviable duty.

61. RIGGING OF FORE TOP-GALLANT AND ROYAL MASTS.—The flying-jib halyard block strop first goes over the funnel on the top-gallant-mast-head; then, fore top-gallant-stay with an eye splice; flying jibstay the same; starboard and port pair of shrouds and starboard and port pair of backstays, the foremost generally fitted as a breast

96

backstay : over the rigging are lashed the blocks for top gallant-studding-sail halyards.

Top-gallant rigging should be set ˜up on the bight; the upper block of the burton fitted with a thimble, through which one shroud is rove, and spliced into the other, well up clear of the thimble; the lower block hooked to the eyes of the rigging close down; the fall always kept rove, and payed down on deck when wanted. When the upper block is seized into the bight of the rigging, it is apt to bring an unequal strain on the shrouds.

Royal-mast.—Stay; starboard pair of backstays; port pair of backstays;—the foremost as breast backstays; truck.

A false royal mast-head, hollowed out to receive the top of the royal pole, which is cut away to fit into it, is used : the rigging and truck are placed on it, and consequently are not disturbed when shifting the mast.

It is now a common practice to split the head of the royal-mast sufficiently to allow the bight of the royal yard rope to un-snatch when the mast is lowered, instead of unreeving it.

62. A TOP-GALLANT STAY—Being placed below the rigging allows the royal to be cut with less roach than it would have if the stay were above.

63. JACKS AND JACK BLOCKS.—Jacks are small iron horns, projecting from an iron band, which is bolted to the rim of a top-gallant funnel. They are principally intended to stand on when crossing royal yards, &c., and are of

97

great assistance in slueing the rigging square when sending up top-gallant masts. The iron band being fitted with eye-bolts, the span blocks, top-gallant buntline and flying-jib halyard blocks can be shackled underneath the rigging; which considerably lightens the appearance of the mast-head. The horns are curved aft to keep clear of the royal when set; and the iron band on the hounds of the top-gallant mast is notched on the fore part, into which a tooth in the iron ring of the jack slips, insuring the funnel being properly placed.

Jack blocks are occasionally used to dispense with the necessity for unreeving the yard-rope, when shifting the mast; and are lashed round and underneath the rigging, the yard-rope being rove in them, instead of through the sheeve in the mast.

64. SENDING STUDDING-SAIL BOOMS ALOFT.—Topmast-studding-boom:—Pay a rope's end down from the top, and bend it to the bolt in the heel; put a whip on the topsail yard to plumb the quarter-iron and bend it to the boom amidships, hitching the heel-lashing to it, to prevent it slipping out; stop the whip out to within three or four feet of the boom-ends, and sway away. Bear the boom-end clear of the topsail-yard, and, when the stop is up to the block, haul up as much as you can get of the heel-rope, take a turn with it, walk back the whip and land the boom across the quarter-iron; cut the stop, pull up on the whip and heel-rope, and launch the boom out.

Top-gallant-boom.—Haul it up into the top, heave a gasket or end of an earing down from the yard-arm, and

98

65.—LININGS OF A TOPSAIL.—The upper corners are called the head earings, and the lower the clews.

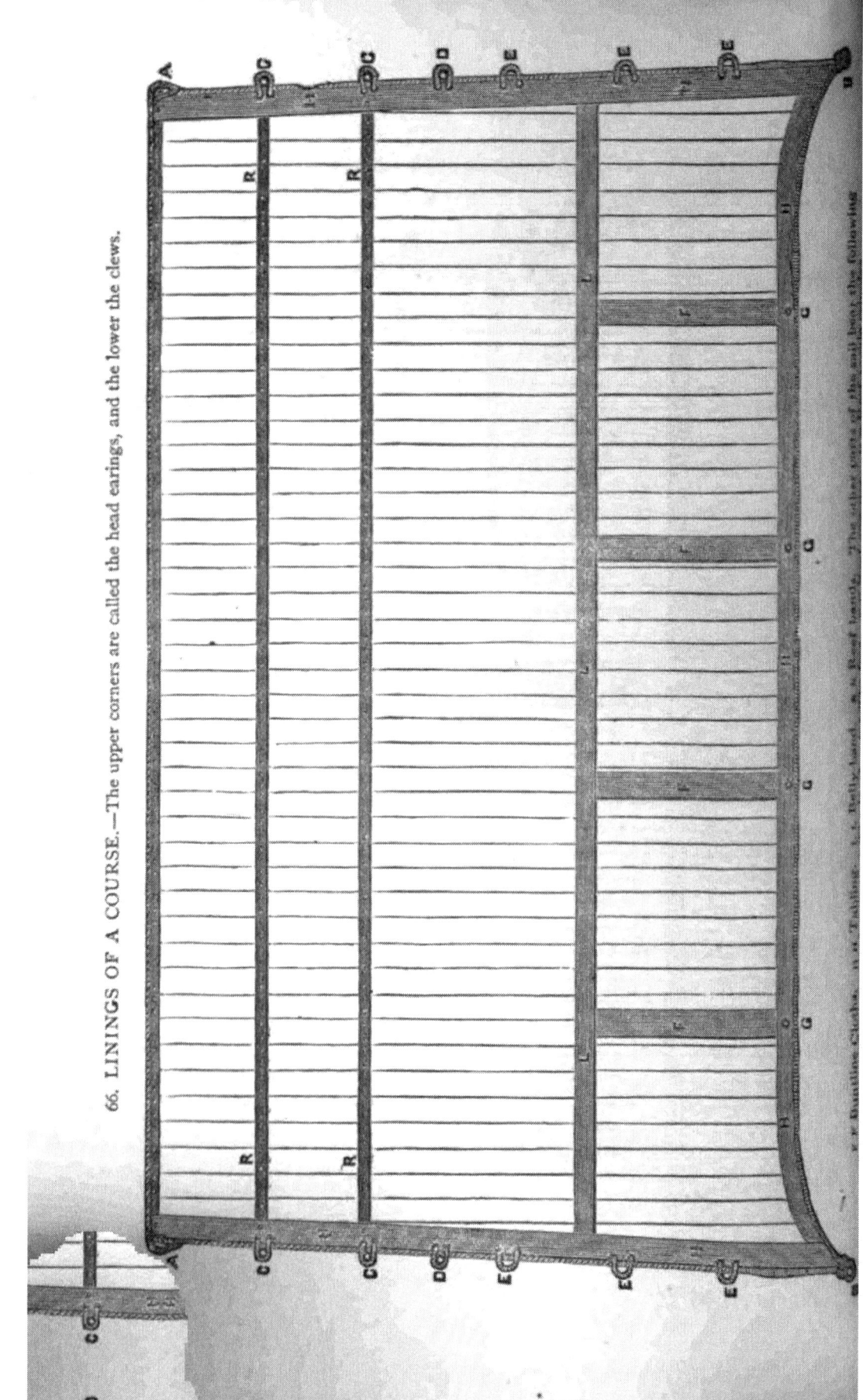

66. LININGS OF A COURSE.—The upper corners are called the head earings, and the lower the clews.

bend it to the boom-end; toggle the boom tricing-line, trice up, and haul out.

Lower booms are got out, abaft the fore rigging, by a whip on the fore and main yards.

67. FIT A TOPSAIL.—Stretch the head of the sail along, fit robands to the eylet holes in the head; the head earings to their cringles. Along each reef band fit the reef-lines, and from the head down the reefs, fit spilling lines.

On the leeches fit third and fourth reef-earings, bowline bridles; span for large reef tackle; beckets and toggles for small reef tackles. In the centre of the sail fit the beckets for the bunt jigger, sew the gaskets on along the head; splice the buntline toggle strops into the foot, and seize in the toggles.

To fit the reef-lines, a small line or *jackstay* is turned into the leech, level with the reef band, on the after side of the sail; another line is then run along the fore side, through each eyelet hole, and round the *jackstay* abaft, hauling taut through each time so as to form a jambing hitch in the eyelet hole; the ends are secured to the leech ropes.

Beckets and toggles must be fitted to the jackstay, on the topsail yard.

The two midship robands are always made larger than the others, to distinguish the centre of the sail in bringing to.

68. FIT A COURSE.—Stretch the head of the sail along, fit the head earrings and robands, put four toggles on the foot for the buntlines, and two on each leech both before and abaft all, for the leech and slab lines to toggle

on to.   A course has only two reefs, which should be fitted in the same manner as those of a topsail.

69. REEFS OF FORE-AND-AFT SAILS.—The points are *crow-footed;* which is done by stabbing a hole in the sail, middling the point, and twisting it against the lay, so as to work the strands out into loops. Put one end of the point through the sail, keeping the loops on one side, which stitch to the sail—one bight being on the upper part of the hole, and the others on each side, and each point on a seam.

70. BOWLINE AND REEF CRINGLES.—Reef cringles, and reef-tackle bridle-cringles have thimbles, which bowline cringles do not require.

71. BOWLINE BRIDLES.—That of the foresail has two cringles; mainsail three; foresail three; main-topsail usually four.   It is a good plan to have the toggle on topsail bowline bridles, fitted with a long drift, as it gives great facility for bending or unbending the bowline, in the top or on the lower yard.

72. CRINGLES IN LEECH OF FORE AND MAIN-TOP-SAILS.—The number is the same in each; for, in the fore-topsail, the reef-tackle bridle hitches to a separate cringle; but in the main-topsail, to the upper bowline cringle.

73. DIFFERENCE BETWEEN CLEWS OF TOPSAILS AND COURSES.—Courses have a clew-rope.

74. HEAD AND LEECH-ROPES OF A SAIL.—The head cringle is first made by splicing an eye in the end of the leech-rope; the head rope is then passed between the strands of this cringle, and spliced into its own part.

102

75. Leech and Foot-ropes.—These are spliced together, just below the lower bowline cringle, with a sailmaker's splice.

76. Sailmaker's Splice.—When a large and small rope are to be spliced together, and they require tapering off to blend their sizes, as in the leech of a topsail, a sailmaker's splice is used.

To form it; unlay enough of the small rope to put the ends in once and a half; but of the large one, unlay for a considerable distance, according to the relative disproportion of the ropes, and the degree of tapering you intend to give them; open out, and bring the parts together, as for a common splice.

Then take a strand of the large rope, cut away about a fourth—from underneath—and put it, *left-handed*, through the corresponding strands of the small rope; cut away a few more yarns, and pass it again, back-handed, *round the same strand* of the small rope; and so proceed—working with the same strand of the large rope, round and round the same strand of the small one, cutting away gradually till it is reduced to nothing. Then, one at a time, put the other large strands through in a similar manner, cutting away more or less of the third strand, as may be necessary to give roundness to the splice. Finally, slue round and splice the small strands into the large rope, as in a common short splice.

77. Cut of Topsails.—If topsails had a straight leech, a greater length of yard-arm would be required to take the reefs in.

103

78. CUT OF TOPSAILS AND COURSES.—Courses are cut with a roach, to clear the boats and hammock-nettings; but topsails have a straight foot.

79. MARKS ON SAILS.—They show, in the case here stated, that the head is of 19½ breadths, the foot of 29 breadths, and drop of the sail 12 yards.

80. REDUCING A TOPSAIL. —If not much reduction is required, a piece may be cut off the head, reducing the size of the first reef; otherwise, it must be cut at the belly-band, to prevent altering the reefs, or lessening the spread of the foot.

81. SERVICE ON THE FOOT OF A SAIL—Keeps the marline from being chafed.

82. ROPINGS OF A SAIL.—Three in a jib—luff and foot, leech, and clew-rope; two in a trysail,—head and foot, and luff, leech, peak-rope, and clew-rope, of the same size; two in a topmast studding-sail,—head, and foot and leeches in one.

83. SIZES OF CANVAS.—

    No 1.—Is used for storm-staysails and courses.
    „ 2.—Fore and main topsails.
    „ 3.—Mizen-topsail.
    „ 4.—Only used for repairing.
    „ 5.—Fore and main-top-gallant sails, fore-topmast staysail, jib, and spanker.
    „ 6.—Topmast, and lower studding-sails.

No. 7.—Mizen top-gallant-sails, royals, flying jib, and top-gallant studding-sails.

„ 8.—For repairing, and boats sails.

Sails are repaired with the next sized canvas smaller than that of which they are made.

84. BREADTH OF CANVAS.—Twenty-four and eighteen inches. The latter is generally number 5.

85. EIGHTEEN-INCH CANVAS.—It is used for the jibs and spanker, as great nicety is required in cutting them.

86. SEWING CANVAS.—Turn the right-hand edge of the first cloth, *a*, over *towards* you, equal to the breadth of the seam ; then lay the next cloth, *b* (working to the right), on the top, and sew its edge to the double part of the first cloth— sewing always from left to right ; rub the seam down, slue over, double the second cloth back from

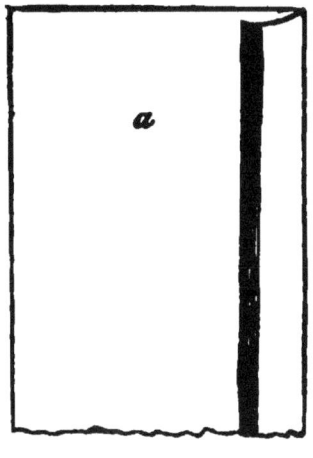

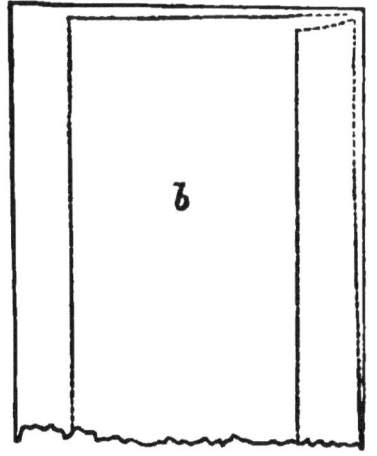

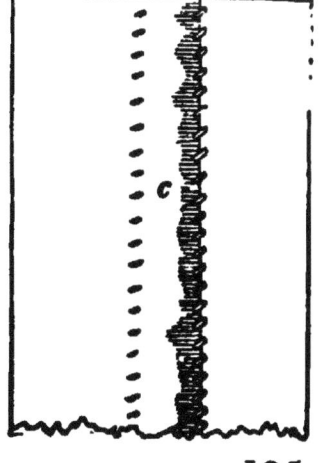

you, and in the same way sew the edge of the first cloth to the double part of the second ; rub down, and it will appear as at *c*.

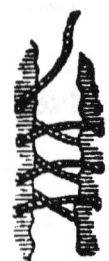

87. HERRING-BONING.—-Is used for stitching up rents and small holes in sails. You begin on the left side, sticking your needle up, then down on the right, and bring the needle up inside the first turn.

88. EYELET-HOLES.—Marline is run along the after side of the sail, and formed in bights over holes stabbed in the canvas, thus :—

89. BREADTH OF SEAMS.—An inch and a half for top-sails and courses, and an inch for top-gallant and smaller sails.

90. DISSIMILARITY IN THEIR BREADTH.—The seams of a spanker are wider at the head and foot than amid-ships ; in a jib they widen at the foot,—the advantage of which, in either case, is not palpable.

91. MIDDLE-SEAMING.—Topsails, courses, and storm-stay-sails are alone middle-seamed.

92. SICK SEAMS—Are those in which the stitches are worn, and given way here and there.

(It is to be regretted that this, and many other expres-sive technical terms, are gradually falling into disuse.)

106

93. LENGTHENING A ROPE WITH AN ADDITIONAL STRAND.—Cut a strand at 1, and lay until you come to 2, and cut another strand; unlay both to 3 (equal to the distance from 1 to 2, or thereabouts), and there cut the last strand; separate the parts and they will appear thus :—

Measure off the increased length required from 1, mark it *a*, and bring the end of the left-hand piece, *b*, down to *a*, and lay it in. The second strand, at 2, must have been cut sufficiently far from *a* to allow end enough for knotting and laying in. Twist the ends *c* and *b* up together, ready for knotting on finishing the splice, and *d* and *e* in the same manner for the present: the splice will then have the following appearance :—

Cut a piece of rope, and unlay a strand sufficiently long to fill in the vacant lay between

f and *g*, and to knot with the ends, *f, g*; lay the strand
in, and finish off as with an ordinary long splice, from
which it will only differ in appearance by its having four
breaks in the rope instead of three. In putting in the
long strand care must be taken to follow the lay along
correctly, or it will not tally with the ends, *f, g*, with which
it knots.

94. TO SHORTEN A ROPE IN THE CENTRE.—Proceed
precisely as in the previous case; but, instead of separat-
ing the strand *b* from 1,—bringing it down to *a, take it up*
on 1 as far as you require to reduce the rope. No
additional strand is used, so knot *b, f; d, g;* and *e, c;*
finish off the ends, and in appearance it differs in no way
from the common long splice.

95. RIGGING FITTED BY THE DOCKYARD.—Everything
is drawn ready fitted, according to establishment, from
lower rigging to a topgallant-studdingsail-halyard-block-
strop. Tackles and other gear are not rove, but all the
blocks are stropped.

96. FITMENT OF YARD AND STAY-TACKLES. — In
stropping the lower blocks, a good drift should be given
between the block and hook, for convenience in hooking
and unhooking and slueing it; and a seizing passed below
the block, and another above the thimble.

The stays should have a short strop with a thimble
seized into it, rove between these seizings, to hook the
yard-tackle to when necessary.

The standing part of the falls should be rove through a
becket in the upper part of the block, and then slipped

over the strop below the block with a running eye spliced into the end, that the standing part may be dipped when turns come in the fall.

97. FITMENT OF BOOM SHEET.—Two single blocks on each side of the boom, the first just outside the rail, and

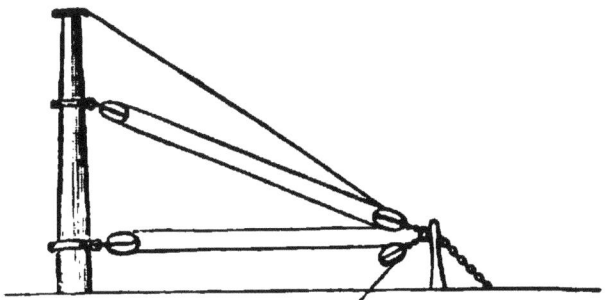

the second half-way between that and the boom-end. An iron spur, on each quarter, with an eye in the end, through which is rove a chain, shackled to a bolt in the quarter, with two short legs on the other end. To the foremost leg a single block is shackled, and to the after one a double block. The fall is then rove, and the standing part spliced into a bolt in the hoop on the boom-end.

98. REEVING ONE ROPE BY ANOTHER.—Put the ends of the two ropes together, and worm three yarns or pieces of spun-yarn between the strands for two or three inches on each side, clove-hitching the ends round the rope, or opening the strands and laying them in.

99. REEVING A NEW COIL OF ROPE.—Dip the end up through the centre, and thus a turn is taken out of every fake.

H 2   109

100. LENGTH OF A COIL OF ROPE.—Hawser-laid rope, 113 fathoms; cable-laid, 101 fathoms.

101. HAWSER AND CABLE-LAID.—Hawser-laid is the ordinary three or four stranded, right or left-handed rope; cable-laid is that of which cables and hawsers are made.

102. FOUR-STRANDED ROPE—Is laid up with a *heart* in the centre.

103. RUMBOWLINE—Is coarse, soft rope, made from outside yarns, &c.; supplied to a ship fitting out, for temporary lashings, and so forth.

104. LACING OF A STAYSAIL—Is rove round and round against the lay of the stay, or the lacing would get into it and hold the sail on setting, or taking it in. After reeving, both parts of the lacing must be seized together, to prevent them tautening up and binding the sail to the stay.

The disadvantage of much lacing consists in the frequent liability of one part to get over the other, which prevents the sail hoisting or coming down; and the objection to many hanks is, that the head of the sail will not stow close down.

105. FITMENT OF STORM STAYSAIL-STAYS.—The fore-stay-sail-stay is fitted with a fork, the eyes of which lash abaft the mast-head, the lower end being rove through a thimble seized into a strop on top of the bowsprit, and set up to a bolt in the stem.

Main staysail-stay is either fitted in the same manner, reeving through a thimble seized into a strop well up the foremast, to allow the foot of the sail to clear the boats, and then setting up on deck ; or else it is lashed on deck after reeving through this strop, the end aloft rove through a clump block at the mast-head, and the staysail halyard block turned into it, so that pulling upon the halyards sets up the stay.

106. FITMENT OF STAYSAILS.—Fore and main staysails may be brought to, with beckets made as follows :—Into one end of a piece of rope splice an eye, large enough to take a mathew-walker formed in the other end ; and when this is done, the becket should be long enough to go from one eyelet-hole, round the stay, and. opposite the next hole, not binding the sail too taut to the stay. Then, beginning at the head of the sail, reeve the beckets, against the lay, round the stay, and the eye put over the knot of the next becket; and so on until all are passed,—all the knots lying on one side. The halyards are double, and reeve through a block at the mast-head ; downhaul as in other sails ; tack lashed to strop round foremast or bow-sprit.

The main topmast-staysail is fitted with throat brails, clew tricing-line and downhaul, and sets on the spring topmast-stay. The neatest way of stowing it, in ships where it is much used, is to fit a couple of catharpin-legs to the after futtock shrouds, the staysail triced up, and stowed on the top of them ; a cover is previously laced to the foremost leg, which is boused up abaft, and peaked like the bunt of a sail ; a bunt-gasket, seized to the after leg, is then passed, and the sail roused up.

The top-gallant staysail sets on the top-gallant stay, when the stay comes down to the lower cap ; but, if to the top-mast-head, a staysail stay must be fitted. It is taken in with a downhaul, and stows up and down the foremast-head to its own stay.

The royal staysail-stay is clenched round the main top-gallant mast-head, reeves through a clump block (which travels with a thimble seized into the strop up and down a jackstay), and thence down on deck. This jackstay is fitted with a running eye round the fore topmast-head, and sets up to the cap; a tricing-line is bent to the clump block, reeves through a block at the topmast-head, and then down on deck; the downhaul block also lashes to the strop of the clump block. The sail is set by tricing it up to the topmast-head, and then setting the stay up. When taking it in, after the sail is hauled down to the clump block, the tricing-line is lowered, and the sail and stay are hauled down to the lower cap It is then stowed up and down the lowermast-head, with the top-gallant staysail in one, covered ; and the centipede passed.

A netting of small rope laced between the man-ropes on the bowsprit, is sometimes used to stow the fore topmast-staysail on ; and is both neat and serviceable.

107. TOPSAIL-TYES—Are cut long, to send the yard up and down by, in addition to the sail-tackle.

108. TOPMAST STUDDING-SAIL HALYARDS.—Lead before the yard ; for the sail, when set, having a forward tendency, would of course bind the halyards if rove abaft.

112

109 JIB-SHEET—leads inside the tack and outside the bowline; and is best fitted, as shown in the cut, where the

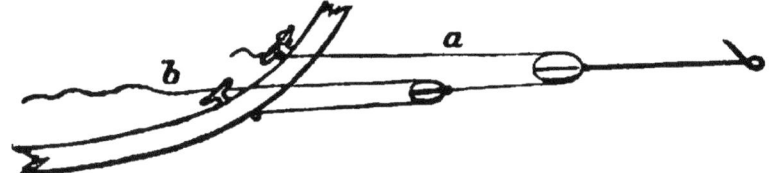

sheet is first steadied aft with the standing part, *a*, and then hauled flat aft by the purchase, *b*.

110. LACING OF A SPANKER—Is spliced into the upper cringle, passed round before the mast, through the next cringle, *back round the mast*, and so on to the bottom. If rove round and round like the lacing on the head and gaff, it would jamb when you want to trice the tack up, or lower the sail down.

111. PEAK HALYARDS.—The advantage of the standing part being secured to the topmast-head, consists, in the counteracting pressure of the sail and weight of the gaff against the forward strain of the topsail braces, which is not fully met by the mizen topmast backstays as they have so little drift; but, on the other hand, an additional strain is brought on the topmast stay, when the yards are swung in working ship.

112. LOWER-TACKS AND SHEETS.—Taper off towards the hauling end, for convenience in handling.

113. SHEETS OF FORE-AND-AFT SAILS.—Should lead in a line drawn direct from the centre of gravity through the clew.

113

The centre of gravity of a staysail is found by bisecting any two sides of the triangle, drawing a line from these points to the opposite angles of the sail, and marking the point of intersection.

Square sails are, first, divided into triangles; then the centre of gravity of each is found, as already shown; and the centre of gravity of the sail is where a perpendicular, drawn from the centre of either the head or foot, intersects a line joining the centres of the triangles.

The centre of gravity of a trysail or spanker is at the point of intersection of two lines—one of which joins the centre of gravity of two triangles, formed by a diagonal drawn from the peak to the tack—and the other joins the centres of two similar triangles, formed by a diagonal from the neck to the clew.

114. QUARTER-BLOCKS.—The sheet is rove through the after sheeve; for, on the *lower* sail being taken in, its clew-line would lead across the sheet, if rove through the foremost sheeve.

115. TOP-TACKLE FALL.—The upper block should be the swivel-block, because the turns are taken in by the pendant.

116. TOPSAIL SHEETS—Are secured with an outside clinch, that they may be clear when required to be let go.

117. TOP-GALLANT AND ROYAL SHEETS—Are bent with an eye, which goes over the toggle in the clew of the sail. The clew-line is often bent round the splice of the eye.

114

118. FORE AND MAIN-SHEETS.—The hook lies with the point up; for, when the sheet hangs in a bight, the hook is liable to cant out, if pointed downwards.

119. MAIN BUNTLINES, LEADING AFT.—Allow the hands to work round from the clewgarnets.

120. CAT AND FISH-FALLS.—The cat-fall is rove through a block on the opposite side of the deck, through the foremost sheeve in the cat-head; and, when rove full, the end is timber-hitched round the cat-head.

The fish-fall is rove through a block lashed to the lower pendant, down through the leading block at the davit head; and, when rove full, is clove-hitched round the shank of the fish-hook, and the end stopped up.

121. CAT-CHAIN—Is a small chain used for catting the anchor, in place of a cat-fall. One length of small chain shackles to the ring of the anchor, and is stopped along the first shackle of cable; another length

115

reeves through an iron block at the cat-head, and before weighing, is led into the hawse-hole, in readiness for shackling to the part stopped along the cable when hove in ; the cat purchase hooks to the inboard end.

122. Number of hempen Cables and Hawsers on board.—*See* Table XVI.

123. Blocks.—Reef-tackle and clew-line blocks are called *strop board;* and fore tack, *shoulder blocks.*

124. Toggles—Are distinguished as *round,* and *ducks-bill;* the latter are also sometimes called *spring* toggles.

125. Gab-rope.—Rove through a block on the bowsprit cap, bent to a cringle in the foot of the jib, and placed so as to bring the foot of the sail taut along the boom ; in bad weather it is the greatest possible assistance to the men engaged in stowing the sail, as it brings in the foot to them, and steadies it there while they gather up.

126. Hiding a Rope—When the nip of a rope always comes in one place, that part must become badly chafed before the rest is much worn ; to remedy this, a strip of soaked hide is worked between each strand of the rope where the nip takes, as at the yard-arm for a top-gallant sheet, or at the thimble for a main bowline.

127. Spider Hoop—Is a general name for any hoop round a mast, except the mast hoops,—such as those with belaying pins attached, or those for awning ridge-ropes ; but the proper spider hoop is the hoop on the topmast head, through which top-gallant rigging reeves.

128. REEF-PENDANTS OF BOOM MAINSAIL.—A mathew-walker is made in one end, and the pendant rove through a hole in the cheek on the side of the boom, with the knot underneath, then through the cringle in the sail, down through the sheeve-hole in the cheek on the other side of the boom ; and a bowline knot, or a hitch with the end seized back, is made in the end, to which the tackle is hooked, and led along the boom.

128. TRIATIC STAY—Is the name given to a schooner's mainstay when it sets up to the foremast-head, or, else, reeving through a strop abaft the mast-head, sets up on deck.   When led straight on deck, two stays are required, the weather one being pulled up, and the lee one over-hauled on going about.

130. DIFFERENT METHODS OF BUILDING BOATS.—1st. Carvel-built, which have fore-and-aft planks, the edges meeting, but not overlapping.

2nd. Clinker built, also of fore-and-aft planks, with the edges overlapping each other.

Diagonal built, having as their name implies, their planking running diagonally, the inside planks running in a contrary direction to the outside ones, and their edges meeting.

131. TECHNICAL PHRASES.—When a buoy leaks, it requires to be *bled* occasionally to let the water out, and is then plugged up again.

A buoy *watches*, while it maintains its position above

117

water, and is not borne under by the strength of the tide or any other cause.

A cable *grows*, in the direction it leads from the hawse-hole, ahead—on the bow—or under foot, as the case may be.

When, from the fall of the tide, the water leaves a ship that is aground, the ship is said to have *sewed* so many feet or inches as the tide has fallen below her original water-line.   The word *sewer* (drain), has the same derivation.

A cask is stowed *a-burton*, when it is stowed athwart-ship.

132. SPARE COMPASS CARDS—Should be stowed with the poles of *different names* next to each other.

133. WIDE CHAINS. — The great objection to their width is, that it lessens the efficiency of your guns by diminishing their angle of training.

134. LARGEST ROPE AND STRONGEST RIGGING.—The fore top-gallant braces, when rove double, are the longest ropes, and the forestays, mainstays, and lower rigging are respectively the strongest pieces of rigging.

135. LARGEST BLOCKS.—Treble and four-fold 30-inch.

136. SPLICING A THREE, AND FOUR-STRANDED ROPE TOGETHER.—For a short splice, divide the fourth strand into three parts, and lay one part in with each of the three

strands.   In a long splice, work three strands in as usual ;
and, when finished, put the fourth strand in where it lies.

137. SPLICING A HAWSER.—Work a long splice, as with
a hawser-laid rope, but, instead of knotting the strands,
unlay them, marry them together, and tuck them in under
the strand that you would reeve them through if you had
knotted them in the usual manner ; under this first strand
of the hawser put all three strands of the strand ; under the
next two only, then one, and, lastly, *back* this one.

Long-splicing the strands can only be done with old, soft
hawsers, which are not worth the trouble, and for these a
shroud-knot, with the ends marled down, and served over,
is the best treatment.

138. SPLICING A THIMBLE INTO A LARGE ROPE.—After '
one half of each strand is put through, it is cut off; and
the other half is opened out, wormed along between the
strands and marled down.

139. ANCHOR-STROPS, &c.—Put the ends in *twice*, don't
cut them off close, but *whip them*.

140. CUTTING OFF ENDS OF LOWER RIGGING—If in
the chains and hemp, saw them off; but,. if you have got
the rigging inboard, turning it in afresh on a platform of
two or three water-casks up-ended, which is the best way,
lay the end on the edge of an axe resting on a block of
wood, and strike down on the rope with a commander ;
wire rigging stretches so little, that it will rarely require
cutting.

119

141. ROGUE'S YARN.—Red, Plymouth; blue, Portsmouth; yellow, Chatham.

142. STRENGTH OF A YARN.—In round numbers you may call it 100 lbs., but the average strength of each yarn, in hawser-laid rope, is found to be greatest in the smaller sizes; thus, for 12-inch rope, the mean average strength is 76 lbs. per yarn; for 6-inch, 78·4 lbs.; for 1½-inch, 93·8 lbs.; for 1-inch, 95·2 lbs.; for ½-inch, 104·5 lbs.*

143. PROPORTIONATE STRENGTH OF ROPE OF DIFFERENT SIZES.—One part of 8-inch is stronger than three parts of 4½inch; for, as the number of yarns in, and therefore the strength (S, s,) of rope of different sizes, varies with their areas, and as the areas of circles are proportional to the squares of their circumferences (C, c,), it follows that,—

$$\frac{S}{s} = \frac{C^2}{c^2};$$

and let n represent the number of parts of the small rope which are equal to the strength of the larger rope, then

$$\frac{ns}{s} = \frac{C^2}{c^2}; \text{ or } \frac{C^2}{c^2} = n.$$

Therefore, to find what number of parts of a small rope are equal to a larger rope—without allowing for the difference of the angle of twist which, as shown above, affects the strength of the rope—divide the square of the circum-

---

* For much of the information regarding the properties of rope which is given in this work, the profession is indebted to Tinmouth's incomparably useful treatise.

ference of the larger rope by the square of the circumference of the smaller, and the quotient will be the number of parts of the smaller equal to the larger.

144. PRACTICAL RULE FOR ASCERTAINING THE STRENGTH OF ROPE.—The square of half the circumference gives the breaking strain of the weakest hawser-laid rope in tons, and is, therefore, a safe rule.   For instance :—

1. *By experiment*, 4-inch rope breaks at a maximum of 5·3 tons, and at a minimum of 4 tons.

By rule, $\left(\dfrac{4}{2}\right)^2 = 4$ tons.

2. *By experiment*, 6-inch rope breaks at a maximum of 11·75 tons, and minimum 8·7 tons.

By rule, $\left(\dfrac{6}{2}\right)^2 = 9$ tons.

3. *By experiment*, 10-inch rope breaks at a maximum of 31·7 tons, and minimum 24·2 tons.

By rule, $\left(\dfrac{10}{2}\right)^2 = 25$ tons.

RULE FOR CALCULATING THE WEIGHT OF ROPE.—Three-strand, hawser-laid, 25-thread yarn, tarred.   Multiply the square of the circumference by the length in fathoms, and divide by 4·24 for the weight in lbs.

Ex. 1. 2-in. rope, 113 fms. $\dfrac{2^2 \times 113}{4\cdot24} = 106$ lbs. Actual weight 105 lbs.

„ 2. 4-in. „   „ $\dfrac{4^2 \times 113}{4\cdot24} = 428$ lbs.   „   „   424 lbs.

„ 3. 12-in. „   „ $\dfrac{12^2 \times 113}{4\cdot24} = 3837$ lbs.   „   „   3840 lbs.

The divisor for hempen cables is 4·79.

Ex. 1. 10-in. hawser, 100 fms. $\dfrac{10^2 \times 100}{4·79} = 2088\,lbs.$ Actual wgt. 2088 lbs.

,, 2- 20-in. cable   ,, $\dfrac{20^2 \times 100}{4·79} = 8351\,lbs.$,,   8352 lbs.

,, 3. 26-in. ,,   ,, $\dfrac{26^2 \times 100}{4·79} = 14113\,lbs.$,,   14112 lbs.

Chain cables are about 2·3 heavier than hempen cables of the corresponding size.

145. HAWSER-LAID ROPE—Is stronger than cable-laid, in the proportion of 8·7 to 6.

146. CABLE-LAID ROPE—Is so laid up to exclude the water.

147. PRACTICAL RULE FOR DETERMINING THE RELATIVE STRENGTH OF CHAIN AND ROPE.—Consider the proportionate strength of a chain and rope to be ten to one,—using the diameter of the chain, and the circumference of the rope. Half-inch chain may, therefore, replace five-inch rope.

The absolute strength of chain, at the *breaking point*, may be found by dividing the square of the diameter in eighths, by 2·4, for round-linked crane chain ; and by 2·7, for chain cable.

Ex. 1. 1½.inch round-link chain.

By experiment, minimum, 58·2 tons ; mean, 62·3 tons.

By calculation, 144 ÷ 2·4 = 60 tons.

Ex. 2. ½-inch ; minimum strength, by experiment, 6·9 tons.

By calculation, 16 ÷ 2·4 = 6·7 tons.

Ex. 3. 2-inch cable; minimum strength by experiment, 96·25 tons.

By calculation, 256 ÷ 2·7 = 94·2 tons.

Ex. 4. ½-inch: minimum strength by experiment, 5·9 tons.

By calculation, 16 ÷ 2·7 = 5·9 tons.

148. STRONGEST DESCRIPTION OF HEMP ROPE—Is untarred, white, three-strauded rope; and the next in the scale of strength is the common three-strand, hawser-laid rope, tarred.

149. USE OF THE ROPEMAKER'S WINCH.—A ship's winch, which will make very fair 2-inch rope, is about 15 inches in diameter. In the frame, which is double, are placed five hooks —the three upper ones for general use, the fourth for four-stranded rope, and the centre one for hardening up large rope 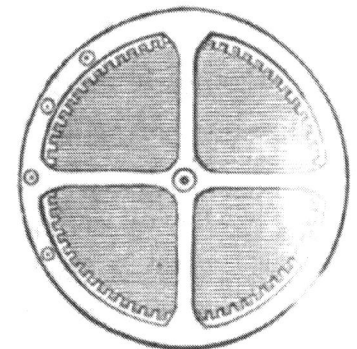 after it has been laid up by the upper ones (the la·ter not being sufficiently strong for that purpose). The sha·ks of the hooks, between the two parts of the frame, ·re inserted in cogged barrels, which are turned by the wh·l, one revolution of which gives nine to the hooks—any ·ne of which can be thrown out of gear by hauling it b·ck close to the after part of the frame.

A *loper* is a swivel-hook, which, by revolving freely, allows the strands to twine up together, by the twist put in them as the top is withdrawn.

I   123

 The *top* is a conical piece of wood, scored on the outside for the reception of the strands. Its use is to keep the strands separate between it and the winch, and to regulate the amount of twist in the rope behind it, by being moved along either slowly or rapidly. When four-stranded rope is required, a hole is bored through the centre, as a lead for the heart.

A length of junk being brought on deck, you proceed to unlay it by attaching the strands to separate hooks, and the loper to the other end—one hand holding back on it, and then heaving back—two hands following the rope down to separate the ends.

Spun-yarn is made by hooking all the yarns that compose it (according to the size required), upon one hook. You then heave round, the reverse way to the lay of the yarns (which in ordinary rope are all right-handed), until there is plenty of back turn in them, holding on the ends by hand ; then rub down, and make it up.

In rubbing down, a boy puts the end of a strand over his shoulder, and walks away with it, another hand holding on the rubber (which is the end of the strand doubled up loose), round the stuff they are laying up.

As many lengths of spun-yarn can, of course, be made at once as there are hooks on the winch.

Nettle-stuff.—Hitch the yarns to separate hooks ; let a couple of hands then take hold of them, and commencing close to the winch, walk back while it is hove round the reverse way ; the yarns are thus hove up the contrary way to what they were originally, to soften them ; for, when drawn out of rope, they are usually hard and angular, and would not lie square, or bear an equal strain, if laid up in that condition. When thus relaid, the ends are knotted together, the loper hooked on—one hand holding on to it, the top put in, the winch hove round the same way as at first, and the top moved along towards the winch. When up to it, the top is taken out, the yarns unhooked, and hitched to a single hook, then the winch hove round the opposite way to what you have just been heaving it, to harden the stuff up, rubbed down, and made up.

Thus, the yarns will be left-handed, and the nettle-stuff right-handed ; for, though the winch is hove round the same way with both, the twist in the yarns causes them to untie abaft the top with the lay of the contrary denomination, and the revolutions of the loper prevents the turn coming out again.

Six (or nine) thread stuff.—Put two (or three) yarns on three separate hooks ; hold on the ends by hand, keeping each of the three lengths separate, and heave round a reverse turn, as with spun-yarn. When sufficiently hove up, knot the ends together, hook on the loper, put in the top, and proceed as with nettle-stuff.

Cable-nippers are laid up the same way.

Hammock lashings are made of three strands of three or four-yarn nettle-stuff, hove round the reverse way, which forms cable-laid stuff, left-handed.

150. THREE-STRANDED ROPE—Is one-fifth stronger than four-stranded.

151. A Splice—Weakens a rope about one-eighth.

For the comparative and actual strength of chain cables, wire and hemp rope, see Tables I, II, III, IV, and V., at the end of the book.

152. A Ropemaker's Eye—Is used for forming the collars of stays. The stay, four-stranded, is unlaid, two strands each way ; then each half is doubled back, and laid up with its own part.   At the fork the four strands are worked in, as in splicing, tapering off by thinning the strands each time they are put in.   The eyes and fork are then served over.

153. Bunting.—At regular intervals, six or seven threads together are worked in of much larger size than the others.

154. Canvas.—Each cloth is marked with a thin waved line of blue paint, being run up and down it.

155. Elliott's Eye.—Put a whipping on the cable a couple of fathoms from the end, and unlay to it.   Splice two strands together with a long splice, making the eye thereby formed equal in length to the diameter of the thimble and the breadth of the seizing ; and splice the third strand to its own part, making an eye-splice equal to the eye already formed.   Place them together, fid them out, put a piece of rope between them to fill up the hollow, and hitch the eye over with small rope.   Seize the thimble in with a round seizing of inch-and-a-half, and heave on a kackling of two-and-a-half-inch rope, two fathoms down from the eye.

126

KNOTTING AND SPLICING.—The important items of practical seamanship here enumerated can only be properly taught by practical demonstration, and I therefore, in this instance, feel disposed to vacate in favour of the boatswain, and to recommend my "young gentlemen" readers to ply their marling-spikes assiduously on those Saturday afternoons so considerately set apart in most ships for that purpose. However, for the benefit of those who cannot, perhaps, avail themselves of the boatswain's assistance, I subjoin a description of all that is of any practical use, omitting that which is either merely fanciful or obsolete.

156. SHEET-BEND.   157. CARRICK-BEND.

158. STUDDING - SAIL BEND.—Two round turns round the yard, then a half-hitch round the standing part and under both parts, and the end tucked in between them.

127

159. ROLLING HITCH.—A rolling hitch is that used for stoppering a rope. It is formed by taking a hitch with the stopper round the rope, then taking another hitch above the first and between the stopper and the rope, and then dogging the tail *back* round the rope *with the lay*.

160. TIMBER HITCH.

161. BLACKWALL HITCH.

162. CLOVE HITCH.

163. A ring-bolt is usually hitched over with either two or three ends. With two ends,—after seizing or hitching the ends you are not working on, to the ring-bolt, you com-mence by taking a left-handed hitch with one of the tails, keeping the cross on the centre of the bolt, which brings the end out to the right ; you then double this end back over its own part to the left, bring up the other tail over this, take a hitch as with with the first, double it back, bring up the first end, and so go on, taking alternate hitches with each, and bringing the end out to the right with each hitch.

With three ends,—you begin by taking a left-handed hitch with the first leg, a right-handed hitch with the second, then left-handed with third, right-handed with first. left, second,—right, third,—and so on, each hitch being passed in the oppo-site way to the preceding one—two ends and one end alternately lying on each side. The ends are finished off by scraping them down, and either passing a whipping, or working a Turk's head round them. When completed, it has the appearance shown in the cut.

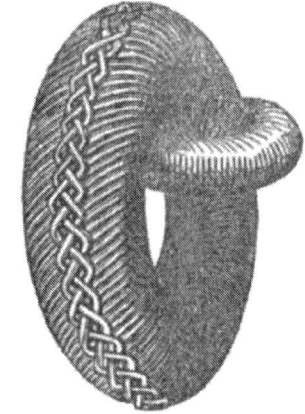

164. A COMMON MARLING HITCH.—Is that used for lashing a hammock up, and is simply thus :—

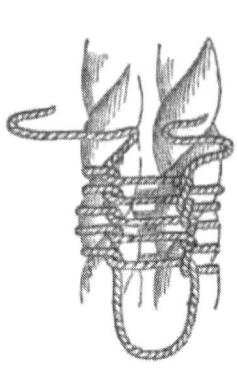

A Marling Hitch for davit-head blocks (fish), &c., is formed by middling the marline, laying the bight along the top, in the centre, and securing it there ; then dipping the right-hand end underneath and taking a turn under, and round the left ; bringing the left up, and taking a hitch over, and through the bight of the right-hand end ; heaving the turns on taut, and keeping them square.

165. KACKLING THE EYE OF A STREAM CABLE. —Secure one end between the parts of the eye, and work on the other end by taking a hitch, alternately right-handed and left-handed, till the eye is covered.

166. ROUND SEIZING.—Splice an eye in the seizing, pass it under both parts of the rope, and reeve the end through the eye; slack up, lay hold of the upper turn and end part with your left hand, and under turn with your right, and work the seizing round left-handed until enough turns—six, eight, or ten— are wound round; then reeve the end back between the upper and under turns, and bring it up through the eye; then heave each turn taut separately, keeping the eye on the left-hand side. When you have hauled the end taut through the eye, pass the riding turns round, in the same direction as at first, one in number less than the inner turns, and hauled hand-taut. When all on, pass the end down between the two last parts of the upper side of the inner turns, between both parts of the rope, and pass two round turns, crossing all parts of the seizing; then slue the rope over, and finish off with a reef-knot on the under side, as in the figure.

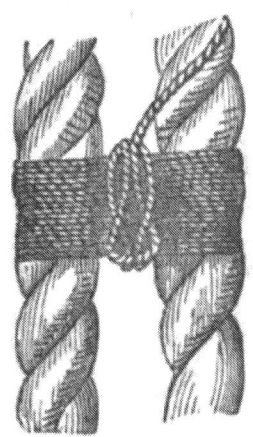

131

167. THROAT SEIZING.— The old throat seizing, used when rigging was turned in with end up, is now seldom required except in seizing a thimble into one of the smaller stays. The end of the rope being laid over the standing part, the seizing is passed, precisely as a round seizing, until you have passed the end down between the two last parts of the inner turns, when, instead of passing the crossing turns right round, you reeve the end between the upper and under turns of the seizing, bringing it out alongside the eye, and so only pass the crossing turns over the upper half, finishing off with the reef-knot on the top of the seizing. Then, when the end of the rope is seized up to the standing part, it will be seen from the tautness of the underneath parts of the seizing, occasioned by the end and standing part of the rope being brought together, that the tension on the crossing turns would be too great if they were passed round all.

168. RACKING SEIZING.—The first turn is passed round both parts of the rope like a round seizing; it is then dipped between both parts, and the the remaining turns are passed as racking turns—over and under. When the requisite number are on, reeve the end down inside the last turn, bring it up outside, and pass the outside turns back towards the eye of the seizing, allowing them to sink in between the parts of the first turns; by which it assumes the appearance of a flat seizing, as

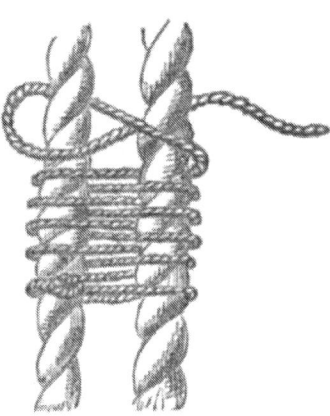

there are in reality no *riding* turns. When down to the eye, dip the end down between the two first turns, and finish off with a reef-knot.

169. A FLAT SEIZING—Is commenced the same as a round seizing, but on the end being rove through the eye, it is finished off at once with a reef-knot without any riding turns.

170. SHROUD KNOT.—Open out the ends of the rope that are to be knotted, put them together as for splicing, and single wall the strands of eaeh end round the main part of the opposite end ; then taper the strands off, marl down, and serve over.

133

171. SINGLE WALL.   172. WALL AND CROWN.

You may now double wall and double crown, by letting the strands follow their own parts round ; first double walling and then double crowning, and cutting the ends off.

173. DOUBLE WALL AND DOUBLE CROWN.

174 FRENCH SHROUD KNOT.—Crown backwards, left-handed, the strands of each end ; then dip the ends that

lie *from* you to the left of those that fall down *towards* you ; haul them into their places, and you will find that they will accommodate themselves to the knot better in this way, than if they were allowed to remain as they came out.   The knot will then appear thus :—

Then tuck the ends in as in splicing (which you can do, also, with the common shroud knot), or tease the strands out and marl down.

175. Matthew Walker.—Put a whipping on (as with all knots), open the strands down to the whipping, and

pass the first end through its own bight, the next through its own and the first, and the third through all three bights ; haul the ends through, work the turns round and place them ;

and the knot will appear as in left-hand figure.

135

176. TURK'S HEAD.—Take two round turns round the rope, pass the upper bight down through the lower, and reeve the upper end down through it; then pass the bight up again, and reeve the end over the lower bight and up between it and the upper one; dip the upper down

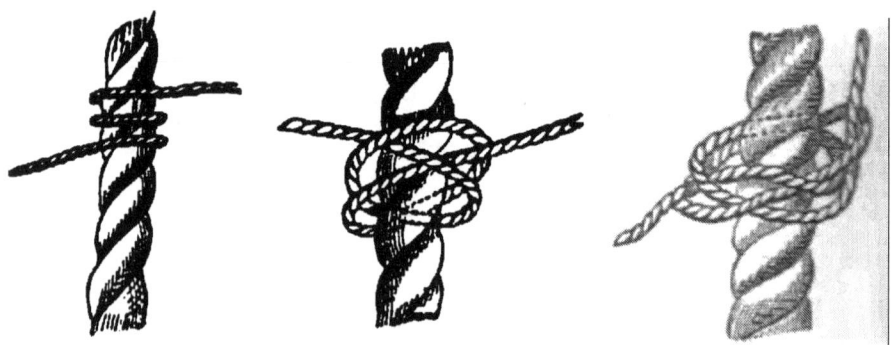

through the lower bight again, reeve the end down over what is now the upper bight, and between it and the lower; and so proceed,—working round to your right until you meet the other end, when you pass through the same bight,

and follow the other end round and round until you have completed a plait of two, three, or more lays, as you wish. The right-hand cut shows a Turk's head of two lays.

177. TURK'S HEAD WORKED INTO A ROPE.—This is done when the knot has to resist a strain, as the rung of a Jacob's ladder. You middle the marline or nettle-stuff that you are working with, and splice a second piece into the centre so as to form a third leg; then pass an end through the rope, and haul it through to the junction of

136

the third leg, which reeve
through the third strand
of the rope, bringing an
end out between each
strand.

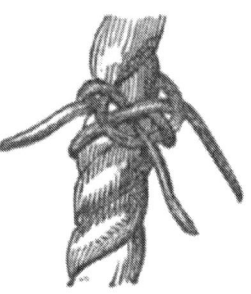

Then crown the ends round the
rope, left-handed; slue round, and
crown them back, right-handed, and
the knot will appear as in the figure.
Follow each part round with its own
end, cut the ends off, and it will be
undistinguishable from the common
Turk's head.   With four-stranded rope, you use four ends.

178. Reef Knot.

179. Stopper Knot.—Double wall, lay the ends up,
put a whipping on, and cut them off.

180. BOWLINE KNOT.   181. RUNNING BOWLINE.

182. BOWLINE ON A BIGHT.—The bight *a* being passed

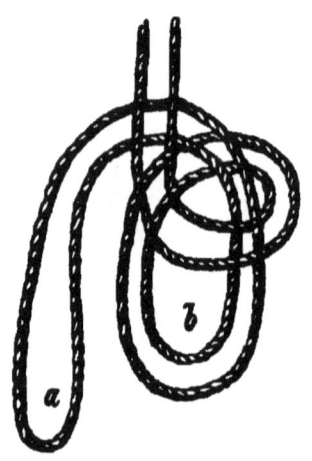

over *b*, forms the knot *c*.

183. FLEMISH EYE.—Put a whipping round the rope,
open the strands out down to it, leave out the outside

yarns and stop them back, and make the rest up into foxes.
Halve them, and put a round piece of wood, the size of

the eye required, between
them on the top, with three
stops laid along it, *S, S, S.*
Knot the centre foxes of
each side, 1 and 2, on *the
top* of the spar, and knot 3
and 8 from you, with a knot
a little round to the left.
Then when all on that side

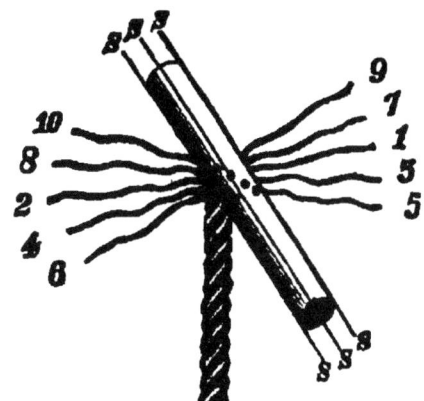

of the centre fox are expended, commence on the other
side, and knot 7 and 4 a little round to the right, towards
you, and 9 and 10 more round, and so on.   When all are
knotted, tie the stops together, to keep the eye from
falling adrift, and take the spar out ; put a seizing round
the foxes close to the shoulder of the eye, and then cut
them off.   Bring the outside yarns over from each side,
placing them in the hollows to round the eye off; tease
the ends out, and worm them in between the strands at
the shoulder.   Then marl all down, fid the eye out,
parcel, and spike-serve it.   When neatness is an object,
graft the eye over with nettles made of two outside yarns.

184. A Fox—is made by rolling a couple of yarns up
the contrary way on your knee, and then rubbing them
down.

A Spanish Fox—is a single yarn rolled up the reverse
way, and rubbed down.

K   139

185. POINTING A ROPE.—Put a whipping on, open out the strands down to it, and form the heart of the inside yarns, tapered off, and marled down hard. Having left out the outside yarns, and laid them up into two-yarn nettles if the rope is not very small, tell them off, one up and one down alternately; knot the filling with a timber-hitch over the upper ones, pass two turns, and dip the end between both to jamb it before hauling the last turn taut; then bring the upper nettles down, and lay the lower ones up, pass the filling, and so proceed, hauling the nettles taut up after each round, and passing the first turn of the

filling under one or two of the upper ends in advance, each time, instead of over them; which allows the lower nettles to hide the hitch when brought up. To finish off, secure the lower nettles with the filling, as shown in the figure. Cut the upper ones off as they are, and the lower ones when you have passed two turns of the filling, hitched it and hauled the bight of the nettles close down.

With large ropes, you secure the upper nettles as well, by taking a hitch with the lower ones round the upper ones and the filling thus :—

Grafting,—in which the rope or strop is covered the entire length, and not at the end only, as in pointing, is performed in exactly the same manner, with nettles laid along it.

140

186. POINTING A LARGE HAWSER.—Clap on a whipping of three-yarn nettle-stuff, snaked. Open out the strands, lay the heart up three-stranded, and splice a becket into it, which has previously been eye-spliced into its own part. Lay the outside yarns up into five-yarn sennit; use, for filling, a two-yarn fox; and continue as already shown.

187. CROSS POINTING.—Commence as for straight pointing and, having laid the nettles, one up and one down alternately, bring an upper nettle down to the *right* of its corresponding lower one, lay the lower one up, and work in this way once round to the right; commence

 again, and bring what are now the upper ones down to the *left* of the lower nettles, lay the lower ones up, and so work round backwards; then, bring them down again to the right, and so go on. Finish off with two turns of straight pointing, as in right-hand fig.

188. HITCHING—Is a very convenient method for covering boats' awning stanchions, &c., and doubtless, many of my readers, when attached to landing parties, have availed themselves of serviceable-looking soda-water bottles, slung and protected in the same manner. The nettles to be used are middled, laid along the article to be covered, and secured in their places with a turn of filling. If working from one end, as in the cut, all the nettles are taken up : if working from the centre towards the ends,

K 2   141

the nettles on each side of the filling supply their own end. The turn of filling being passed and hitched as in pointing commence hitching the nettles round the filling, hauling 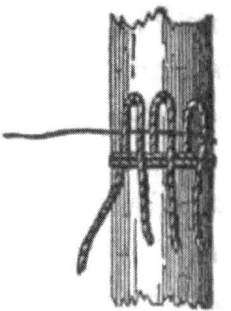 each taut separately, working to the left, keeping the filling taut, and going round and round. If what you are covering contracts in circumference, you must leave out a nettle occasionally, and cut it off; and, should it increase, lay fresh ones in. It is finished off by keeping the bights of the last round slack until you have passed a couple of turns of the filling and hitched it as in finishing off pointing, when in the same manner haul the bights close down, and cut the ends off.

189. ROSE LASHING.—Reeve through the eyes to be lashed, middle it, and pass racking turns, leaving off with the ends in the same bights; pass each end between the bights of the lashing on either side of the crossing, as shown

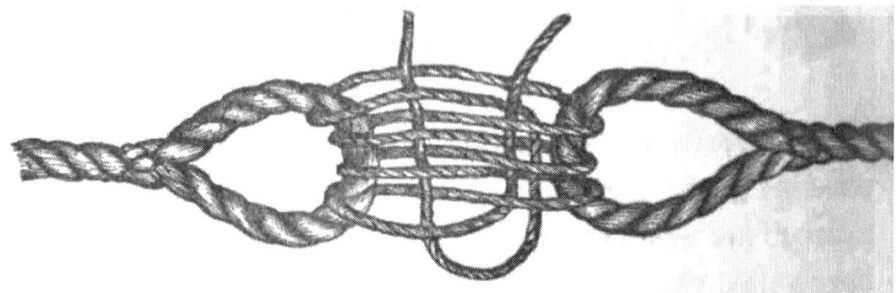

in the cut. Then take two or three round turns, passing them opposite ways, haul them well taut, and knot the ends.

190. A NETTLE—Is made of two or three yarns, laid up with finger and thumb, keeping the lay in the yarn, and is left-handed stuff.

142

Thumb Line—Is made of yarn twisted up the reverse way, and is right-handed.

191. WHIPPING A ROPE—In the ordinary manner, is done by laying the end in the lay of the rope, pointing up towards the end, passing a few turns round the rope, binding the end of the whipping; then laying the other end on the turns already passed, pointing downwards, passing the remainder on the bight, round the rope and the last end part, hauling through on the end part, and cutting off.

A West-country Whipping—Is that used for putting a mark on the fore brace, for instance; and is done by middling the whipping, and half-knotting the ends on each turn, on opposites sides of the rope; and finishes by knotting the last turn with a reef-knot.

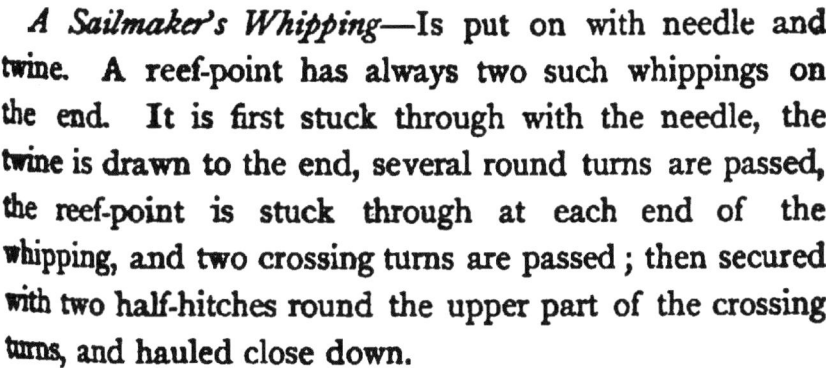

A Sailmaker's Whipping—Is put on with needle and twine. A reef-point has always two such whippings on the end. It is first stuck through with the needle, the twine is drawn to the end, several round turns are passed, the reef-point is stuck through at each end of the whipping, and two crossing turns are passed; then secured with two half-hitches round the upper part of the crossing turns, and hauled close down.

Crowning the End of a Rope—Is a rough substitute for whipping; and the strands are then tucked in twice or thrice, as in splicing. Lead lines are generally served in this way.

143

192. A GRUMMET.—Take a strand, three times the round of the grummet required, with end enough in addition for tucking in for finishing ; middle it, lay the right-hand

end over the left, and follow the lay round with each end until the rope is re-formed; then tuck the ends in where they meet, as in splicing.

193. A SELVAGE STROP—Is made of spun-yarn, or small rope, according to the size required, warped off, and marled down.

194. COMMON SENNIT—Is made with an odd number of nettles. If, however, an eye is to be formed, you commence with an even number—one being a short one ; and after the eye is formed, the short end is worked in, or, if too long, left out and cut off,—leaving an odd number to go on with. We will suppose that a reef-point is to be made of seven parts of spun-yarn :—Cut off four lengths (one being but little more than half the length of the others), middle them, toggle the bights through a becket

triced up before you, halve the nettles, lay the right-hand nettle over the next one to it, bringing it over to the left, making three now on your left, and one on your right ; bring the outside nettle on the left over two, which will equalize them again ; then the right over one, left over two, and so on alternately till you have worked length enough for the eye ; next bring all eight parts together, halve them and go on as at first—right over three, and left over four. When two or three lays are worked in this way, leave out the short end, and continue with seven parts,—right over

three, and left over three in succession. Finish off by forming a bight of the left-hand nettle when you bring it over, laying the end up ; and as you work the remaining nettles in, point them down through this bight ; and, when all are in, secure them in their places by hauling the bight taut through upon them and cutting the ends off, as in the left-hand fig.

195. FRENCH SENNIT—Like common sennit, is made with an odd number of nettles. If about to make a harbour gasket for a royal yard in this manner, of nine parts of nettle-stuff, cut off five lengths (one being a short one),

middle them, put a seizing round the bights to form the eye, which marl down, and serve over; then bring all nine parts together (having left out the short one after the seizing was passed), and divide them with five to the right, and four to the left; weave the outside one on the right, over and under the nettles on its own side, bringing it out to the left, then do the same, with the outside nettle on the left, and lay it out to the right, when there will

be again five on the right, and four on the left, and so
continue the mat in the same manner.

196. ROUND SENNIT—Is used for man-ropes, yoke-
lines, &c. Stretch a heart of small rope taut along between
two belaying pins, or other convenient fixture; take 8 (12,
16, or more) nettles, put the whipping round the heart and
ends, to hold them, divide them into fours of 2 (3, 4, or
more) parts each; then lay No. 1 pair
over the heart, to your left; then No.
2 to your right, crossing the 1st pair;
next No. 3 pair under all to the right,
and over No. 2;
No. 4 round under
all to the left, and
over No 3. Then
No. 1 round to the
right, under 2, and over, 4, 2 round
to the left, under 3, and over 1;
and so on, always bringing the upper pair on the opposite
side, to cross over the pair last passed. Finish the end
off by pointing the heart with the nettles made into smaller
ones; and finish the top by walling and crowning the
heart, covering it with duck to round it, then double-
walling and crowning the nettles over the heart knot, previously whipped underneath, with a Turk's head to cover
the whipping. Or, after forming the knot of the heart,
and covering it, and putting the whipping round the nettles
underneath, you may cut them off, and cover the knot
with Turk's heading of mackerel line, begun very slack,

146

and spread over the knot, by passing with a sail needle, as many lays in the plat as will be required to cover the knot.

197. SQUARE SENNIT—Is used for the same purposes as round sennit, and also by engineers, as packing for their pistons. It is made somewhat in the same manner as round sennit but without a heart. Nettles are used in the same ratio, increasing by fours, but are worked singly instead of in pairs. Having put a whipping round the (eight) ends, divide the nettles, and lay half on each side : bring the uppermost left-hand nettle round underneath all, and up inside two, of the right-hand ones—crossing over the latter ones to the left, and making four on each side again ; then take the uppermost of the right-hand nettles, pass it underneath, and under two and over two of the left-hand ones— still keeping four on a side, because the nettle taken up always comes round to its own side again. To proceed, take the upper nettle on each side alternately, and finish off as you finish round sennit.

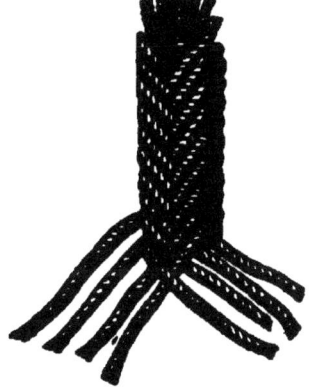

198. SWORD MAT.—At a distance apart, equal to the length of the mat, sling a couple of bars in a horizontal position. Hitch one end of the warp to the bar at the end on which you intend to terminate the mat ; take up the loom, which is made of a sheet of copper perforated with holes and slits alternately, reeve the other end through

147

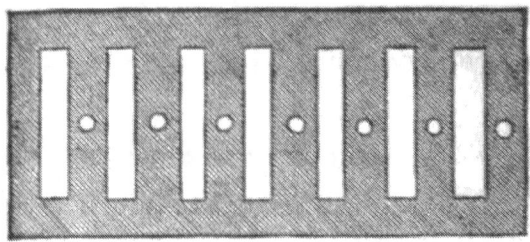

the first hole, over
and under the bar
at which you intend
to   begin, back
through the first slit,
under and over the
other bar; and so wind off as many parts as are required
for the breadth of the mat, the last turn being rove through
a slit, and secured to the bar, at which you finish off. This
done, lift the loom up, middle the filling, and lay it between the upper and under parts; then lower the loom,

and the parts that were lowermost will rise in the slits,
become the uppermost, and thus put a cross in the warp.
Next put the sword, made of hard wood in the shape of
a knife, in between the upper and under parts, and drive
the crossing close up towards the bar, and harden it well
up; then pass a turn of filling to secure the crossing,
reeving the ends through contrary ways, haul it taut, take
out the sword, lift the loom up, and go on again. When
you come to the last turn of filling half knot it with two
turns.

If you have to make a mat for which your loom is not

large enough, you rig a fiddle, by slinging a handspike athwartships to the main deck beams overhead; pick up every other part of the warp, and, with a piece of nettle-stuff passed over the handspike with *two round turns*, and rove round the alternate parts of the mat, trice them up. The upper parts will thus cross the under parts before and abaft the fiddle, and you will require two swords. Reeve the filling, and secure the first crossing already formed, by the parts being triced up, in the ordinary manner, hardening it up with the first sword; now, put the second sword in between the crossing and the bar abaft the fiddle, give the mat a shake to disengage the parts, and with the sword lift the upper ones up; the crossing will thus be extended before the fiddle, so withdraw the first sword,

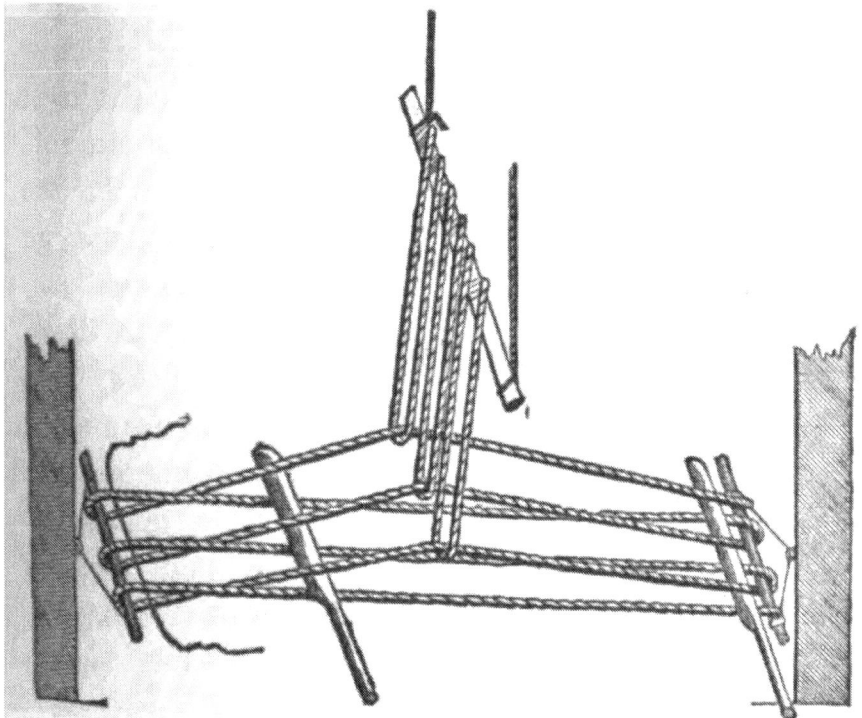

149

put it in abaft this crossing, drive it up and secure it with
a turn of filling; again lift up the fiddle, keeping the
second sword fast (which is never removed); a crossing is
again formed at each end; and you again repeat the
operation.

With a heavy boom-mat five or six feet wide, you require
a second fiddle underneath, to rouse the parts through.
A couple of hands jump down on the handspike; and the
upper one, which is triced up by a couple of jiggers, is
lowered at the same time.

To finish off or *selvage* the mat :—After passing the last
turn of filling, and securing it with a half-hitch with two
turns, you lay the lanyard across on the top of the filling,
and commence unreeving again the front row of nettles,
one at a time, beginning on the right. As you withdraw
them you bring the corresponding nettle, at the back, over
the lanyard, and filling, and reeve it back through the hole

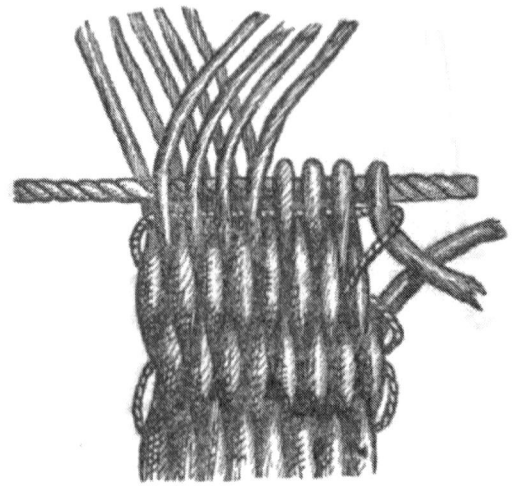

left vacant by the one
hauled out, thus : go
right across, and haul
the bights taut down
to the lanyard. On
slueing the mat round,
you will find that this
will leave the second
row of filling bare ; so
go on withdrawing the
same ends again,
along the second row, and pointing the same reeving ends

150

as at first, through the holes the others came out of, covering the filling and complete four or five rows of this in the same manner. Then, to cover the last row of filling, and to secure the ends of the nettles, you lay them up and down alternately, the long ends that you have withdrawn going up, and the short ones that you have been reeving, laying down ; haul them taut, beat them in, and then tuck them under the bights of the next lay, the lower ones left-handed through the bights to the right, and the upper left-handed to the left. Beat the mat down and cut the ends off.

To finish off by *shouldering*, as for the upper part of a lower rigging mat (when, after reaching the top of the dead-eye it is contracted in order to cover the shroud for a few inches), you leave as many nettles out at each edge of the mat as will reduce it sufficiently, then lay the lanyard (to secure the mat above the dead-eye) along the top of the last turn of filling, and go on working on the centre nettles that you have retained, as far up as you intend to go. Knot the filling, tease the ends of the nettles out a bit, place them round the shroud and serve them over. The ends that you left out, on each side, you finish off by selvaging, as already explained. As the rigging stretches, turn the bottom of the mat up, with the end inside.

151

199. SPLICING A SWORD MAT.—Unlay six or eight inches of each mat, open the ends out, marry them together, laying one up and one down flat along the mat, withdraw the nettles on one side of one (No. 1) mat, and point the nettles of the other mat (No. 2) through the holes they come out of; all ends will then disappear from that side, and there will be four rows of ends on the other. Slue over, pick out the proper nettles of the side, which have been married together, withdraw the ends belonging to No. 2 mat, and introduce the corresponding ends of No. 1 through the holes. The same operation has now been performed on each mat, and on each side there are now two rows of ends; marry those together on each side, laying one up and one down, and go on splicing by withdrawing and reeving, for two or three rows more in each mat. Leave off with the ends all out on the same side, and finish off as with selvaging.

A Cobbler's Stitch—Is used for joining the sides of mats together. Take a filling of roping twine, middle it, and reeve each end through two bights in each mat, (if a heavy mat, through three bights at each edge,) then reeve the lowermost end back through the same bights as the upper end, which will bring the ends out at opposite sides; draw the mats together, and reeve both ends through two turns in each mat again, passing each other through the same hole opposite ways; and so work on, like a cobbler stitching a sole. Finish off each end, by taking a hitch through a bight in the mat of the next lay above, and cut the ends off.

200. PAUNCH MAT.—For heavy rigging mats, strands of 3-in. or 3½-in. rounding would be used for foxes, with a lanyard of 2½-in. Stretch the lanyard along at a convenient working height, middle the foxes and lay them across it, and, commencing on the left, lay up one turn in the first pair, right-handed. Repeat this with the second pair, and lay up the nettle that comes round to the front and left, one turn with the underneath nettle of the first pair, which was brought out to the right; then lay this latter up, one turn with the other nettle of its own pair, and take a hitch with it,—which do with the two last nettles on the left, each time that you work down to them, to keep the mat from unlaying again. Now commence with the third pair,—take the underneath nettle round the upper one, which lay up with the underneath and right-hand nettle of the second pair, which lay up with the other one of the second pair, which lay up with the under one of the first pair, which lay up with the left-hand nettle of all, which lay up with two or three turns to prevent unlaying, round which take a hitch. So proceed until all the nettles are brought in,—a second hand holding them back as you lay up, and when you have come to the last, and the full breadth of the mat is formed, go on in the same way, working down for length. When you have obtained this on the left edge of the mat, it will appear as

153

in the figure; and you then begin to work down square, taking a hitch with each pair as you have finished with them, to prevent them unlaying.

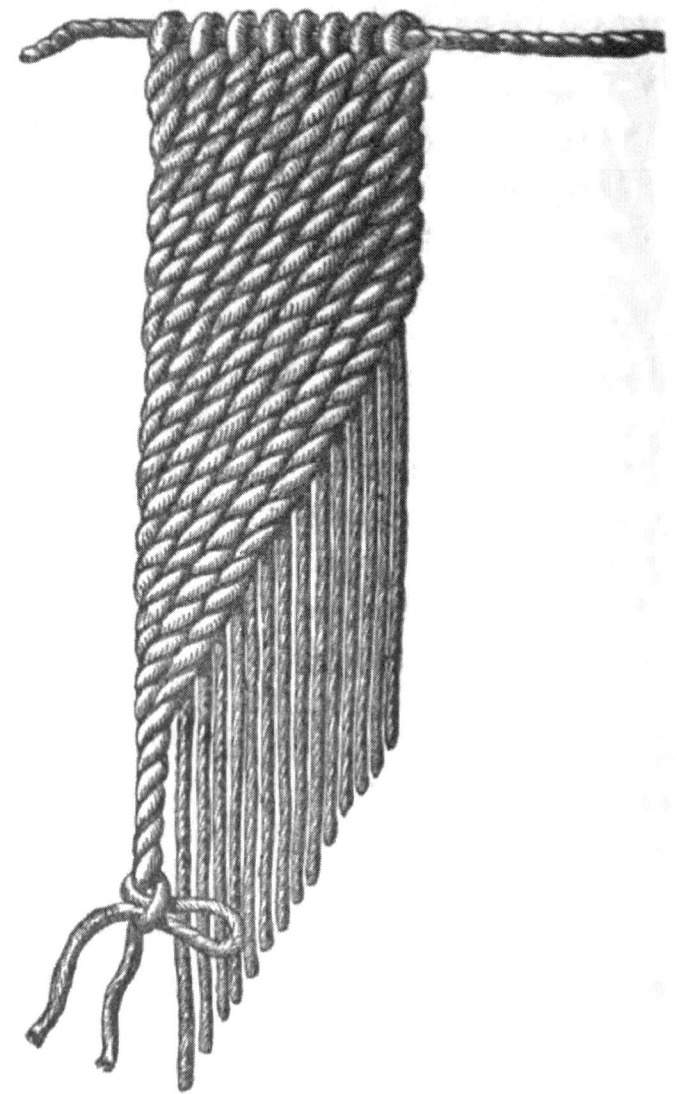

To selvage it, take it down, and lay it on a grating; commence with the first left-hand fox, which bring round under the next one, and lay up along the mat, laying the

154

ne that it comes round (which is the second fox) down-
rards, and in this manner go right across; then stretch·
he lanyard along the nettles where they, cross, and hitch
he ends to the grating. With the first fox laid upwards
ake a right-handed hitch round the lanyard and the first

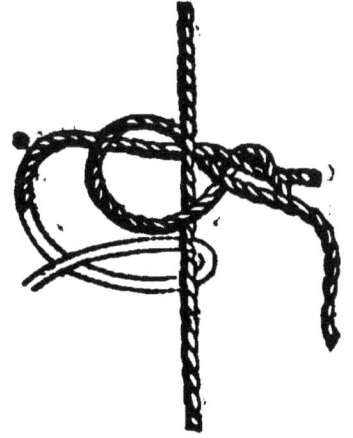

me down, then take the down
me, *a*, dip it back under the
anyard and haul it taut down,
mother hand at the same time
hauling back on the upper one
and so knot the foxes right across.
When done, haul all the lower
ends taut up, and, beginning on·
the left, cross the upper nettle
(which is on the left of the lower)
over it, and reeve it through the bight in the mat in the
immediate lay to the right, bringing the end out to the
left : (rove left-handed.) Beat the hitches down, and cut
the ends off, but not close ; for if left of the proper length,
they will form two rows of thrums. Tuck a thrum in every
third bight up, and in every other lay across, which is
quite thick enough ; and beat down the bights in the mat
that they are rove through, each time separately.

To make a Breeches Mat.—Mats of this shape are used
for the collars of stays ; the broad part lying over the
crutch, and the legs lacing round each fork. You work
the mat down square as far as you require it, then halve
the foxes, and work each part down separately for the
legs.

L   155

You may convert an ordinary mat into a breeches mat by cutting the midship fox across at the head, and simply unreeving it down as far as is wanted; then crossing the ends, and tucking them into adjoining bights.

To repair a Rigging Mat—That has had a hole chafed through it. Stick sufficient foxes through the bights of the mat at the top of the hole, to cover it, lying well over the edges, and back clear of the hole, and middle them. Bring the left-hand fox round the next one to it, lay its end up, and the one it comes round downwards, like the commencement of selvaging; go right across and secure it by sticking the left-hand nettle, right-handed, through a bight in the mat in the edge of the hole, and the right-hand nettle, left-handed, through a similar bight, the ends of each pointing outwards; then work the next and succeeding rows as a paunch mat is worked, but working square across, laying one fox up with its next only, and securing each row as it is completed, by tucking the right, and left-hand nettles in as you did with the first row. When you have thus covered the hole, stick all the ends through the bights below them left-handed once or twice, and cut them off; then slue the mat over, and either stick the broken ends into the new piece, or bring the edges together with a lacing,

201. DRAWING AND KNOTTING YARNS.—Having taken the twist out of the strand, let a couple of hands lay hold of the ends, and beat it on the deck to loosen the yarns, which

156

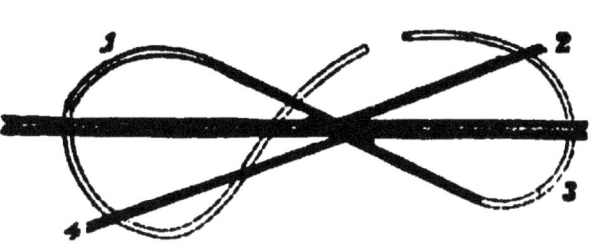

re then drawn
out. They are
knotted toge-
ther, for rope-
making purpo-
ses, by splitting
the ends, scraping them down, and marrying the forks
together.   No. 1 end is then brought underneath towards
you and half-knotted to No. 3 end, which is passed
underneath, from you, giving it somewhat the appearance
of a reef knot; then tauten it to jamb the knot, and cut
the ends off.

202. A SPANISH WINDLASS—Is used for heaving two
parts of a shroud together
at the nip, before passing
the seizing; and for
many other similar pur-
poses.   A strand is laid
on the top; the ends are
crossed underneath, and
brought up on opposite
sides, the bights taken
round a bar, or lever, laid on the top, a twist is taken in
them, and a marlinspike is inserted in the bights at each
end, and hove round upon.

203. WORM, PARCEL, AND SERVE.—A rope is wormed
in order to give it a round snug appearance; the ends of
the worming are seized round the rope, or tucked in, and
then wound along the lay.   After being passed by hand,

L 2

worming is hove on by a soft strand knotted and taken round the rope ; a bolt is then passed through the bights and the strop twisted up and hove round the rope, which tautens the worming as it proceeds. With very large rope, the worming requires backing on each side with smaller stuff, in order to fill it up properly. If the rope is not to be served, a seizing, snaked, should be put round the worming at intervals, to keep it in its place, as it is liable to work slack.

Parcelling, which is employed to preserve the rope from wet, is made of tarred canvas, and is passed with the lay of the rope, with the edges overlapping.

Service is used to protect the rope from chafe, and is passed against the lay of the rope. It is commenced by passing the first turns over the end, and finished by slacking up the last three or four turns, dipping the end through them, hauling them taut singly, and then drawing the end through.

Spike-serving—Is used when you have a small eye or similar piece of gear to serve. The turns are passed by hand ; and each is hove taut separately by taking a marlin-spike hitch over a marlinspike, and with the point prizing it against the rope until the service is taut.

204. A MARLINSPIKE HITCH—Is used for heaving the turns of a seizing taut, for steadying the point of the marlinspike when going aloft, &c., &c. The marlinspike

is laid over the lanyard, the
part that is towards you laid
over the other part, crossing
the marlinspike, the bight
thus formed doubled over,
the marlinspike withdrawn
and stuck in between the
midship part and the bights,

in which position it will resist any strain ; and, directly it
is drawn out, allows the knot to fall adrift again.

205. SHORT SPLICE.—Unlay the ends, marry them together, lay the strands of one end over the strands of the
other end that are to the left of them, and under the next
strand to the one passed over.   Slue the rope round, and
do the same with the other strands ; then put the strands
on both sides, over one, and through the next again, or
else put them in " once and a half "—(they have already
been put through once, so you, in that case, halve the
strands, put the upper half through, and leave the under
half out, which hides it ;) then stretch the rope, and cut
the ends off.

206. LONG SPLICE.—Unlay the ends alike, but for a
much longer distance than for a short splice, and marry
them together; unlay a strand on each side, and lay the
strand of the other end, that is opposite to it, up in the
lay that it comes out of, making both equidistant from
the centre pair of strands, which you do not touch.

Twist each pair up as you have done with them, to keep them in their places, and cut off the spare ends; grease the strands, *whole-knot* them together, stick them in once and a half, and cut the ends off. For a large rope, such as the fore brace, instead of knotting the strands, merely lay them alongside each other in the score of the rope, then put the ends in once, a half, and a quarter, and *back it* with the remaining quarter of a strand to taper it off. In splicing, instead of laying a strand over one, and under the next, you *back*

it by putting the strand in, left-handed, under the strand you would otherwise have laid it over; which gives it an exceedingly neat and serviceable finish.

207. EYE SPLICE.—Unlay the end, and lay the strands on the rope the required length of the eye down from the bend; stick the midship strand under the strand of the rope on which it lies; lay the next end over this last strand, and under the next one; slue the eye over and stick the third end in under the third strand, put the ends, or half the ends, in again, and cut them off.

160

208. CUT SPLICE.—Unlay the ends, place them alongside each other in opposite directions, the one overlapping

the other equal to the length of the eye required. Splice the strands of each end in, as for an eye splice, and serve them over.

209. HORSE-SHOE SPLICE is formed like a cut splice, but differs in shape, one leg being longer than the other.

210. GRECIAN SPLICE.—Say that the rope to be spliced is a 7½-inch topmast backstay. Put a whipping on, unlay the ends, lay the four strands up into ten yarn foxes, short-splice the hearts together, and serve them hard over with yarn. Then marry the foxes, and pass the ends that lie upwards over the next downward one on the right, and

161

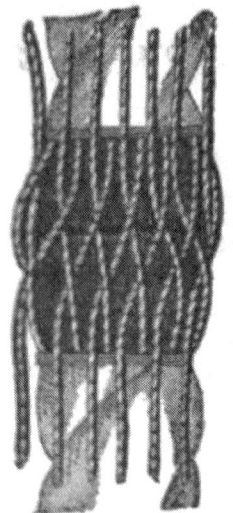

under the bight of the second downward one, working round to the right. Haul all parts taut, scrape the ends down, marl over hard, parcel well with tarred canvas and serve. This splice is particularly neat; and, as there are no bends in it, it is necessarily much stronger than a shroud knot.

211. Splicing Hemp and Chain Cables together.—Three chain tails being shackled to the chain cable, pudden, by laying strands of yarn along them; lay a 3-inch rope tail in with each; then marl down, parcel, and marl over. Put a whipping round the hemp cable, unlay the end, and unlay each strand; pick out the outside yarns, lay the strands of each strand up again, splice a 3-inch tail into the three strands of the cable, make the outside yarns up into sennit, and graft the splices of the tails over. Being now ready for splicing, lay the chain tails up for a short distance, and then short-splice each cable into the other in the ordinary way. Three seizings are next put on over the splice, the centre one of 2 inches, and the quarter ones each of 1½ inch. The tails are wormed along the cable, and secured with a couple of flat seizings, snaked.

212. A Deep-Sea Lead-line—Should be laid up, one end with the other, for three or four inches before splicing; for, being hard stuff, it is liable to draw.

The marks should be tucked under a strand, after each knot is put in, and then they will lie flat along the line, and run no risk of fagging out, or being torn off, which they are subject to if the marks hang loose.

213. CAT'S PAW.—Lay the bight of the rope over the end and standing part, as in left-hand figure; then, with a bight in each hand, take three or four turns in them by twisting them from you; bring the bights together and hook on.

214. SHEEP-SHANK.—By laying the bight of the rope up

alongside the standing part, shorten it up as much as you require; and then take a hitch with the standing part and end round the bights.

215. SLINGING A CASK—With butt slings. Reeve the end through the eye in the slings, slip the bight over one end of the cask, pass the slings round the other end, and take two half-hitches round its own part.

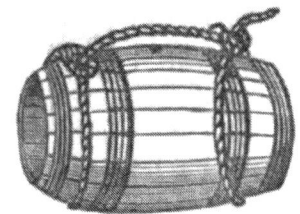

With Bale Slings.—Lay the slings on the deck, roll the cask over them, lift the bights up and pass one through the other, spreading them out well, and beating down as you get the weight of the cask.

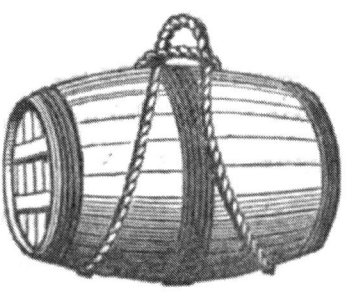

With a Rope's-end.—Make a bowline knot in the yard-whip, and stick the end back so as to form a short bight, to which bend the stay whip. Turn the bight of the bowline over its own part, and slip each bight thus formed, over one end of the cask.

With the head knocked in.—Slip the bight of the whip under the cask, take a hitch with each part over the head, and knot them together above.

216. To SLING A MAN—In the most secure manner: make a bowline on a bight, shorten one of the bights up, seat him in the long bight, and put his arms through the short one.

217. BENDING TWO HAWSERS TOGETHER.—A *reeving*

(line) *bend* is about the best, with the ends seized back; or instead of that, a half-hitch through the bight of

each hawser is frequently used. If the bights are bowline knotted, instead of being hitched and seized, the end should be thrust back between the standing part and upper bight, to prevent it jambing, in the same way that a toggle is often used with this knot; but with a heavy strain a bowline-knot often capsizes. If in a hurry, a carrick-bend may be used for small warps.

218. Bending a Hawser to the Ring of an Anchor. —A fishermen's bend, which is the same as a studding-sail bend without the end tucked back, is what is generally used, but it becomes hard jambed with a strain. A *round turn*, a half-hitch, and the end stopped up, is far preferable; and I may here remark, with reference to all purposes in which they can be used, that *two half-hitches will never either slip or jamb.*

219. Reeving the Turns of a Seizing through a small Eye.—After reeving a turn of the seizing, splice the end you are working on into the bight; or, if you have already rove several turns, splice it into the bight last passed, then work all parts round and round until sufficient turns are completed, draw the splice, and secure the seizing.

165

220. WORKING A CRINGLE IN A ROPE.—Unlay a single strand from a rope of the size that the cringle is required to be; begin on the left, and put this strand under two strands of the rope you are working it on; divide it into thirds and haul two-thirds of it through, so that the long leg is from you; lay the two parts up together so as to form sufficient for the round of the cringle, but always with an odd number of turns, ending with the long leg towards you; stick it from you under

two strands; bring it round and work back to the left; put it under two strands towards you, leaving one strand intervening between the place you entered it, then back over one, and down under two. Now tuck the short end

in under the same two strands in the rope as the cringle is already worked through, then over one, and under two; cut the ends off, and serve the cringle over.

If a cringle is to be worked into the leech of a sail, the

strand is taken round the rope and through the eyelet hole
in the sail ; and the ends are finished off by taking a hitch
round all, and then passed under two, over one, and under
two, as before.

 221. NET-MAKING.—Fill the needle,
stretch the head-rope along, and begin
on the left by securing the end of the
twine to it.   Regulate the size of the mesh by taking it
over your finger, and then clove-hitching it to the head.
When you have worked as far to the right as the head is
intended to extend, get round on the other side of the
net, and work back again ; but this row of meshes, and
all the subsequent ones, are formed by hitching them to

the upper row with a sheet bend.   When the second row
is finished, shift round to the other side again, and work

167

the third row. The last row is hitched to the foot-rope, which is weighted with leads ; the head-rope is floated with corks ; and side-ropes are afterwards seized on.

To repair a seine, you cut it away until you get a straight row of meshes, and replace them as you at first made them.

A shot, or treasure-net, is made like a cabbage-net ; the head-rope is circular, the meshes are formed in the usual way, and the circumference of the net is reduced as you work down, by bringing two meshes into one, at regular intervals ; at first, one mesh in a row ; in the next row, two meshes ; then taking up every fourth mesh, next every 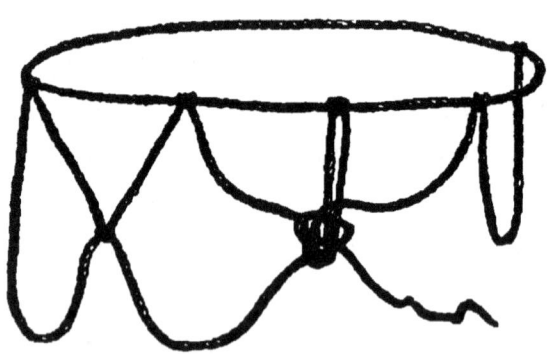 third in a row, and so on. Finish off by working a small grummet through the meshes at the bottom, to keep them together ; and reeve two strops through the head for beckets, so that by hauling them apart, the mouth of the net is drawn up.

 **222. BOATS' FENDERS.**—A paunch mat fender is made of a piece of mat rolled up taut, with the ends of the foxes placed in the centre ; the end is sewed to the part of of the mat where it terminates, and the edges are laced together. The lanyard of the mat forms the lanyard of the fender.

168

The usual fender for boom-boats is made of as many parts of spun-yarn as will give it the requisite dimensions.   These are middled and doubled over the lanyard, and a small grummet is driven over the

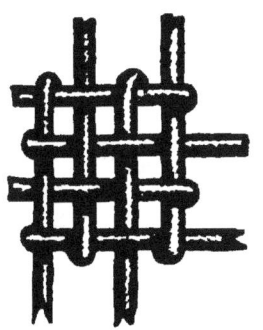

bights to make them snug. as in making a swab. It is then grafted over, either with sennit of foxes, and finished off as grafting is usually finished; or by crowning the end over with the foxes, as is shown in the left-hand figure. .

You can crown in this way with any number of ends that are a multiple of four, by dividing them into four parts, and laying a part down on each side ; then bringing 1 over on side 6, keeping the bight up, laying 6 over between 1 and 2, bringing 2 over between 6 and 5, and laying 5 over outside 2 ; then laying 7 over 1, under 6, over 2, and under 5 ; 4 over 5, under 2, over 1, under 6 ; then reeving 8 across, and lastly

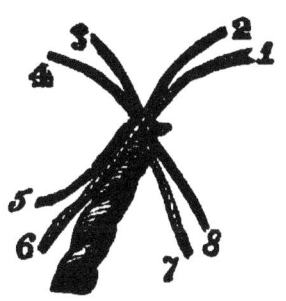

3 ;—when it will be found that all the ends are secured. Haul the bights taut down, and either put a whipping round underneath, or tuck the ends under the grafting and cut them off.

A grummet fender is merely a rope grummet grafted over.

A canvas fender is stuffed with oakum, roped at the

edges, and has a small grummet sewed on the centre, to keep the chafe off.

Leather fenders are used for gigs.

223. A CLINCH.—Is termed an inside, or an outside one, according to the position of the end. In an inside clinch, *a*, the end is protected, and the clinch looks snugger. An outside clinch, *b*, is used for a cable, and in any case where the rope is not permanently secured, and where the strain is such as would jamb an inside clinch.

224. HAMMOCK CLEWS.—Take twelve lengths of nettle-stuff, middle them, serve round all at the centre, and pass a seizing to form the eye ; then lay one up and one down, as for a sword mat, bring the outside nettle on each side across for filling and leave it out ; form the other rows in the same manner, and when reduced to two, knot the last pair.

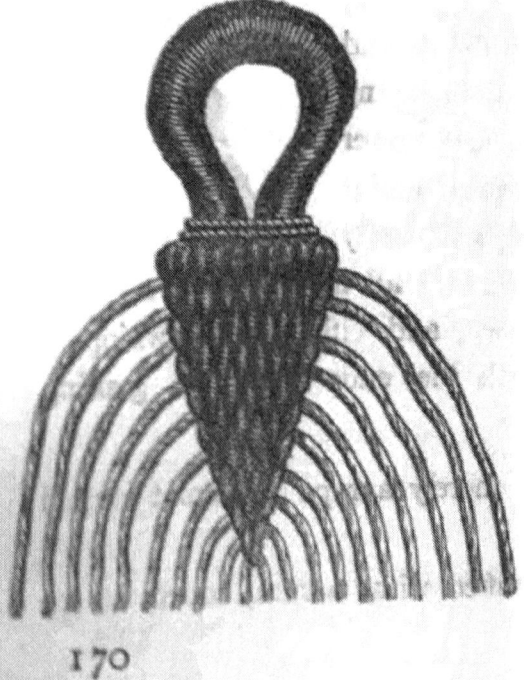

170

Spanish Clews—Are without plaiting, and are made by serving the nettles round below the seizing, leaving one out on each side, at regular intervals.

225. SENNIT FOR HATS.—Split the grass up, take a couple of lengths, cross one over the other, double, the underneath one over the upper, then the right-hand one over one and under the other two, 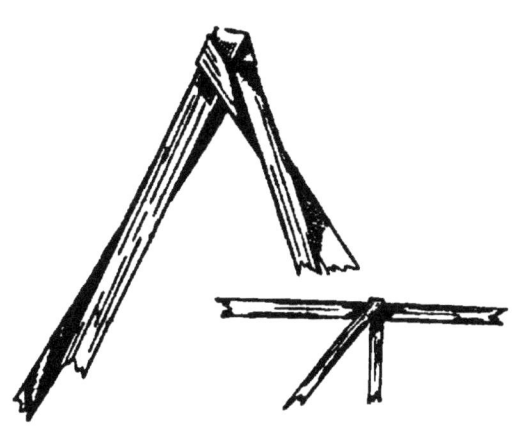 and what is now the right-hand one over two and under one, then the left-hand one over one and under two, and again the left over two and under one ; then work two in on the right, and so on. Join the grass when you come to an end, by laying the end of another piece on the top,

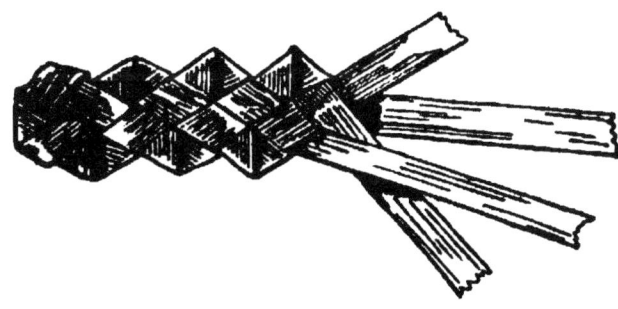

and then go on working it in ; and always join on the upper side, because the under side is the proper *right* side of the sennit. Afterwards clip all the ends off, and rub the sennit down smooth with a bottle, or anything hard.

The button is formed of a broader piece of grass. It is first doubled short over itself, then 1 under 2, leaving a space, then 2 over 1, and down through the centre of the triangle; next 1 over 2, and down through the centre, coming out on the opposite side, and so on until an octagonal figure is formed.

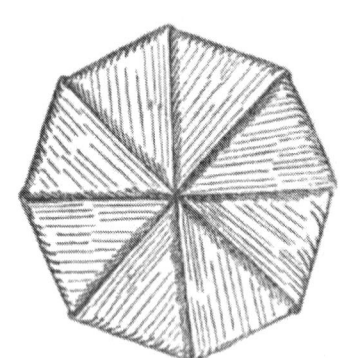

The hat is begun by stitching the sennit to the button, commencing at the end finished off with, and working round left-handed. The sennit is kept as slack as possible, and stitched through every other corner for the first few rounds; then afterwards through three thicknesses of sennit, and through every corner, the stitch being kept out of sight, by the needle being pointed underneath the strands of the sennit.

226. COIR BRUSHES.—Shape a piece of hard wood for the back (stave of a salt-meat cask, for example), burn out the holes in rows with a marlinspike ; and out of another piece of wood cut a *former*. Make the coir up into filling

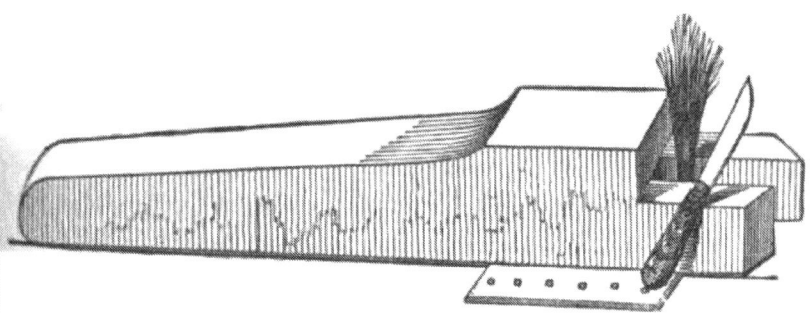

proportionate to the size of the holes, pass the bight of the marline down through the first hole, slip it over the filling, take a turn or two round the former, and heave the bight of the filling through the hole, up to the level of the top of the back ; then slue over,  put the filling between the notch of the former, and cut it off square, dip the bight of the marline down through the next hole, and in the same manner proceed with each, until all are filled in.

227. Units of Measurement.—The size of spars, dead-eyes, and chain, is expressed by their diameters; of rope, by its circumference ; blocks by their length ; hand masts (Norway spars), by their circumference, in hands, four feet from the heel (the hand being four inches).

228. Berthing Ship's Company.—Begin on one side, forward, and number off right across 1, 2, 3, 4, &c. ; in this way when one watch is on deck at night, you have every other hammock empty, and the same number of men off each side of the deck. Fifteen inches is the general rule

for the distance apart of hammock hooks, allowing when practicable, more room for petty officers—boatswain's mates near the hatchways, boys, with a ship's corporal, and the seamen schoolmaster on one side of the main deck. The guard, quarter-masters, signal-men, &c., who have to keep night watch, placed where they will be as little disturbed as possible, if the hands should be turned up early. Each man should have his bag given him, marked with his number on the ship's books, on the bottom.

229. MESSES.—Every mess should have the same number of men from each watch belonging to it, so that the weight may be equal when one watch is on deck; also, that you may have enough hands in the watch below to clean it. Marines and stokers have messes to themselves; boys, daymen, &c., should be equally divided amongst the messes.

230. PROVISIONS.—Wet provisions are salt beef, pork, suet, vinegar, lime juice, and rum. Dry provisions are peas, flour, raisins, tea, sugar, chocolate, and oatmeal.

231. HOISTING IN PROVISIONS.—The "quarter," and small stay tackles, should be used; the lower block of the "quarter" should be worked with a light whip on the yard. The quarter is taken round the yard and hooked to its own part after being triced up by a whip on the lower lift.

232. OLD PROVISIONS—Should always be cleared out of the holds before stowing the new; when the new are

174

)wed, the old must be stowed on top, to be consumed
st.

233. How, and where Stowed.—Provisions should
: stowed in the holds, so that each kind can be got at,
 due proportion without breaking bulk ; and as much
accordance with the following plan as possible.　　.

Wet provisions being the heaviest form the ground tiers,
e dry provisions on the top ; beef and flour on the star-
)ard side, pork and pease port side.

Casks are stowed fore-and-aft, bung up, fire-wood or
mnage being placed under the *chines*, to prevent their
uifting.

In the spirit room, the casks are stowed bung up, and
llge free ; spirits should be carefully guarded, until the
ey is turned in the lock of the spirit room.　Biscuit is
:owed in bags in the bread room.

Before commencing to stow, the holds should be
1oroughly cleansed, and white-washed

234. Casks Marked.—Each cask has the contents,
nd date of package marked on it, the bung is found
etween the rivets of any two opposite hoops.

235. Slops—Consist of bales of cloth, flannel, drill,
luck, jean, silk handkerchiefs, and bedding ; casks of
;hoes, marine clothing, soap and tobacco.

236. Size of water tanks.—The largest tank contains
)oo gallons, is 4 feet 1 inch square at the ends, and 6 feet
1 inch in height, the next size contains 500 gallons, and is
4 feet 1 inch, by 5 feet 1 inch ; and the 400 gallon tank

175

4 feet 1 inch square ; these tanks, empty, weigh ten, eight, and six hundred-weight, respectively, the bilge tanks have their lower outer edge taken off, otherwise they are of the foregoing dimensions.

237. STOWING TANKS.—Tanks are stowed on a skeleton platform, built at the bottom of the hold, placed with their tops level, and with the corners in which the manholes are, adjoining, so that when watering, or pumping out, four tanks can be filled or cleared without shifting the hose more than a foot or two.

They should be wedged up taut, and caulked in. Tanks are slung with a toggle in the manhole, and placed with levers and tackles.

238. STARTING A TANK.—In one corner of the tank is a rod, the lower part of which acts as a plug, and screws into a socket in the bottom. The upper end comes up through the top of the tank, and turns with a key, which lets the water out below ; and to keep it fair over the hole for screwing in again, it traverses between two iron stays near the bottom.

239. BALLAST.—There are two sizes, weighing $1\frac{1}{2}$ and 3 cwt. each, they are six inches square at the ends ; the largest is three feet long, the smaller of course half that length.

240. IN STEAM LAUNCH.—Get her alongside, and with the watch hoist out the engine ; and, if necessary, the coal boxes and water tanks. The engine is slung with

176

chain slings, having four legs to it, and is hoisted in with
the main-yard and stay-tackles. Then "hands in launch;"
top-gallant yardmen and topsail sheetmen "away aloft"
coming in the starboard side—"starboard lifts"—"top
away," at once, and haul taut the topsail sheets. "Belay
the lifts"—"lay out." Two burtons are hooked to each
lower yard; haul taut and frap the burtons, lifts, and
topsail sheets, together with a small line from the top.
"Trice up, brace in," on which the stays are triced up;
yard tackles lowered and the yards braced, so as to plumb
the boat as much as possible, while still allowing her to
clear the ship's side; braces and trusses hauled well taut.

"Lay in," "down from aloft"—hook the yard and
stay-tackles; "haul taut the yards;" away with the yards
taking down the slack of the stays. When high enough,
"turn with yards," "away with the stays." Heave a line
out of the boat for a luff to bring her into place, and a
fore and after forward to steady her. "Turn with the
stays;" "man the rigging;" "lower of all," "away aloft."
Let go the burtons, topsail-sheets, and rolling tackles;
top away on the port lifts and get the squaring marks
down at once. Then, "trice to hand"—"lay out."
Unhook the stays, man the braces and bill and quarter
tricing lines; "hold fast on the lower yards;" then
"lower and square." "Square yards," and "down from
aloft." When another boat has to follow, hook the stays
to the slings, and the yards to the stays, the yards can
then be unhooked and passed over again, whilst the first
boat is being placed.

177

241. SHIP ROLLING HEAVILY.—The great thing to look out for is to keep the boat from being stove, while hoisting; therefore, take a whip to the bows of the boat, from the lower boom end. Run the guns in, lower the ports, be prepared to fend her off well. When well up to the nettings, hook the opposite stays crossed, and use bow and stern guys, from both sides of the deck.

242. YOU TOP UP FIRST—Because, otherwise, the lifts and burtons would bind against the topmast rigging, on pulling up.

243. CHAFING GEAR.—Paunch mats on the bunt of all yards between the yard and masts, well greased. A mat on the quarters of the topsail-yards in wake of the rigging. Breeches mats on the collars of lower stays (but here and elsewhere, bamboo scotchmen are preferable, when they can be obtained). A mat on lower yards to protect the sail where it takes the stay, when braced up. A mat under each leech-line block; hanging mats (or a hide) on the lower rigging, where the yards bind; on topmast backstays, for the same purpose, and in the wake of staysail pendants; on foremost swifter of lower rigging where the foot of the courses takes, and on the lanyards where the sheet chafes; on crossjack yard-arms, for the preservation of the spanker; and on the horns of the crosstrees, for the protection of the top-gallant sails. Battens should be permanently fitted on the sheet-anchor stocks, to prevent the hoops cutting the fore sheets; or a mat should be laced on.

178

An Account of the Fitting out of H.M.S. " Bellerophon."
This affords a brilliant example of what *can* be done in
the Navy, when a ship's company are commanded by
officers possessing the requisite union of due seamanlike
and administrative qualities, and I give it as a high standard by when all such work may be measured, and as an
appropriate pendant to the first section of our subject.

On March 7th, 1847, orders were unexpectedly received
for the 90-gun ships " Rodney," Captain Edward Collier,
C.B., and " Albion," Captain Nicholas Lockyer, C.B., to
fit out respectively, the " Bellerophon " 78, and the
" Calcutta," 84, then lying up in ordinary, the former in
Portsmouth, and the latter in Plymouth harbour.

These ships, in common with all the " advanced " ships
in ordinary, had their lower masts, gun-carriages, chain
cables (in 12-fathom lengths), stowed in their tiers, and
the lower tier of water-tanks on board ; which state the
" Bellerophon " was in when the " Rodney's " *commenced*
work on Monday morning, March 9th. On the same
evening the topmasts were fidded, and mizen top-gallant-
mast pointed. By Tuesday evening the top-gallant-mast
were fidded, running gear rove, and sails bent. At half-
past ten on Wednesday morning she hauled off from the
jetty, and that evening saw her at Spithead with three
months' provisions and stores on board, awaiting orders
to proceed to sea.

The ship's company went ashore every evening, and
had their full time for meals every day ; and thus a line-
of-battle ship was fitted out for a three months' cruise, in

every way ready to engage an enemy, in thirty working hours.

H.R.H. Prince Albert having visited the ship, and expressed his admiration of the skill and energy exhibited in the accomplishment of so unexampled a result, she was dismantled and returned again into ordinary.

244. WEIGHING.—Put the slip on, unbitt, and bring to (this is with a patent capstan) heave round, off slip, keep paying down the slack chain ; hauling the cable from the capstan with chain hooks, and aft with hook ropes ; when up to the bows, avast heaving on slip, haul enough cable forward for bitting and catting, bit the cable, bowse to to the compressor.

Hook the cat, haul taut, keep hauling, off slip, surge the cable, and away with the cat.   When up to the cat-head, pass the ring stopper, hook the fish, ease up the cat, put on the stock pendant and bowse on it, haul away the fish. When high enough, turn with the fish, walk away the topping lift, pass the shank painter, ease up, and unhook the fish, and bowse in the slack chain.

245. SECURE AN ANCHOR FOR SEA.—After catting and fishing the ring of the anchor, will be the drift of the cat-block below the cat-head, and must be boused close up ; to do this hook the cat to a strop round the lower arm of the stock ; and bouse close up to the cat-head, haul taut the ring stopper, and unhook the cat ; there are various ways of passing lashings when securing for sea round the stock and shank, which must depend much on the shape of the bow.

180

SECTION II.

AT SEA.

RULE OF THE ROAD.

246. CLOSE HAULED ON OPPOSITE TACKS.—The ship on the port tack is always to give way, if necessary, either by keeping away, or going about.

247. SHIPS WITH THE WIND FREE.—Give way to those on a wind ; therefore, the ship on the port tack stands on.

248. TWO SHIPS HAVING THE WIND LARGE,—And meeting nearly end on, are to pass on the port side of each other ; therefore the ship to the eastward keeps away, and the other hauls up.

249. UNDER STEAM,—And *nearly* end on to each other, both port their helms and pass on the port side (*see the order in council of the 30th July, 1868, respecting port helm*), when meeting not end on.

250. A STEAMER—Always gives way to a sailing vessel, and it must be remembered that every vessel under sail, with steam ready, though not using it, is considered a steamer in the event of collision.

251. EVERY VESSEL UNDERWEIGH—Is to carry a green light on the starboard, and a red light on the port side ;

steamers in addition carry a white light at the foremost head. The side lights to be fitted with inboard screens, projecting at least 3 feet forward from the light, so as to prevent the light from being seen across the bow. Vessels towing, carry two white mast-head lights.

252. DURING FOGS—Vessels under steam are to sound a steam whistle; vessels under sail to use a fog horn; at anchor, ring a bell.

These signals to be sounded once at least every five minutes.

253. MAKING PLAIN SAIL.—"Clear lower deck;" "make all plain sail, starboard tack;" "upper yardmen aloft;" man the topsail sheets and halliards; "away aloft;" "trice up, lay out;" "hoist the jib;" "let fall, sheet home;" upper sails to be kept up until the topsails are nearly mastheaded; then let fall by order, sheeted home and hoisted.

As each sail is let fall, the loosers should lay in, and move smartly down from aloft.

"Port braces"—"fore and main tacks;" "brace forward;" "let run, haul on board"—when the sails are set, and yards braced up; "haul taut weather braces, lifts, and trusses;" coil down ropes.

254. TACKING.—Keep the ship full for stays, and give the word "Ready, O!" to enforce attention. *Ease* the helm down, that her way may not be too suddenly checked. Haul over the boom; and, when the helm is down,

"Helm's a-lee!" on which the fore and head sheets are let go and overhauled. When the wind is out of the mainsail, "Raise tacks and sheets," keeping the fore tack fast till the main-yard is hauled, for as the foresail bellies in to the mast (which it always does to a certain extent when the fore tack is let go), it becomes a back sail, and retards the ship in coming to. This is still more the case when, in a strong breeze, it becomes necessary to check the fore bowline, to relieve it of the undue strain brought upon it. The top-gallant bowlines at the same time are let go, the lee main tack shortened in, the weather after (preventer) braces, and lee maintop bowline manned ; and when the wind is ahead, as a general rule, or, in quick working ships, a little before, taking the main top-sail as your guide,— the weather leech of which will be well aback, or, in a dark night judging by the shaking of the spanker—"Haul well taut ; mainsail haul !" The after yards are swung and braced up as far as the fore yard will allow—the lee head braces, in short ships, being checked for that purpose, the maintop bowline run away with, and a turn taken before the main-yard can fly back again, main tack boarded, and sheet gathered aft, head sheets shifted over, and boom sheet eased off. When all safe, and the after sails begin to fill, the head bowlines are let go, the head yards braced round, and the fore tack boarded, to the order "Fore tack, head bowlines—Of all haul ;" if, however, she has paid off too rapidly, the head yards should not be braced up till she has come to, or is coming to the wind. The main yard is now braced up, and the sheet hauled aft. The helm is righted if she loses her way, and shifted over if she gathers sternway. The lee breast back-stays, when used, are borne abaft, and the weather one crutched and pulled up in stays. Finally, the yards are all trimmed, the weather braces hauled taut, the weather lifts bowsed up, and the bowlines hauled. When done, pipe the sweepers, call the hammock stowers and coil down ropes—every man a rope, and every rope on end.

255. TOP-GALLANT BOWLINES—Are let go, when you raise tacks and sheets, because, when the sails are aback, if the lee braces are not quite taut, the whole strain of the top-gallant sail, and great part of that of the topsail would come upon them; and, also, that they may be cleared away in good time before the yards are hauled.

256. THE LEE FORE TACK—Is not shortened in like the lee main tack, because, by doing so, you would make a back sail of it, and prevent the ship coming to.

257. TACKING IN LIGHT WINDS.—Keep away a little, and get as much way on as possible, before putting the helm down.

Man the head sail downhauls; ease the helm down; check the lee head braces, and head bowlines.

"Helm's a-lee;" haul down the head sails; brace the head yards up as she comes to the wind; when nearly head to wind, brace round the yards on the mizen mast; and when the wind is fairly round on the other bow, haul the main yard, and hoist the head sails.

258. MISSING STAYS.—On port tack.—Haul aft the head sheets, put the helm a-starboard, raise the main clew-

184

garnets, brail up the spanker, and square the after yards. Then, when she fills, either brace up again on the port tack, and try it again ; or, let her come round on her heel, squaring the head yards when the wind comes aft, shifting the helm as she gathers way, and bringing her to the wind on the starboard tack.

259. DANGER ON THE LEE BEAM.—Run the weather braces in, and make a stern-board till clear.

260. TACKING IN A BREEZE.—Ease away the weather head-braces with a' turn, keeping a strain on them when the yards fill, and standing by to belay in time ; for, if let go and overhauled, as in moderate weather, a sprung yard would be the possible consequence.

261. THE LARGER HELM—Carried in the freshening breeze, is occasioned by the increased immersion of the bow, which throws her up into the wind ; and, owing to the oblique direction given to the rudder as the ship heels over, much of the effect is lost, and a greater helm is required in consequence.

262. ABOUT SHIP, UP MAINSAIL.—Instead of " raise tacks and sheets ;" it will be, " raise the fore-tack ;" " up mainsail " and " maintopsail haul ;" instead of " mainsail haul."

263. THE DISTANCE GAINED TO WINDWARD.—When lying within 5½ points. of the wind, is 47 per cent. on the whole distance run ; as you will see by reference to a transverse table.

185

264. THE ACTION OF THE RUDDER—Causes a ship to rotate on an axis before the centre; the exact position of which depends upon the build and rig of the ship. A Chinese cargo-boat will fly round with the bow almost stationary.

265. A SHIP HEELS OVER—At first from the sudden action of the wind upon the sails; and she rights as she gathers away, from the increased lifting pressure of the water on the lee side.

266. TO FORE-REACH IN STAYS.—Ease the helm down very gradually, haul the main yard the moment you can insure her staying, and, in a fresh breeze, keep fast the fore sheet if the ship works well.

267. TO AVOID FORE-REACHING.—Round to quickly, check the lee head-braces, and make a late haul of the main yard.

268. STEAM AND SAIL.—Tacking with the watch, look out and haul the after yards quickly, or you will have a bother with both them and the head yards if she gets on the other tack before you.

269. TO WINDWARD.—Your companion is the weather-most, for a line drawn from her at right angles to the wind will fall to windward of you.

270. TAKEN ABACK.—As she will lie her course on the other tack, pipe "Watch about ship;" raise tacks and sheets, brace round the after yards, board the main tack, attend to the helm, and haul the head yards as in tacking.

Should she refuse to come-to to starboard, and has lost her way, port the helm, up mainsail, in spanker, square the after yards, and wear round.

When taken aback with the wind on the lee bow, there is, of course, no help for it but to go round ; but if the wind is ahead or on the weather bow, and you do not wish to go on the other tack, you box her off with the head yards ; that is, if flattening in, easing the boom over, &c., are not sufficient.

271. WEARING UNDER PLAIN SAIL.—Up mainsail and in spanker : put the helm up. " let go the bowlines—round in the after yards;" keep bracing in as her head pays off, shivering the mizen topsail, but keeping the main just lifting.   When the wind is aft, "raise the fore tack"—"square the head yards."   Brace forward the after yards and bring her to the wind ; haul out the spanker, brace up, set the mainsail, and haul aft the head sheets.   It is a good plan, particularly if wearing with the watch and using steam, to brace the head yards right up on the new tack, after squaring them, before manning the after braces.

272. WEARING SHORT ROUND.—Starboard tack before going round.   Throw the ship up in the wind to deaden her way ; haul up the mainsail, and brail up the spanker ; brace the head yards a-box, and square the after yards ; put the helm a-port when she gathers stern-way, amidships when she loses it, and a-starboard when the after sails fill and she gathers headway.   Square the head yards as in wearing, and when you have brought the wind on the port

N   187 quarter, brace up the after yards, haul out the spanker, and board the main tack.

273. WEARING IN A GALE—With a heavy sea running, requires great care, and a temporary lull in the weather should if possible be taken advantage of. Trusses, preventer braces rolling, and relieving tackles, must be carefully attended, plenty of way should be kept on the ship, that the helm may be well answered.

274. WEAR IN A STORM, WHEN ALL OTHER MEANS HAVE FAILED.—By manning the fore rigging as thickly as the men can pack, ships, under the circumstances stated in the question, have wore when all previous attempts were unsuccessful.

But a sea anchor, or stop water, with a hawser from the quarter, will do better, if you can launch it.

275. SHIFTING OVER STORM STAYSAIL-SHEETS.—The general plan, and I think the best, is to haul down the sail, shift over the sheet, steady aft and hoist, but it may be done by using luffs as sheets from the opposite sides.

276. WEARING UNDER STAYSAILS.—Put the helm up, brail up the after trysails, and turn the yards as with sail set. In a very heavy sea it may be necessary to drop the reefed foresail for the purpose of keeping way on the ship, and preventing her being pooped, even at the risk of not being able to furl it again. In the mean time shift the sheets over, and steady them aft; when before the wind set the after sails, and haul down the fore and main

188

staysails, setting them again as soon as the sheets are shifted over.

277. SETTING STUDDING-SAILS.—"Hands trim and make sail—studding-sails both sides·" "Away aloft." "Main clew-garnets and buntlines, spanker brails." "Up mainsail, brail up." "Weather braces, lifts and trusses. Raise the fore tack, round in." When ready with the studding-sails, "Boom topping-lifts, fore guys, topmast and top-gallant studding-sail halyards." "Haul taut." "Rig out, trice to hand." On which the lower booms are topped up, and hauled forward, topmast and top-gallant studding-sail booms rigged out, topmast and top-gallant studding-sails triced up to the yards, head stops cut, sails launched over the brace blocks, and the slack of the tacks taken down. The lower halyards are then manned by the hands from the topping-lifts and fore guys, and at the word "Hoist away," everything goes out together.

Otherwise, "Boom-jiggers, topmast and top-gallant studding-sail halyards." "Rig out, hoist away." The sails are then set as quickly as possible independent of each other: and when set, and the lower studding-sails ready, "Boom topping-lifts, fore guys, lower halyards." "Top up, hoist away."

278. TAKING IN STUDDING-SAILS.—"Hands shorten sail—studding-sail downhauls." "Away aloft." "Top up the lower booms." Lower studding-sail tripping lines, topmast and top-gallant studding-sail downhauls, boom jiggers and after guys manned ; then "Haul taut, trip up the lower studding-sail, shorten sail."

It may not be out of place here to make a few remarks upon the fitment of studding-sail gear.

Lower studding-sail tripping-lines are best rove from aft (commencing at the clew), through an eyelet-hole in the centre of the sail, and up before all through the block on the inner yard-arm.

Lower studding-sail yards, half the usual length, make the sail much easier to handle.

A long lizard for the lower boom topping-lift, rove through a block at the fore yard-arm, through a block at the slings, and thence on deck, is preferable to the usual lizard taken out by hand.

Lizards, both for topmast and lower studding-sails, are an improvement on rope-yarn stops. For this purpose a strop, with a thimble seized in, should be fitted to the outer arm of the topmast studding-sail yard, and the lizard spliced close outside it, round the yard. After the sail is rolled up, a turn is taken round the sail and halyards, and through the thimble, passed along the sail to the bunt, and hitched round the sail; the bight being jambed between its own part and the sail, so that when hauled upon, or a turn taken round the lower lift and the halyards hoisted on, it comes adrift. For the lower studding-sail, a strop attached to the lizard is merely put round the sail; a toggle, into which the lizard is spliced, put through the bight, a turn taken on the forecastle when high enough, and the sail hoisted.

An enlarged topmast studding-sail may be set by means of a jack yard laced to the outer part of the foot, the

190

tack bent to the centre ; and a fore topmast studding-sail tack may with advantage be kept rove through a tail-block in the bunt of the fore yard, where, practically, whatever it may do in theory, it requires no attention when trimming sails ; and abaft, there is only one rope, the boom-brace, to attend, instead of two.

Instead of taking a burton out on the topsail yard, let a pendant be fitted, rove through the span-block (double), at the mast-head, with a hook on one end to take out on the yard, and a thimble at the other to hook the burton to, the single block of which is hooked to a strop round the eyes of the lower rigging.

Let the topmast studding-sail downhauls be led through a tail-block on the topsail-sheet or some convenient place ; which slip directly the yard comes down to it, running away with the downhaul, and bringing the sail in without a check.   The deck sheet should be rove through a leading-block.

Have top-gallant studding-sail downhauls bent to the inner yard-arm, and rove through a timble in the inner leech.

279. AFTER SETTING A TOPMAST STUDDING-SAIL.— Steady taut the deck sheet, get hold of the short sheet, reeve it through a tail-block on the quarter iron, bend it to a ropes-end out of the top, haul it up, haul aft and belay it ; *then* come up the deck sheet, bend it to the downhaul, and pay them down before all ; afterwards, shift the boom jigger for rigging in,—or, instead of shifting it, overhaul the hauling part, hitch it to the heel of the boom, and rig in with the single part.

280. AFTER TAKING IN A TOPMAST STUDDING-SAIL.—
Unbend the tack and halyards, and bend them together;
swing the halyards in to the hands on the yard, who haul
them up, dip them abaft, and pay them down, when they
are again bent ready for setting; take the burton off the
topsail yard, and shift the boom jigger for rigging out.

281. FLYING LOWER STUDDING-SAIL.—Take the sail in,
and run a few eylet-holes along the foot a short distance
in from the outer clew. Lace it to a jack yard (a small
studding-sail, or boat's yard will do), fitted with a span;
and, as the outer leg should be somewhat longer than the
inner one, put a seizing round both parts. Bend the tack
to the bight, and set the sail again. A deep sea lead on
the clew will imperfectly answer the same purpose.

282. FORE TOPMAST STUDDING-BOOM UNCLAMPED.—
Round down on the lower halyards, put a knot in them,
pull up and lift the boom, leaving end enough below the
knot to round down again.

283. HEEL LASHINGS.—That of a topmast studding-
boom is secured round the quarter iron; of a top-gallant
studding-boom, through the quarter strop and round the
jackstay.

284. THE ADVANTAGE OF A STUDDING-SAIL BEND—
Is, that it lies close to the yard, and consequently permits
of little or no drift between the yard and block.

A strop to go two-thirds round the yard—a small iron
toggle spliced into the end of the halyards—the halyards

rove through the bights of the strop, and toggled—is equally secure, equally neat, and far more convenient for bending and unbending, which you must do every time you take in the sail.

285. DIPPING A TOPMAST STUDDING-SAIL BEFORE-ALL.—Send a couple of hands on the lower yard : lower the sail well down, and let them gather it in until they get hold of the outer leech which is then gathered down, until the inner yard-arm can be canted before the leech of the topsail, then let go, and hoist away.

It should be remembered that a touch of the helm may help a good deal in setting and taking in studding-sails.

286. DIPPING A TOPMAST STUDDING-SAIL ABAFT-ALL.—Gather down on the *inner* leech.

287. HITCH WITH THE DOWNHAUL ROUND THE CLEW.—Let the boom come in, gather in on the foot, lay hold of the clew, and then clear the downhaul.

288. GEAR TRICING-LINE.—The lower studding-sail tripping-line is used, bent to a strop and toggle. The studding-sail gear should be kept aft, stopped along the waist ridge ropes, and merely triced up, instead of being stopped along the fore yard.

289. SETTING STUDDING-SAILS—*With a swell on*, without much wind to steady the sails, haul taut the buntlines and bowlines before laying out on the yards.

193

290. REEFING TOPSAILS—Topmast studding-sail set; lower the topsail *when the burton or preventer lift is off the yard*, the studding-sail being in.

291. COMING TO THE WIND.—Take in the royals, and one or two reefs; the jib, and a reef in the spanker if necessary. While reefing, bring the ship to the wind under the courses.

292. GETTING SHEETS HOME.—Always get the lee sheet home first; then ask the officer of the watch, if necessary, to give her a luff up, and get the weather sheet home while the sail is lifting.

293. LEE BOOM-SHEET.—By hauling it taut, you would endanger the boom.

294. LIFT AND BRACE OFF.—Lower the sail, get hold of the leech, cant the yard, and rig it from the topsail yard.

295. BREEZE FRESHENING.—1st. In royals and flying jib. 2nd. In first reef of topsails. 3rd. In second reefs, and mizen top-gallant sail. 4th. In fore and main top-gallant sails, jib and spanker.—Set fore topmast-staysail and mizen. 5th. In third reefs and reef of courses. 6th. Close reef the topsails, down fore topmast, and set fore staysail. 7th. In mizen topsail. 8th. In fore topsail, courses and mizen.—Set main staysail, and mizen trysail. 9th. In main topsail—if you think it advisable. Yards and masts sent down, and other precautions are of course supposed to be taken.

194

296. REEFING TOPSAILS.—" Clear lower deck," " reef topsails," " two reefs ;" " weather topsail braces," " hands by the topsail halyards," " away aloft ; " " let go the top-bowlines, round in ;" " lower the topsails," then haul out the reef tackles, turn the yards to the wind, and haul taut the braces, steady taut the top-gallant clewlines to keep the sheets clear of the men reefing ; " trice up, lay out ;" the sail is then lighted out to windward, the weather earing hauled out, then to leeward ; pass the beckets through the reef-line and toggle them ; " lay in down from aloft," let go the reef tackles, attend the braces." " Hoist the topsail."

297. REEF-TACKLE CARRIED AWAY.—Clew the sail up, pass the leech along and reeve the reef-tackle afresh; haul out, take the reef in, and sheet home.

298. PASSING AN EARING.—Haul the reef close out by the outer turn, passed down abaft, through the cringle, up before the yard, over the cleat, down abaft, and the bight passed through the cringle, leaving the end abaft the sail. Pass the bight up before and over the yard, rousing the reef well up, then haul back on the end till the bight lies close down on the yard; pass the end through the bight from abaft, haul well back and hitch it. For a third or fourth reef, as many inner turns are passed as the cringle will admit of, and are passed on the end—not on the bight.

299. FITMENTS OF EARINGS.—Those of the first and

second reefs are usually formed of two pieces of small rope; the longest spliced into its own part, forming an eye two-thirds the length of the earing; the other, spliced into each part of this eye, at equal distances apart, the bight of the two parts lying square with each other. This tapers the earing, the end consisting of one part, the third quarter of two, the middle of three, and the part which forms the first turn of the earing, of four parts. All are marled together; and a seizing is put round the bights, making an eye to go over the yard-arm.

The third and fourth reef-earings are formed of a single part, and are spliced into the eyelet-hole in the sail through which the lower turns of the cringle are passed, and seized up outside the cringle.

300. AFTER TAKING IN A THIRD REEF—Get the preventer braces and preventer parrals on.

301. TAKING IN A CLOSE REEF.—Man the weather brace, rolling-tackle, and clewline, round in, lower the topsail and clew down ; check the lower braces if on a wind, haul the reef-tackles close out, easing the sheets, and hauling up on the clewlines at the same time ; haul taut both buntlines, secure the yard (not forgetting to haul taut the halyards, as it is hanging by the lifts), trice up and lay out.

A close reef-earing is usually passed abaft all, as there is such a mass of sail and leech-rope on the fore part, but it is nevertheless doubtful whether the usual plan is not the best for all reefs.

196

302. REEFING COURSES.—Haul the clew-garnets two-thirds up, and haul up the reef-tackles and buntlines.   If on a wind, round in the weather-brace, to clear the sail of the stays; haul taut both lifts, and rolling tackle if on, and truss to; lay out and light over.

303. TAKING IN A COURSE.—Man the weather clew-garnet and leechlines, and both buntlines; ease off a fathom of the main sheet, before starting the tack, lest you spring the yard by suddenly relieving it of so great a strain; then ease away the main tack and bowline, and haul up the weather clew, take in the lee clew, haul the gear close up, round in the weather brace, and secure the yard for furling (which may be done over all, without tricing the booms up).   When furled, place a mat, or old hammock, over the sail in the wake of the stays, previous to bracing up.

304. SETTING A STORM STAYSAIL.—Haul the sheet aft before hoisting, having seen the hook moused; ease away as you hoist, and haul aft again.

305. SENDING TOP-GALLANT MASTS DOWN AT SEA.—Get burtons on the backstays, to ease away as you sway to unfid and to steady taut as you lower.   Send the mast down through lubber's-hole with a heel rope rove through a block on deck abreast of the mast, well manned, and kept taut as the mast comes down.

306. SET THE FORE STAYSAIL,—*Then* shorten sail in the usual manner.

197

307. TAKING IN A JIB IN A BREEZE.—Keep the ship away, and make use of the gab-rope.

308. WEATHER MAIN-TOPSAIL BRACE GOES—On a wind, put the helm down, let go the lee main brace, square the main-yard and bring her to the wind with the topsail aback, lash the yard to the topmast rigging, lay out, and put on the preventer brace.

309. WITH THE WIND ON THE QUARTER.—Watch trim sails ; keep her away, let go the halyards, bring the wind on the other quarter, get a preventer brace on, trim and make sail.

310. PREVENTER BRACES.—Yard-tackles for the lower yards, and the long 3½-inch top-whips for the topsail yards.

311. WEATHER MAIN-TOPSAIL SHEET AND CLEWLINE GONE.—Haul up the buntlines, reef-tackles, and lee clew-line ; hand the leech in, pass a gasket round the sail to steady it, and reeve the clewline afresh. If, however, you cannot get hold of the leech, unreeve the main top-bowline from the fore top, send a hauling-line down for the end, reeve it through the quarter block, haul it up, and so confine the sail till you have passed a gasket, when reeve the bowline again, and the new clewline and sheet.

312. PARRAL OF MAIN-TOPSAIL YARD GONE ; BEFORE THE WIND.—Haul taut both clewlines and topsail lifts to steady the yard, and see that the braces bear an equal strain ; but do not clew up, as the great object is to keep

the yard as steady as possible. Without delay, hang the top-gallant mast rope at the cross-trees, unreeve it altogether, dip it under the rigging, and make a running bowline with it round the mast and topsail-tyes; open it well out, send a hand down with it, and slip it over the tye-blocks. In the mean time, hands are employed reeving the hauling part through a leading block abaft; clap the watch on, and truss the yard to; get up the spare parral, and set the sail again. If the yard complains, ease off the topsail-sheets, hauling taut the clewlines.

As before remarked, we are not bound to assume that from want of proper care these accidents occur. Therefore, if such a case were put as the carrying away of a parral *in a gale of wind*, we should merely suggest that a new one be fitted and got up, and another preventer passed in the mean time; for the sound preventer parral, that under the circumstances would be on, would relieve us of all apprehension.

313. Parral gone, on a Wind.—Heave the sail aback and clew the yard down, hook a couple of jiggers from the cap for rolling-tackles, clew up if necessary, and get the preventer parral on.

314. Topmast-stay carried away.—Keep the ship away, shorten sail, get up and haul taut the sail-tackle; and replace the stay with a hawser, bowline-knotted round the mast-head.

315. A Bobstay gone.—Take in the top-gallant sails, head sails, and spanker, haul up the mainsail, lower the

199

fore topsail, and keep away if necessary. Send a hand down to knot both parts of the bobstay together—forming a strop ; hook the double blocks of two luffs to it, and the single blocks to a strop through the heart in the bobstay collar ; reeve the falls through blocks on the bowsprit, set them up and make sail, keeping away and getting a pull of them occasionally.*

If the shroud be gone close to the cutwater, it must be cut away with an axe, and a strop rove through the hole, if it can be got at. But, if in such weather that you cannot send a hand down, you must send the fore top-gallant mast on deck, get the jib-boom in—if it is safe to start it, and the runners and tackles up to relieve the stays, and ease the sail carried, until the weather is fine enough to secure the bowsprit effectually. I cannot see that a hawser, taken round the bowsprit and led in through the hawse-holes, would be of any utility, from the small angle it forms with the bowsprit ; and in bad weather you would not be able to keep the hawse plugs out.

316. JIB-BOOM CARRIED AWAY.—So much depends upon ever-varying circumstances, that what is recommended in this and similar cases, must only be considered as generally applicable, and not suitable or necessary on all occasions. As a general rule, therefore, heave to and get the wreck in, taking in the top-gallant sails, and housing the fore top-

---

* NOTE.—This is the correct answer without doubt, but the reviser has seen two bobstay collars out of three, gone in a heavy gale of wind, and nothing the worse, though they could not be replaced until the weather moderated.

gallant mast.   If you bear up, or stand on, you will knock the bows about with the broken spars, and find great difficulty in getting hold of them.

317. JIB-SHEET CARRIED AWAY.—*Mind your weather-helm*, haul down the jib, trice the tack of the spanker up, and clear away the fore topmast-staysail.

318. MAIN TACK AND CLEW-GARNET GONE.—Bear up, or wear, and haul the sheet aft.

319. TILLER-ROPE CARRIED AWAY.—When this occurs, it may be assumed to be blowing fresh.   The first thing to be done, therefore, is to steady the rudder, which, in a sea-way would fly from side to side with great violence. The quickest way of doing so will be by means of the remaining rope; and, as the chances are that the weather wheel-rope will be the one to go, jamb the helm down, shorten sail, and heave to with the head yards a-box, if you do got want to come round-   Otherwise, if there is a ship close astern of you, for instance, haul the mainsail up, and square the main yard in stays.   Should the lee rope go, put the helm up, heave to on the other tack, and shorten sail as soon as possible.   If unsafe, from the position of the ship, to do either, chock the rudder up (which, by the way, is not done in a moment when the tiller has taken charge); man the head sheets and cross-jack braces, and steer the ship by the sails.   In moderate weather, the relieving-tackles will probably be hooked before it will be necessary to touch anything.   In all cases send hands down to hook, and work them, and reeve new wheel-ropes.

320. LOWER SHROUD CARRIED AWAY, AND NOT LONG ENOUGH FOR TURNING IN AFRESH.—Turn the dead-eye out, strop it with rope of equivalent dimensions, and seize a large thimble in ; knot the shroud, reeve it through the thimble, and seize the end up ; reeve the lanyard again, and set the shroud up.

321. JIB DOWNHAUL CARRIED AWAY.—Unbend the lee top-gallant bowline, make a bowline round the stay, and haul down. Should it carry away, send the downhaul up by the weather bowline used as a hauling-line, bend it round the stay, and assist it, if the lacing jambs, by hauling down six feet at a time with a rope's-end rove through the lee bowline block at the boom-end.

322. MAIN YARD SPRUNG ON THE WEATHER QUARTER; SHIP ROLLING HEAVILY.—Unbend the sail, clew up the top-sail, reeve the jeers and take them to the capstan. Send the studding-sail booms down to lighten the yard, and to get them out of the way. Send an up-and-down on each side through lubber's-hole, lash them to bolts in the cap, and hook them to butt slings round the quarters of the yard. A little further out, on each quarter, hook the top burtons to strops on the yard, and on deck to bolts in the fore part of each gangway. Lower the yard-tackles down, cross them and hook them in to the ship's side abreast of the mast. · Unshackle one truss, and reeve a stout piece of rope down through one thimble, abaft the mast, under the necklace, and up through the other thimble of the truss stop ; to each end hook a burton from the

202

cap, haul taut, and unreeve the other truss. Heave round the jeers, swaying on the quarter tackles at the same time, knock the slip off, and walk back, attending the lifts, yard tackles, preventer truss, and braces, and steadying the yard forward by the burtons. Land it across the nettings, and lash it there. Strip it of everything in the slings, and knock off the battens and casing to have a good overhaul. If found sprung where it was supposed, place a topmast studding-sail boom on the top of the yard, and another on the fore side—supposing the fracture to have occurred there ; fill the space up above and below the spring with capstan bars, and handspikes, &c. Get up 230 or 240 fathoms of 3-inch and 3½-inch rounding, or unrove rigging, if you have it ; divide it into six lashings, three on each quarter, outside the clothing. Pass the lashings on both ends, each turn bowsed well taut with a jigger, rack each turn as it is bowsed taut by driving nails through it into the yard, and, when finished tautened up with wedges. Then put on the slings, which will require lengthening ; lash the clothing on, having tailed the lashings ; and sway the yard up, in the same manner in which it was lowered down.

For a slight spring, an iron fish will probably be sufficient to prevent it opening out and spreading further.

323. FORE YARD CARRIED AWAY IN THE WEATHER QUARTER.—Clew the topsail up, confine and steady the weather yard-arm by slip-ropes, and unbend the sail the best way you can ; hook an up-and-down from the cap

to the weather quarter, bend the fore bowline round it, and land it on the forecastle. Reeve four parts of the jeers, and send the lee yard-arm down. Land a spar on the knight-heads, and lash it to the foremast on the lee side, level with the nettings, and across it lay the lee portion of the yard. On another spar from the knight-heads, on the weather side, suspended by a luff from the rigging, and steadied by guys, place the weather yard-arm. Bring the broken parts together by luffs and burtons, crossed from opposite sides of the deck, and fish the yard with studding-sail booms. Place one on the after side, above the batten, another on top of the yard, and a third on the fore side; fill up with capstan bars, would the whole together, and wedge it up taut. While this is being done, the fore tacks and sheets may be singled and shackled to the clews of the fore topsail, and the sail set flying. When finished, sway the fore yard up, bend, and set the sails.

324. SWIFTING IN.—Reeve a rope through a block on each shroud, and bowse on it till the rigging is taut.

325. MAINMAST GOES OVER THE SIDE IN A STORM.—Wear, if possible, and bring the wreck to windward; cut away, and get clear of it as soon as you can.

326. BOWSPRIT BADLY SPRUNG.—Shorten all necessary sail, according to the breeze; send fore top-gallant mast down, secure foremast with runners and tackles, and top-

mast with sail-tackle, and slacken up the stays, if circumstances require it. Get head sails and flying-boom in; and, if the bowsprit is so badly sprung as to lead you to think that it would be unsafe, when fished, to carry the jib with the boom rigged out the full extent, rig it in for a fish until the heel buts the stem. Place the flying-boom on one side, and a topmast studding-sail boom on the other, and would all together, wedging and chocking up between. Out of the head-ports on the forecastle, rig, on one side, the spare jib-boom, and, on the other, a handmast, or spare mizen-topmast; secure the heels inboard, and lash the heads securely to the head of the bowsprit on either side. Round the centre of one of the shores, secure the standing part of a lashing; reeve it down through the gammoning hole in the cutwater, up and over the opposite shore, down through the cutwater again, over the first shore, and so on until sufficient turns are passed, finishing off with a few frapping turns round the lashing and over the bowsprit. The jib may still be set outside the bowsprit cap.

If you intend to get the jib-boom out again, fish the bowsprit with one or two spare anchor stocks hollowed out, assisted with the shores as before.

327. BROUGHT BY THE LEE.—Put the helm down, and brace round directly, unless in the mean time she answers the helm, and brings the wind on the weather quarter again; though the probability is that you will either lose the masts or be thrown on your beam-ends.

328. Laying a Ship to.—Haul the foresail up; and, if you find that you can run her with safety, for a short time under the topsail and staysail, furl the foresail before bringing her to the wind. If, however, there is such a sea running, that you cannot keep before it after shortening sail, look out for a smooth, down with the helm, and round short to, to avoid exposing her broadside to the sea a moment longer than is absolutely necessary.

329. Broaching to—Is synonymous with coming up into the wind; but is exclusively applied to a ship in bad weather, when it becomes a situation of great danger to the ship and spars. When running free, with the sea on the quarter, want of attention at the helm is the common cause of such a mishap. Put the helm up, lower the topsails if they are standing; and, if she does not pay off, box off or brace up, as the occasion demands. Should, however the ship be going over, let fly everything, of course, instantly.

330. Preparations for a Hurricane.—Have plenty of steam up; get the jibboom whiskers and dolphin striker in; send upper yards, masts and rigging on deck, studding-sails out of the rigging, and booms off the yards. Rolling tackles, preventer braces, and parrals on. Storm staysails bent and ready for setting. Sails close reefed, yards well secured, and rigging mats properly placed to prevent chafe. Gratings, tarpaulins and battens ready for the hatchways. Life-lines along the decks; guns, shot, bucklers, and hawse plugs, boats, booms and anchors well lashed and secured. Ports examined and well barred

in. Relieving tackles, spare wheel and binnacles ready. Try the pumps to insure their being clear and ready for working.

Cook two or three days provisions in advance. Set the storm sails, and take in the topsails in time; see them well furled with sea gaskets. Register the barometer every half hour; make yourself all clear " on the law of storms ;" and place your ship on the right tack.

331. THROWN ON YOUR BEAM-ENDS.—Let fly everything—when, if she does not right, or continues to go over, there is no resource left but to cut the lanyards of the weather rigging, if you have time, and let the masts go over the side ; at the same time cutting the lashings of the booms, and clearing away the boats. If in soundings, letting go an anchor will bring her head to wind and probably right her.

332. DANGER OF FOUNDERING.—Rig a sea anchor, with three spars in the shape of a triangle, and lash a sail across it; at one corner sling a weight proportionate to the size of the spars, launch it overboard, and ride by it until jury-masts can be rigged. If unable to do this, letting go an anchor, and veering a long scope (if possible of hemp cable), will in some measure steady the ship by bringing her head towards the sea.

333. WATER GAINING ON THE PUMPS.—Heave what guns you can overboard, and otherwise lighten the ship as circumstances will admit.

207

334. THE LAWS OF STORMS.—The culpable disaster detailed in the question resulted from disregard, or ignorance of these well-known laws, which, had they been attended to, would not only have enabled your friend to avoid all danger from the approaching storm, but would have taught him how to profit by it, and unhesitatingly to turn it to his own advantage. I have space here only to touch on the first principles of this very attractive science; and, for its interesting particulars, must refer the reader to the standard works of Piddington and Reid.

But five-and-twenty years have elapsed since Mr. Redfield, of New York, first drew public attention to the rotatory and progressive motions of storms, which resulted in the discovery of the following laws:—

1. That, in the northern hemisphere, their axial rotation is in a direction contrary to that of the hands of a watch, or W. 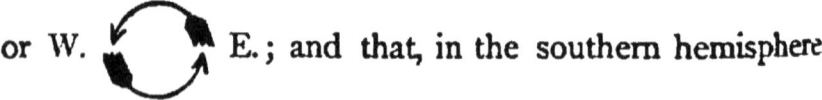 E.; and that, in the southern hemisphere,

they rotate with the hands of a watch, or W.  E.

2. That, though some cyclones are almost stationary storms, the majority move onward on a curved track, at a rate varying from one to ten miles an hour in the Southern Ocean, and from ten to forty in the West Indies; that, near the equator, their course is nearly west, diverging to the north in north latitudes, and to the south in south latitudes, until they cross the tropics, when the curve becomes more rapid, and they finally re-curve to the east-

208

ward. Their dimensions vary from 200 to 600 miles in diameter in the South Indian Ocean, and from 100 to 1,000 miles in the Atlantic. The usual typhoons of the China Sea are from 60 to 300 miles in diameter.

3. That there is generally a calm space in the centre, where sudden and terrific gusts break the unnatural repose, with a confused and dangerous sea running.*

4. That in the northern hemisphere, the centre bears eight points to the left of the wind, your back being to it; and, in the southern hemisphere, eight points to the right of the wind.

5. That cyclones are almost always preceded by a falling barometer.†

6. That, to avoid them, you should, when to the right of the cyclone's track, or in the right-hand semicircle, lie to on the starboard tack ; and, in the left-hand semicircle, or to the left of it, on the port tack, in both hemispheres. But this, as will subsequently be seen, only holds good when you are far enough from its path to be out of harm's reach, for it then insures you against closing within dangerous limits, and from being taken aback from the shifts of wind, which, if this rule is attended to, will always be aft.

---

* In the hurricane that passed over Martinique, October 11, 1831, 9,000 people perished ; and at St. Pierre the sea rose to a height of 25 feet, and 150 houses along the beach disappeared in a moment.

† In the hurricane at Havannah, on October, 12, 1846, the fall of the barometer was so sudden, in the vortex, that the windows of the houses were forced *outwards*.

When before, or near its track, it is necessary to increase your distance by bearing up or standing off, as the case may be, until the cyclone has passed, when you may resume your course with caution.*

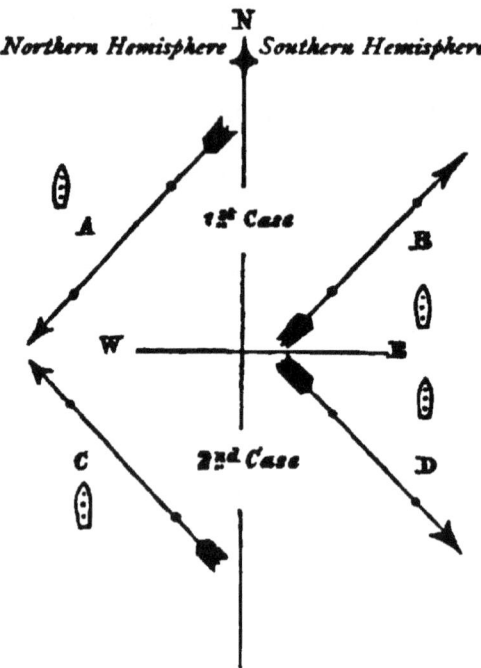

By projecting the track of a storm by the bearing of the centre, it will be seen,— firstly, that when the shifts of wind in either hemisphere occur in the direction N.E.S.W. you are in the right-hand semicircle ; and, secondly, when the wind veers in the contrary direction N.W.S.E., you are in the left-hand semicircle. Consequently, in the first case (see diagram), in north latitudes, the cyclone is travelling from eastward to westward, and in south latitudes from westward to eastward.

In the second case (see diagram), in north latitudes, its course is from eastward to westward, and in south latitudes, from westward to eastward.

In Diagram A, the ship { at first has wind North, when Centre would be East
afterward.........East ....South

---

* In the memorable gale after Rodney's action of the 1st April, 1782, upwards of 3,000 seamen alone are computed to have perished in the fleet and convoy. *They were hove to on the wrong tack....Reid.*

In Diagram B, { at first ....North ....West
afterwards.........East............................North

In Diagram C, { at first ....North ....East
afterwards.........West ....North

In Diagram D, { at first ....North.........................West
afterwards.........West ....South

It will be observed that the wind is here spoken of as changing in a direction contrary to that of the storms themselves, which in north latitudes has been stated to be

W. E., and in south latitudes W. E. ; for, in the first case given above, the shifts of wind are assumed

to occur in the direction W. E. ; and, in the

second case, in the direction W. E. In the first

case this is contrary to the rotatory motion of northerly storms, and in the second case contrary to that of southerly storms.

The reason of this will be seen if we draw a circle, N.W.S.E., to represent the body of a storm ; with a ship anywhere within its influence, as at A. Assuming the ship to be in north latitude, the cyclone will be revolving in the direction shown by the curved arrows, and the wind in each quarter of the storm circle will blow in the direction shown by the straight arrows ; for, though it sweeps *round* the storm's axis, it may, from the small segment occupied by a ship, be represented, as far as she is concerned, as a tangent to the circle.

211

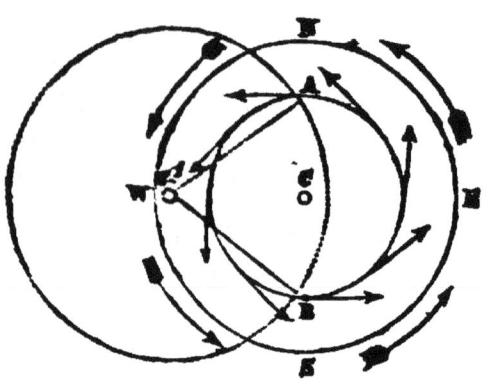

At A, therefore, she will have the wind from the eastward, and the centre of the storm will be eight points to the left, or south of her. If it is travelling from east to west, the first shift of wind she will experience will be from S.E.; for while moving on its course in the direction, C,C', it will be changing the bearing of its centre from the ship, which, when at C', will be S.W. of her, with the wind from the S.E. So that, though the storm is revolving in the direction W.  E., the wind is shifting in the direction W.  E. But if the ship, on the contrary, be in the other semicircle, say at B, she would have the wind at west, and when the centre reached C', at S.W.; consequently, the change being from west to S.W., would *coincide* with the rotatory motion of the storm.

The figure will also show why, if induced to cross the path of a hurricane with a fair wind, you will be deceived by finding it coming round against you as you enter the other semicircle.

Now, if we apply these principles to the case in point, it will be seen that at 8 P.M., 16th, the prize got the first hurricane-wind, the true nature of which might have been conjectured from the atmospheric appearances, the fall of the barometer, the easterly swell (cyclones in these latitudes usually travelling from the E.N.E.), and from the time of the year (the month of February being that in which the greatest number of hurricanes occur in those latitudes). However, at this early stage to have failed in interpreting these signs is very pardonable; and the reason that nothing further occurred during the night was owing to her steering a course in advance of that of the storm. At 6 A.M., 17th, however, it was gaining on the ship, which brings the wind further forward; and, on tacking, and finding the wind increasing and veering in the order to be expected, they should have been on the alert, have carefully watched the barometer, registering it every half-hour and been prepared to escape from the anticipated danger, which would soon unmistakably have declared itself. At 7 or 8 P.M., at the very latest, they should have bore up north and afterwards N.N.E., or thereabouts, as the wind drew forward, and ran, until told by a rising barometer, a moderating gale, and the wind's direction that the storm had passed. By noon, 18th, they would probably have run far enough, the wind being W.N.W., and it would have been safe to have hauled gradually round again, keeping away S.E. till the wind was N.W., which they would have got—say about 7 P.M., taking care not to draw too close upon the storm again, nor yet to get beyond its influence. They might then have braced forward on the starboard tack and resumed the voyage, parallel, but in the rear of the storm, with a fine, fresh breeze. Its track would probably have soon curved away rapidly to the southward, and carried them five or six hundred miles upon their course; and when their road and the storm's no longer agreed, they might have parted company at their own discretion.

In connection with this subject, the following remarks, taken from the "Meteorological Papers" published by the Board of Trade, will be found of great value.

WIND AND WEATHER.

"Some persons attribute influence to the moon in respect of weather, and say a change may be expected within a few days of the moon's phases. But the interval between one and another phase of the moon is but seven days, and "a few" of these days *must* be a time near one phase or another. Accidental coincidences are generally allowed to influence the mind, because, when they occur, they mark any event more particularly. Similar to these are the prejudices against sailing on a Friday, which used to be so general.

"Continued comparisons of changes of weather or wind during many consecutive years, in various parts of the world, have proved decidedly that there is no regular correspondence between the lunar phases and atmospherical changes.

"The following are a few of the more marked signs of weather :—

"Whether clear or cloudy, a rosy sky at sunset presages fine weather; a red sky in the morning, bad weather, or much wind (if not rain); a grey sky in the morning, fine weather; a high dawn, wind; a low dawn, fair weather.*

" Soft looking, or delicate clouds, foretell fine weather, with moderate or light breezes; hard-edged, oily-looking clouds, wind. A dark, gloomy blue sky is windy; but a light, bright blue sky indicates fine weather. Generally, the *softer* clouds look, the less wind (but perhaps more rain) may be expected; and the harder, more 'greasy,' rolled, tufted, or ragged, the stronger the coming wind will prove. Also a bright yellow sky at sunset presages wind; a pale yellow, wet; and thus, by the prevalence of red, yellow, or grey tints, the coming weather may be foretold very nearly; indeed, if aided by instruments, almost exactly.

" Small inky-looking clouds foretell rain; a light scud, driving across heavy clouds, wind and rain; but if alone, wind only.

" High upper clouds crossing the sun, moon, or stars, in a direction different from that of the lower clouds or wind then blowing, foretell a change of wind (beyond tropical latitudes).

" After fine clear weather, the first signs (in the sky) of change, are usually small, curly, streaked, or spotty clouds, followed by an overcasting of vapour that grows into cloudiness. This murky appearance, more or less oily or watery, as wind or rain will prevail, is a sure sign. The

---

* A high dawn is when the first streaks of morning light appear over a bank of cloud, instead of near the horizon, as is usual when there are no heavy clouds.

higher and more distant the clouds seem to be, the more gradual, but extensive, the coming change of weather will prove.

"Generally speaking, natural, quiet, delicate tints or colours, with soft, undefined forms of clouds, foretell fine weather; but gaudy, or unusual hues, with hard, definite outlines, presage rain and wind."

THE USE OF THE BAROMETER.

"By attention to the following observations (the result of many years' practice, and many persons experience), any one not accustomed to use a barometer, may do so without hesitation or real difficulty.

"In all parts of the world, towards the higher latitudes, the quicksilver ranges, or rises and falls, nearly three inches, namely, between about thirty inches and eight-tenths (30·8), and less than twenty-eight inches (28·0) on extraordinary occasions; but the usual range is from about 30·5 inches, to about 29 inches. Near the line, or in equatorial places, the range is but a few tenths, except in storms, when it sometimes falls to 27 inches.

"If the barometer has been about its ordinary height, say near thirty inches, at the sea level,* and is steady, or

---

* In different latitudes the ordinary, mean, or normal height may be less, or even more than 30 inches, though *seldom* the latter, except from the tropics to about the thirty-fifth parallel. It stands lower, about a tenth of an inch for each hundred feet of height directly upwards, or vertically, above the sea; when its average height, on the Thames, in England, is 29·94 inches (at 32°).

rising, while the thermometer falls, and dampness becomes *
less, north-westerly, northerly, or north-easterly wind, or
less wind may be expected. †

" On the contrary, if a fall takes place, with a rising
thermometer and increased dampness, wind and rain (or
snow) may be expected from the south-eastward, southward, or south-westward.

" Exceptions to these rules occur when a north-easterly
wind, with wet (rain or snow), is impending, before which
the barometer often rises (on account of the *direction* of

---

* If a thermometer have a piece of linen tied round the bulb,
wetted enough to keep it damp by a thread or wick dipping into a
cup of water, it will show less heat than a dry one, in proportion to
the dryness of the air and quickness of drying. In very damp
weather, with or *before* rain, fog, or dew, two such thermometers will
be nearly alike.

Hence, for ascertaining the dryness or moisture of air, a ready and
sure method is the comparison of two thermometers, one dry, the
other *just* moistened and *kept so*. Cooled by evaporation, as much
as the state of the air admits, the moist (or wet) bulb thermometer
shows a temperature nearly equal to that of the other one, when the
atmosphere is extremely damp or moist ; but lower at other times in
proportion to the dryness of air, and consequent evaporation, as far
as twelve or fifteen degrees in England, twenty, or even more, elsewhere. About six degrees of difference is considered healthy in a
temperate climate.

Pouring water over the bulb, instead of merely moistening it,
imparts to the mercury the temperature of the water, which *may* be
higher than that of the air.

† In the southern hemisphere, for North read South, and for
South put North, in these pages.

the coming wind alone), and deceives persons who, from that sign only (its rising), expect fair weather.

" When the barometer is rather below its ordinary height, say near twenty-nine inches and a half (at the sea level *only*), a rise foretells less wind, or a change in its direction towards the northward, or less wet; but when the mercury has been low, say near twenty-nine inches, the first rising usually precedes, and foretells strong wind (at times heavy squalls) from the north-westward, northward, or north-eastward, *after* which violence a rising glass foretells improving weather, if the thermometer falls. But if the warmth continue, probably the wind will back (shift against the sun's course), and more southerly, or south-westerly wind will follow.

" The most dangerous shifts of wind, and the heaviest northerly* gales happen after the mercury first rises from a very low point.

" It may be repeated that indications of approaching changes of weather, and the direction and force of winds, are shown less by the height of mercury in the tube, than by its falling or rising. Also that a height of about thirty inches or upwards (at the level of the sea) is indicative of fine weather and moderate winds.

" A rapid rise of the barometer indicates unsettled

---

* Southerly, in south latitude. The movements are the same with east and west winds in both hemispheres; but if there be a rise in an instrument with a north wind in the northern hemisphere, it sinks with a north wind in the southern, and *vice versâ*. The same occurs with south winds.

weather. A slow rise or steadiness, with dryness, shows fair weather.

"A considerable and rapid fall is a sign of stormy weather and rain. Alternate rising and sinking show very unsettled weather.

"The greatest depressions of the barometer are with gales from the S.E., southward, or S.W.; the greatest elevations with winds from the N.W., northward, or N.E.

"Although the barometer generally falls with a southerly, and rises with a northerly wind, the contrary *sometimes* occurs; in which cases the southerly wind is dry and the weather fine, or the northerly wind is wet and violent.

"When the barometer sinks considerably, high wind, rain, or snow will follow. The wind will be from the northward, if the thermometer is low (for the season) from the southward, if the thermometer is high, for the time of year and the locality.

"Sudden falls of the barometer, with a westerly wind, are sometimes followed by violent storms from N.W. or north.

"If a gale sets in from the eastward or S.E., and the wind veers by the south, the barometer will continue falling until the wind becomes S.W., when a comparative lull may occur; after which the gale will be renewed; and the shifting of the wind towards the N.W. will be indicated by a fall of the thermometer, as well as a rise of the barometer.

"As a general rule, the wind usually veers, shifts, or goes round, *with the sun* (right-handed in northern places, left-handed in the southern parts of the world), and when it does not do so, or backs, more wind or bad weather may be expected, instead of improvement.

" This veering of the winds is a direct consequence of the earth's rotation, and currents of air from the polar regions alternating or contending with others from the equator. The polar currents are cold, dry, and heavy. Those from the equatorial parts of the world are warm, moist, and comparatively light. Their alternate or combined action *(foretold* by the glasses and other signs), solar heat, and electricity, cause all the varieties of weather that we experience.

" In a barometer the mercury begins to rise occasionally before the conclusion of a gale, sometimes even at its commencement, as the equilibrium of the atmosphere begins to be restored. Although the mercury falls lowest before high winds, it frequently sinks considerably before heavy rain. The barometer falls, but *not always* on the approach of thunder and lightning, or when the atmosphere is highly charged with electricity. Before and during the earlier or middle part of severe and settled weather, the mercury commonly stands high and is stationary.

" Instances of fine weather, with a low glass, occur exceptionally ; but they are always preludes to a duration of wind or rain, *if not both.*

" There may be heavy rains or violent winds beyond the horizon, and the view of an observer, by which his instruments may be affected considerably, although m particular change of weather occurs in his immediate locality.

"The caution already given should be specially remembered, that the longer a change of wind or weather is foretold by the barometer before it takes place, the longer the presaged weather will last ; and, conversely, the shorter the warning, the less time, whatever causes the warning, whether wind or a fall of rain or snow, will continue.

"The tides are affected by atmospheric pressure, so much that a rise of one inch in the barometer will have a corresponding fall in the tides of nine to sixteen inches, or say one foot for each inch.

"Vessels sometimes enter docks, or even harbours, where they have scarcely a foot of water more than their draught ; and as docking, as well as launching large ships, requires a close calculation of height of water, the state of the barometer becomes of additional importance on such occasions."

TABLE SHOWING THE FORCE AND VELOCITY OF THE WIND.
BY SIR W. SNOW HARRIS.

Pressure in lbs. per Sq. Foot.	Velocity in Miles per Hour.	Popular Descriptions.	Pressure in lbs. per Sq. Foot.	Velocity in Miles per Hour.	Popular Descriptions.
0·002	0·68	Gentle airs (unappreciable by gauge).	1·042	15	Fresh breezes, top-gallant sails and royals.
0·004	1		1·170	16	
0·005	1·06		1·250	16·5	
0·019	2	Light airs (just appreciable by gauge); would fill the lightest sail of a yacht.	1·302	17	Fresh winds; reefs.
0·028	2·5		1·430	17·8	
0·032	2·66		1·470	18	
0·043	3		1·563	18·67	Strong winds; treble reefed topsails.
0·052	3·3		1·630	19	
0·065	3·8		1·790	20	
0·071	4		1·820	20·14	Gales; close-reefed topsails and reefed courses.
0·090	4·5		2·084	21·47	
0·100	4·75	Light breezes; such as would fill the lightest sails of a large ship.	2·600	24	
0·112	5		3·126	26·40	
0·130	5·38		3·647	28·52	Strong gales; close-reefed topsails, and staysails.
0·136	5·5		4·168	30·56	
0·162	6		4·689	32·34	
0·228	7		5·200	34	
0·260	7·6		7·800	41	Heavy gales and storms.
0·291	8		10·400	48·2	
0·364	9		13·000	53·91	
0·390	9·27	Moderate breezes, in which ships can carry all sail.	15·600	59	
0·452	10		20·800	68·18	Very heavy gales; great storms; tempests.
0·521	10·77		26·000	76·18	
0·551	11		31·200	83·6	
0·650	12		36·400	90·12	Tornadoes; cyclones; hurricanes.
0·780	13		41·600	90·34	
0·830	13·6	Fresh breezes, top-gallant sails and royals.	52·000	107·7	
0·884	14		62·400	120	
0·910	14·25				

335. THE LAWS OF STORMS (*continued*).—In this case had the subjects of it, as late as 9 A.M,, when their apprehensions were first awakened, shortened sail, brought to on the starboard tack, and made the necessary prepara-

tions for a heavy gale of wind, which they still would have had, they would have escaped uninjured. The centre of it would have approached as near to them as it subsequently was about 1 P.M.; and then, gradually receding, would have allowed them to proceed on their voyage. Instead of which, lured on by the prospect of a good run to the southward, and entertaining the erroneous idea that running before it was the most likely means of running out of it, they hit upon the most direct method for running headlong into it, which they accordingly did, and, as we have seen, narrowly escaped with their dismasted ship.

This being an example of a cyclone in north latitudes, at 3 A.M., therefore, if the ship was within its influence, the centre must have bore E.S.E., or eight points to the left of the wind; consequently the course steered, S.E., tended to lead her directly for it, if, as was afterwards proved to be the case, the track of the cyclone, in conformity with their usual course in these latitudes, was to the westward; and the fallacy of running *from it*, as they supposed, is fully evident.

There having been little difference between the progressive motion of the storm and the speed of the ship, no considerable alteration in its bearing occured until 1 P.M., when the wind, having come round to N.E. by N., showed the bearing of its centre to be S.E. by E. As they closed, these changes necessarily occurred more rapidly; and hence the danger, when on the wrong tack, of being taken aback, as they in this instance were.

In the morning, the wind having drawn round to the southward, showed that the storm had passed away to the westward, and that no further mischief was to be apprehended from this formidable meteor.

336. SHIPS CLOSING IN A CALM.—Send the boats of both ships to the smaller, or to the one whose head is in the best direction.

337. TO ASCERTAIN THE ANGLE OF THE YARDS.—Paste on a looking-glass a paper semicircle with the degrees marked. Draw a fore-and-aft line along the deck ; on it place the side of the semicircle, under the yard ; and the reflection will indicate the angle.

Or, if the ship is upright, you may ascertain it by dropping a plumb-line from two points along the yard, and running a line along the deck between them, which, cutting the fore-and-aft line, will denote the angle by Gunner's quadrant.

338. WHY UPPER YARDS, ON A WIND, BEAR BRACING IN ABAFT THE LOWER YARDS.—The smaller the sail the more taut it can be set, and the less belly is given to it in consequence ; therefore the plane of such sails make a larger angle, when the angles of the yards are equal.

339. THE AFTER YARDS BRACE UP SHARPER THAN THE HEAD YARDS,—And they "touch" together, because

224

:he eddy wind, out of the sails on the foremast, striking the after sails, renders it necessary that they should be braced sharper up in order to receive the true wind less obliquely.

340. STRAIN ON A WEATHER BRACE.—On first strik- ing the sail, a current of air presses with equal force on all parts of the surface; but the moment it meets with the resistance offered by the sail, it escapes by passing away to leeward; and this stream passing off the weather side of the sail, neutralizes the direct effect of the wind to lee- ward, and so relieves the lee yard-arm.

341. WHY A SHIP GOES TO WINWARD.—Let AB represent one of the yards of a ship that is close- hauled. C*d* the direction, and CD the force of the wind; CE the effective force of the wind upon the sail (=CD × cos. DCE), commu- nicated in the direction C*e*, perpen- dicular to its surface.

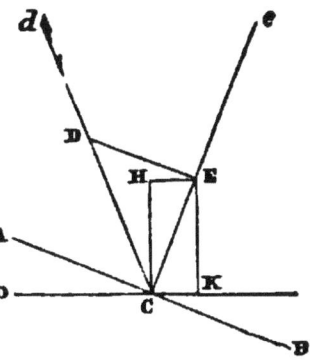

Resolve the force CE into its equivalents CK, CH (the one in the direction of the keel, and the other perpendicu- to it), and the former will represent the force exerted to drive the ship ahead in the direction CO, and the latter to set her to leeward.

The direct force is equal to the lateral force when the wind will admit of the yard being trimmed at an angle of 45° with the keel; but it will decrease as the yard is braced forward to that point.

The ship is forced ahead—notwithstanding the excess of lateral force, because the resistance offered by the bow is so much less than that presented by the broadside. Evidently therefore (leaving leeway out of consideration), as a ship will sail at a less angle to the wind than eight points, she will, on each tack, go to windward of a line drawn from her position at right angles to the wind, and by thus working, will actually approach the quarter from whence the wind is blowing.

342. FORE CHAINS CARRIED AWAY, AND CHAIN-PLATES DAMAGED.—Set the rigging up with luffs to the bolts in the ship's side, placed there for that purpose; two luffs to a shroud. Replace what chain-plates require it with spare ones, and keep them out in their place with a chock of wood between them and the ship's side; then set the rigging up properly.

343. GETTING QUARTER AND STERN BOATS IN-BOARD.— Quarter boat. Wooden davits. Run the sail-tackle up to the main topmast head, abaft the mast, and hook it to the foremost slings; haul taut, take the weight of the boat, and come up the fall. Hook an up-and-down from the mizen-mast head to the foremost davit, pull up, knock the bolt out, unship the davit, and then fleet the up-and-down to the after slings. Pull up the sail-tackle and get the bows of the boat in, clear of the backstays; then pull up the up-and-down, overhaul the after fall, unhook it when in-board, and transport the boat where you please.

Stern boat. Shift one of the boom topping-lifts (which

226

should be fitted to unhook), to the boom end, top it well up, and hook a burton and a jigger to a strop on the end of the boom. Sling the boat a little before the centre, and hook the burton. To the bolt in the stern hook the jigger. Haul both taut and unhook the falls; lower the jigger, cant the stern of the boat out, and the bows in; then pull up on the burton, haul forward on the painter, and get the bows in on the rail; pull up on the jigger, light to the burton, and lift her in on the deck.

A cover laced over a boat will prevent her filling, when in danger of being washed away, and you are unable to top her up or get her inboard.

344. PREPARE FOR ACTION.—Have steam ready for full speed, unbend sails, get top-gallant masts on deck, send down studding-sail booms, top-gallant rigging, and as much running gear as possible; get the topsail yards and mizen topmast on deck. House the fore and main top-masts, rack the top tackle pendants and unreeve the falls; lash the heads and heels of the topmasts to the lower mast, that they may help to support it if wounded; run in jib-boom and bowsprit if so fitted; it would also be advisable, I think, if the weather will permit, to clear away some of the lanyards of the lower rigging, and have every-thing clear for cutting away the lanyards left secured.

Brace the lower yards sharp up, and hang them, also take any other precaution that may suggest itself to you, in order to ensure the masts, if they should unfortunately be shot away, going clear of the ship at once, instead of falling alongside, masking your guns, or worse still fouling

227

the screw, the very life of the ship, and without which you must fall an easy victim to the ram or guns of your opponent. If the sails cannot be stowed away below, they should be well wetted, and rolled taut up. Boats' davits should be topped and secured; spare wheel ropes rove, relieving tackles in readiness, rudder pendants cut adrift, and led in-board; yards and stays ready for hoisting out boats. Before commencing an action, decks should be wetted and sanded; bulkheads triced up, tubs of water distributed about the decks, pumps tried, hoses screwed on to the steam main, and every possible preparation made against fire.

The unrove running rigging may be worked into rope mantlets, which, when hung up to the ship's side between the guns, prove a most effective protection from splinters, small fragments of iron, &c.

345. ENGAGING AN ENEMY.—No positive rule can be laid down, as so much must depend upon circumstances, and the nature of the opposing ships. But this may be said, that the windward position allows better pointing and the smoke clears off instead of blowing into the ports. In ironclads, especially turret ships, the more oblique angle of side you can expose to the shot of your enemy, while keeping your own guns bearing, the greater will be the defensive power of your plating, and the more favorable position will you be in, should a chance of using the ram occur, while your rudder and screw are safe from injury if you attack in this manner bow on.

346. CHASING TO WINDWARD.—Work up, as close as

possible, in a line dead to leeward of the chase, because, the longer you stand on beyond this, the better you will lie on the other tack (and consequently are doing so much the worse on the present tack). Therefore, tack as frequently as you can on either side of that bearing from the chase which coincides with the direction of the wind.

Let A represent the chase at noon, ten miles dead to windward of the chaser B.

B¹. The position of the chaser, at the rate of four miles an hour, when she tacked at 12.30 P.M.

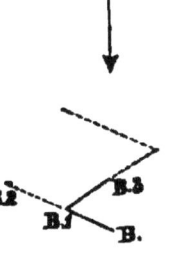

B³. Her position at 1 P.M., and

B². Her position at the same time, supposing her to have stood on (under a popular motion), until she had brought the chase abeam.

Now, from B¹ the chase bears N. by E. seven points from the course the chaser is lying. The latter consequently tacks, and lies up on a course five points off the chase, which, of course, is better than standing on as she was. Supposing, however, that she ignorantly stands on until she brings the chase abeam B², and the chase also tacks, her position then would be a mile further from the chase than if she had tacked earlier, for she would then, as has been shown, have been at B³, steadily following the chase up without giving her a chance of escape.

347. ON THE CHASER TACKING WHEN SHE CAN FETCH THE CHASE.—Whether the chase should tack, also, depends upon whether the chaser is astern of her, or on the

bow ; if on the lee bow, the chase should tack also, for, if she stood on, she would close her pursuer until they met, if the chase tacked at a proper time. But, if coming up astern, she should stand on, for, were she to tack, she would near the chaser until she arrived in the wind's eye of her, when any shift of wind whatever would be greatly to her advantage. In either case *the chase should keep on the same tack as the chaser*, who then only by superior sailing will be enabled to close.

348.—CHASING TO LEEWARD OR A STEAMER.—Steer, by a rough guess, the course that you think will enable you to intercept the chase, and take her bearing. If you find that she is heading you, it shows that you have kept away too much, and should haul up a little ; but, if dropping, you may edge away a little more. Consequently *the direct course, for the point at which you would meet, will be that on which her bearing remains the same*, should her course not be altered, or your relative rates of sailing vary. She should be closely watched ; and if she alters her course, you must at once adopt a fresh one.

If the chase sail better than ships in general with the wind abeam, quarterly, aft, or on a wind, as the case may be, she should be ready to take advantage of it, if there is any considerable distance between you, by gradually bringing you on that bearing which will enable her to steer directly from you on that particular point of sailing she has an advantage in. If, however, she has little choice in that respect, she should endeavour to gain ground by watching her pursuer narrowly, and gradually altering

230

her course when she observes that she has hit off the proper bearing.

349. HOW GRENVILLE FOUGHT THE SPANIARD.—"In August, 1591, Lord Thomas Howard, with six English line-of-battle ships, six victuallers, and two or three pinnaces, were lying at anchor under the islands of Florez. Light in ballast, and short of water, with half their men disabled by sickness, they were surrounded by a Spanish fleet of 53 ships. Eleven out of the twelve English ships obeyed the signal of the admiral, to cut or weigh their anchors, and escape as they might. The twelfth, the 'Revenge,' commanded by Sir Richard Grenville, of Bideford, was unable for the moment to follow, of her crew of 190, ninety being sick on shore, and, from the position of the ship, there being some delay and difficulty in getting them on board. But Sir Richard was in no haste to fly. He first saw all his sick on board and stowed away on the ballast, and then, with no more than 100 men left him to fight and work the ship, he deliberately weighed, uncertain, as it seemed at first, what he intended to do. The Spanish fleet were by this time on his weather bow, and he was persuaded (we here take his cousin Raleigh's beautiful narrative and follow it in his words), to cut his mainsail and cast about, and trust to the sailing of the ship.

"But Sir Richard utterly refused to turn from the enemy, alleging that he would rather choose to die than to dishonour himself, his country, and her Majesty's ship, persuading his company that he would pass through their two

231

squadrons in despite of them, and enforce those of Seville to give him way ; which he performed upon divers of the foremost, who, as the mariners term it, sprang their luff and fell under the lee of the ' Revenge.'

"The wind was light ; the 'San Philip,' 'a huge high-carged ship, of 1,500 tons, came up to windward of him, and taking the wind out of his sails, ran aboard him. The Spanish ships were filled with soldiers, in some 200, besides the mariners ; in some 500, in others 800. * * * * After many interchanged volleys of great ordnance and small shot, the Spaniards deliberated to enter the ' Revenge,' and made divers attempts hoping to force her by the multitude of their armed soldiers and musketeers; but were still repulsed again and again, and at all times beaten back into their own ship or into the sea.'

" All that August night the fight continued, the stars rolling over in their sad majesty, but unseen through the sulphur clouds which hung over the scene. Ship after ship of the Spaniards came on upon the ' Revenge,' 'so that never less than two mighty galleons were at her side and aboard her. Before morning fifteen several armadoes had assailed her, and all in vain ; some had been sunk at her side ; and the rest, so ill approving of their entertain-ment, that at break of day they were far more willing to hearken to a composition, than hastily to make any more assaults or entries.'

" All the powder in the ' Revenge,' was now spent, all her pikes were broken, forty out of her 100 men killed, and a great number of the rest wounded. Sir Richard,

232

though badly hurt early in the battle, never forsook the deck till an hour before midnight; and was then shot through the body while his wounds were being dressed, and again in the head, and his surgeon was killed while attending on him. The masts were lying over the side, the rigging cut or broken, the upper works all shot in pieces, and the ship herself, unable to move, was settling slowly in the sea ; the vast fleet of Spaniards lying round her in a ring, like dogs round a dying lion, and wary of approaching him in his last agony. Sir Richard seeing that it was past hope, having fought for fifteen hours, and 'having, by estimation, eight hundred shot of great artillery through him, commanded the master-gunner, whom he knew to be a most resolute man, to split and sink the ship, that thereby nothing might remain of glory or victory to the Spaniards ; seeing in so many hours they were not able to take her, having had above fifteen hours time, above ten thousand men, and fifty-three men-of-war to perform it withal, and persuaded the company, or as many as he could induce, to yield themselves unto God and to the mercy of none else ; but as they had, like valiant resolute men, repulsed so many enemies, they should not now shorten the honour of their nation by prolonging their own lives for a few hours or a few days.'

" The gunner and a few others consented. But such δαιμοί'νη α'ρετή was more than could be expected of ordinary seamen. They had dared do all which did become men, and they were not more than men, at least than men were then. Two Spanish ships had gone down, above fifteen hundred men were killed, and the Spanish admiral could not induce any one of the rest of his fleet to board the 'Revenge' again, 'doubting lest Richard would have blown up himself and them, knowing his dangerous disposition'! Sir Richard lying disabled below, the captain, finding the Spaniards as ready to entertain a composition as they could be to offer it, gained over the majority of the surviving crew ; and the remainder then drawing back from the master-gunner, they all, without further consulting their dying commander, surrendered on honorable terms ; 'the ship being marvellous unsavourie,' Alonzo de Bacon, the Spanish admiral, sent his boat to bring Sir Richard on board his own vessel. Sir Richard, whose life was fast ebbing away, replied that ' he might do with his body what he list, for that he esteemed it not ;' and as he was carried out of the ship, he swooned, and reviving again, desired the company to pray for him. In a few hours, Sir Richard, finding his end approaching, showed not any sign of faintness, but spoke these words in Spanish, and said, ' Here die I, Richard Grenville, with a joyful and quiet mind, for that I have ended my life as a true soldier ought to do that hath fought for his country, queen, religion, and honour. Whereby my soul most joyfully departeth out of this body, and shall always leave behind it an everlasting fame of a valiant and true soldier, that has done his duty as he was bound to do.' When he had finished these, or other such-like words, he gave up the ghost with great and stout courage, and no man could perceive any sign of heaviness in him.

" Such was the fight at Florez, in that August of 1591, without its equal in such of the annals of mankind as the

234

thing which we call history has preserved to us. At the time, all England and all the world rang with it. It struck a deeper terror, though it was but the action of a single ship, into the hearts of the Spanish people; it dealt a more deadly blow upon their fame and naval strength than the destruction of the Armada itself; and, in the direct results which arose from it, it was scarcely less disastrous to them. Hardly, as it seems to us, if the most glorious actions which are set like jewels in the history of mankind are weighed one against the other in the balance,—hardly will those three hundred Spartans, who, in the summer morning, sate ' combing their long hair—for death,' in the passes of Thermopylæ, have earned a more lofty estimate for them- selves than this one crew of modern Englishmen.

"After the action there ensued 'a tempest so terrible, as was never seen or heard the like before.' A fleet of merchantmen joined the armada immediately after the battle, forming, in all, 140 sail; and of these 140, only 32 ever saw Spanish harbour. The rest all foundered, or were lost on the Azores. The men-of-war had been so shattered by shot as to be unable to carry sail; and the ' Revenge ' herself, disdaining to survive her commander, or, as if to complete his own last baffled purpose, like Samson, buried herself and her 200 prize crew under the rocks of St. Michael's."*

After reading this, each man's feelings will be the best comment; but, if his patriotism be not stimulated, his motives purified, and his spirit fired by such an example, he is not to be envied; for it stands alone, even among

---

* England's forgotten worthies.— *Westminster Review.*

those marvellous exploits—

> " That fill
> The spacious times of great Elizabeth
> With sounds that echo still."

WITH A SQUADRON.

350. IN OPEN ORDER.—The ships will be four; and in " Close Order," two cables apart.

351. COLUMNS APART.—The distance should be twice the number of ships in the longest column in cable's lengths; thus, with four ships in line, the columns would be eight cables apart; but cruising in " Open Order," ten cables is the distance usually preserved.

352. FLEET NUMBERS.—A number is given by the Admiral to each ship, it indicates her station in column. The fleet is also divided into divisions and sub-divisions.

353. COLUMNS OF DIVISIONS AND SUB-DIVISIONS —Are the terms used to denote that the ships composing the fleet are formed in divisions or sub-divisions, whether in line ahead or otherwise; for instance, "Columns of Divisions in line abreast."— " Columns of Sub-divisions in quarter-line," etc.

" Columns of Divisions in line Ahead."

" Close Order."

Scale—Half-an-inch to one cable.

By altering course together eight points, the ships become formed in "Columns of Divisions in line-abreast.

236

354. LINE-ABREAST.—A column is in "line-abreast" when the ships are ranged in one line abeam of each other.

"Single Column line-abreast."

Alter course eight points together, and the ships become formed in "Single Column line-ahead."

355. QUARTER-LINE. —A column is said to be in "quarter-line," when the ships are ranged in one line, abaft each others beam, but not right astern.

"Column in quarter-line."

Generally this line is formed four points abaft the beam of the leaders.

Q 2

"Column in two quarter-lines."

A column is said to be in "two quarter-lines" when the ships are ranged on each quarter of a single ship.

"Column in two bow-lines."

A column is said to be in "two bow-lines" when the ships are ranged on each bow of a single ship.

238

356. DIRECTION OF A COLUMN—Is the bearing on which the ships are formed from their leaders.

357. TACKING IN SUCCESSION.—The leading ships put their helm down together, the other ships at the moment that will allow them to fetch into the wake of their next ahead when on the other tack.

358. LINE OF BEARING—In the old sense meant that the fleet were sailing on a bearing, which, if they hauled their wind, or tacked together, would put them in "line of battle," or, as it is now termed, "line-ahead." It may be generally understood to mean that ships are on a bearing from each other; into which they have been thrown by altering course together.

The following definitions of the technical terms connected with fleet sailing, may be of use to those who have not access to the general signal book, from which they are taken.

A Column means any number of ships in a distinct group, whether in line-ahead, abreast, or otherwise.

The Leading Column is the headmost column in any formation.

The Starboard Wing Column is the column on the extreme right of any formation.

The Port Wing Column is the column on the extreme left of any formation.

The Rear Column is the sternmost column in any formation.

The Leader of a Column is the headmost ship.

239

The *Starboard Wing Ship* of a column is the ship on its extreme right.

The *Port Wing Ship* of a column is the ship on its extreme left.

The *Rear Ship* of a column is the sternmost ship.

The ship *next ahead* of another, is that immediately before her, or before her beam.

The ship *next astern* of another, is that immediately behind her, or abaft her beam.

The " *Starboard Columns* " of a formation are the alternate columns, commencing from the right.

The " *Port Columns* " of a formation are the alternate columns, commencing with the second column from the right.

The foregoing terms when used in the evolutionary signals refer solely to the position of the ships at the moment of making the signal, and no ship or column is ever alluded to by a term expressive of position, unless such ship or column actually holds that position at the time.

The formation or disposition of a fleet is termed its *order*.

The term *Commander of Column* indicates the senior officer in that column.

The following remarks in connection with steam evolutions may perhaps be found of some interest to young officers who have not had much experience with large squadrons.

The speed of a fleet steering a course is limited to that of its slowest ship.

The speed at which a fleet can manœuvre must be still less, to ensure the slow vessels the power of preserving their station with facility.

At a given speed, the rapidity with which an evolution involving a large alteration of course can be effected, will be governed by the ships of the most inferior steering power.

From the foregoing can be gathered the great importance of the ships composing a fleet assimilating each other, both in speed and handiness.

Accurate station can be best preserved by making moderate, not extreme, changes of speed or course, which latter renders the station of the ships following you most difficult to keep, besides increasing the expenditure of fuel.

Before commencing steam evolutions, each vessel should be aware of the revolutions of the screw per minute, required by her to go the same speed as any other ship whose revolutions are known; this can be best done by obtaining a co-efficient of revolutions.

A general comparison of the angle of helm that can be given, with the diameter of the circle described, will be found most useful.

In the presence of an enemy, owing to the great uncertainty of signals being seen and correctly interpreted, and in the absence of a pre-concerted plan of attack, it is improbable that any but the most simple and easily executed manœuvre would be attempted; the more complicated may be regarded rather as affording an exercise necessary to the attainment of skill and precision in handling the ships, than for their elaborate performance in the face of a hostile fleet.

Smokeless coal is an absolute necessity in a fleet.

359. WEARING IN SUCCESSION.—Your ship being well round on the other tack, the after yards should be kept in until the last ship in the line has passed, lest, by coming to the wind too soon, you do not allow room for the other ships to pass ahead of you ; whereas, with the after yards well in, you are all ready for keeping away in case of accident.

360. FOG AT NIGHT.—Use the fog horns, or if under steam, the steam whistle ; stop all unnecessary noise, note the last bearing and distance of the Admiral, and your next ahead ; have a watch with second hand, and a slate ready to note any gun signals the Admiral may make ; avoid making any sudden changes of speed if possible.

361. THE ADMIRAL'S MOTIONS—Should at all times be immediately followed, unless ordered to the contrary.

362. TRIAL OF SAILING.—To ascertain the results, you assume your own ship throughout the trial to be a fixed point, and lay off from it, at the commencement and end of the trial, the bearing and distance of the ship or ships with whom you are competing. The bearing is obtained by compass ; and the distance is deduced from the masthead angle, the height of the mast-head being previously ascertained.

242

Trials of sailing resolve themselves into two classes— on and off the wind. The test of the former is limited to the direct distance gained in the wind's eye; while in the latter the whole distance run determines the result.

A single example of each will be sufficient to explain all that need be said upon the subject.

ON A WIND.

Let it be supposed that at half-past seven, on the morning of October, 3rd, 18—, Her Majesty's ships " Pallas," "Minerva," " Nymphe," and " Cleopatra," on signal from the former, made all sail and hauled to the wind preparatory to trying rate of sailing; that at 8 A.M. the signal was made to take bearings and angles, and that the following was the result on board the " Minerva," then, and at the close of the trial at 11 A.M., the other ships at the same time making similar observations, and arriving thereby at independent conclusions.

It must be borne in mind that, on every shift of wind, you must take fresh bearings and angles, and either commence a new trial or close it.

When many ships are concerned, it is advisable, to avoid confusion, to protract a separate diagram for each position, and not to unite two as has been done above.

The senior officer should signal to take bearings and angles simultaneously every hour, so that, should any alteration for the better or worse take place in any ship's sailing, the cause may be ascertained from knowing the time when it originated. Also, in the event of any mis-

243

take occuring or accident happening to any particular ship, you may, on subsequent consideration, find it judicious to close her part in the trial at one of the intermediate hours, which you have therefore an opportunity of doing.

In taking angles, the mast-head should be brought down to a point level with the observer's eye, otherwise the angle at the base is more, or less, than a right-angle. Consequently, the angle subtended by the mast-head and hammock-netting, when the observer is on the deck of his own ship, is more correct than that between the mast-head and water-line. The distance, moreover, between the latter is not a constant number, being affected by the distance the ship is from you.

Time.	Ships.	Bearings.	Angles.	Wind.	Remarks.
8 A.M.	Pallas	N. 73° W.	2° 40'	N.N.E.	10h. 15m. Tacked together.
	Nymphe	N. 49 W.	1 10		10h. 20m. Cleopatra unable to carry royals.
	Cleopatra	S. 55 W.			
11 A.M.	Pallas	N. 40 W.	1 35	,,	Steady breeze throughout.— Rate of sailing, 5½ to 6 knots.
	Nymphe	N. 67 W.	0 46		
	Cleopatra	S. 62 W.	0 52		

Height of mast-heads.... { Pallas........167 feet.
Nymphe ....140 „
Cleopatra ..140 „

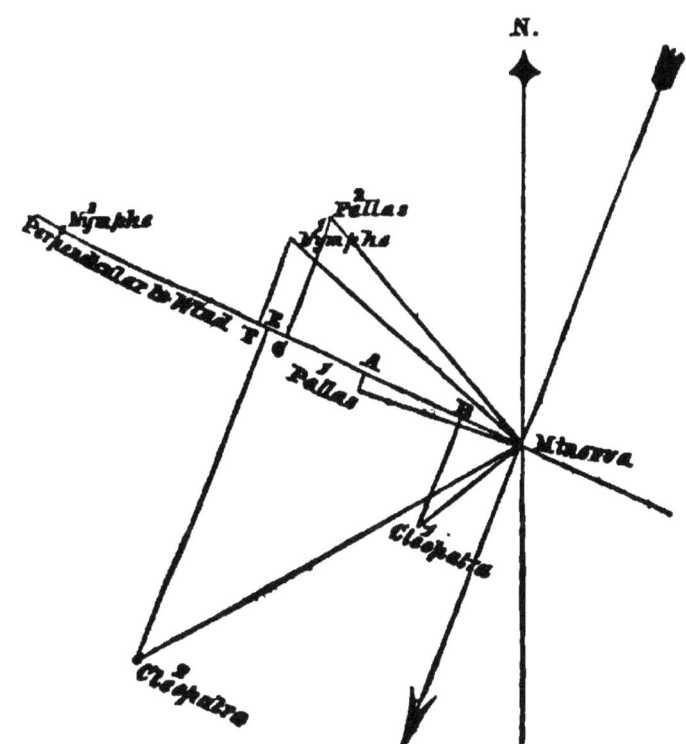

"PALLAS."

Positions at 8 A.M.	Positions at 11 A.M.

167 feet and $\angle$ 2° 40′ gives MP¹ = 597 fathoms   167 feet and $\angle$ 1° 35′ gives MP² = 1009 fathoms

NMA (90° − 22½°) = 67½°   AP¹ = MP¹ × sin. AMP¹   NMP² = 40° .... GP² = MP² × sin. GMP²

NMP² (73° ...... 2·775974   GMP² (67½° − 40°) = 27½° ...... 9·664406

AMP¹ (73° − 67½°) = 5½° ...... 8·981573   3·003891

57.........1·757547   466.........2·668297

Commencement of Trial........ 57 fathoms to leeward of "Minerva."

End........................ 466 fathoms to windward.

Gain on "Minerva" in 3 hours.. 523 fathoms.

"NYMPHE."

MN¹ = 1046 fathoms........FN¹ = MN¹ × sin. FMN¹   MN² = 1744 fms.   Deduced from mast-head angle·

NMN¹ = 49° .... 3·019532

FMN¹ (67½° − 49°) = 18½° ...... 9·501476

332........ 2·521008

Commencement   ·   332 fathoms to windward.

End of Trial, equal,   ·

Loss on "Minerva"   ·   332 fathoms.

"CLEOPATRA."

MC¹ = 445 fathoms........BC¹ = MC¹ × sin. BMC¹   MC² = 1542 fathoms.   EC² = MC² × sin. EMC²

2·648360   3·188084

BMC¹ (180° − 55° + 67½°) = 57½° ... 9·926029   EMC² (180° − 62° + 67½°) = 50½° 9·887406

375........ 2·574389   1190 ...... 3·075490

Commencement of Trial   ·   375 fathoms to leeward of "Minerva."

End   ·   1190 fathoms "

Loss   ·   815 fathoms.

246

OFF THE WIND.

To illustrate a trial of this description, let it be assumed that in the afternoon the same ships took up position east and west of the " Pallas," and when, at 1.30 P.M., all were fairly started under all sail, that the bearings and angles by signal were taken ; were repeated at 2.30, and again

Time.	Ships.	Bearings.	Angles.		Course.	Wind.	Remarks.
1.30 P.M.	Pallas	S. 85° W.	5°	54´	South	North	All ships carried studding-sails both sides
	Nymphe ..	West	2	20	7·5 knots	6, b. c.	
	Cleopatra	N. 81 E.	4	30			
4 P.M.	Pallas	S. 39 W.	4	15			3 P.M. "Cleopetra" carried away part fore topmast studd.-sail boom ; 3·20 sail set again
	Nymphe ..	N. 47 W.	1	50			
	Cleopatra.	N. 29 E.	2	18			

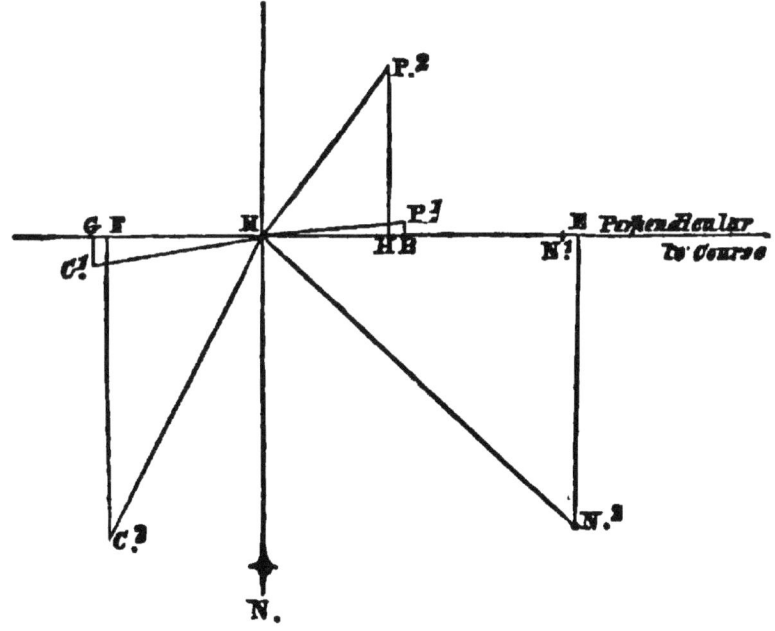

POSITIONS at 1'30 P.M.	POSITIONS at 4 P.M.

"PALLAS."

$MP^1 = 250$ fms. $BMP^1 = 5°$ $BP^1 = MP^1 \times \sin. BMP^1$ $MP^2 = 366$ fms. $HMP^2 = 51°$ $HP^2 = MP^2 \times \sin. HMP^2$

$$
\begin{array}{ll}
2\cdot397940 & 2\cdot563481 \\
8\cdot940296 & 9\cdot890503 \\
\hline
22\ldots\ldots1\cdot338236 & 284\ldots\ldots2\cdot453984
\end{array}
$$

Commencement of Trial......22 fathoms ahead of "Minerva."
End ....284 fathoms   "

Gained on "Minerva" ....262 fathoms.

"NYMPHE."

$MN^2 = 729$ fms. $EMN^2 = 43°$ $EN^2 = MN^2 \times \sin. EMN^2$

$$
\begin{array}{l}
2\cdot862727 \\
9\cdot833783 \\
\hline
497\ldots\ldots2\cdot696510
\end{array}
$$

At commencement of Trial.........abeam of "Minerva."
At conclusion ......497 fathoms astern.
    Therefore "Minerva" beat her that distance.

"CLEOPATRA."

$MC^1 = 296$ fms. $GMC^1 = 9°$ $GC^1 = MC^1 \times \sin. GMC^1$ $MC^2 = 581$ fms. $FMC^2 = 61°$ $FC^2 = MC^2 \times \sin. FMC^2$

$$
\begin{array}{ll}
2\cdot471292 & 2\cdot464176 \\
9\cdot194332 & 9\cdot941819 \\
\hline
46\ldots\ldots1\cdot665624 & 508\ldots\ldots2\cdot705995
\end{array}
$$

At starting.........46 fathoms astern of "Minerva."
At close.........508 fathoms   "

Lost on "Minerva" ......462 fathoms.

248

at 4 P.M., when the trial closed; and that the following observations were made by the "Minerva." (The intermediate ones are not noticed.)

The "Pallas," therefore, proved herself the best ship on both points of sailing; the "Minerva" second; and, of the other two, the "Nymphe" best on a wind, and "Cleopatra" before it.

363. TOPSAIL-YARD SPRUNG IN A TRIAL.—Fish it temporarily with a couple of capstan bars.

364. MAIN TOPSAIL SPLIT ACROSS THE HEAD.—Take a reef in.

365. STOPPERING THE LEECH OF A TOPSAIL.—Settle the halyards, cut a piece of rope long enough to connect the parts of the leech-rope, work a knot in each end, send a hand down in a bowline, and pass a seizing round the leech and under each knot.

366. MAINSTAYS CARRIED AWAY.—Bear up, trice up runners and tackles, then haul your wind.

367. RUDDER DISABLED.—Veer something astern by a hawser, bend a couple of guys to the hawser, and lead them through a block on each quarter, rigged out if you have time, and get a tackle on in-board. Veer the bend a short distance astern; and, to port the helm, haul in on the starboard guy, easing the port, and *vice versâ*.

Under other circumstances, the end of the hemp sheet-cable alone may be used.

249

368. USE OF RUDDER-CHAINS.—These are intended as a substitute for the tiller, when it is damaged and cannot be replaced, or when the rudder-head is injured; and are worked by a tackle from the end of a short spar, rigged out of the aftermost broadside port.

369. RIGGING-STOPPER.—Two pieces of rope, the required length, are middled, the dead-eyes seized in, and the tails coach-whipped. The lanyard is rove, and an eye spliced in each end, as either end becomes the standing part, according to whichever happens to be put on uppermost. The rigging is brought to by taking a half-hitch with each tail opposite ways round the shroud, dogging the upper tails upwards, and the lower ones downward along the shroud, above and below the part that is wounded, and securing it with a nettle in each tail. The double block of a stout jigger is then hooked to a selvagee strop round the shroud, above the stopper, and the single block to the eye in the lanyard in the lower dead-eye. The eye in the other end, bringing up against the dead-eye, acts as a knot; and the shroud is then set up.

370. WITHOUT A COMPASS.—A piece of hard iron or steel held in a perpendicular position (or more correctly speaking, in a position in which it points to the magnetic pole), and struck smartly with a hammer, will acquire and *retain* the magnetic property. In the northern hemisphere the north pole will be the

250

end which was lowest, and in the southern hemisphere that which was held uppermost. The sun by day and the stars by night are the only other guides you have.

In Captain Golowin's narrative of his captivity in Japan, in 1811—13, he relates how they imparted magnetism to to a needle by rubbing it with a stone. " The proverb that necessity is the mother of invention," he observes, "was fully realized ; for Mr. Chlebnikoff even managed to make a compass. We requested our attendants to let us have two large needles for mending our clothes, and afterwards pretended that we had lost them. The Japanese sometimes fasten together the beams of their houses with copper; this had been done in our house, although the copper was very rusty. Mr. Chlebnikoff cleaned a piece of this copper, in the middle of which he bored a hole, so that a needle might be placed upon it. By frequently rubbing this needle on a stone. which he selected for the purpose, he succeeded in magnetising it, and finally gave it such a degree of polarity, that it pointed, with tolerable accuracy, towards the north."

371. NECKLACE ON THE FOREMAST CARRIED AWAY.—
If unable to stand on the other tack, lower the topsail, run a hawser up to the topmast head, pass it round, pay down, hook the single blocks of a couple of luffs to bolts in the chains, bring to, snatch the falls, set the hawser up, and seize both parts together below the cross-trees. If the breeze is fresh, get a sail-tackle up in addition.

If unable to replace or repair the necklace, either fit a rope one, or bring together all the futtock shrouds that re-

R   251

quire securing, shackle them to a spare anchor-shackle or otherwise, and set them up with a couple of up-and-downs hooked at the partners, and then frap them in to the mast aloft. The spurs through the links will hold the necklace on the opposite side to where it is carried away ; and it is not probable, either, that both necklaces on the mast will carry away at the same time.

372. TAKING IN BOOM MAINSAIL.—In lowering away, mind and keep the jaws below the peak, or you will not get the sail down.

373. STOWAGE OF BOOM MAINSAIL.—Pass the leech along the gaff, taut in from the gaff and boom ends, with the exception of a foot or two of slack, which the outer hand keeps back for a skin to stow the foremost part of the clew in, close under the gaff end : the slack sail is then passed forward, gathered up and stowed in the head cloths. When the gaskets are passed, the gaff is lowered with the sail just touching the boom.

A cutter's mainsail is frequently stowed on the foot.

374. TRIMMING SAILS, SHORT-HANDED.—If the wind draws aft, trim the after yards first ; if forward, the head yards.

375. REEFING TOPSAILS IN STAYS.—According to the old song, you

"Away aloft" when the helm is put down ;
"Lower away the the topsails," as the main yard flies round ;
"Trice up," and "lay out," and take two reefs in one ;—

For all in one moment this work must be done.
Then, man your head braces, your halyards, and all,
And as you "hoist away the topsails" you "let go and haul."

But a better plan is to "lower the topsails" when you "raise tacks and sheets," laying the yard square. Haul the main yard at the proper time, regardless of the men on the yard, provided the topsail braces are kept taut. Take the reefs in pioperly, "hoist the topsails" when the men are off the yards, and "haul of all" as usual.

The watch on deck and idlers reef the topsails, and watch below put the ship about.

376. MAN OVERBOARD.—*Plain sail, on a wind.*—Let go the life-buoy, put the helm a-lee, call the boat away, and direct the signalman not to lose sight of the man. Bring the ship up into the wind, to deaden her way (taking care not to bring her round or to give her sternway), square the main yard, haul the mainsail up, and shorten whatever sail is necessary. The practice of going about, under these circumstances, is in many respects very objectionable. The cry of "man overboard!" in the most perfectly disciplined ship, is sure to be attended with some confusion at first, which becomes "worse confounded" when followed by the pipe of "hands about ship!" repeated and spun out by half a dozen boatswain's-mates. How much more quiet and simple is the order "square the main yard!" But the great and conclusive objection to it is, that, ten to one, the cause of it all will be lost sight of—in the literal sense; and, after getting the ship round and lowering the boat, *then* will arise the

R 2   253

question of "Where's the man?" The signalman will
say that he was last seen on the quarter, but, as the
quarter in the interval has been performing a circuit, the
reply becomes anything but satisfactory.   The boat in the
mean time is probably vaguely striking out astern, and
some with the hailing here and answering there, anarchy
in the end is pretty sure to reign triumphant. What a
contrast has heaving-to present. The boat shoves off,
un-embarrassed by doubt; the signalman has had nothing
to distract his attention; and should the former pull half
a point wide, a flag over the stern will correct her course.
At all times at night, and more especially in the event of
the lifebuoy not being fired, the above remarks apply
with still greater force.

It may be urged that by going round, the ship is placed
to windward of the man before the boat is lowered, and,
therefore, she will reach him quicker than she would were
the ship hove to on the original tack.   But, granting that
she does reach to windward of her former position
(although the main yard is squared in stays), where is the
gain? Though the boat in this case pulls to leeward, it
must not be assumed that, when the ship does not put
about, her boat must pull to windward; for, as the man
falls from the ship and is in her wake, the boat must
necessarily have the wind and sea abaft her beam; and in
either case the ship can bear up, if necessary, and get to
leeward of her boat to pick them up.

Letter M means "pull to starboard," N "pull to port,"
and O "keep as you are going."

Plain sail, before the wind.—Put the helm over, and come to the wind with the head yards aback, hauling up the foresail, and setting the spanker.

Studding-sails on one side.—Put the helm-a-lee, trip up the lower studding-sail, or let go the outer halyards, let fly the studding-sail tacks, brace up the after yards, and bring her to the wind with the head yards square. The studding-sails will fly before all, where they will be becalmed, and must be hauled down principally by the deck sheets. If you put the helm up to take the studding-sails in to leeward, you run a most unnecessary distance away from the man; whereas, even in a fresh breeze, you run no risk by letting fly the tack of a weather studding-sail, for the sail flies to leeward clear of everything.

Studding-sails, both sides.—Round to with all despatch, but in this case you must take everything in properly; for, if you let fly tacks and so forth, before the controlling gear can be manned, you will find "the more haste" to be "the less speed.

In each of the above cases, both quarter-boats, when possible, ought to be cleared away and lowered as speedily as possible, and the life-buoy let go instantly, except in a very light breeze and when the man falls from forward, when you should hold on a little to come up to him, and then let go. Beware, too, of committing a blunder, which I once saw nearly perpetrated, of dropping the buoy upon the man's head.

Cases are not uncommon of men being drowned after they have been seen to get hold of the life-buoy; and, as

255

on two occasions, I have seen it turn over with a man, it is very probable that to that cause such accidents are owing—the man being in an exhausted state and unable to get hold again. The proper way to hold on, is to put the feet on the rest at the bottom, one on each side, and throw the arms over the cross-piece; whereas an attempt to get *on* it will result in a capsize.

The circular cork life-buoys are so handy for *throwing* to a man, that is well worth while to carry one on each quarter for that purpose.

Boat's gripes, instead of being secured to an eye-bolt in the chains, should be set up to a strop with a thimble in it, passed through the eye-bolt, and retained thereby by a slip-toggle a lanyard attached; which has therefore merely to be hauled upon to free the boat.

The steadying-lines should be of chain, with a hook on the ends; rope ones give, and are seldom hitched square. If they are too taut, an undue strain is brought upon the gunwale; and if too slack, the boat is not steadied.

To hoist a quarter boat up in a sea-way, there is no combination of "gil-guys" that you can invent equal to jackstays from the davits, set up to bolts at the water-line. A lizard is fitted to each, which travels up and down; a turn whipped round the thwarts, and the boat run up, clear of the side, without further ado.

377. TREATMENT OF A MAN APPARENTLY DROWNED.— The following directions are those issued by the Royal National Life Boat Institution :—

" 1. Treat the patient instantly, on the spot, in the open air, exposing the face and chest to the breeze, (except in severe weather.)

" To clear the Throat.

" 2. Place the patient gently face downwards, with one wrist under the forehead, in which position all fluid will escape by the mouth, and the tongue itself will fall forwards, leaving the entrance into the wind-pipe free ; assist this operation by wiping and cleansing the mouth.

" If there be breathing—wait and watch; if there be no breathing, or if it fail, then—

" To excite Respiration.

" 3. Turn the patient well and instantly on the side, and—

" 4. Excite the nostrils with snuff, hartshorn, volatile salts, or the throat with a feather, &c., and dash cold water on the face previously rubbed warm.

" If there be no success, lose not a moment, but instantly—

" To imitate Respiration.

" 5 Replace the patient on the face, raising and supporting the chest well on a folded coat or other article of drsss.

" 6. Turn the body gently on the side and a little beyond, and then briskly on the face, alternately ; repeating these measures deliberately, efficiently, and perse-

257

veringly, about fifteen times in the minute, or every four seconds, occasionally varying the side."

[*By placing the patient on the chest, it is compressed by the weight of the body,* expiration *takes places; when turned on the side, this pressure is removed, and* inspiration *occurs.*]

" 7. On each occasion that the body is replaced on the face, make uniform but efficient pressure, with brisk movement, on the back, between and below the shoulder-blades or bones on each side, removing the pressure immediately before turning the body on the side."

[*The first measure increases the expiration, the second commences inspiration,*]

. The result is—respiration, or natural breathing— and, if not too late, life.

" 8. After respiration has been restored, promote the warmth of the body by the application of hot flannels, bottles or bladders of hot water, heated bricks, &c., to the pit of the stomach, the arm-pits, between the thighs, and to the soles of the feet.

" *To induce Circulation and Warmth.*

" 9. During the whole time do not cease to rub the limbs upwards with firm, grasping pressure, and with energy, using handkerchiefs, flannels, &c."

[*By this manner the blood is propelled along the veins towards the heart.*]

" 10. Let the limbs be thus warmed and dried, and then clothed, the bystanders supplying the requisite garments.

258

" Cautions.

" 1. Send quickly for medical assistance, and for dry clothing.

" 2. Avoid all rough usage and turning the body on the back.

" 3, Under no circumstances hold up the body by the feet ;

" 4. Nor roll the body on casks ;

" 5. Nor rub the body with salts or spirits.

" 6. Nor inject tobacco-smoke or infusion of tobacco.

" 7. Avoid the continuous warm bath.

" 8. Be particularly carefull to prevent persons crowding round the body.

" General Observations.

" On the restoration of life, a teaspoonful of warm water should be given, and then, if the power of swallowing have returned, small quantities of wine, or brandy and water, warm, or coffee.   The patient should be kept in bed, and a disposition to sleep encouraged.

" The treatment recommended should be persevered in for a considerable time, as it is an erroneous opinion that persons are irrecoverable because life does not soon make its appearance, cases having been successfully treated after persevering several hours."

378. LETTING GO LIFE-BUOY.—As you face aft, the right hand fires, and the left lets go.

379. TOPMAST SHATTERED BY LIGHTNING.—Lash a light spar on each side of the mast, and unfid.   Cut away these

259

spars as you lower, lashing the topmast to the standing part of the hawser as it comes below the cap.

(I see that this wrinkle is already before the naval world in Captain Liardets work ; but, as I heard of it several years previously, it is doubtless public property.)

380. TOPSAIL ON FIRE.—*Fore Topsail.*—Bear up, haul down and stow the head sails, clew the topsail up, keeping it mast-headed, and cut the foresail adrift. Then lower the topsail yard, and play upon the fire with engine and fire-buckets.

Main Topsail.—Take in all sail but jib and spanker, and bring the wind abeam.

With mizen topsail on fire, come to the wind.

381. MAKING UP A TOPSAIL FOR BENDING.—To bring a sail to, furled, it is, of course, indispensably necessary to lighten the yard-arms as much as possible, and, consequently, to throw all the weight you can into the bunt, which is kept up by the sail-tackle. Having, therefore stretched the head taut along the deck, roping downwards, and gathered back from the head, you bring the second reef up to it to form the skin ; then lay the leech from the second reef-cringle to the reef-tackle cringle, along the head, gathering all the slack sail into the bunt ; the reef-tackle bridle is left out, the cringle being brought up to the head cringle, and the clews carried in and laid out over the head on each quarter. The buntline toggles are brought in amidships, and seized to the head, so that,

260

directly they are bent and a turn is taken with them, the sail-tack can be walked back, and the strop cut adrift. The bowline toggles being left out, the foot-rope and all slack sail gathered in amidships, the sail is rolled up and the gaskets are passed; and the clews, of which there is considerable drift left out for convenience in handling aloft, are passed from the fore side of the sail, underneath, and stopped up on the after side. Seize the strop on, and pass the head-earings in to the bunt, handy for laying hold of and passing out, when the sail is swayed up to the yard; and, with heavy sails, it may be necessary to hitch the buntlines round the quarters, to keep them up.

382. MAKING UP A COURSE.—Reef-tackle cringles are worked into the leeches a couple of feet below the head, to which the reef-tackles are hooked for hauling out when bending, and shifted down to their proper cringle below the reef, when the earing is secured.

Stretch the head taut along, gather back, and bring up the second reef to form the skin; bring the leech taut along from the cringle, to which the reef-tackle is to be hooked; lay the leechlines toggles out, and seize them to the head, and they will thus be in their proper places, close under the blocks, when the sail is hauled out; bring the buntline toggles close in amidships, drag all the slack sail into the bunt, and lay the clews out like those of the topsail; roll up, pass the gaskets, stop the head-earings up in a coil, seize the strop on, and seize the head of the sail to the after part of the strop, that when the strop seizing is cut, the head of the sail may be kept up until brought to.

261

383. MAKING UP A JIB.—Stretch the foot of the sail along; pass a reeving-line through the hanks and lacing, and knot the ends together, after bringing up the bights of the head and lacing one by one; put a stop round every other cloth, and it is ready either for stowing away or bending.

384. SHIFTING A TOPSAIL.—" Watch shift main topsail," "topsail clewlines and buntlines," "away aloft," "clew up and furl the sail." The sail-tackle in the mean time is cleared away, triced up, and hooked round the top-mast head, and its lower block hooked to a strop, which is seized round the bunt of the new sail.

When the old sail is furled, unbend the topsail sheets, clewlines, bowlines, reef-tackles, robands, and head earings; hitch the buntlines round the sail, secure the bunt robands to them, ease in, and lower the sail down on the weather side by the buntlines.

While you have been doing this, the new sail has been swayed up, carefully kept on the right slue, until the second reef-tackles can be bent; then give the order—" haul out," and lower the bunt of the sail level with the yard. Secure the bunt robands and head earings, and bring the sail to; bend sheets, clewlines, robands, reef-tackles, and buntlines; clear away the gaskets, "let fall," "sheet home," and "hoist the topsail." If blowing hard, the requisite number of reefs should be taken in the new sail before it goes aloft, so that the reef beckets may be rove and toggled before letting fall.

385. SHIFT MAINSAIL.—"Watch shift mainsail;" "away aloft;" take in and furl the sail; unbend the reef-tackles and over-haul them down on deck; unbend buntlines, leech-lines, slab-lines, tacks and sheets—cast off head earings and robands, ease in, hitch the midship buntlines round the sail, and lower it by them.

The new sail is swayed up, *furled* by the stay whip, and the yard arms are hauled out with the reef-tackles; this done, bring to the head of the sail, bend tacks and sheets, buntlines, leech-lines, and slablines; cast off the gaskets, let fall, and set the sail.

386. SHIFTING JIB.—Haul down, untoggle the purchase, cast off the tack and jib pendants, and bend the reeving-line, (kept fitted), either with a seizing passed between the eyes, to allow it to pass through the sheave-holes, or with a small clasp hook fitted to the reeving-line. With a piece of sennit, kept seized on the stay under the sail, take a hitch round the stay, above the sail, to prevent it slipping down the stay in coming in, and to keep it in its place on going out. If blowing, a gasket must be passed round the sail. Bend a clew-rope from inboard to the clew, pull up the halyards, ease away the downhaul, and haul in on the clew-rope,—a hand at the boom-end lighting the stay through. When inboard, unreeve the stay, reeve it through the lacing of the new sail, and the downhaul through a couple of thimbles on the luff, take a hitch with the sennit, pull up the halyards, haul away the reeving-line and downhaul (the latter manned best,), easing the halyards and clew-rope; toggle the stay and pull up on the

263

purchase, shackle the tack, toggle the pendants, let go the downhaul, and hoist away.

The stay purchase is fitted with a strop, long enough to allow the bight of the stay to go through ; a toggle is then put through the bight, and both parts of the stay are seized together. The halyards are fitted with a clasp-hook, and the tack secured to a strop, which is passed down through the afterpart of the sheeve-hole, and toggled underneath the boom.

A jib-stay is sometimes seen fitted in two parts ;—the shorter part, from inside the head where it sets up, reeving through the sheeve-hole in the boom, and having a thimble spliced into the end ; while, to the lower end of the long part, a clasp-hook is fitted, to take the thimble in the other part. Thus, it becomes unnecessary to unreeve the stay through the boom ; for, directly the sail comes in on the foreacstle, the two parts are unhooked, the long end hauled through the lacing, rove through the new sail, hooked to the short part, and hauled out. Or it may be fitted to set up abaft the mast, and with a slip-shackle at the boom end.

A T-chain may be used for shackling the pendants to the clew of the sail ; it is perfectly secure, and can be disengaged in a moment. The broad end of the large link should be bent up, to allow the centre of the cross bar to lie close up to it.

264

387. How to tell the Head from the Tack of the Sail in the Dark.—By the roping being on the port side, which is the case in all fore-and-aft sails.

388. Shift Jib-boom.—Strike the fore top-gallant mast, get in the jib and flying-jib, unreeve the jib-stay, in flying jib-boom and leave it resting on the spritsail gaff and bowsprit shrouds. Hook the topmast staysail halyards to a strop round the end of the jib-boom, haul them taut and keep them manned, haul taut the heel rope, ease up guys, back-ropes and jumpers ; slip the heel chain and crupper, ease the boom in by the heel rope, pulling up the staysail halyards as the boom comes in ; leave the funnel and rigging resting on the spurs fitted to the bowsprit cap. A jigger on the forestay with a shifting strop round the boom is used to take the weight off the end as it is run in. In the mean time the new boom has been shouldered and carried forward, with its head resting on the knightheads. Shift the heel rope and jigger with shifting strop, from the old boom, to the new ; haul away the heel rope when pointed and rigged, hook the staysail halyards as before, only keep easing them as the boom goes out. When out, on crupper and heel chain, fid the fore top-gallant mast, pull up back-ropes and jumpers, reeve and set up jib-stay, out flying jib-boom. Set the jib and flying-jib.

389. Shifting a Top-gallant Mast.—Furl the upper sails, stop the yard-ropes out, unbend the gear, and send the yards down. Land the royal yard in the top, unbend the yard-rope, and unreeve it in the top, keeping the end at the cross-trees. As soon as the top-gallant yard comes

265

down, carry the lower yard-arm aft and land it; do not unbend the yard-rope as with the royal yard, but snatch the bight and run away with it. Sway on the mast-rope, the hands stationed at the rigging and stays clearing them away; unfid and lower away. By this time, the end of the yard-rope is within a few feet of the mast-head, when a hand on the cross-trees checks it with a stopper, and unreeves the rest by hand; and when it is clear, lower away roundly, keeping the funnel fair as it comes off. As soon as the royal sheeve-hole comes below the cap, pass the lizard, securing it with a couple of half hitches, and lower away through lubber's hole; land it on deck with the heel aft, unsnatch the mast-rope. In the mean time, the new mast has been cleared away, laid alongside the old one, and *placed on the same slue;* so, that directly the mast-rope is unsnatched, it can be snatched again without any deliberation, or fear of mistake; hitch the lizard, and sway away, easing the heel forward with a slip rope. Cast off the lizard as soon as the royal-mast-head is between the trestle-trees, sway, place the royal rigging and truck, reeve the royal yard-rope from aft forward, rounding down by a reeving-line in the top; place the top-gallant rigging as the mast goes up, reeving the top-gallant yard-rope forward aft, as soon as the sheeve-hole is above the cap. The reeving-line, which has been paid down on deck, as soon as it has been bent to the becket in the yard-rope aloft is run away with, and the yards are swayed aloft directly the fid is entered; the top-gallant rigging falls being paid on deck, and jiggers on the backstays all ready for pulling up at the same time.

266

Top-gallant masts fitted with snatches may be closed either with a slide to slip in a groove on each side of the sheeve-hole, by a strong iron pin, or with a couple of metal clasps across the snatch, which, by a pin behind each, are prevented from opening except towards each other, when, to free the yard-rope, one must be close down before the other can be started. When there is not a lug, an eye-bolt should be driven into the heel on the fore side of the mast, to catch the inside of the cross-trees, and prevent the mast being swayed through them, and also to bend a heel-rope to, by which to steady the mast at sea in going up or coming down. Just above the square of the mast a hole should be bored to receive an iron bolt with a shoulder to it, and an eye in it to attach a lanyard to; which preventer-fid should be kept at the mast-head, and entered directly the hole appears above the trestle-trees, in order to catch the mast in the event of the mast-rope carrying away when fidding. A hole may also be bored, with advantage, about four feet below the royal sheeve-hole, for the lizard to reeve through, which allows it to be passed on sending the mast down, while the truck and rigging are being taken off, and the yard-rope unrove; and, in going up, to place and reeve the same without " avast swaying."

For expedition, in bending and unbending the gear, fit the top-gallant yards with chain quarter-strops, and the quarter-blocks with clasp-hooks. By having the chock in the cross-trees, which confines the heel of the top-gallant mast, made to ship and unship, the mast can be sent down before all—to leeward, without the necessity for lowering the topsail.

S

390. SHIFTING A TOPSAIL YARD.—Take the sail in, unbend it, and haul it into the top. If, on the port tack, you are shifting the main topsail yard, stowed starboard side—port yard-arm aft, you must haul the mainsail up, and send it up before the main yard ; and the same forward, on the starboard tack, fore topsail yard stowed port side—starboard yard-arm forward ; unless you wish to keep the courses set, when you bring the yards over to windward. Pay down the sail-tackle whip, trice up the sail-tackle, round it up and hook it to the slings lashed out on the quarter; unlash the quarter-blocks, cast off the standing part of the clewlines, and the standing part of the reef-tackles, unreeving the upper one, but allowing the lower one to go down with the yard-arm, making a knot in the end ; unsnatch top-gallant sheets, untoggle studding-sail tack blocks, and trice the booms up and down the topmast rigging, easing them in off the yard by a reef-earing. Hang the fly-blocks with jiggers to the topmast rigging ; unshackle the port tye-block forward, and starboard one aft, and cast off the standing part of the starboard tye at the fore topmast head, and port tye at the main, round the tye down, and take a couple of half hitches with the end round its own part close down to the tye-block, then haul taut and take a turn with the halyards. Single the parral lashing, man the sail-tackle, attend the braces and sway away, easing the lower and topping on the upper lift ; then lower away, unrigging the upper yard-arm in the top, and the lower one on deck. Bend the top-bowline to the yard in order to send it down for the new yard, to guy it clear of the lower yard or top

268

rim ; if the yard is coming up to windward, the bowline must be dipped under the lower yard. As soon as the lower yard-arm is unrigged, land the goose-neck in a shoe fitted for it with a lanyard, and haul it along the gangway, where land it. Shift the sail-tackle and topsail-tye to the new yard, bend the bowline to the upper yard-arm (which is better, I think, than putting the guying-block of the sail-tackle on—at least, when sending it up to leeward ; but, when to windward, the bowline perhaps may be dispensed with, and the block used instead). To the lower yard-arm hook a luff from the fore or main rigging, according to the yard, to ease it forward or aft and keep it off the deck ; sway up-and-down, and rig the yard-arms. Send a hauling-line down from the top for the end of the reef-tackle, as soon as it is rove through the lower yard-arm, which haul up and reeve through the block on the sail. Man the sail-tackle and halyards, led on opposite sides of the deck, and sway away when ready, taking through slack of lower lift. When the slings are above the cap, take a turn with the halyards, walk back the sail-tackle and top on the lower lift, attending the braces. Pass out the earings and ends of the reef-tackles, haul out and bring the sail to. On quarter-blocks, send the booms out, bolt the tye-block, and secure the tye, sheet home, and hoist away.

The topsail tye is not always used.

391. SHIFTING MAIN TOPSAIL YARD IN A GALE.—Lower the yard by hand, unbend the sail and send it on deck. Lash the slings out to leeward, if you are trimmed

S 2

at all forward; hook the sail-tackle, get the booms off
the yard, and the gear unrove.   Put two burtons on the
main yard-arms, overhaul the starboard one up (supposing
the yard to be coming down the starboard side), and hook
it to a strop half way out on the starboard topsail yard-arm,
and the port one up under the main stays, and hooked to
the same place.   Overhaul a guy (fore tackle falls, or a
small hawser), from a leading block in each gangway, and
bend them to the starboard yard-arm outside the burtons,
and the main top-bowline to the starboard quarter.   Man
the sail-tackle, port lift, burtons and guys. and sway away.
Unrig the yard, let go the guys as they cease to become of
use. land the yard, and use the same precautions in sending the new one up.

On such occasions, great difficulty is always found in
steadying the yard to get the parral passed.   To obviate
this, before you sway across, hook a couple of jiggers from
bolts in the cap to the slings of the yard, with which rouse
the yard to.

392. A SAIL TACKLE—After use, requires over-hauling
along the deck before stowing away, in order that it may
reach the hatchway when triced up again.

393. BLOCK OF SAIL-TACKLE COMES OUT.—Rack both
parts together below the pendant, send a snatch-block up
to the mast-head, snatch the fall, cut the racking, and
sway away again.

394. MAKING UP A SPANKER.—Make it up on the
head, doubling the leech in to bring it square with the
head, then roll up.

270

395. MAKING A TOPMAST STUDDING-SAIL UP.—Lay the yard on the deck with the fore side of the sail downwards, gather back from the head to form a skin, then bring the leeches and sail up to the yard a foot or two at a time, bighting the downhaul along with the outer leech equal to the whole length of the leech; pass the remainder along the sail to the inner leech, and leave it out with the sheets; then roll up.   When setting stops are used, one is passed round the sail amidships, and another round the outer yard-arm, confining the halyards.

396. A LOWER STUDDING-SAIL—Is rolled up on the head, and doubled in the length of the cover in which it is stowed.

397. STOWAGE OF SAILS.—When the sail-room will admit of it, topsails and courses should be stowed with the bight doubled back between the yard-arms, which, when roused out lies in the square of the hatchway ready for whipping up, and all the time and labour usually lost in breaking out, when the sail is stowed the whole length of the sail-room, is thus avoided.   As the arrangements of ships, below, vary so greatly, it is useless to particularise any special disposition of the sail to facilitate removal.

398. TOP-GALLANT MAST-ROPE.—The hauling part is rove through the lizard; for, if the standing part were used, the mast would be swayed up heel foremost.

399. THE STANDING PART—Is secured to that bolt in the cap which will keep the mast rope in a line with the

271

sheeve. In the main, it will be the foremost bolt on the starboard side ; and in the fore and mizen, the foremost bolt the port side.

400. TOP-GALLANT MAST GONE SHORT OFF.—Send a snatch-block up to the topmast-head, snatch the yard-rope, and pull up,—which will bring the mast in ; then lash the yard, unbend the yard-rope, send the mast first down, and then the yard.

401. STOWING A JIB.—In harbour, when you stow the head sails in a cloth, if covers are not used, gather up from the foot, using the after cloths of the leech to form the skin, a little slack sail being gathered up to cover the hanks, &c., at the head, and stopped close down, and the clew hauled up and equalized along the boom. At sea, get hold of the leech of the sail, gather it on the boom, and pass the gasket.

402. MARKS AND DEEPS.—The marks are leather at 2, 3, and 10 fathoms, the two-fathom mark having a hole in it ; white at 5 and 15 ; red at 7 and 17 ; blue at 13 ; and two knots at 20 fathoms. The intermediate fathoms are deeps.

403. DEEP-SEA-LINE.—Two knots at 20 fathoms, three at 30, and so on up to 100, when you commence again. Between every ten fathoms there is a single knot.

Mark it, by passing the line through a strand of the lead-line, and take a knot in it ; then pass it through the next strand and make another knot; and so on, as many as are required.

If a patent lead, or a buoy and nipper are used, there is no necessity for heaving to ; but, if in deep water with a fresh breeze you want to get an up-and-down cast with a common lead, you will be obliged to do so ; though, if not going very fast through the water, a luff up will in most cases answer the purpose.

When the lead is armed, carry it forward to the cat-head, pass the line forward from the weather quarter and bend it ; place hands at intervals along the chains and quarter-boats, and let them coil up in their hands the quantity of line you require forward,—according to the depth of water. Let go, when ready ; and as the line passes each man in succession, he calls out to the next,—"Watch there, watch !" should he not feel bottom. The quartermaster attends aft ; marines hold the reel ; and the line is snatched and walked in. Sounding with the patent lead, care must be taken not to check the line.

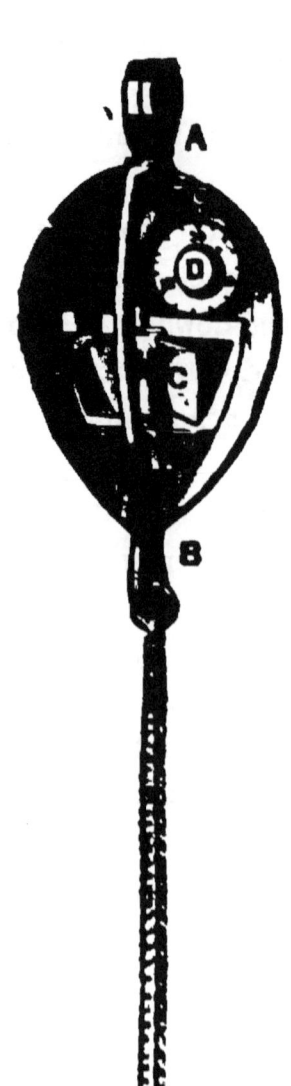

WALKER'S HARPOON SOUNDING MACHINE.—The first wheel makes one revolution in 30 fathoms, and the second one in 150.

Attach the sounding line to the Machine by the hole A, and a ship's lead to the lower hole B, by a looped or endless rope about three feet long.

Before throwing out the Machine (which must be done with plenty of rope), set the dials, by turning the button D, on the first dial, until the pointer is opposite the number 30, and the index of the wheel on the other side of the Machine points to 150.

For additional satisfaction, two or more Machines may be used at the same time, by having a looped line about three feet long between each.

404. VERY DEEP SOUNDINGS—In a steamer are taken with much greater facility from the bow, as it enables you to avoid getting over the line.

405. MARKING A LOG-LINE.—The length of the glass being 28 seconds, the length between each knot must bear the same proportion to 28 as 3600—the number of seconds in an hour, does to 6076—the number of feet in a nautical mile. Therefore, as 3600 : 28 :: 6075 : 47·26 ; or 47 feet 3 inches.

A short glass, of 14 seconds, is used when the ship is going upwards of five knots ; in which case, to give the true rate, the number of knots that are run out must be doubled.

The knot, not the line, is divided into tenths ; and, to assist in calculating the distance that the last knot is over the taffrail, a single knot is placed midway between the knots. This of course is equal to five-tenths, but, when it is not brought exactly on the taffrail the difference is guessed at. *Stray-line* is allowed before the knots commence, to let the log-ship get clear of the eddy in the ship's wake, previous to turning the glass, and is proportionate to the height of the ship.

Log-lines should be wetted before marking, or correcting the marks, to allow them to take up, as they are always wet when in use.

275

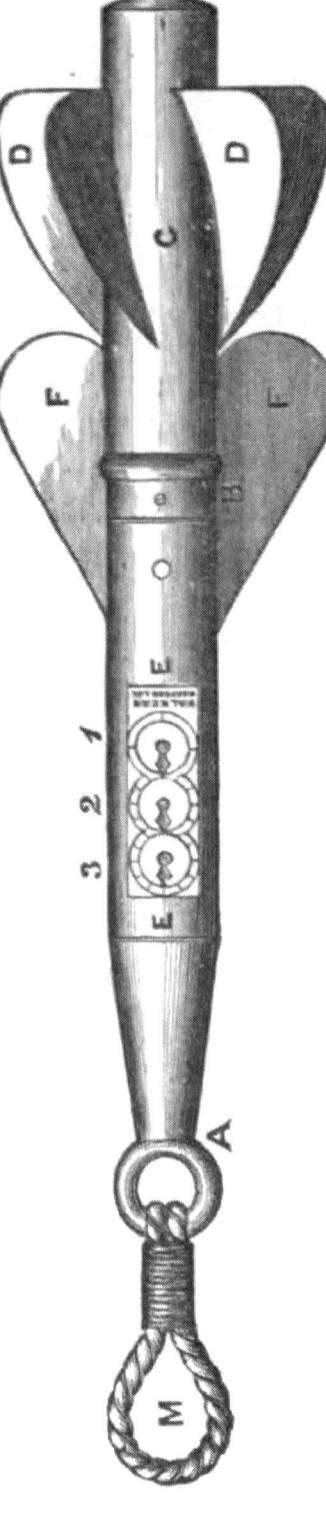

WALKER'S PATENT HARPOON SHIP-LOG—The part marked A and B in the above figure does not revolve as it passes through the water, but contains the wheel-work for registering the number of revolutions of the Rotator C, which is caused to revolve as it passes through the water, by the oblique position of the vanes D D. The angle of the vanes is so adjusted to the wheel-work of the Register, that when the machine has passed through one mile, the finger of the first dial will have made one revolution ; the finger of the dial No. 2 will have made one-tenth of a revolution, and index No. 3 will have made one-hundredth of a revolution, or in other words, the first index goes round one mile, the second index in ten miles, and the third in 100 miles.

It will be seen that in this Log the Rotator and Register are combined, the Rotator being a continuation of the Register or part that holds the wheel-work. By this arrangement, not only is the machine made more compact, but the Rotator is protected from all front-end pressure, thus removing the principal cause of friction, and thereby enabling the Log to register *with equal accuracy at all speeds.*

It will be observed that the float-plate F causes the Machine to travel horizontally at all speeds; the side pressure, and consequent friction on the Rotator Spindle, being thereby reduced to a minimum, and the durability of this, the only wearing part of the Log, greatly increased.

Directions for Use.—When the Log is to be used, con-nect it to the tow-line at M (the tow-line should be about 50 fathoms long), then place the first finger to 1, the second to 10, and the third to 100.

Before throwing the Log overboard, *be sure to cover the dials and the oil-hole* by turning the sliding-case E E, in order to prevent any dirt from getting into the Machine.

406. A SQUALL CLOSE UPON YOU.—Haul the mainsail up; lower the topsails, haul the reef-tackles out, and the buntlines taut ; and, if likely to head you, keep the ship away a little to be prepared. If the jib and spanker are set, take them in, and set fore topmast staysail.

Under ordinary circumstances in squally weather, the invariable cry is, "Hands by the top-gallant (or royal) halyards !" Accustomed to the order from long habit, it is repeated without reflection, from a vague notion of

safety in the measure, and to be in accordance with rule
in the event of anything going.   As midshipman of a
boat, you would not keep the sheet belayed, in breezy
weather, and station a hand, in preference, to the halyards.
Neither should you do so as officer of the watch, for you
know that the heavier the squall is the firmer the yard
will bind, and consequently, that letting go the halyards
before the sheet is eased off will relieve nothing.   For the
future then (if you have hitherto been misled, by custom,
to the contrary), place hands by the lee sheets, and let the
alarm of "Hands by the royal halyards !" henceforth die
out with you.

407. TAKEN UNPREPARED.—Put the helm up, and ease
over the boom.

408. SETTING FORE TOPMAST STUDDING-SAIL IN A
BREEZE.—See the yards properly secured, the lifts and
trusses of the fore yard well taut, the topsail yard well in,
a jigger on the topsail lift, and the burton well up; if necessary get a preventer brace on.   As soon as the boom
is out, and the heel-lashing well secured, martingale it
down with a knot in the lower halyards ; steady taut the
boom-brace, keep away and trice to hand.   When above
the fore yard, get the tack out and hoist away.   The best
knot for the lower halyards is a short sheepshank.

409. TAKING IT IN.—Keep away, ease off the short
sheet, lower the halyards and walk away with the downhaul.   Do not start the tack till the yard is close down to
the boom-end ; nor rig in, till the sail is well below the

278

ore yard.   The deck sheet should be led through a block
on deck, and well manned.

410. A Ship in tow of another.—When the ship
ahead puts her helm down, to go round, the ship in tow
puts her helm up, and always endeavours to keep directly
in her leader's wake.

411. In Tow of a Steamer.—The steamer appointed
to tow you, having hoisted your pendants at the fore,
waits till you hoist your own pendants in reply, to indicate
that you are ready, and then takes up a position ahead.
You then send your hauling-lines on board, by which she
hauls the towing hawsers in ; and it is directed that the
"starboard towing-cable, in all cases, is to be the best,
and brought to the capstan of the ship towed for the
purpose of equalising the strain upon the towing-cables, as
well as to assist in steering the steamer."   A longer scope
in a breeze than in a calm, is of course necessary ; mats
should be placed in the hawse-holes, the palls of the capstan all down, and bars swifted.

In a tideway, or in a breeze, the steamer first anchors
ahead, and takes in and secures hawsers ; then the ship
weighs, lastly, the steamer.

Should the breeze freshen and the sea get up, direct
the steamer to veer a breaker astern, which hook and take
in, that, in the event of a hawser parting, there may be no
delay in hauling on board another.

When towing alongside, fore-and-aft springs should be
passed in addition to the bow and quarter lashings; one

279

hawser going from the after part of the ship to the fore part of the steamer, and the other reversedly.

412. ROUNDING THE HORN IN THE WINTER MONTHS.—Bend a new suit of sails; reeve new braces and tacks and sheets if necessary; send topmast studding-sail booms on deck; caulk the ports in; fit the second reef of the courses; reeve the topsail bunt-lines double, through a thimble seized into the foot, the standing part taken abaft the sail to the yard; fit leechlines to the topsails; secure the boom-boats well; top the quarter boats up, and secure them; get stern boat inboard; unbend cables, fit standing preventer braces and trice them up to the quarters of the yards when not in use; seize strops to the parrals of topsail yards, to hook the rolling-tackles to, and, when all finished, you will be tolerably snug.

413. CLUBHAULING.—When a ship, working off a lee shore, has not room to wear, and is unable to tack, in consequence of the heavy sea, her only resource, in the event of not anchoring, is in clubhauling.

A hawser is passed out of the lee quarter port and secured to the ring of the lee anchor, the helm put down, and the anchor let go and veered on; the cable is then unshackled ready for slipping, and slipped when the ship cants the right way. When all safe, cut the hawser, or let it go, buoyed, if you intend at any time to return to recover the anchor.

414. GROUNDED.—Clear away kedge, or stream anchor, according to circumstances, and get ready for laying it out

at once, whether you are likely to do without it or not. Heave all aback, watch the lead, to see if she goes astern; and, if on a sandy or muddy bottom, let every man take a shot in his hands, and sally together from side to side: by which means she may work herself loose.   If of no avail, shove off with the anchor; if necessary, start your water; but should the wind be on shore, heave a good strain on the hawser or cable before doing so.   If aground forward, and there is deep water astern, run the guns aft, and *vice versâ.*

415. WITH A RAPIDLY FALLING TIDE.—If unable to move the ship, you must prepare to shore her up, to prevent her falling over on her broadside; and therefore, supposing that on the port side the water is shoalest, give her a list over to port by running the starboard guns in, passing the shot over, &c.   By means of the fore and main yards and stays, get the spare fore and main topmasts over the port side, with their heels weighted with shot to sink them; bend fore-and-aft guys to the heels to place them, and let their heads take underneath the fore and main chains. As soon as she begins to settle down the right way, run the port guns in, close the ports, secure everything in its place, and send top-gallant masts on deck.   In the mean time, lay the stream and kedge out on the starboard side, abreast of the fore and mainmasts, lead the hawsers in there, and heave well taut, for the purpose of steadying the ship and relieving the shores.

Be careful not to list her over more than is sufficient to prevent her falling over to starboard, for the shores are

281

only intended to keep her upright; and not to support her weight, which must rest upon her keel and bottom.

416. SHIP FALLS OVER AND FILLS.—This happened to the "Samarang," 26, which ship was eleven days immersed in the Sarawak river, under the circumstances stated; and the following description of the means adopted to raise her is derived from Sir Edward Belcher's "Voyage of the Samarang."

The crew and stores were landed as soon as possible, the ship cleared of her top-hamper, and before the next spring tide the following preparations were made:—

Three upright spars, *a, a, a,* were placed respectively abaft the fore chains, between them and the gangway, and on the fore side of the main chains—on the starboard side. The heads of the two latter were crossed; and between them and the foremost one, a spar, *b,* was lashed, to keep them steady in their places.

To the heads of these heavy purchases were attached, with the lower blocks lashed to the bights of the breeching hawser, passed through the main-deck ports, and over the skid beams.

From the fore and main mast-heads, on the port side, tackles were taken to a cable ashore, which was secured to the trunks of trees.

On the starboard side, a powerful raft was constructed, of spars and water-casks, and across it were laid two trees, *c, c,* seventy feet in length ; their heels being lashed and cleated to the foremost and after skid-beams on the port side ; and to the ends of these outriggers, which were

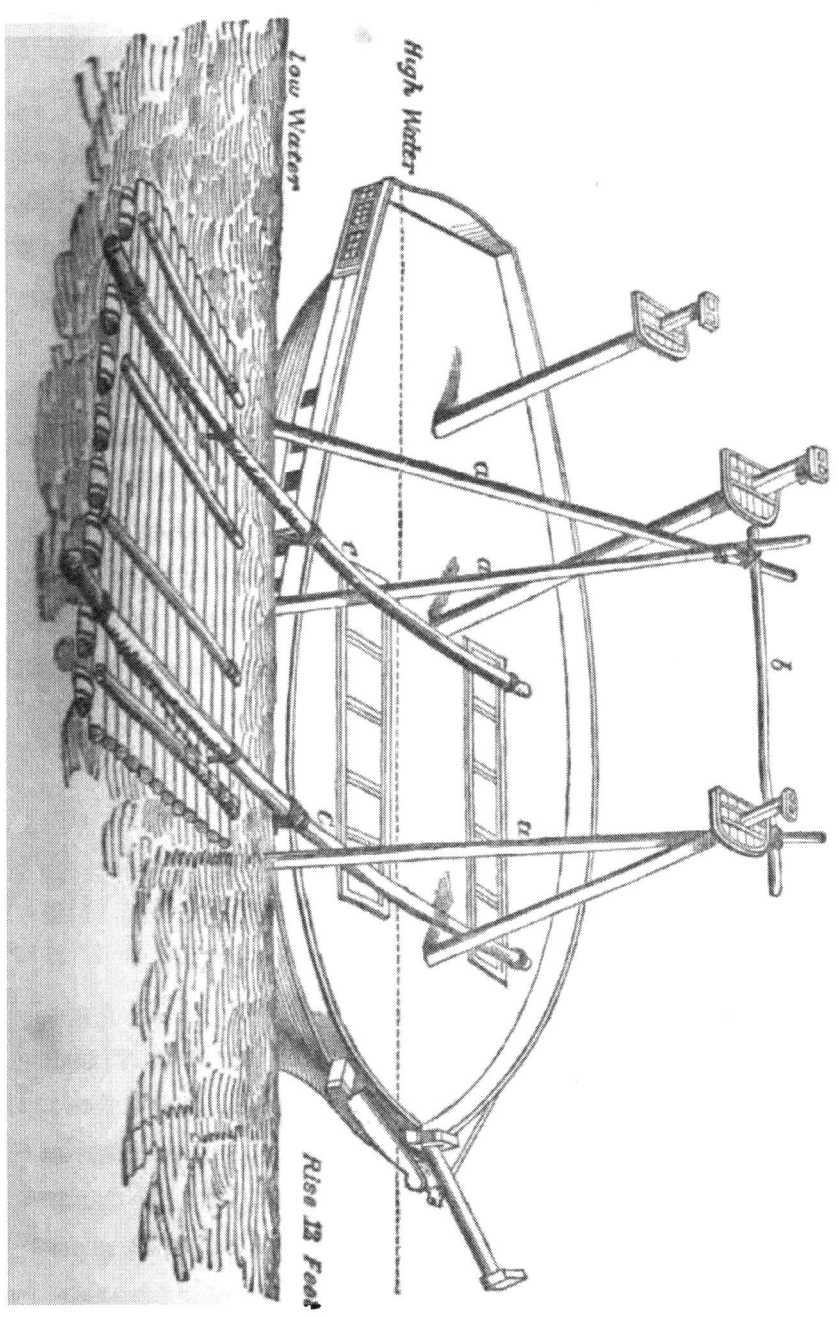

lashed close down at low water, purchases were attached from the heads of the shores, to act in conjunction with the power of the raft.

These arrangements proved entirely successful. As the tide rose, on the day the attempt was made, the ship gradually assumed an upright position, and, being hove off to her anchor, was shifted to a safer berth.—July, 1843.

417. CARRYING ON.—The resistance by which a moving body is opposed, in passing through wind and water, varies as the square of its velocity; and since the power to be exerted depends on the product of the resistance and the velocity, the power varies as the cube of the velocity. Hence, to ascertain the alteration in the rate of sailing which will be produced by increase or diminution of sail, say—

As the area of sail, then set,
Is to the area of canvas about to be set;
So is the cube of the speed, then shown,
To the cube of the speed to be produced.

And, in the present instance, the speed will be found to be only accelerated ·8 of a knot an hour.

If, then, so large an amount of sail as sixteen hundred yards, equal in this case to the main topsail and fore and main top-gallant-sails, prodnce so small a result; how little except in emergencies, will a smaller amount of canvas cracked upon a ship to the endangering of the spars, compensate for the trivial gain in speed obtained at such a hazard.

284

As a general rule, therefore, the moment a spar complains, in with the sail ; and thus, knowing the futility of pressing a ship, you will be relieved from those unpleasant moments of hesitation, when tempted to hold on against your half-formed convictions to the contrary, you stand, with anxious glance aloft at every lurch and bound, the image of hapless indecision.

418. UP SCREW.—Lifting screws are fitted in a banjo frame, and require to be slewed with the blades up and down before raising. Reeve the screw pendants and falls ; the pendants are rove by reeving lines, which are always kept rove through the sheeves in the banjo, and cross-piece, or sheer-head, as the case may be ; the standing part of the pendants are secured on deck with a round turn, half-hitched, and the ends seized down. Deaden the ship's way if necessary ; man the falls equally, walk away steadily, when high enough, put in the chocks, walk back the falls and unreeve the pendants.

To get the screw down, reverse this operation.

419. DIS-CONNECT THE SCREW.—This is done in the screw passage generally, by removing the connecting bolts ; if you are going fast, the speed should be reduced before dis-connecting.

Few screws will commence to revolve under a speed of four or five knots, it is therefore a good plan if on a wind to keep away a little after dis-connecting, and so start the screw.

In a feathering screw the blades can be turned so as to offer very little resistance to the water.

420. BACKING ASTERN—Will, if there is any wind, always bring the ship's stern up to it, and of course throw her head off the wind.

421. TWIN SCREWS—Are right and left-handed, so that when working they revolve in opposite ways, and do not affect the steerage; their advantages over the single screw are that the ship can be turned in a smaller space, though not quicker, also that you still have the power of steaming with one if the other should foul, or its engines break down. The disadvantages are, that from their position they are more liable to be fouled, and that under canvas they impede the ship more than a single screw. Ships fitted with twin screws, when cruising with a squadron, should never back or stop one screw without the other, and both screws should, when moving, make the same number of revolutions, not only for your own sake, but for the benefit of your next astern.

422. COMING IN FROM A LONG CRUISE.—A day or two before getting in, have the paint-work well scrubbed and cleaned, especially under the bows and chains; studding-sail booms sent on deck and lightly planed over, then sent up and the ends painted. Chafes on boats and lower booms touched up, lizards and ladders ready for going on, and, if in fine latitudes, ship's side painted as low down as possible, having first been well scrubbed. Masts fly-blocks, &c., scraped, and chafes on rigging blacked. The morn-

286

ing before going in, holystone decks, scrub windsails, boats' gear, and sails. Sling clean hammocks the evening before, if they at all require it. Accomodation-ladder holystoned and in order ; top-gallant masts fresh stayed, and squaring marks of lifts, braces, and buntlines looked to. As you near the port, down hanging-mats, off sea and up harbour gaskets, or, if used on the head of the sail, they will require blacking afresh ; single the tacks and sheets, off spans of topsail buntlines, see cables and anchors clear, buoy-rope ready and buoy blacked, chains to rights, and nothing hanging overboard. If coming to, under sail, on approaching the anchorage, turn the hands up, shorten sail, not forgetting to have a boat's crew warned to shove off and square yards directly you come to ; upper-deck sentries ready for going on, and stage party and stage ready with paint, &c., for going round directly the sails are furled. A harbour furl of the head sails, if they are not wanted ; then, if the topsails are sufficient to come to under, " Fore clew-garnets, top-gallant and royal clewlines, studding-sail downhauls ;" " Shorten sail." Let go the weather anchor when you reach your position, veer away and stand on till far enough, when clew up the topsails and let go the other anchor, giving her a sheer over the right way, so as not to cross the cables, and hold on till you heave in, to avoid fouling the anchor. Furl sails and moor ship.

In an open roadstead, moor with open hawse to the prevailing wind, if there is a predominating one ; otherwise, with open hawse to seaward. If in a tide-way, lay the anchors for the flood and ebb, up and down the river.

287

Let me here recommend the plan of squaring yards with flags, as it possesses so many advantages over the general method. It saves the lungs of the boatswain, allows him to go to any distance from the ship, is not liable to be misunderstood, is far more expeditious, and, in a close harbour, saves all the intolerable bawling that follows the close of any exercise with the fleet.

Three small flags are required, bent to short staves,—red, white, and blue. Red stands for main; white, fore; blue, mizen. Boatswain faces the ship, and holds the flag on the side the yard requires to be topped. For lower yards the flag is held horizontal; top sail yards, flagstaff perpendicular; top-gallant yards, he stands up in the boat, and holds the staff at an angle of 45°; royal yards, flagstaff at the same angle, but the arm lowered. Masts can be stayed in the same manner. The flag need not be kept up all the time the yard is being topped on; but it can be lowered directly the boatswain's mate, on the jib-boom end, hold his hand up to show that he understands it, and should be waved when the yard is square.

423. MANAGEMENT OF CHRONOMETERS.—We will suppose that you anchor at Hong Kong, November 30th, 1856, with the chronometers run down; that they are numbered 2103, 742, and 254, and that their hands point respectively to 8h. 17m. 10s., 3h. 57m. 43s., and 9h. 30m. 22s. You therefore wind up one, 2103, shortly before 4 p.m. (time of place), by which you will set it to approximate Greenwich time (Hong Kong being about 7h. 27m. east of Greenwich); but as it is considered injurious to

touch the hands of chronometers, and with many you are unable to get at the face to move them, you wait till it is 9h. 30m. by 2103, and then wind up 254; and, when nearly 4h. by these two, wind up the third, 742; thus, for the sake of convenience in computing their differences, bringing them all near to each other.

On the following morning land with one, 2103, and ascertain its error by A.M. sights, or equal altitudes (Inman, art. 253—260), taking several sets. Repeat this on the succeeding day; and, if these agree with the former, and no inaccuracies are detected, an interval of a week at a time may elapse between the subsequent observations for rate.

Prepare a "CHRONOMETER JOURNAL" according to the following form, in which you note down the comparisons taken every morning when you wind up, and by which you see how the watches are going with each other.

The error of 2103 from the 1st to the 21st is that found directly from sights; and the error of the other chronometers, in the adjoining columns, is obtained by applying the comparison; thus—

DECEMBER 1st.

m. s.		*m. s.*
2103......4 30 Slow of G.M.T.		2103......4 30 Slow of G.M.T.
Comp. ...0 21 Fast.		Comp. 21 0 Slow.
742 ..... 4 9 Slow of G.M.T.		254..... 25 30 Slow of G.M.T.

The daily rate on the 8th, 14th, and 21st, is found by dividing the difference between the error on those days,

Dec. 1856.	TIME BY		2103.−742.	TIME BY		2103.−254.	TIME BY		742.−254.	
	2103.	742.	Daily Difference.	2103.	254.	Daily Difference.	742.	254.		Daily Difference.
	h. m. s.	h. m. s.	sec.	h. m. s.	h. m. s.	sec.	h. m. s.	h. m. s.	m. s.	sec.
☽, 1 ...	12 16 0	12 16 21	21	12 16 20	11 55 20	21 0	12 17 0	11 55 38	21 22	—
♂, 2 ...	12 29 0	12 29 22	22	12 29 20	12 8 13	21 7	12 30 0	12 8 30	21 30	8
☿, 3 ...	12 4 0	12 4 23	23	12 4 20	11 43 5	21·15	12 5 0	11 43 22	21 38	8
♃, 4 ...	12 15 0	12 15 24	24	12 15 20	11 53 58	21 22	12 16 0	11 54 13	21 47	9
♀, 5 ...	—	—	—	—	—	—	—	—	—	—
♄, 6 ...	—	—	—	—	—	—	—	—	—	—

290

On the opposite page keep a Table of "RATES AND ERRORS" for bringing up the time daily, as under :—

Dec. 1856.	2103. Slow.	Daily Rate. Losing.	742. Slow.	Daily Rate. Gaining	254. Fast.	Daily Rate. Losing.	Hour of Winding.	REMARKS.
	m. s.	sec.	m. s.	sec.	m. s.	sec.		
1	4 30	—	4 9	—	25 30	—	8. A.M.	By sight at Kowloon Pt., Hong Kong. Lat. 22° 17' 6" N., Long. 114° 10' 12" E.
2	4 32	2·0	4 6	3·0	25 25	5·0	"	
8	4 47·5	2·5	3 46·6	3·2	24 52·4	4·7	"	
14	5 5·1	2·7	3 24·8	3·4	24 28·9	4·7	"	
21	5 24	2·7	2 59	3·5	23 56	4·7	"	
22	5 26·7	"	2 55·5	"	23 51·3	"	"	Sailed from Hong Kong.
23	5 29·4	"	2 52	"	23 46·6	"	"	
24	5 32·1	"	2 48·5	"	23 41·9	"	"	Exercised firing at a target.

and the error found on the 1st by the number of days in the interval; the error found on the 1st being used in each case, because the longer interval gives the better average.

After the 21st, when the last rate was obtained, the error is brought up by applying it daily; retaining it until you have an opportunity of correcting your rates again at a place whose position is fixed, unless, by scanning the daily differences, you are led to suppose that the rate of any watch is altering, or has jumped into a different rate, when you alter the rate accordingly.

When at sea, find once a week the Greenwich time by all three watches; and repeatedly do so, on approaching land, scrutinizing the longitude given by each. But, as you cannot practically catch them all at the same instant, without an observer to each, you find the time shown by each watch, at time of sights, by applying the comparisons; for example—

A.M. MARCH 2nd, 1857.

	h.	m.	s.	
2103............4	10	20		Time observed for sights.
	7		39·5	Error, fast.
	16	2	40·5	G.M.T. (1st).

742.

h.	m.	s.	
4	10	20	Time shewn by 2103.
	+	21	Comp. between 2103 [and 742.
4	10	41	742 at time of sights.
	7	41·2	Error, fast.
16	2	59·8	G.M.T.

254.

h.	m.	s.	
16	10	20	Time shown by 2103.
3	21	0	Comp. between 2133 [and 254.
12	49	20	Time shown by 254.
3	13	23·8	Error, slow.
16	2	43·8	Greenwich Time.

You would, therefore, use the mean of 2103 and 254, seeing that they differ but three-quarters of a mile, and would reject 742, which differs 4¾ miles from 2103, and four miles from 254, unless you had very strong ulterior reasons for relying upon it.

If you have only two chronometers, and you find, when bringing them up weekly, that the longitudes differ, take the mean, unless you have good reason to prefer one to the other.

In comparing more than three chronometers, select one for a standard, and compare each of the others with it, instead of with each other.

SECTION III.

ON GENERAL SERVICE.

424. CUTTING AWAY MASTS.—You first pass a hawser outside the lanyards of the rigging on the side you intend the masts to fall over. If the port side, cut away the mast on the starboard side, as high as you can, for the stumps will be of service in securing your jury-masts; and, when you have weakened it sufficiently, cut away all but a pair of shrouds on each side—guided by circumstances; then get out of the way and cut away the remaining starboard rigging, keeping fast the stays till the mast has fallen, when you free them immediately, and cut the port pair of shrouds adrift, which you will be able to get at, by their being kept up by the hawser.

If all three masts are to go, commence with the mizen-mast, and work forward; although, when at anchor, it is generally not advisable to cut the mizen mast away, as it is of great service in keeping the ship steady, head to wind.

425. ANCHORING WITH GUNS.—You have still your guns left, and, having hauled in each cable as it parted, shackle them altogether, point the end out and haul it aft, outside, by a hawser passed forward. When aft, lash the end with a good cross-lashing to the muzzle of the after-most of the guns you intend to use, and also to the neck-ring, and at the same time get on lashing the remainder in the same manner, allowing a drift of cable between each, equal to the depth of water, in order that the first gun going down may not tear the others out of the ports : and, commencing aft, heave them overboard without loss of time.

Should you have the good fortune to weigh them again, hook on the cat as they come up to the bows, and get them in through the bow port, if it will admit of its being done. By having a good drift between each, you will only have the weight of one at a time to heave up.

Should the guns not bring her up, you may be able to select the spot to go on shore on, by getting up a short pair of sheers, setting a staysail on them, and slipping the cables.

To heave a Gun overboard.—Cast loose, lay the gun horizontal, and ease her out, so that the muzzle may be just clear of the inside of the port. Hook two side-tackles to the housing bolts, and to a short strop under the neck, haul them well taut and keep them manned. Hook a train-tackle to each rear loop, and to the train-tackle bolt in the deck, haul taut and attend them. Unreeve the breeching, place a capstan bar on the steps of the carriage on each side, with the small ends under the gun, ready to elevate. When ready, throw back the cap-squares, look out for the roll, and at the order "Heave and haul," haul upon the side-tackles, heave on the capstan bars, and ease the carriage out by the train-tackles, the port being hauled up at the same time. In ironclad ships none but upper deck guns could be thrown overboard through the ports, owing to the small size of the latter.

In the event of a ship getting ashore, and having to heave her guns overboard to lighten her, they should be slung by a single part of the breeching, for weighing; the clinch secured to the button, and then lashed out to the muzzle; using a breast-frapping for a buoy-rope and a truck for the buoy.

The reviser at first fully intended to erase the foregoing answer, but on second thought determined to retain it, as it may perhaps occur, that a ship should be obliged to use guns in place of anchors; though under the circumstances detailed he would feel more inclined to select the softest spot on the beach.

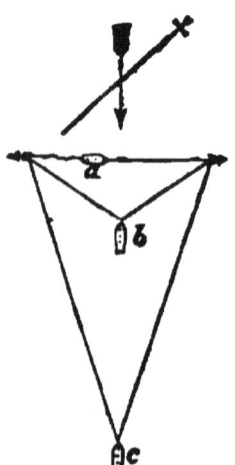

426. MOORING WITH OPEN HAWSE TO ANY BEARING.—Drop the anchors N.E. and S.W. of each other—at right angles to the prevailing wind; and, as the usual rule for veering cable is, to three times the depth of water, moor with about three shackles on each anchor, as at *a*, where she is shown lying with the wind from the N.E. When it shifts to the N.W. she will tauten both cables, and if not moored too taut, will drop down to *b*, in which position she will ride with safety in all ordinary weather. If the wind increases to a gale, you veer to *c*, with eight or nine shackles on each, previously dropping a third anchor if you think you will require it.

427. ANCHORING WITH A SPRING ON YOUR CABLE.— Supposing the wind to be directly on shore, and you wish, on coming to, to bring your port broadside to bear upon it: you pass a hawser or stream-chain from the starboard quarter, in through the starboard hawse-hole: run a range of cable up before the bitts, and shackle or bend the stream or hawser to it, which on the anchor being let go and veered on, you work with a deck-tackle, and so you will be able to spring your ship to a nicety, providing there is no great shift of wind. Should this be an undesirable contingency, you must, of course, anchor by the stern, with kedge, stream, or sheet anchors, according to the strength of the wind, and the importance of the case. If there is no immediate hurry, bend the spring after the anchor is let go.

428. ON COMING TO WITH A WEATHER TIDE.— Look out and give her a good sheer, to avoid being driven back over your anchor.

429. AT THE ORDER "STAND CLEAR OF THE CABLE,"— Besides doing so, and standing by the compressor-tackle ready to bowse to, the chocks of the tumbler should be taken out, but the pins kept in till the order—"Let go the anchor," when they are taken out; but the lever is kept back, by hand, till the boatswain gives the word—"One, two, three—let go," at the last sound of which the anchor is freed by a rouse on the jigger.

430. PARTS OF AN ANCHOR.— In the Admiralty anchor, here shown, the stock is in two pieces, which are not

297

brought close together, in order that they may spring against the hoops, and keep them taut.

In Rodger's anchor, the palm is smaller; and the stock which is solid, rests on a shoulder on the shank, and is keyed on the top by a bolt passing through the end of the shank.

a. Shackle, or
    Ring.

b. Stock.

c. Shank.

d. Crown.

e. Arm.

f. Pea
g. Palm. } Fluke.

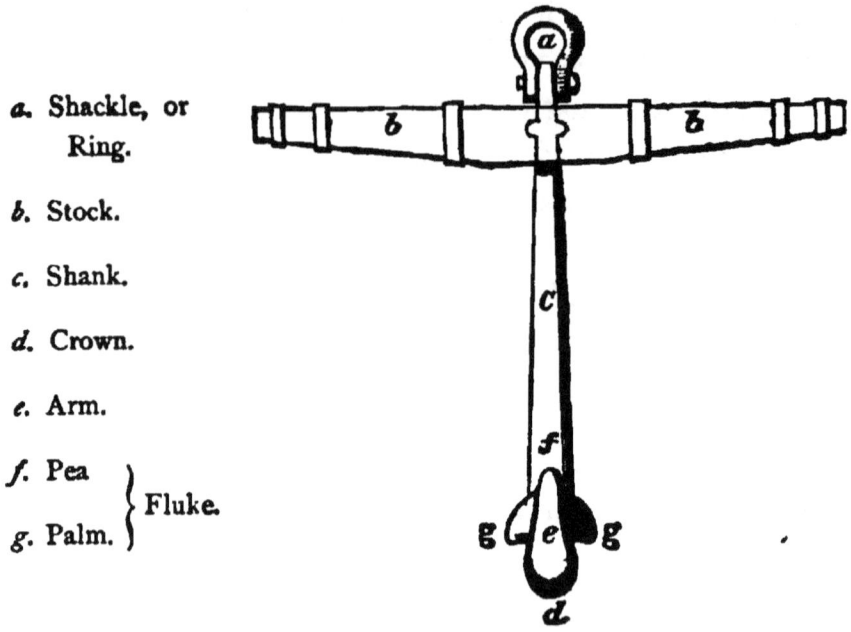

431. BACKING AND FILLING, AND DREDGING.—When, with a foul wind, but with the tide in your favour, you are in a river that is too narrow to admit of the ship beating down, "backing and filling" must be resorted to. If only at one or two points the river contracts so as to render this necessary, you may handle her by hauling the main-sail up, taking the spanker in, and bracing the head yards a-box, as you approach the narrows; squaring them if she falls round off—bracing the after-yards aback, if

298

requisite, filling if you wish to forge across the river, or bracing aback, when necessary to near the other bank.

In some rivers, however, as that, for instance, on which Shanghai is situated, you are compelled to keep in mid-channel from the anchorage to the embouchure, and therefore should weigh under as small sail, only, as is sufficient to keep her under control. Under ordinary circumstances, the jib and main topsail are the handiest sail to work under, though you would increase it if the wind fell light. Under this, back and fill, ease off and haul aft, as requisite.

In the event of the wind failing entirely,

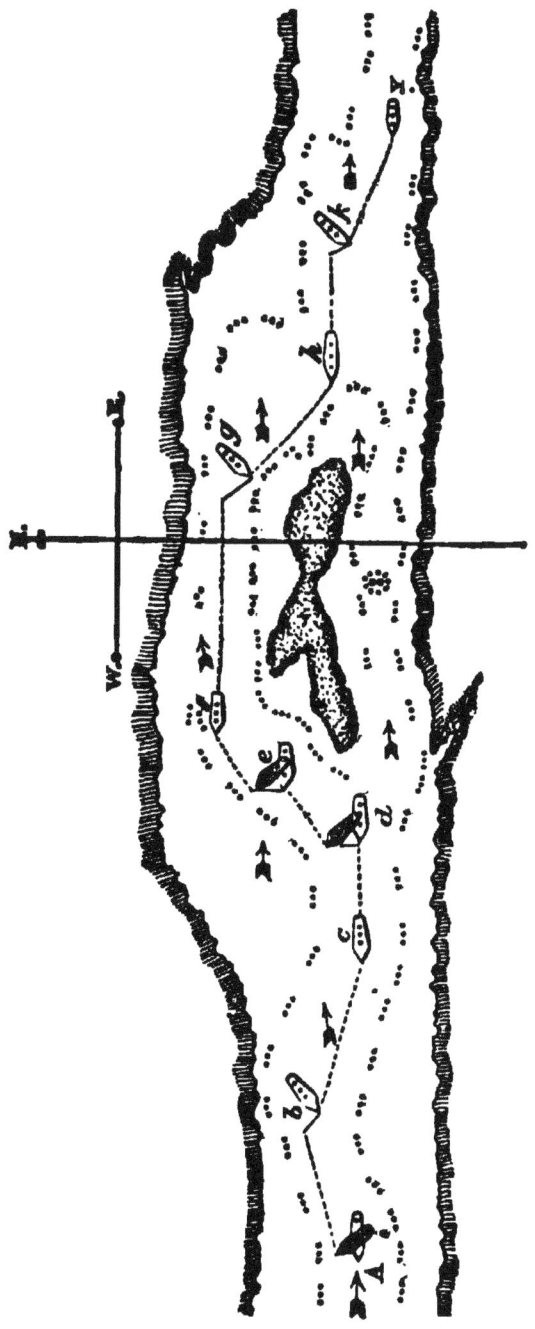

U

the ship, necessarily would drift at the mercy of the current, unless some other aid than that of sail were called into play, to enable you to keep her in the fairway and to avoid the shoals and dangers in the route; and through the instrumentality of the anchor it is that this is effected by what is termed "dredging." In narrow waters no manœuvre requires so nice an exercise of judgment, and under no circumstances are a quick eye and a clear head more requisite. While dropping down, the anchor is kept hanging by the slip, just clear of the bottom, and it is let go, and a fathom or two veered according to the strength of the tide, when it becomes necessary to sheer over to one bank or the other. The capstan is kept manned; and, as soon as the anchor is dropped, the cable is brought to again, ready for tripping the moment she is sheered over into the position required.

To illustrate this, let us suppose that a ship at A wishes to drop down to Y; that the three-fathom mark, represented by the dotted line, is less than her draught of water; that there is a dangerous bank midway; and that the arrows denote the direction of the tide.

On heaving up and down at A, the helm is put a-port and she is sheered over in the position of the shaded figure; the anchor is tripped, and with her head the same way— the helm being kept over while heaving up—she is dropped down to *b*. Here it becomes necessary to sheer her over to the south bank ; the anchor therefore is let go, the helm put a-starboard, and she is sheered over to *c*, thence allowed to drop down to *d*. From this position, by successive

300

stages, she is sheered by the helm right across the stream, and, on arriving at *f*, proceeds as at first, till she reaches her destination.

432. A NUN BUOY.—Iron nun buoys are now supplied fitted with a ring and swivel at either end, to which the buoy rope is bent, with a sheet bend, and the end scized. There are two other ways of slinging it. The first commences by placing a strop or grummet round the buoy, on

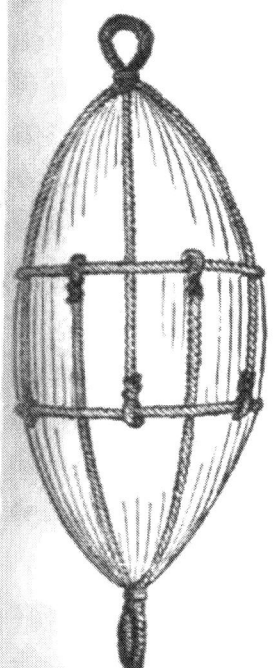
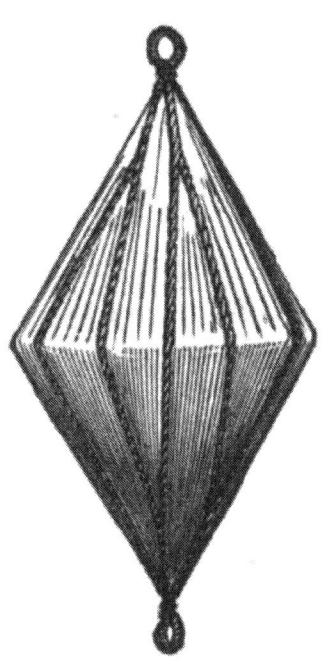

each side of the centre; next, middling two pieces of rope, laying the bights on the top, and the ends down the buoy under the strop on their own end, and spliced round the strop on the opposite end; then, with two other pieces of rope, the same thing is done on the other end, the strop roused taut up by a jigger hooked to the bights of the slings, and a thimble seized into each end, which tautens the whole. The legs and strops are served, and the eyes hitched over.

In the second place, four pieces of rope are middled, and the bights of two laid over each end, forming the same number of legs as in the first; but no strops are used. Each leg of one end is spliced into the next right-hand leg of the other end; scores are cut in the buoy for their reception, and a seizing round the eye tautens them up.

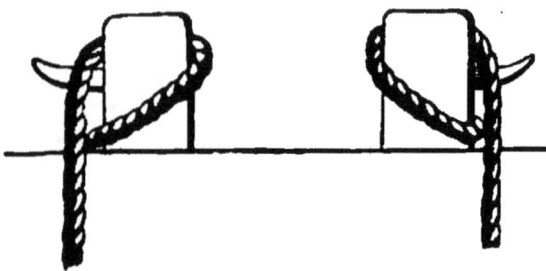

433. BITTING CABLES. — Both chain and hemp cables are bitted the same way. Facing forward, as in the cut, the starboard cable is bitted with the sun, and the port against it; the cable from the hawse-holes leading under the cross-piece or battledore, on the outside of the bitts, and the bight thrown over the bitt-head. A bitting-tackle is used to rouse the bight up; the pendant rove through a swivel-gin over the bitts.

434. PASSING NIPPERS.—The *rationale* of passing a nipper rests upon the necessity for bringing the messenger to the cable, as you cannot bring the cable to the

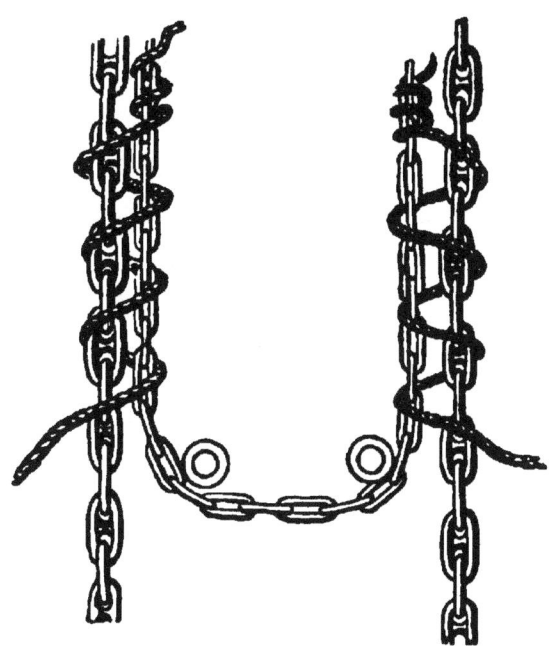

messenger, and at the same time rousing the messenger up to prevent its getting underneath the cable. Two or three turns are first taken round the messenger by a hand inside; the coil is then passed over the cable to the hands outside, who, facing aft, pass it round, messenger and cable, as the latter comes in; on the port side with the sun, and on the starboard side against it, rousing each turn taut as it is passed. The end is then dogged round the cable, and twisted up with the end of the next nipper; both ends are held on by a hand who walks aft with them, and, when far enough aft, the nipper is started and passed forward again.

435. HEAVING THROUGH ALL.—Strew well with sand, pass the turns thick, and, if that is not sufficient, take here and there a *round turn* round the messenger, and another round the cable, passing racking turns between.

When obliged to use a deck-tackle to break out, heave on the capstan and haul on the tackle *together*, giving the time by a *slow* pipe. It is amazing the difference that this makes.

303

436. A DECK TACKLE—Consists of a runner and long tackle, separately fitted, the double block of the tackle hooks to the runner, the single block and the other end of the runner are secured abaft. The block of the runner is secured to the cable ; the tackle may be used without the runner. Small vessels not fitted with capstans usually have the double block of the tackle fitted with a claw to hook over a link of a chain.

437. BRING TO, PATENT CAPSTAN.—Brown's patent capstans are now in general use, and the days of messengers

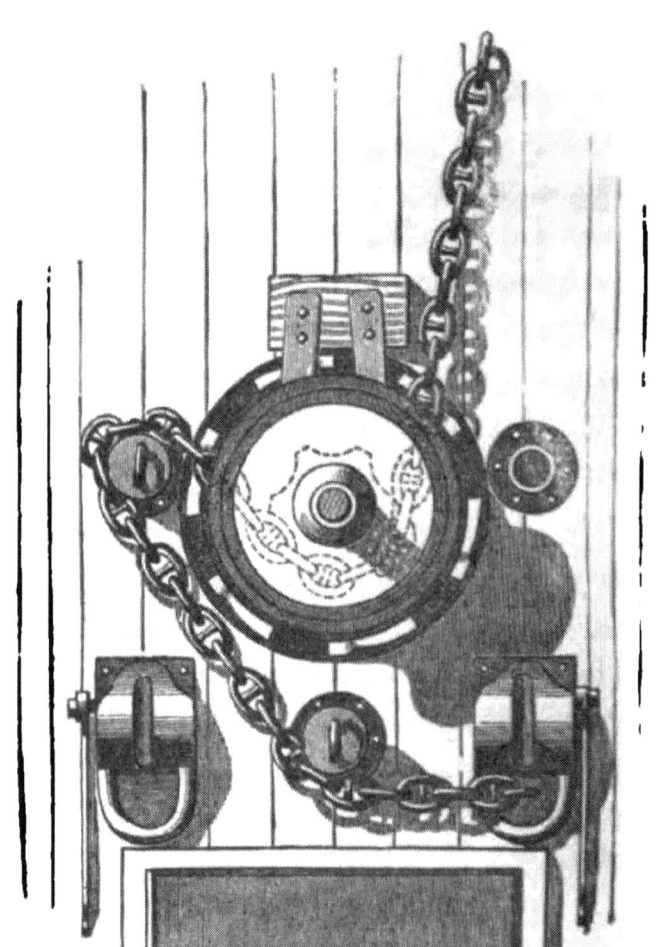

and nippers, are fast coming to an end. These capstans are fitted with sprocket wheels, corresponding to the links of the cable, each link in turn binding in its corresponding indentation.

To *bring to*, put the slip on, unbit, and haul the bight of the cable, round abaft the capstan, drop in the roller, and lift the chain into the sprocket wheel; the slack chain is

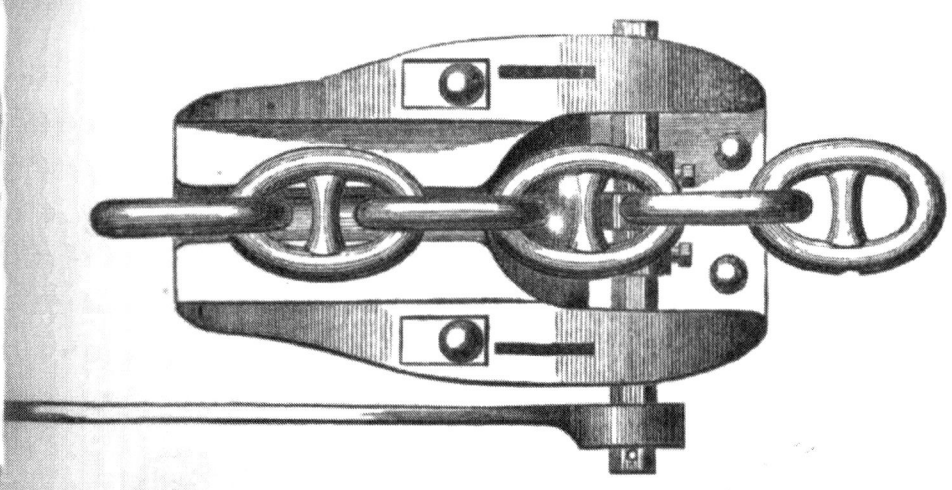

hauled clear of the capstan with iron chain hooks. Ships fitted with these capstans, also have a controller, into which the links of the cable successively sink as you heave in, and which of course relieves the capstan of much strain, the cable is thrown in or out of the controller by a lever at the side.

305

438. NUMBER OF SWIVELS IN A CABLE.—One in every other length.

439. A LENGTH OF CHAIN CABLE—Is 12 ½ fathoms. They are marked inboard from the shackle, and sometimes on both sides, with a piece of wire or tin round the stay-pin of the link, a link for every shackle ; the one next the shackle without a stay-pin not being reckoned. At the tenth shackle, when the cable is of that length, you commence again (though a cable, as supplied, is only of eight lengths).

440. STAY-PINS.—Without them, the cable would become full of kinks ; and, were they removed, the links would also collapse.

441. A GANGER—Consists of one or more lengths of chain, shackled to the sheet anchor and brought into the hawse holes, or just outside, and renders the operation of bending or unbending sheet cable much easier.

442. ADVANTAGE OF HEMP CABLES.—The one great advantage is, that they allow an anchor to be laid out farther from the ship by boats, being much lighter than chain, but in other ways they are more difficult to handle than chain cables.

443. STOWAGE OF HEMP CABLES.—Coiled with the sun ; the starboard cable in the port tier, and the port cable in the starboard tier. When both ends are fitted with an Elliott's eye, the end is generally attached, by a

306

slip-shackle, to a chain strop round an orlop-deck beam. When not fitted with an eye, chain tails are shackled to the strop, and spliced into the cable.

444. STOPPERING HEMP CABLES.—In addition to the deck-stoppers used for chain cables, bitt, ring, and hatch-way stoppers are required.

A bitt-stopper is a stout piece of rope, middled, with an eye which goes over the bitt-head above the cable, made by seizing both parts together. The ends are selvageed, brought aft and under the cross-piece, and dogged round the cable before the bitts.

A ring-stopper is a piece of rope middled, with the ends coach-whipped or selvageed. The bight is laid over the cable abaft the ring; the ends passed through the ring and dogged round the cable.

A hatchway-stopper is a piece of stout rope middled, and the ends coachwhipped. The bight is laid over the cable inside the hatchway, and the ends are passed through a hole in each side of the corner and dogged round the cable outside; so that, the greater the strain on the cable, the harder the stopper will jamb.

445. HEMP MESSENGER.—The ends are fitted with long lashing eyes, with the splice grafted over; but they are not brought close up to each other, as they would not lie fair round the capstan, the crown of the eyes, when brought together forming so great a rise: a drift of two or three feet is, therefore, allowed between them. Four turns are

taken round the capstan, the heaving-in part being the lowermost. When the opposite cable is to be brought to, the ends must be unlashed and passed the contrary way, which may be done, without heaving the turns off, by slacking them round the capstan, and dipping the aftermost end through; the parts then placed fair, and the ends relashed. Hands must be stationed to haul back on the upper part as it comes round the capstan.

446. AFTER UNBITTING—You lift the cable up on the cross-piece, or battledore, on which the messenger should be already placed for facility in passing the nippers.

447. HEMP CABLES—Are stoppered below, round an orlop-deck beam, for bringing up at a short or long service, according to whichever it is intended to ride at; the bight, round which the lashings are passed being left outside so as to be easily got at. If intended to veer to the latter, the first must be previously taken off, and, when a longer scope is required, one abaft should be passed before the second is slacked off.

448. PREPARING FOR LETTING GO.—Run up a range of cable, before the bitts, sufficient for the depth of water; and, according to the weather, get a long range up abaft. Stand by to clear away in the tiers, lead the hook-ropes along, see stoppers attended, and a good kackling on where required in bringing up.

449. THAT END OF A CABLE—Is shacked to the anchor, which brings the bolt of the shackles and the *cup of*

the swivels aft;—otherwise, they would catch the bitts, &c., in running out.

450. BEFORE SURGING—The cable should always be bitted; and also stoppered if the cat-fall is old.

451. PUTTING A SWIVEL ON.— Veer, or heave in on the riding-cable, if necessary, in order to bring the shackle, where you intend to put the swivel on, before the bitts.   On slip before-all, unshackle and shackle the ends to an upper and lower link.   Stopper the other cable inboard, or hang it by the small slip attached to a length of stream chain, unshackle, haul each end in alongside the riding-cable by a small hawser passed round the cut-water,—the

bight being kept up by a bull-rope from the bowsprit, and shackle the ends to the remaining links of the swivel.   Off stoppers of both cables (that of the riding-cable last), veer the swivel out clear of the hawse-hole, haul in the *slack* of the other cable, and make all fast.   Ride, in this way, by one cable inboard, for, when the swivel is hove up amidships, the copper corrodes the cable, and the cable chafes the copper.   In fine weather, as soon as the swivel is put on the riding-cable, it may, if you prefer it, be eased out, and the other cable shackled in a boat under the bows.

Though it is customary to shackle both inboard ends to the swivel, the propriety of doing so is not quite clear, for should it come on to blow, and you find it necessary to veer, you pay overboard the second cable without deriving any advantage from it whatever.

452. TAKING IT OFF.—Bring to the riding-cable (say B.B.), stick out S.B—hauled out clear of the cutwater by a bull-rope from the bowsprit, and heave swivel and all parts in through the starboard hawse-hole. It is immaterial which cable you clear first ; but, supposing it to be S.B., put the starboard slip on the outer part of the port cable, unshackle from the swivel, shackle both ends together, off slip, and let run. Then put the slip on B.B. before the swivel, unshackle, and shackle the ends again, bowse to the compressor, and off stopper.

If you think it undesirable to heave in, you can unshackle it in a boat out-board. Riding, therefore, as before by B.B., and with the swivel hove up on the starboard side, pass the small slip attached to a length of stream chain, out of the spare hawse-hole, and put it on the port cable below the swivel; heave taut on it, unshackle, shackle the ends, and off slip. Proceed in the same manner with the riding-cable, hanging the swivel with a hawser to rouse it in by.

453. THE CUP OF THE SWIVEL—Should be kept up, and tallow put into it occasionally.

310

454. MOORING WITH A SWIVEL ON.—You render it impossible, by any amount of heaving, to do as you intend, for you have made no allowance for the depth of water. If the cables were laid taut along the ground in a direct line, the fourth shackle of each, under the circumstances stated, could of course be joined—on the bottom; but, when attached to the bows of a ship, the difference between the base and the other two sides of the triangle is the measure of the increase of cable required to unite them. In this case, therefore, you would have to veer another shackle on one cable, mooring with five on one and four on the other; or, else, weigh the second again, and drop it closer to the first.

By running out seven shackles in the first instance, before dropping the second anchor, then veering four, and heaving in three, you would have been moderately taut moored. The time of tide is also to be considered (at Portsmouth, the rise and fall of spring tides; being twelve feet).

455. UNMOORING, WITH A SWIVEL ON.—If the cables are up and down, there may be a cross in them below water; and, therefore, if you have nothing to guide you, you will likely enough shackle the ends of different cables together; but, by remembering which legs of the swivel the cables were shackled to when you put the former on, you cannot misplace them. For instance, if the long legs were both on one side, and the B.B. shackled to them, you at once know which is the starboard cable. If either of the cables is taut, of course there is no difficulty.

311

456. TWO CABLES WEAKER THAN ONE.—In reference
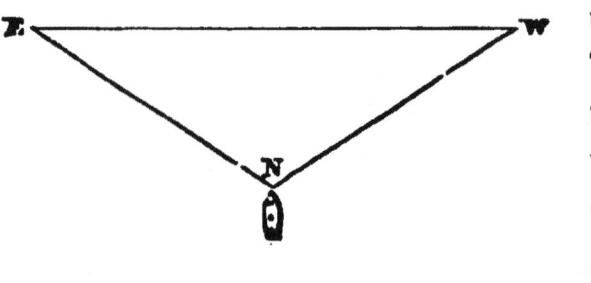
to this subject,
Tinmouth has
the following
valuable remarks
on the nature and
properties of a
span :—

" Supposing a ship to be moored between two anchors
laid out east and west, with the wind blowing at
right angles to that line, I have calculated that supposing a ship could be maintained in a position in which
the angle EWN is 5°, the whole amount of support which
the two cables would give to the ship is $\frac{17\cdot4}{100}$ parts, or
about one-sixth the strength of one cable,

At the angle of 10° it would amount to $\frac{34\cdot7}{100}$ parts.

15°   „   „ $\frac{51\cdot7}{100}$ „

20°   „   „ $\frac{68\cdot4}{100}$ „

25°   „   „ $\frac{84\cdot5}{100}$ „

30°   „   „   the strength of

one cable.

" Many experiments have been made with pieces of
rope, of various sizes, to determine this question, and in

312

every case it has been clearly proved, that when a span is so placed as to have a less angle than thirty degrees, the strength of the two parts of rope or chain, of which it is composed, is less than the strength which one such part would have if placed in a direct line with the strain.

" In order to prevent the numerous, and in some cases fatal accidents which occur in the use of a span, it is necessary to investigate the peculiar character of a rope in this position, that by the evidence of established mechanical laws the reader may be enabled to understand why the small force of a few pounds, applied to a rope or chain when in use at a flat obtuse angle, shall produce the astonishing strain of eighteen hundred per cent. upon it.

" Let a rope be extended from A to B with any degree of tension ; if a force, however small, be applied at any part of the rope, in any direction out of the line AB, it will cause a deflection, increase the tension on the rope.

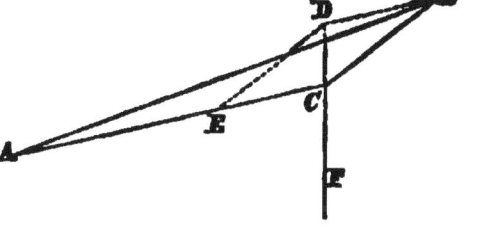

" Let the force F be applied at C in the direction D C F, and let the rope take the position A C B. Let any length, C D, represent the force F; draw D B parrallel to A C, and D E parallel to C B; then C B will represent the tension produced by F on the part C B of the rope, and C E that produced on the other part of the rope A C.

313

$$EC = F \times \frac{\text{sine } DCB}{\text{sine } ACB}; \text{ and } CB = F \times \frac{\text{sine } DCA}{\text{sine } ACB}$$

"Suppose F be taken = 10 lbs. ; the angle A C B = 175° ; and D C B = 50° ; then the angle D C A will = 125°, and E C, or the tension on the part A C of the rope = 10 lbs. $\times \dfrac{\text{sine } 50°}{\text{sine } 175°} = 87\cdot8$ lbs.   C B, or the tension on the part B C of the rope = 10 lbs. $\times \dfrac{\text{sine } 125°}{\text{sine } 175°} = 93\cdot9$ lbs.

" Hence, the greater the obtuse angle A C B, the greater the tension on the part A C, or C B, or on both parts, according to the direction of the force applied.

" If the force F, and the angle A C B, be supposed to be constant, the effect of varying the direction of the force may be seen.

" Thus, if D C F, the direction of the force, bisects the angle A C B, the tension of A C is equal to that of C B; and the tension on the whole rope A C B is a maximum.

" Again, if D C F be perpendicular to the part A C of the rope, the maximum tension is produced on the other part C B; and if D C F be perpendicular to C B, the maximum tension is produced on the part A C of the rope.

" It will be seen by this example that the small force of 10 lbs. applied to this span produces an effect of 87·8 lbs. upon one part of the rope, and 93·9 lbs. upon the other part; the whole effect being 181·7 lbs., that is, upwards of eighteen times the force applied. A still greater effect might be produced by a more obtuse angle."

314

457. KEEPING A CLEAR HAWSE IN A TIDEWAY.—We will suppose the river to run north and south, on which bearing the anchors are laid out; and that you are riding by the B.B. with the ebb and wind from the northward. On the tide turning, you will, therefore, bring a cross in your hawse if you swing with her stern to the westward. To avoid this, set the spanker and haul the boom over on the port quarter; put the helm a-port when the flood begins to make, and take the spanker in when the wind is brought on the starboard quarter.

Before the ebb makes again, you must be prepared to cant her back to the eastward, now riding by the S.B., with the wind still from the northward; therefore, set the spanker, ease the boom over on the port quarter, and attend to the helm.

In the first case, riding to the ebb by the B.B., should the wind shift to the eastward, you cannot avoid canting to the westward, and, on being tide-rode, you will ride with a cross in your hawse; but this will be taken out on the flood making, should the wind remain the same.

The head sails will assist in canting, or at any rate, will prevent her swinging back again when the spanker is of no further use—the contrary sheets to that of the boom being hauled aft. But it must be borne in mind that the great canting power is the spanker, the boom being hauled right over on the weather quarter; and, if this will not cant her, you must be moored too taut.

458. CLEARING HAWSE.—Bring the small slip on a length of stream chain, out through the spare hawse-hole,

and put it on the dipping-cable (being the one she is not riding by), below the turns.   If they are not above water, you must heave in on the riding-cable, and bring them up; and, if they still run below water, you must lash the cables together as far down as possible, clear what are above the lashing, heave up to it, and put the small slip on if you can, but if not, lash again, and, lest the lashing should slip after you have unshackled the end, put a bolt through the links of both cables and pass the lashing round it. Bowse taut the small slip and belay it; put the slip-stopper on, and unshackle the cable at the nearest shackle abaft the slip, which, on mooring, should always be veered before the bitts, in anticipation of clearing hawse.   Pass the bow-line (which is a small hawser rove through a block on the bowsprit, and leading in on the forecastle) through the hawse-hole, and bend it to the end of the cable; then bend a stouter hawser to the same end, knock off the slip, and haul out on the bowline.   When outside the hawse-hole, unbend the hawser and dip it round the riding-cable the contrary way to the turns, the bight of the cable hanging by the bowline.   Haul the cable taut in from the small slip, by the hawser, unbend the bowline, and the turn comes out.   If there are any more, bend the bowline, and repeat the operation.   When finished, put on the slip, un-bend the hawsers, and shackle the cable, take off the small slip and finally the slip-stopper.

459. KEEPING A CLEAR ANCHOR IN A TIDEWAY.—In the by-gone days of hempen-cables, owing to the injury done to them when lying on a hard bottom, and the

facility with which, on account of their buoyancy, they fouled the anchor, tending it properly became a matter of serious importance; blunders were considered very discreditable; and the management of the ship at turn of tide required close attention and considerable experience. But now, thanks to chain cables, a ship with a long scope of cable out, may lie for months in a roadstead without approaching her anchor, and in a tideway, as mooring is not the tedious operation of former times, and a foul hawse can be cleared in one-tenth the time, ships seldom remain for any lengthened period at single anchor. However, when it is of importance to keep it clear, and an anchor-watch is kept for the express purpose of preventing a foul anchor, there can be no reason why greater attention should not be paid to it than is generally the case; all that is requisite being a knowledge of the effect of the stream on the rudder, and of the head and after sails on the ship.

Supposing a ship to be riding by her S.B., with the ebb tide and wind from the northward, she requires, when the tide turns, to be sheered so that the bight of the cable may not fall over her anchor, which would be the case were she left to herself to drift up with the flood.

Before slack water, therefore, put the helm a-port, for, as a ship in a strong tide ought to lie with a slight sheer to keep her steady, you will not require to describe so great a circuit, by canting with her head to the eastward, as you would if you went round the other way. Hoist the jib or staysail, according to the force of the wind, and haul the port sheets aft, or to windward. When the flood makes, shift the helm, and let draw and haul aft the head sheets as soon as they will take, which will set her ahead with a taut cable. As soon as it is brought at right angles to the wind, the tide, acting on her lee broadside, will drive her over, or to windward of her cable, when the head sails become of no further use, and are hauled down : the helm is kept a-starboard, to check her, and to keep her with her head sheered to the eastward directly the cable brings her up ; in which positions she will lie till the tide again turns.

When the tide turns, the wind remaining the same, set the jib and spanker and sail her round her anchor, head to the eastward, taking them in when they cease to be of service, and you will lie as before to the ebb tide, with the helm a spoke or two a-port.

Let the wind now shift to the westward ; you must therefore, before the tide ceases, shift the helm a-starboard, and, as the tide slackens, she will come head to wind ; then hoist the jib with the starboard sheet aft, or to windward, and, as the flood makes, her stern will cant, and, dropping round to the northward—to leeward of her anchor, and head to the flood, the head sails will keep her steady and the cable taut. When the tide has fully made, haul the jib down.

It is needless to place the ship in any other relative position to the wind ; for, after what has already been said, the right mode of proceeding, in such cases as slightly deviate from the above, will at once be seen.

318

460. LETTING GO SHEET ANCHOR.—The cable being shackled and clear inboard, out all stops of the ganger but one or two outboard; clear away the berthing, see the anchor clear, jigger hooked to the slip, &c., and guns run in that are likely to be caught by the cable. From forgetfulness of this, a ship some few years ago, letting go the anchor in a hurry, had a gun dismounted, the carriage disabled, and a beam sprung, by the cable falling across the muzzle.

461. VEERING CABLE IN A GALE.—If B.B., brace the yards for casting to port, hoist fore topmast staysail with the sheet to windward, put the helm a-port, and veer away by short drifts at a time, having the lanyards of the deck-stoppers merely eased up, and kept manned ready for rousing taut. By thus canting her broadside up to the wind, she will drift slowly, and take the cable easily.

462. WHY YOU VEER CABLE IN HEAVY WEATHER.—The chapter *On the Properties of Chain Cables*, in Mr. Tinmouth's work, to which the reader is referred, is the best answer to this question.

• "The hemp cable," it is here remarked, "is well known to possess the valuable quality of elasticity sufficient to accommodate itself to any variety of strain when used as a cable, but the chain is, on the contrary, so stubborn and unyielding, that nothing but a long scope can render it safe; this is equivalent to additional strength, it permits

---

* Abridged.

the ship to rise over each succesive wave, under the constant pressure of a great strain, preventing entirely the danger of sudden jerks, which, of all other trials, is the greatest and the worst to a chain.

" It is a prevalent but fallacious notion, that, even when used in deep water and with a severe strain, the curvature or deflection of chain is considerable, and that near the anchor it rests upon the ground undisturbed by either the pitching motion of the ship, or the tension which she causes. At a testing strain of 630 lbs. per circular $\frac{1}{8}$th inch, the utmost deflection was found to be only 10 feet upon a length of 100 fathoms, in 10 fathoms water, with the hawse-hole a fathom above the surface ; the diameter of the chain being 1 ½ inches, and the strain 40½ tons.

" In a common gale, which would produce this strain, not one link of the 100 fathoms of chain will quietly rest upon the ground ; on the contrary, it will be found by the experiments on a depth of 10 fathoms, that 127·98 fathoms of chain are required to form a semi-catenary* when suspended in air, and 137.03 fathoms when in water, the buoyancy of which must at all times have its influence. If the strain be less than that mentioned, the curvature will be greater, and no danger need be apprehended; but in a severe gale, the force of which may be supposed equal to, or nearly equal to, a breaking strain, it must be evident that a long scope is the only way to prevent a

---

* A catenary is the curve into which a flexible chain of uniform density and thickness forms itself when suspended, or allowed to hang freely from two points.

fatal result ; and any man in charge of a ship at anchor, with the necessary quantity of chain cable on board and space astern to allow him to make use of it, but who neglects to do so, must be considered the author of his own misfortune, whether it may amount to the loss of his anchor or the loss of his ship."

463. MESSENGER CARRIES AWAY.—Bowse to the compressor, stopper the cable, and get up a span-shackle,—a long or a short one, according to the link carried away,

464. ANCHOR COMES UP WITH THE STOCK GONE.—Cat it, and rig a stage over the bows, and no difficulty will be found, under favourable circumstances, in driving the hoops on the new stock.

Otherwise it must be hoisted inboard.

465. FOUL ANCHOR.—If with the flukes uppermost, pass the end of a hawser up the fore-scuttle ; get an anchor-strop on the arm which is most convenient, hook the cat to it, run it up to the cat-head ; hang the anchor by the hawser passed over the thumb-cleat, and with the end hitched round the cat-head ; haul taut, unhook the cat and shift it down to the ring ; ease down the hawser, away with the cat, and clear the cable, using ring-ropes when wanted, and, when clear, haul in the slack of the cable.   Slue-ropes on the stock are often of great assistance in clearing the chain.

When an anchor comes up foul, with a turn round the stock, and you cannot clear it at the bows, or hook the cat to the ring, you hook it to an anchor-strop passed round the anchor so as not to jamb the chain ; and, when up, clear it by dipping or unshackling it.

466. THE CAT IS HOOKED—from out—in, because it is thus the more easily lowered and pointed through the ring of the anchor. The fish is hooked to the inner arm from forward—aft. (Cat-chain, see answer 121.)

467. CAT-BLOCK GONE.—Replace it with the spare one.

468. LETTING GO FROM THE BOWS.—Before letting go, you must put the slip on, take the nippers off, bit the cable, and haul the compressor back.

469. SWEEPING FOR AN ANCHOR.—Divide one or two deep-sea lead-lines, according to the depth of water, between two cutters. Pull to windward of where you suppose the lost anchor to be (knowing your former bearings) ; drop the bight, weighted with leads at intervals, and open out. Pull gently down to leeward, keeping the leads at the bottom until they catch the anchor ; then cross the boats and haul up to it.

If there is much cable attached, see if you can get hold of it with a creeper near the end ; and, if you succeed, take it in through the hawse-hole, shackle on, and weigh the anchor. In case you should be too far off to weigh it from the berth in which you then are, get under weigh again and warp up.

If unable to get hold of the chain, send barge and pinnace away with a 9-inch hawser, and, guided by the

322

cutter which has got hold with the lead-line, drop the bight of the hawser over the anchor ; knot a piece of rope round both parts of the former, as close as you can without having it so taut as to prevent its running down ; sling a couple of shot to it, and, in order to jamb both parts and prevent the anchor slipping out of the bight when heaving up, let it slip down the hawser. A large anchor-shackle may be used instead. Pass the ends of the hawser in, clap a deck-tackle on one part, take the other round the capstan, and heave the anchor up. Or, connect the lower and main-deck capstans, and take one end round the capstans, on each deck.

470. Cat-head and Boomkin carried away.—Brace forward the fore yard, and secure it as for hoisting the launch in. Lash a top-block on the yard to plumb the bows, and through it reeve the top-tackle pendant, passed over the cap and hitched round the quarter of the fore yard. Reeve the top-tackle purchase on deck (splicing two together if necessary), take the cat for the lower block, to which secure the standing part, and reeve the hauling part either through a leading-block or the upper block, and thence on deck through a block on the cap. Trice the purchase up by the yard-tackle—lashed in, and hook it to the pendant. Overhaul down, hook the anchor and hoist it up; fish and secure it in the usual manner, except that the ring is brought in to the side by the cat-head stopper taken round the timber-head.

323

Rig the fish-davit out for a boomkin, and martingale down where most convenient.

471. GETTING A SHEET ANCHOR INTO ITS PLACE.— Cat the anchor, hang it by a hawser rove through the ring and unhook the cat. Pass an anchor strop over the flukes, slip it up the shank, and lash it up to the upper stock. Put another strop round the crown. Trice the purchases up, and secure the yards as for getting the launch in, but bracing the main yard forward, and getting a sail-tackle up from the bowsprit cap for a preventer fore brace. Hook the fore yard-tackle to the strop on the stock, the fore purchase to the ring, and the main purchase to the strop on the crown.

Ease away the hawser, keeping the bight of the chain up by a burton from the fore yard ; haul away the purchases ; have a stock-tackle led along the deck ready to clap on if required, a tackle from the main chains to rouse aft if wanted, and a stay-tackle to lift the flukes in if the drift from the main yard is very great.

The sheet anchor is sometimes got into its place by a couple of fish-davits ; or by the fore yard and fish-davits.

472. TRANSPORTING WAIST ANCHOR TO THE BOWS.— The quickest way is to let it go, then weigh and cat it.

473. COMING TO WITH AN ANCHOR THAT HAS ONLY ONE ARM.—Cock-bill the anchor before going in ; hang it from the cat-head by a hawser through the ring, and reeve the buoy-rope through a block on the bowsprit. Reduce speed, and, on the ship getting stern-way, ease the anchor down

324

square by the hawser and buoy-rope, with the fluke forward ; veer cable on reaching the bottom, and, when you find that it holds, unreeve the hawser and stream the buoy.

474. WEIGHING UNDER SAIL IN A FRESH BREEZE, WITH A VESSEL CLOSE ASTERN.—Heave in as short as safety permits ; loose the courses, jib, and spanker, brace the yards for casting, set the foresail, and hoist the jib with the sheet to windward. Trip your anchor, attend the helm (the watch below and idlers remain at the capstan, watch on deck make sail), board the main tack, and brace round the head yards when she pays off, haul out the spanker, let draw the jib-sheet, cat the anchor, and loose the topsails.

475. A SWELL ON THE PORT BOW, AND NOT ROOM TO CAST TO STARBOARD.—Lay a kedge out, buoyed, on the starboard beam ; pass the hawser out of the starboard quarter port, reeve it through a strop and toggle on the ring of the anchor, and bend it to the crown. Bend a lanyard to the toggle, and let the boat that lays the kedge out hold on to the buoy, and stand by to slip the toggle. Shorten in, spring on the hawser, weigh under the jibs, slip the toggle, trip the kedge and run it up to the quarter, hoist your boat up, loose, and make sail.

476. WEIGHING IN A WEATHER TIDE, WITH THE SHIP TAUT AHEAD OF HER ANCHOR.—The ship will not lie broadside to the tide, because the effect of the tide on her broadside may be greater in proportion than that of

325

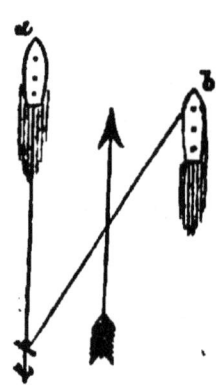

the wind; and she may still under the same circumstances remain ahead of her anchor, because the wind acts with greater force on the ship's stern and on the squared yards, than the tide does upon the bow. Riding then by the S.B. at *a*, port the helm and sheer her over to *b*, where she will remain at a taut scope, stemming the tide; then heave in.

477. WEIGHING UNDER SAIL FROM A CLOSE BERTH.— Make sail, weigh, and cast to port with the head-yards a-box, and the after-yard square, towards the object you wish to clear, with the helm a-port; for, as you necessarily

get sternway in casting, you recede from the danger by turning her head towards it, as is shown by the ship *a*. Starboard the helm as she gathers way, brace up the after yards, and come to the wind on the port tack.

Were you to cast to starboard, or from the danger, you would back into it, stern foremost, as the ship *b* has done.

478. THE ANCHOR SHOULD NOT BE TRIPPED—Until you see that the ship is canting the right way; and, if coming to the wrong way, you must hold on till she casts as you require.

479. WEIGHING UNDER SAIL IN HALF A GALE OF WIND, CLOSE TO A LEE SHORE.—Pass a stream-cable from the quarter port, forward, on the side of the tack which you intend to stand on, and shackle it to the bower cable, in or outboard as most convenient. Send hands aloft to be in readiness to make sail, taking in such reefs as are necessary; man the topsail sheets and halyards, having braced the yards about a point forward; veer gently on the cable during a lull, heaving round on the stream till the wind is nearly abeam; sheet home the topsails and hoist them; and, as the sails will be shaking, little strain will be brought on anything, nor much additional pressure on the ship. Be ready to slip the cables, man the lee braces, mizen sheet, and fore topmast staysail halyards; brace up, hoist away and haul aft; man the fore and main tacks, slip the cables, and haul aboard.

480. BACKING AN ANCHOR.—If in preparation for hurricane weather, heave in or veer away on the anchor down, say B.B., till you bring the fourth shackle some few fathoms abaft the bitts; put the slip on, unshackle and unbit; pass the end out and shackle it to the ring of S.B., which has been eased down to the hawse-hole; off slip, and ride by S.B. cable, with its anchor at the bows until the gale comes on, and then veer it down to the ground. Should the gale pass off, you can hang the B.B. cable outside by the clear-hawse pendant, and replace both in their original position.

If, on veering to 50 fathoms on S.B., you found the gale still increasing, shackle the remaining hundred fathoms of the B.B. to it (supposing that there are three cables divided between the two bowers, as is usually done),—let go starboard sheet anchor, and veer away on both. Finally, if compelled by the violence of the storm to make the utmost of your resources, shackle the other sheet cable to the end of the one already down, and veer away on both to within a few fathoms of the clinch, keeping that in to freshen the nip of the hemp cable with. You will then, it is to be hoped, ride it out with three anchors down, and 500 fathoms of cable ahead.

With more than two cables ahead there is little probability of the strain being equally divided, unless they are systematically laid out in fine weather ; and, with four anchors down, ships have snapped their cables one after another, partly from the same cause, and partly from the fatal effects of sudden jerks upon a short scope—such as a hundred fathoms would be in a gale of great severity. But an anchor is backed only when the holding-ground is bad.

A length of 250 fathoms on one anchor is perhaps unnecessarily long, though in the above case it was demanded by the position of the sheet anchor, which you were obliged to veer on, because (as generally happens in practice), it was not dropped until, having veered on the riding-cables, you were compelled, on account of the increasing wind, to let it go. But, to ride a storm out, you should certainly not have less than 150 fathoms of chain on each anchor, in 10 or 11 fathoms' water; and, if no chain is expended in backing, you can afford this on each of the bower anchors when dropped near each other: veer then, three shackles on each, and hold on at this as long as you can. When the gale has set in, let go the sheet, and veer away on all three anchors; shackle the two sheet cables together, and you will then lie with three anchors ahead, with a cable and a half on each, which is probably the best disposition that can be made.

481. TO MAKE A SMALL KEDGE MORE EFFECTIVE.—
Lash a pig of ballast, or other convenient weight to it.

482. LAYING A BOWER ANCHOR OUT BY A LAUNCH USING TRUNKS.—There are many different plans of carrying out an anchor, and each has some special advantage to recommend it, but should your launch be fitted with trunks, and the water where the anchor has to be placed, not very shallow, I believe there is no plan better than the following:—Reeve the cat and fish falls, and put the stock tackle on, haul taut these, slip the shank painter, cockbill the anchor, off ring stopper, and stock tackle. Ship the midship trunks, windlass, and anchor davit in the launch; and haul her before or abaft the anchor as the case may

329

be, taking care that her head is to the sea, and her stern near the anchor.

When you have placed the boat, put the bight of a stopper over the nearest fluke, half knot it—or better still—cross and seize the parts close to the fluke, bring the ends up through the trunks, and with the windlass heave the anchor close up to the boat, lowering the cat at the same time. Then take another stopper through the ring of the anchor,—one end is taken over the roller in the stern davit, and led through the ring-bolt of the after slings with a round turn, and secured to a thwart; the other may be led over the stern, and set up with a luff hooked to the ringbolt of the foremost slings, rouse the ring of the anchor close up to the launches keel, after having unhooked the cat.

Send as much cable with the anchor as the boat can safely carry, and make fast another boat astern of her with the remainder.

Meanwhile, the cable has been stoppered at frequent intervals; and a cutter has been dispatched with a kedge and hawser for them to warp out by. This kedge should be placed well ahead of the position in which the anchor is to be dropped, otherwise it will come home before the launch gets there: the cutter should then return on board with the hawser. Pass the warp into each, let all hands clap on, haul away, and pay out the cable to the bottom as you go. If each fake is stoppered to a *thwart* or ring-bolt in the boat as it is coiled away, there will be no danger of its taking charge when you pay out.

330

As soon as you have warped up to your position and all
the cable is payed out, ease down the luff until the anchor
is clear of the boat, have a sharp axe ready in case of anything holding, stream the buoy, and slip the stoppers together at the order " let go."

As chain cables are nearly twice-and-a-half the weight
of corresponding hemp ones (being in the proportion of
16.4 to 6.7), the latter should be used in preference when
it is necessary to lay out upwards of 70 or 80 fathoms, or
in bad weather, when any considerable load would endanger the boats.

If you hold on the cable till the anchor is let go, and
then pay out as you return on board, you must first ease
down sufficient to reach the bottom, or the anchor on
being let go, will take the boat with it.   For this purpose,
a bight of chain is usually stopped round outside the boat,
ready for dropping; and, if this is not enough, more must
be payed out.

If you have to warp out against the wind and sea, lay
the cable down on your return; if before it, pay out as
you go.

WITHOUT USING TRUNKS.—Rig the fish-davit; sling
the flukes with a span formed of two stout pendants;
hitch one round each arm of the anchor as it lies on the
bill-board, close up to the palms and splice a long-eye
into the other ends (all of which can be done while the
davit is being rigged); nail a couple of cleats, to form a
fork, on each end of a small spar or oak plank, about
eighteen inches longer than the beam of the boat amid-

ships; place this in the span, allowing sufficient drift fo
the boat to pass between it and the anchor; toggle th
eyes of the span together with a large toggle, fitted with
stout lanyard, and seize each end of the stretcher to th
span, to prevent it slipping down when the anchor i
lifted. Hook the fish to the span, and the cat to the rin
of the anchor. Pass a strop round the shank, and lash
up to the upper stock, leaving the bight above the lashin
just long enough to come in over the boats stem. Cr
the gunwales down, midway between the two after-thwar
to receive the stretcher (which scores may afterwards b
fitted with shutters, to be ready for future use on a simila
occasion). When a span is not used, the lashings fo
slinging the anchor should cross inside the boat, to fra
the sides together.

Haul taut cat and fish, slack up ring-stopper and shan
painter, and ease the anchor down. The moment it is lov
enough, the launch hauls up, stern foremost, passin
through the span, and bringing up with her stern agains
the stock. The slip-rope is rove through the ring-bolts ir
the stern and keel, lashed down and well parcelled in th
wake of the latter one; the ends are knotted, and th
bight is toggled to the bight of the strop on the stock
The stretcher is then lashed down to the boat, and the ca
and fish are unhooked. Connect both toggles by the same
lanyard; form an eye in the bight, by crossing and seizing
both parts together, so that a jigger from the bows of the
boat, hooked to it and hauled on, will bring an equal strain
on each part. To let go, proceed as already described,
only man the jigger in place of slipping the stoppers.

332

With a heavy wash under the bows, so that the launch could not lie under the cat-head with her stern forward, the anchor must be cock-billed, the cat hooked to the span, and the fish to the ring, the cat-head-stopper eased up, the anchor squared with the flukes forward, and the launch veered aft by a boat-rope from the jib-boom end, steadied, if necessary, by a whip from the fore yard-arm, braced forward.

Should you find, on easing down, that the boat will not carry the anchor safely, take the weight off it again, and lash as many water-casks under the bilge as you think will be sufficient (the buoyancy of a butt being eight cwt., and that of a puncheon upwards of five).

It must be borne in mind that the weight of an anchor in the water is less than what it is out of the water, by the weight of water that it displaces. The specific gravity of wrought iron is 7·788, and of salt water 1·026; therefore, the specific gravity of iron in relation to water—7·788 ÷ 1·026, is 7·59. The largest wooden stocked bower anchor weighs 95 cwt. with the stock; but, as the oak and hoops are, as nearly as possible, of the same density as water, the stock—five cwt., need not be taken into consideration. Consequently, the weight of the anchor, minus the stock, divided by 7·59, gives the decrease of weight when the anchor is submerged; in this case equal to 11·86 cwt.

Or, the decrease of weight consequent on the immersion of a body may be found by calculating its cubic contents, and then ascertaining the weight of its equivalent bulk of water.

Y 2

90 cwt. = 161280 oz., which, divided by 7788 (the specific gravity of iron reduced to the same standard), gives a quotient of 20.7, being the cubic contents of the anchor in feet. Now a cubic foot of salt water weighs 64·2 lbs.; and, therefore, 20·7 cubic feet weigh 1329 lbs., or 11·86 cwt. as before.

483. LAYING SHEET ANCHOR OUT BETWEEN TWO BOATS IN HEAVY WEATHER, BACKED WITH THE STREAM.—Hoist out the two pinnaces: send one away to run out a kedge, and in the mean time, get the stream anchor and part of the stream chain cable into the other. To the stream cable lash a block, large enough to take a 7-inch hawser, at a distance from the anchor equal to about twice the depth of water in which the anchor will be let go. Reeve and middle the hawser, and pass both ends inboard. Warp the boat out by the kedge, and let go the stream anchor well in advance of where the sheet is to be dropped. Leave a cutter to buoy up the cable when the block is lashed, and come on board.

While this is being done, the yard-tackles are got down, the anchor slung and lowered down square, stock athwart ships. Two spars being prepared, the pinnaces' gunwales are cut down amidships where the foremost spar lies, and the aftermost spar is lashed across the sterns. The boats being hauled up on either side of the anchor, it is slung with a long strop round the upper fluke, passed over the foremost spar, and toggled to a strop, round the shank abaft, which is passed over the after spar; and the stock, lying across the sterns, is lashed to each boat to keep it steady. The

334

7-inch is then made fast to the boats, and they are hauled out on board the ship to where the cutter is buoying up the stream cable.   This they take in, and send the cutter back with the end of the 7-inch.   When they get hold of the hawser on board, it is bent to the end of the sheet cable (the ganger being unshackled); then the hawser is manned, and the cable hauled out to the boats and shackled to the anchor.   The stream cable is then hitched round the shank, and seized, and allowed to slip down to the crown; the stock lashings are cast off, and the anchor is let go, with the ring towards the ship, by a jigger on the lanyard of the toggle.

484. TO FIND THE NUMBER OF CASKS REQUISITE TO CARRY OUT A 95-CWT. ANCHOR.—A butt holds 110 gallons, and a gallon of (distilled) water weighs 10 lbs.; therefore, 110 x 10 = the floating power, 10 cwt. nearly.

The weight of the casks themselves need not be considered, as when they are submerged it is inappreciable. The anchor, as has been shown, loses nearly 12 cwt. by immersion; and, as the weight of the stock—5 cwt., is not felt, eight butts should be *sufficient* to support it, though doubtless ten would be safer.

A spar (spare jib-boom) would be required to secure the casks to.   They should be whipped over ready slung, and placed at each end, and in pairs on each side of the spar, leaving the centre clear for the anchor.   Hang it by the ring, with a small lashing round the spar and ends of the stock, to keep the latter fore-and-aft. Cast these off before letting go.   If the water be very shoal, or circum-

335

stances otherwise unpropitious, it may be necessary to sling the anchor flukes forward ; in which case it will be hung by two lashings, instead of one—a disadvantage when the operation of letting go is performed with an axe.

485. TO CALCULATE THE CAPACITY OF A CASK.—Multiply half the sum of the areas of the two interior circles, viz., at the head and bung, by the interior length, for the contents in cubic inches ; which, divided by 277·27, the number of cubic inches in a gallon, reduces the result to that measure.

Supposing that the casks at your disposal measured 21 inches in diameter at the bung, 16 inches at the head, and 28 inches in length ; then 346·4 and 201·1 would be the respective areas, and their half sum—547·5 multiplied by 28, and divided by 277·27, would give 27·65 gallons for the contents, which is the capacity of a beef-barrel.

486. TO ASCERTAIN THE NUMBER OF 4-FT. TANKS REQUISITE TO CARRY OUT THE SAME ANCHOR.—The cubic contents of the tank being 64 ft., and a cubic foot of (distilled) water weighing 1000 oz., or 62 ½ lbs. ; 64 × 62·5 = floating power, minus the weight of the tank (which in water would be about 6 cwt.), or 30 cwt. nearly. Three tanks, therefore, would be the number required.

487. TO CALCULATE THE FLOATING POWER OF SPARS, FOR THE SAME PURPOSE.—Try the three spare topmasts ; the main being 64 ft. long (exclusive of mast-head) ; diam. 22 in. ; fore, 57 ft., diam. 22 in. ; mizen, 45 ½ ft., diam.

336

in. The weight that they will sustain, is the difference between their own weight and that of the water they displace.

To ascertain the weight of a spar : multiply the square of the diameter by ·7854 (the area of a circle whose diameter is one inch), to find the area ; multiply the area by the length, to obtain the cubic contents ; and the product by the weight of a cubic foot of the material, ascertained by experiment.

Main topmast.—The greatest diameter being 22 inches, the proportion of diameter at 1st quarter is $\frac{60}{61}$; 2nd quarter, $\frac{19}{21}$; third quarter, $\frac{8}{9}$; equal to 22 in., 21·6 in , 20.9 in. and 19·5 in., respectively ; consequently 21 in. is the mean diameter.

64 ft. = 768 in., and 21^2 × ·7854 × 768 ÷ 1728 (the number of cubic inches in a foot) = 154 cubic feet.

Fore topmast—57 ft., in like manner gives 137 cubic feet ; and

Mizen topmast—45·5 ft., with a mean diameter of 16·2 in., is equal to 65 cubic feet.

Total, 356 cubic feet.

356 × 64·1 (the weight in lbs. of 1 cubic
   foot of salt water)...   ...   ·= 22819 lbs.
356 × 36·3 (the weight in lbs. of 1 cubic
   foot of Norway spars) ...   = 12923 „
   _____

   Floating power of spars   ...   9896 = 88 cwt.
   _____

337

488. OUT STREAM ANCHOR AND CABLE.—Drop the launch alongside; put the gear into the lumber-irons; unship the rudder, as you will steer with an oar, and see luffs, strops, and davit in the boat ready for weighing, and lead and line for sounding. Lay the ends of two capstan bars over the stern, spread out, and rest the other ends, lashed together, on the bights of the cable when it is coiled away, over the after-thwart, ready to receive the anchor. Clear away the anchor in the chains, stop the yard-tackle in with a strop round the pendant, bend on a fore-and-after from the gangway, lift the anchor out with yard and stay, stock it with a whip and burton from the main yard, reeve the buoy-rope double through a block on the crown for weighing, and lower it down with the stock athwartships, resting on the capstan bars, and the flukes up and down the stern. In the mean time the end of the cable has been passed up, taken from the hatchway round the fore bitts, and so walked round, instead of being roused up by standing pulls from the hatchway to the port. Coil the cable away on the top of the thwarts, stopping the last fake outside the boat under the rowlocks, in preparation for letting go, as cable equal to the depth of water must be payed overboard before the anchor is dropped, to prevent the gunwale being torn away. Send boats ahead to take the launch in tow, and shove off. When required to let go, cut the stops of the cable outside, stream the buoy, and ease the anchor over on the capstan bars by lifting the crossed ends.

To weigh the stream anchor in a launch, ship the davit

338

the stem of the boat; lift the cable over its end and lap the double block of a luff on the cable, and the single block is hooked to the bows of the boat; it is best to use two luffs fleeting them alternately, and if the anchor is hard to break out, put one luff on the fall of the other.

489. IN EXPECTATION OF BEING FOULED BY ANOTHER SHIP.—Send hands aloft to drop the foresail, put the slip on, unshackle the cable, bend on a hawser, and, as your friend approaches, off slip and give him a wide berth. In a fresh breeze, stand by to veer instead of unshackling.

If collision be unavoidable, get the swinging boom alongside, lower the quarter-boats and ports, overhaul lifts and trusses, and brace the yards up on the tack opposite to the side the ship is on.

490. ANCHORING IN A BOAT ON ROCKY GROUND.— Bend the cable to the crown of the anchor, and stop it to the ring before letting go. Should the anchor catch when you weigh again, a heavy strain will come on the stop, which will carry away, and enable you to break out flukes uppermost.

491. AWAY WITH A SEINING PARTY.—A ship's seine is about 360 feet long by 12 deep, with a purse in the centre, about 16 feet deep, to confine the haul. To each end of the seine a staff is seized, weighted just sufficient to sink it; the lower part is square with the foot of the seine; and to one end of each pole a line, from 80 to 100 fathoms long (top-gallant studding-sail tacks and halyards), is bent, and spanned out to the other end. This being done, the

339

seine is payed down, and coiled away in the stern sheets of the boat; and a dingy accompanies the latter to under-run the seine, should it catch against rocks on the bottom. On reaching the beach, a few hands remain in the boat, and the remainder stand by to man the hauling-lines. The end of one line is hove on shore, and held on to; the boat pulls out to the extent of it, and then shoots the seine in a direction parallel to the shore, or round the space you intend to sweep, taking care that the bunt goes out clear, with the mouth open to the shore; when all out, the boat pulls in with the other hauling-line; then both are manned and walked away with, closing as you go. When you get hold of the poles, the lower ends are canted in, and the foot of the seine held down as it comes up.

Succeeding hauls are made in the same manner, and the ground is shifted as the fish become thinned; pipes and fires are lit, and a broil accomplished on the embers, &c.

492. To ascertain the Quantity of Water a Boat will bring off.—A butt holds 110 gallons, and a puncheon 72 gallons, and, by Admiralty Circular, water is computed at 210 gallons to a ton. The boat, conse-quently, stows 2,404 gallons, or nearly 11½ tons.

Hoist out empty casks by a toggle in the bunghole; the toggle attached to chain or rope legs of unequal lengths, that the casks may hang clear of each other.

Under some circumstances, ships may water expeditiously by means of a guess-warp from the ship to the shore, unreeving the running gear, and knotting it together, when the distance is considerable, and the boats warping up thereby.

493. KNOT IN A HAWSER, UNDER THE CIRCUMSTANCES DESCRIBED.—Open it out, and pass the boat through it. This actually happened in a ship that I belonged to.

494. CANVAS TANKS—Are supplied to nearly all ships, and are made to fit under the thwarts of a launch, it is a much cleaner and safer plan than watering in bulk, although the boat will not bring quite so much water on board at a time. The tanks when done with, are usually run up by a whip on the foreyard, until dry.

495. BRINGING OFF WATER IN BULK.—See the boat clear and free from leaks, pump some fresh water into her the night before, but dry the boat out before sending her away; and keep the bottom-boards, and a few oars or thwarts loose in her, to prevent the water surging about when she is loaded.

496. RAFTING WATER OFF.—Knock the outer hoops off each end of the casks, and drive them on again with a becket underneath, for a hauling-line to pass through between the beach and the boats anchored outside the surf. If not worth while to fit beckets, you may sling the casks instead. Parbuckle them into the boats, over the stern, if the water is smooth, and pull on board.

497. BOATS' RAIN-AWNINGS.—Fit three or four stretchers for each side, to step in the bottom of the boat, lash down

341

to the gunwale, and project two or three feet beyond it.
Through a thimble seized to the end of these outriggers,
or through a hole bored in them, reeve the ridge-rope,
and set it taut up.　Then haul the awning out to the
stanchions (which must be of good height), and the side
stops to the ridge-rope.　It may also be worth while to fit
a curtain in addition.

When the rain is over, and the awning made up, this
ridge-rope, with the outriggers kept fast, forms a capital
clothes-line for drying your wet things on, and ought not
at any time to interfere with the oars.

**498. BOAT STANDING FOR THE SHIP AND UNABLE TO
FETCH UP.**—The safe plan is to send a boat away with a
small hawser to meet her, and then haul up both together,
giving way at the same time.　This saves a vast amount
of trouble in the end, for, when a boat-rope is veered by
a breaker, it requires buoying up at intervals to keep the
bight from sinking, and even then will be carried very
slowly astern—to add, probably, another proof to the
universal proposition, that *half-measures are always failures.*

A small coir hawser should be kept (with a breaker
attached to it) aft, on the upper deck of every ship, it
will be found to save endless trouble with boats in a tide-
way.

**499. CAUGHT IN A FOG, AFTER TOWING A SHIP OUT OF
HARBOUR.**—Go on board the ship you have been towing,
and take the bearing of the harbour, which you know from
the course you have been steering : note the relative di-

rection of the wind, if it is steady, and shove off, keeping
it on the same bearing till you get inshore or fetch the
harbour.   Should there be no wind, from the boats in line,
standing for the harbour, when, if each boat keeps in the
wake of his leader, the leading boat will be enabled, by
keeping the line directly astern of him, to steer a straight
course for their destination.   The soundings, also, will
tell you whether you are approaching or pulling away from
the shore ; and, if the ship will heave to, and fire guns at
intervals till you have time to get in, you cannot well go
wrong.

500. Sent away to set Fire to a Ship or Buildings.—Take with you a lighted slow-match, and a port-
fire. (A port-fire requires scraping on the top, but you
can ignite it with a slow-match.)   If you are away without
either, the quickest way of making a fire is by mixing a
couple of cartridges up into a *devil*, and setting fire to it
by means of a piece of paper, smeared over with wet
powder, fired out of a musket with a half charge.   A cap
stuck on the point of a knife, with a piece of this touch-
paper, in it, will ignite the latter if struck against anything
hard, when the report of the musket would be inconvenient.

501. A Gale of Wind in an Open Boat.—Lash
your masts, bottom-boards, and oars together ; hang the
boat's anchor to them, to weight them ; span them with
the boat's hawser, and pitch them overboard.   This will
not only keep you head on to the sea, and form a break-
water, but will prevent you drifting so fast.   Pass the other

343

end of the hawser round the boat outside, guy it down here and there, by passing the bight of a rope over the bows, and slipping it aft under the bottom; lay the sails over the fore part of the boat, and lace them down outside to the hawser; raise the after part up a little by sticking a stretcher up under it, and you will thus keep the seas from breaking into the boat, and have a shelter from the weather. Bung the breakers well up, run a piece of rope through the beckets to form a life-buoy, and keep the boat baled out.

502. "WATER, WATER, EVERYWHERE; AND NOT A DROP TO DRINK."—Twice a day dip your clothes overboard, and put them on wet.

503. LANDING, AND GETTING OFF IN A SURF.—Pull np to the rollers, and, if you are not going to beach her, let go the anchor, back astern, and go in after the third, which is the heaviest one, jerking the looms of your oars down to keep the blades out of the water. Let those who intend to land jump out as soon as possible, toss your oars in, and haul out through the surf before the next heavy sea comes in; if you are going to remain, go in of course bow first, jumping out and hauling the boat up before a sea comes over the stern and fills her. A steer oar through a grummet in the stern-ring should be used, as the rudder cannot be relied on. The best surf-boat is a whaler *with paddles*.

504. TRACKING.—Land all but one hand to steer the boat; pass your grapnel out, and track her up. If you have

344

far to go, make tracking belts to go over the shoulder, of any small stuff you may have in the boat, and hitch them to the boat-rope;—slipping the bight into the fore-most rowlock, if, from the shallowness of the water, it is necessary to track at a broad sheer.

505. CAUGHT IN A SQUALL.—Down with the helm and throw her up into the wind, without waiting for the sheet to be let go, although there may be a hand attending it; then lower away and reef.

506. FIRE-ARMS.—Before returning on board, be most particular in seeing all the rifles unloaded; for innumerable have been the accidents resulting from passing loaded fire-arms up a ship's side.

507. HOISTING BULLOCKS IN.—Hook on the yard and stay to a strop round the beast's neck, putting his fore leg through it to prevent it choking him. Cattle should be hoisted in by the horns only when the latter are very strong, and the animals themselves very small.

508. HOISTING HORSES IN.—If troublesome, cover his eyes, hobble him, and sling him with a broad mat, or canvas slings, under his belly ; with a crupper from his haunches round the chest, to keep the slings from shifting. Lead the halter through a ring-bolt on deck, and take the slack through as he comes in. A strop round the nose, hove taut with a short stick or toggle, will rapidly tame an

unmanageable horse.* Horses should be kept slung in their stalls at sea, with their hoofs just resting on the deck.

509. UP-ENDING A LARGE CASK.—Lay a capstan bar under the bilge on each side, span them together under the chimes of the cask, at each end ; man the bars, and up with it, sticking to it on the opposite side to prevent it going over.

510. CONDEMNED ROPE—Is returned into store in five-fathom lengths.

511. MOUNTING A 64-PR. GUN WITH ITS OWN TACKLES. —The side and train-tackles supply you with nearly thirty fathoms of three-inch rope, which is capable of supporting a weight, *suspended to it*, of 50 cwt. Therefore, if it is possible to apply the power necessary to lift the gun to three parts of rope attached to it, their can be no doubt of their capability to sustain it, more especially when applied as a parbuckle.

If the gun is lying with the vent up, scoop the earth

---

* To see how defective all rules and specific directions may be, unless seconded by mother-wit and dexterity, read this Crimean anecdote of an embarkation of horses on board the " Ganges."

"One horse," writes the ' Staff Officer,' "would not allow the slings to be put under him, and kept on lashing out with one hind leg in a most furious manner (it was too rough for him to kick with both, as he would have fallen). This beast was delaying the embarkation of the other horses ; so one sailor called out, 'Jack, next time he kicks lay hold of his leg !' which Jack very coolly did, and, to our utter astonishment, the horse stood perfectly still, and only snorted ; in another second he was swinging in the air, half-way up the ship's side.

346

away from under one of the trunnions, and roll it over with the vent down. Lift the carriage on the top, lock the cap-squares, reeve and middle the breeching, pass the ends over the rear axle-trees, and secure it so as to confine the breech to the carriage; then haul over the latter on its flat. Hitch the side-tackles to the upper fore axle-tree, and the train-tackle to the rear axle-tree, and reeve them under the carriage and over the gun. Clap on all three parts as many hands as can get hold, assist with the handspikes on the opposite side and rouse away, chocking her up with stones at every inch you get.

512 GETTING A GUN UP A HEIGHT.—Dismount the gun as you mounted her, easing her over by a hawser passed the opposite way, and landing the breech and muzzle on some large stones to keep her off the ground. Then unlash the carriage, and wedge the gun up in a cask, woulding staves round it beyond the cask, and making it as round as possible. Parbuckle it up with the hawsers, and haul the carriage up afterwards.

513. PLACING HEAVY GUNS IN A LAUNCH FOR LANDING. —Cut a spar or oak plank, to lie on the gunwale inside the upper streaks, over the after-thwart; and place a couple of spars fore-and-aft, resting on this and on the stern. Land the guns athwart these, and stow the carriages and gear forward.

514. MOUNTING THEM WITH A SMALL TRIANGLE OR GYN.—Hook the tackle to a strop through the neck-ring, and weigh the breech off the ground high enough to allow the carriage to be run up with the trunnion-boxes under

z   347 the trunnions, the muzzle still resting on the ground ; then lower away roundly, and the gun falls into its place.

515. A PARBUCKLE—May be worked on the bight, or on the end.

On the Bight—Middle the hawser, pass the bight under the gun, haul back and slip it over a fixture ; open the ends out under the gun, to keep it square, and walk away with it.

On the End—When you have nothing to make the bight fast to in the direction in which you want to move the gun, middle the hawser (or less, according to the distance to be moved over), and take two or three turns round the gun amidships ; then let a few hands hold back on the underneath end, which is taken up as the part you haul on comes off,—the hands that hold on the end following the gun up at the same time. Skids must be laid along, to keep the trunnions off the ground.

When a gun has to be taken a considerable distance, shut it vent up, bend on to the neck-ring, and clap on plenty of hands.

516. FIGHTING A GUN WITHOUT A CARRIAGE.—Rig a triangle, sling the gun round the trunnions and over the button, hooking on the purchase so as to give the required elevation, in which it has an advantage over a carriage, inasmuch as there is no limit to it. To check the recoil, reeve the breeching through a block or thimble on two legs of the triangle, with a large net full of shot slung to the ends. Sheer-head guys will perhaps be found necessary.

348

Otherwise, build the trunnions up, and regulate the elevation by a small triangle over the breech. But by this plan you can only fire at a fixed object, as the direction cannot be altered.

517. LANDING FIELD-PIECE FOR EXERCISE.—Haul the boat up alongside, and place the large end of a capstan bar on the gunwale on each side of the stem, projecting a foot or two over, the inner ends being secured. Hoist the gun out, ready mounted, on the field-carriage, and land the axle-tree across the capstan bars, outside the stem, with the wheels on each bow. Bear down on the trail, and lash it to a thwart. Place the limber in the stern-sheets, and afterwards hoist the boxes over.

On reaching the shore, land the field-piece party, hook on the drag-ropes and man them, launch the capstan bars out, and plant them as skids, lashing the inner ends to prevent them slipping. Bend a rope's-end to the trail to ease it down by. Haul away on the drag-ropes handsomely until the wheels take the ground, and then run the gun up. Pass out the boxes and land the limber.

518. IN THE FACE OF AN ENEMY.—Fight the gun on its slide in the boat as long as it is available, land the covering party, cease firing, in tompion and vent-plug, unreeve the breeching, slip a short strop over the breech and another over the muzzle, bringing them together at the trunnions, carry aft the runners of the foremast, top the bowsprit up for a derrick (previously fitted for that purpose), hook a tackle from the derrick-head to the strops,

Z 2

bend a drag-rope to the breech-ring, whip the gun out, drag it ashore and mount it. Hands in the mean time have got the carriage and limber ashore and ready, the wheels having been slung outside the boat, the trail and limber fore-and-aft, and the boxes in the stern-sheets.

Boat-keepers haul the boat off to her anchor, leaving a line ashore to haul in by when wanted.

519. HOISTING IN GUNS.—The gun you wish to hoist in is an 8-inch, and weighs 9 tons. Top the main yard and brace it, so that it will plumb the port or hatchway through which the gun has to go ; put burtons on the yard as preventer lifts, haul the lifts, preventer lifts, trusses, braces, and topsail sheets well taut, lash the bunt of the main yard to the mast with a cross lashing, hook a luff tackle on the opposite side to the rolling tackle strop, and to another strop round the mast, haul it taut. Lash a top block on to the yard far enough out to allow the gun to clear the ship's side while hoisting ; take the end of a 7-inch or 8-inch hawser from the opposite side of the deck over the lower cap, and through the block lashed on the yard, then take the end on deck and secure to it the upper block of your yard purchase, round it up sufficiently high, and secure the hawser on deck, well parcel the hawser in the wake of the cap, and wherever it is likely to chafe.

For both yard and stay purchases, two three-fold blocks must be used, with five or six inch falls rove in them, the hauling parts should be led through leading blocks at the mast-head before going on deck; top-tackle blocks can be used for the purchase blocks.

The gun is slung with a chain strop, having a seizing on one bight, leaving an eye large enough to fit over the button of the gun; the other bight to which the purchase blocks are hooked, is well lashed to the gun outside the trunnions.

The main hatchway of ships carrying heavy guns on the main deck, is generally fitted with moveable combings or iron plates, that fit across the hatchway, allowing the carriage to be placed so that the gun can be lowered into it at once; great care should be taken in transporting the gun to its port, or you will find the deck much cut up by the iron carriage.*

For guns under 6½ tons in weight, secure the main yard as you would to hoist in a launch. Reeve the end of a top-tackle pendant through a top block, take the end over the lower cap and secure it on deck, lash an up-and-down tackle to the main yard arm, and to the top block on the pendant to be used as an outhaul; reeve a top-tackle fall, hook the upper block to the pendant, and lead its hauling part through a leading block on the strop of the upper block; through another at the cap, and then on deck.

To get the Gun in through a Port.—When slinging the gun, allow a good drift outside the lashing, to give play to

---

* *To hoist in heavier guns, see answer number 534.*

the gun when the purchase block binds against the upper port-sill; line the port, to prevent injury to it, hook the purchase, and hoist away. When up to the port, ease in the up-and-down, pass the gurnet out, and hook it to the neck-ring, haul in on the gurnet, ease away the purchase, and land the gun on the carriage run up to receive it. Unhook, and overhaul down for the next.

The gurnet—consists of a pendant and tackle, and is best fitted so that it can be worked under the eye of the officer superintending the mounting, and for this purpose, a clump-block with a double strop should be fitted, and the bights either slipped over the dismounting bolts, or toggled through the deck. The end of the pendant is fitted with a hook or shackle to take the neck ring of the gun.

Boats guns are slung with their breechings, and hoisted in with the yard tackles.

520. To Calculate the Weight of a Gun.—Rule: Divide the gun into as many sections as its form requires, to enable you to obtain the true dimensions, and ascertain the weight of each part separately. To do this:

1st. Find the area of the base of the cylinder, by multiplying the square of the diameter by ·7854; or by multiplying the square of the circumference by ·07958.

2nd. To find the solidity of the cylinder, multiply the area into its length.

3rd. Add the contents of each section thus found, for the whole contents of the cylinder, supposing it to be a solid mass.

352

4th. In the same manner find the contents of the bore of the gun, assuming it to be a solid cylinder.

5th. Subtract this from the solid contents of the gun, previously found, to obtain the actual contents, and—

6th. By Table VIII, obtain the weight of a mass of metal of the dimensions ascertained.

$7.125^2 \times .07958 \times 8.5 = 34.34$ ft.   Contents of 1st section, from base to trunnions.

$6.146^2 \times .07958 \times 11.333 = 34.06$ ft.   Contents of 2nd section, from trunnions to muzzle.

$.75^2 \times .7854 \times 19.833 = 8.75$ ft.   Contents of bore.

$68.4 - 8.75 = 59.65$ ft.   Cubic contents of gun.

$59.65 \times 524.8 + 5$ cwt. $= 14$ tons, 4.5 cwt.   Total weight of gun.

521. To find the Solid Contents of a Sphere.— Multiply the cube of the diameter by $.5236$; or the cube of the circumference by $.01688$, and, by Table VIII, find its weight.

$8.7^3 \times .5226 \times 4.171 = 90$ lbs.   Weight of the shot.

522. Getting a New Mast in by the Old One.— Let the mast be 128 feet long; viz., 40 feet from the heel to deck, 67 feet from deck to trestle-trees, and 21 feet the length of the head.   Diameter, 40 inches; and weight, 20 tons.

Get the main yard, lower cap, and top on deck; fish the mast where the decay or spring has taken place, and

353

on that side—say port side—prepare to get the new mast in. Set the stays and starboard rigging well up; lash a runner and tackle on the fore and after side of the masthead, set them up well forward and aft on the port side of the deck, and come up the port rigging. Lash the purchases above the rigging, taking for the main purchase the four and three-fold purchase blocks with the $7\frac{1}{2}$-inch shroud hawser for the fall; and for

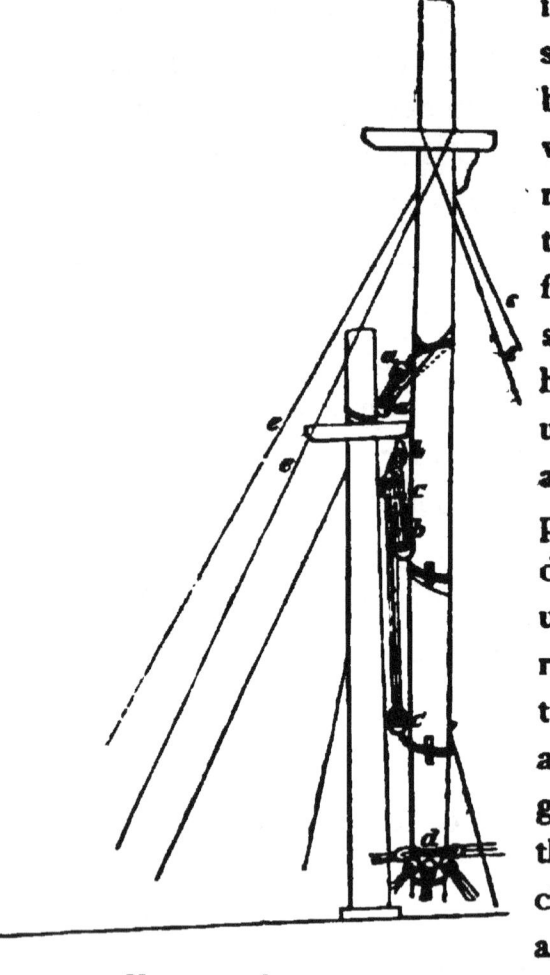

a. Upper purchase.
b. Main purchase.
c. Lower purchase.
d. Heel-tackles.
e. Mast-head guys.

the upper purchase, two three-fold top-tackle blocks, with a tail of $6\frac{1}{2}$ inches. Bring the new mast alongside with the head forward; lash the main purchase a little above

354

the centre (of gravity), towards the head, and the upper purchase half-way from that towards the heel. Sway the heel up clear of the main chains by the upper purchase (capable of lifting 40 tons), rousing it forward by a tackle if necessary; and then, with both, sway the mast up square. Ease it inboard by hawsers from the main-deck ports, and land it on the deck.

Slack up the main rigging, and saw the mast through close off to the deck, wedging it up as the saw enters. Shore the deck up most carefully abaft the mast; place a bed for the heel level with the line of section, and nail it down, as it would be impossible to cut it off quite close to the deck. Get powerful deck-tackles on the heel, reeve appropriate mast-head guys, overhaul the rigging, and fleet the mast abaft the mast-hole. Set the rigging up again, shortening up the after-shrouds, if necessary, and support the mast further with the fore and main runners and tackles, two forward and two aft; and secure the heel in its place by shores, fore-and-aft and athwartships, from the hatchways and ship's side. Nail a large bolster across the trestle-trees, on the fore side of the mast, for the purchase-block strops to lie on, that the blocks and falls may not bind against the mast. Relash the purchases, with a lower purchase in addition, similar to the upper one, hanging down well clear of the main purchase. Sling the stump of the old mast, and hoist it out. Lash the strops upon the new mast,—that for the lower purchase, about twenty feet from the heel; main purchase about 45 feet from the heel; upper purchase about 50 feet from the head; strops for heel-tackles a foot or two clear; all well cleated.

355

Over the mast-head, middle and hitch a couple of 6-inch hawsers; take two ends forward and two aft; toggle the main and upper purchases, bring them to the main and lower-deck capstans, and heave round. When high enough to need it, hook to the heel six up-and-downs, or luffs, and attend them and the mast-head guys carefully as the mast goes up. When the upper purchase comes two blocks, stopper, and belay it to the bitts; toggle and bring to the lower purchase, heave round, and ease away the upper purchase. Rouse the heel over the mast-hole, and walk back, with the mast-head guys manned, and heel-tackles ready between decks. Unrig the old mast, and hoist it out with the new one.

523. GETTING MAIN YARD FORE-AND-AFT THE DECK. —Coming down port side. The ordinary plan is to top yard to starboard, by a sail-tackle from the topmast-head, hauling forward on the preventer brace and lowering the jeers, to clear the top rim; hauling aft by mizen burton to port yard-arm, and then with a luff on starboard yard-arm, rousing it over into the gangway, when lowered clear of the main stays.

In a ship with short lower masts, it may happen that there is not sufficient drift for the yard-arm to come in over the nettings or through the gangway; in which case, having rove the jeers, unrove the after braces, unbent the sail, and sent the booms down, you hook a tackle to the bunt of the yard from the starboard side of the forecastle, and, alongside it, a runner and tackle from the foremast head, the pendant being taken under the top,

356

and secured close down to the eyes of the rigging. To a strop round the starboard yard-arm hook the port up-and-down inside the quarter-iron, and outside the quarter-iron, on the port yard-arm, hook the port main tackle: these support the yard-arms when fore and aft, and the lifts are unrove. From the port fore rigging, hook a burton to the starboard yard-arm, where the fore tackle is attached. Then heave taut the jeers, off slip, turn out the trusses, and lower the yard partly down, rousing it bodily forward by the runner and tackle, and bracing the starboard yard-arm inside the fore rigging by the burton and preventer brace; turn with the runner, walk back the jeers, and haul forward on the fore-and-after till the port yard-arm is clear of main rigging and mainmast, attending, at the same time, to the fore and main tackles; rouse the yard-arm over by a luff, lower of all, and land the yard, allowing it to come aft as far as convenient.

524, UNBENDING SAILS.—Words of command.—"Unbend sails." "Away aloft." "Lay out on the lower yards and unclamp." (Laying in again.) "Trice up—lay out." "Ease in." "Stand by booms and buntlines." "Sails and booms—lower away."

If top-gallant and royal yards are across, yards, sails, and booms may be lowered together.

525. SHIFTING BOWSPRIT CAP—Rig the jib-boom three-fourths in, and pass a lashing round the head and heel to keep it in its place when the cap comes off; pull up on the sail-tackle (from mast-head to boom-end), to

357

take the weight of the cap when it is started: unreeve the heel-rope, sling a spar on each side of the bowsprit, lash a couple of leading-blocks to the jib-boom, close to the cap, and through them reeve a rope's end to the heel of the spars; with these, bump the cap off, the bolt, which secures it to the bowsprit (fore-locked on the top, abaft the foremost hoop), being driven out; carpenter's assisting with their mauls. When off, sling it, rig the boom in altogether, and hoist the cap in with a couple of luffs on the fore stay, the sail-burton taken off the boom, and with the fore up-and-down.

Or, it may be got off by drooping a pair of sheers formed of topmast studding-sail booms, supported by a sail-tackle from the mast-head, the heels stepped on the bees, and the cap slung, while being bumped off, by a couple of luffs from the sheer-heads; and transported in as before. In this manner, it may also be sent out, and placed again.

The jib-boom may be used for getting the cap on, by resting the heel against the stem, topping it up with the sail-burton, and swaying the cap up by a tackle from the boom-end.

Or, it may be sent out as far as the collars of the fore stays by the luffs, and there lashed to a topmast studding-sail boom pointed through the round hole; a guy on each side taken to it from the cat-heads, the sail-tackle hooked to the end of the boom and pulled up, and the boom rigged out by heel-ropes—easing the guys and sail-tackle.

358

526. SHIFTING BOWSPRIT.—A bowsprit may be got out either with a main topmast as a derrick, or with the two fore topmasts as sheers. If by the latter means, strike the fore topmast and land it on deck; get the spare one up alongside of it by an up-and-down; open out the heels—resting on shoes, cross the heads and lash them. Secure the foremast with runners and tackles, strip the bowsprit, and house main and mizen topmasts. Lash a top-block to the sheers'-head for the topping.lift, and a couple of blocks to the fore-mast-head just above the rigging, so that they will clear the top when the topping-lift is rove, using for it a 7-inch hawser, with the standing part secured to the sheers'-head.

Lash a three-fold top-tackle block at the sheers'-head, and reeve the main jeers for a purchase, the lower block being either a top-tackle or a cat-block. Secure the pendant of the launch's purchase to the foremast-head, lead it over the sheers'-head, so that the block will be close up when they are drooped, and lash it out on the bowsprit ten or twelve feet inside the cap, for a cap purchase, a turn or two of the lashing being taken to the cap, to prevent it slipping in. Lash the purchase out between the gammonings ; two or three turns round the bowsprit not being taken over the hook of the purchase block, in order to jamb the lashing. Mark the bowsprit where the sheers'-head should plumb when drooped sufficiently, which should be as far outside the lashing as the bowsprit houses inboard. Haul forward on the purchase and droop the sheers till a plumb-line from the purchase block comes over the mark on the bowsprit. Lead the fall through a leading-block hooked to a lashing passed over a toggle inside the hawse-hole, and long enough to allow the fall to lead fair, through the main deck bow port to the capstan. Bend a rope's-end, through a block on the cat-heads, to the man-ropes, for head-guys; hook a luff to the bowsprit from the head-knee, close to the stem on each side to assist in clearing the heel by hauling out, if necessary—slipping the strop down as the bowsprit goes out; also, in the same manner, hook a luff from the bows on each side, to steady the heel when swayed out.

The heel-lashings should be passed only temporarily till the sheers are drooped, and then lashed properly; and the space between the upper part of the heels and the deck should be well wedged up and attended to.

Knock out the wedges, and, when ready, heave round on the purchase, easing the cap purchase as the mast goes out, and keeping it from binding in the bed.

Get the new bowsprit in by the same appliances, attending to the directions given in Art. 2.

527. SHIFTING LOWER MASTS WITH YOUR OWN SPARS.—Sheers are sometimes formed of the fore and main yards, with fishes lashed to the yard-arms, but the two main topmasts are better adapted to the purpose.

To give sufficient droop, it will be necessary to cross the sheer-heads two-thirds down the mast-heads, and to plant the heels (stepped in the lower caps), a third of the deck in from the ship's side. In other respects proceed as in Arts. 2 and 522.

In June, 1857, H.M.S. "Nankin," 50, was employed in dismantling the wreck of the "Raleigh," 50, sunk off Macao; but being unable to start the wedges of the masts, as the water rose to the upper deck port-sills, and never fell at low water below four feet on the main deck, they were induced to attempt what most men would have considered an impossibility; and to the great credit of those officers of the "Nankin" on whom the duty devolved, they succeeded, with sheers formed of the "Raleigh's" main topmast, in drawing the lower masts through orlop, lower, and main-deck wedges, and in getting them overboard without an accident.

When sheers are very disproportionate to the length of the mast you are getting out, the purchase would be two blocks when the heel but just clears the upper-deck partners, as you would not be able to take it higher on account of the great top weight : it consequently would be too low to clear the upper works unless lowered in an athwartships direction, and then roused over bodily before lowering the heel. This, however, would be a work of great danger and difficulty, as the heel-tackles would be eased up, and the whole leverage of the top-weight thrown on the upper purchase. Under such circumstances, the mast should be sent over on the opposite side, head downwards ; easing up the head-tackles and lowering the purchase.

528. HOISTING OUT A PADDLE SLOOP'S PINNACE.—The boat is slung with a fore-and-aft span, and lifted by a stay-tackle from a span between the fore and main-masts,

plumbing the boat ; then hauled out by the fore-yard purchase, either before or abaft the fore rigging, according to
the position of the paddle-box. In addition to the burtons, the fore yard is secured by a preventer brace from
the bowsprit.

529. HOISTING IN A LONG SPAR.—Trice up yard and
stay-tackles, cross the stays, and brace the yards in ; pull
up the after end best, until the foremost end is inside the
fore rigging, backstays being frapped in ; then lower the
after end, and haul forward.

530. HOGGING SHIP.—Wedge a large grating full of
broom stuff ; bend a weight to the bight of a hawser, and
dip it under the ship's bottom ; haul up on one end and
bend on the hog at the bight. Reeve a hawser, inboard,
through a block on the bowsprit and spanker-boom ends,
and bend the ends to the hog ; give the thwartships
hawser into a boom-boat on each side ; and if the hog is
over the starboard side, and you are going to hog that side
first, let the port boat haul up on the hawser until the hog
is brought close down to the keel, and, when down, and
a taut turn has been taken in both boats, man the fore-
and-after and walk it forward and aft the whole length of
the ship. The port boat then eases up the breadth of the
hog, the starboard boat takes in the slack, the fore-and-
after is hauled on, and another longitudinal section cleaned,
and so on with both sides. By heeling the ship over, you
may clean a short distance below the water-line by means
of small hogs with poles stuck into them.

362

531. INTERNAL ECONOMY, &c.—HAMMOCKS.—As the neatness of the hammocks adds as much to a ship's appearance as their slovenly condition detracts from it, it is necessary that they should be carefully inspected by the midshipmen stationed to nettings, previous to being stowed. To permit of this, the men, on coming on deck, should fall in abreast of their nettings in the rear of each other, according to their numbers; the foremost hammock of each netting always commencing with the same number on the watch bill, and continuing consecutively, the men keeping rank, and closing up as the foremost hammocks are passed in. The first turn of the lashing should be rove through two holes in the tabling, close to the midship seam; no wrinkles allowed in the head, nor in any other part of the hammock; the ends of the nettles carefully laid along, and hitched over inside, and a twist taken in the clews and hauled taut along the hammock by the lanyard of the opposite clew. A hand should attend the gage while stowing; and the lashings of the waist hammocks should form one uniform line, inside and out, by being squared after they are stowed.

To insure regularity in the distance of the turns, and in the position of the numbers, an iron scale should be used like that in the cut. It is there placed on a starboard watch's hammock, and must be turned over to mark those for the port watch. Seven holes are punched in it, where it lies on the seam; and when these, with the oval for the number, are pencilled round, the scale is removed. A stitch or two is then passed through the seven dotted

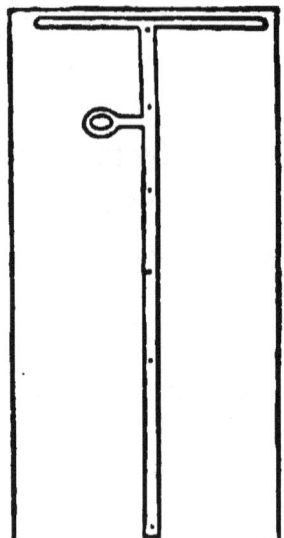

marks, which show, when lashing up, where the turns should come; and the patch is painted with black numbers, on a white ground bordered with a black line, for one set of hammocks; and with white numbers, on a black ground bordered with a white line, for the second set Two good stops, whipped, should be spliced into the head of each hammock, and two in the foot, for stopping to the gantlines; the centre stop for the head being a fixture in the gantline.

When hammocks have a tendency to exceed their stipulated dimensions, a hoop is held for the hammocks to be passed through as they are stowed.

On piping down when hammocks have been covered, the men, after taking them below, should return on deck, and form in line round the ship facing the nettings, abreast of where their hammocks have been stowed, ready to man the nettings for furling, when they have been reported clear by the young gentlemen stationed to them.

————

MIDSHIPMEN'S DUTIES.—While touching on this subject, I am reminded of a very laconic, but comprehensive summary, issued by the captain for their guidance, in a ship of some note.

" Their duties," it ran, " in one sentence, are *to do as* they are ordered, in a smart and intelligent manner.

364

"They are to see all orders carried into effect. That the men are at their stations. That they perform the duties of their stations. That all ropes are coiled down directly they are belayed. That all dirt, or spots on the deck, are instantly removed. That rope-yarns, or other rubbish, are removed from wherever they may have chanced to accumulate.

"When sent on duty, they are never to quit that duty. They are never to leave their boats, nor suffer any of their crew to do so. They are not to allow spirits or wine to be brought to their boats' crews; and are to report any man who may have misbehaved.

"They are at all times to appear properly dressed, and are to avoid incurring debt.

"They are constantly to keep in mind that, unless they conduct themselves to my satisfaction, they will not receive a certificate; without which, when the time arrives, they will not be examined touching their qualifications for a commission."

Furthermore, the officer of the watch is ordered by the captain "on all occasions to be most strict with the midshipmen, and is authorized to punish either of them by giving them an extra watch for any fault not sufficiently grave for him to interfere with." The officer of the watch is also directed "not to allow the midshipmen of strange boats to remain on board after they have delivered their messages, but to make them lie off, or hang on to the boom."

2 A 2

The first lieutenant is to "take care that they are kept strictly under instruction during school-hours; and they are never to have leave unless they are clear of debt, and unless they perform their duties in a diligent and attentive manner."

The character of a ship can always be told by her boats and boats' crews; therefore the officer of a boat should not only consider himself answerable for her cleanliness and good order, but that the crew are properly dressed, orderly, and respectful, and that they *always give way,*—setting the same example of respect to officers of other ships, as would be required of him and his men by those of his own. As a general rule, boats are better manned and cleared from booms, instead of from the gangways. Under ordinary circumstances, every man should be on deck in a minute from the pipe; and the first person up should be the midshipman of the boat.

As midshipman of a top, he should exert himself to maintain the most perfect silence; to see, in furling sails, that the men keep within the marks which should be painted on the yards, until ordered to lay out; and that as they come in off the yards, none land in the top except the men stationed there for squaring yards. As the booms should not be lowered until every man is in, he should see that the quarters of the yards are smartly cleared, to make way for the outside hands, with the exception of the yard-arm man, who remains out to foot the boom clear. In reefing, he should be particularly careful that the boom-tacks and tricing-lines are properly attended, and are not started until every man is in. In crossing yards, and shortening sail, that the squaring marks of lifts are expeditiously got down; and, on all occasions, that a *second* hail from the deck is never necessary.

As midshipman of the watch, he is to have his watch bill always with him : and, as it should be a standing order that no man is to *walk* when called, working ship, &c., so the young gentleman should at all times set the example of a like prompt and ready obedience. On the school a youngster is brought up in, his future character depends.

———

To mates of decks the following receipts may be of use :—

For guns.—4 oz. resin, 2 oz. lamp-black, 3 oz. bees-wax (2 oz. shellac), 1 quart linseed oil. Boiled 50 minutes, and, when taken off, half a pint turpentine added.

This is to be laid on as a first coat, and afterwards kept up with ordinary bees-wax and turpentine. For bronzed guns, omit the lamp-black, and previously apply a solution of sal-ammoniac, after scraping.

White varnish for range-tables, &c.—White resin and turpentine, dissolved in a close bottle, placed in hot water on a stove.

Cement for cracks in woodwork, &c.—Four parts of bees-wax to one of resin, melted together, and tinted with Indian red and yellow ochre.

Leather belts, &c., may be stained black with a solution of copperas.

367

For steamers' funnels, the same in whitewash turns it a buff colour.

Varnish for spars.—Boiled linseed oil and resin, warmed till the resin is dissolved.

Mast colour.—Dockyard-yellow, a little white, and warmed up with Venetian red.

Black stain.—Into a breaker put 2 lbs. copperas, 2 lbs. nut-gall, 8 lbs. alum, pounded up ; 8 lbs. old iron, and 25 pints of vinegar. When wanted, boil as much as is required and lay on hot. It is better to make a large quantity at first, as the longer it is kept the better it becomes. Three or four coats are necessary.

French polish.—5 oz. naphtha, 1 oz. shellac, 10 grains of isinglass, 1 dram of myrrh, and 6 drams of olive oil.

Whitewash.—The best is made from quicklime, for it will not rub off, and if kept in a tank, there can be no danger from it. To keep whitewash in good order, all marks should be rubbed out, and the whole smoothed down with hard canvas rubbers on sticks, before going over it at any time.

Scraping masts and booms.—Instead of going through the scraping process every Saturday, and covering your deck with chips, send the booms down on deck when they want it, and scrub them with sand and canvas ; both lowering them down, and swaying them across together. The dirt should merely be scraped off the top-gallant masts as an ordinary practice, and a light plane-over given to

368

them at long intervals after a general refit, which is infinitely less injurious to them, at any time, than scraping with knives.

Though the "watch-mark" on the arm is usually a sufficient indication; "Which watch on deck?" is a question often asked when the hands are employed; therefore have a brass S or P hung upon the wheel, and turned at the end of every watch.

Washing-tubs.—The lower hoops should be knocked up an inch or two, when drawn, or your decks will be marked.

A large dirt-tub on the main deck, to collect the rubbish of all decks, whipped up at the end of each watch, and capsized with a slip-toggle, is far better than a head-shoot dangling from the bows.

Holystoning, *too frequently*, makes the deck rough. A sprinkle and scrub at seven bells in the forenoon, with hand-brushes, cloths, or hand-swabs, dries rapidly in warm weather, and renders it less necessary.

Instead of lowering the duty cutters on alternate days, keep each at the davits for a week at a time. On Saturday, keep the boat up that has done duty for the week; clean, and paint her bottom, if it requires it : and you have then the ensuing week to touch her up and put her to rights ready for relieving the other cutter. With boom-boats the same; for, if they are worked indiscriminately, they can never be kept in proper order.

In a small vessel never be induced to advocate the relinquishment of mess-tables and stools. Men sprawling

369

on the deck among their beef and pork has a dirty, demo-
ralizing effect ; which has only to be witnessed to convince
one of.

Saturday being the great cleaning and renovating day,
it is a good plan to muster the watch in the morning in
their clean working rig, duck jumper and trowsers (the
coaling rig of steamers), which though tarred and stained,
may nevertheless be kept scrupulously clean.

Sunday, the blessed day of rest, is too frequently a day
of bustling, fatiguing duties, and the most undesired of all
the seven.   From the hour of commencing work in the
early morning, until the pipe to dinner at last releases you
there is often no cessation.   To those on whom the work
of the ship devolves, Divine service is no relief, for it is
then felt to be part of a relentless routine that has to be
gone through, and they are only too glad when what,
week after week, seems an interminable repetition, is
brought to a close.   I know of no remedy for this serious
evil short of a total change in the character of the day, as
it is at present viewed.   Instead of looking upon it as the
first day of a new week, with your hands clear until the
work of the week on the morrow commences, it is generally
considered the winding-up day of the previous week,
when all its accumulated details have to be examined and
gone into.   On Sunday, the paymaster makes up his
books, and gives in his report ; warrant-officers' accounts
and midshipmen's logs are written up and sent in ; de-
faulter's book and defaulters examined ; Articles of War
read ; ship's company mustered by open list ; and the

whole ship—decks, holds, and store-rooms, minutely and rigorously inspected, after a laborious preparation, which is then followed up by a lengthened service of prayer and homily.

Unless the above necessary duties are transferred to another day, Thursday for instance, I cannot see how the sacred nature of the Sabbath is to be maintained. Holystoning decks and crossing upper yards, on Sunday morning, may now be counted as things of the past; but to be consistent in this, the rigorous Sunday inspection, with its jading, temper-breaking preludes and accompaniments, should be simplified as much as possible. By all means muster at divisions : but leave the general inspection of the ship for a week-day. *A well-regulated ship should always be ready*; but the usual Sunday spruceness, obtained at so great a sacrifice, is frequently on a great deception, and by it, that which is known by the name of " Divine Service," is rendered a soulless and compulsory piece of acting.   Under such circumstances, no one for a moment can imagine that men, who from their habits are totally unaccustomed to any but the briefest contemplation or connected thought on abstract subjects, can give their minds, for an hour and a half, to the devotions they are assembled to take a part in.   Of course, such a startling improbability *is* not entertained by any one, and we are therefore driven to the conclusion that " Divine Service " is often only maintained for the mere sake of keeping up appearances, and to be in accordance with the " Articles of War."

I would beg of my young readers to treasure up, and abide by those few wise words, which, often quoted, are known as " the golden maxim " of the great Sir Matthew Hale :—

A Sunday well spent,
Brings a week of content,
And health for the toils of the morrow ;
But a Sabbath profaned,
Whatsoe'er may be gained,
Is a certain forerunner of sorrow.

He made this his rule of life, and hear what he says as it was drawing on to its close :—

" I have found by a strict and diligent observation, that a due observation of the duty of this day, hath ever joined to it a blessing upon the rest of my time ; and the week that hath been so begun, hath been blessed and prosperous to me : and on the other side, when I have been negligent of the duties of this day, the rest of the week hath been unsuccessful and unhappy to my own secular employment ; and this I do not write lightly or inconsiderately, but upon a long and sound observation and experience."

CAPITAL PUNISHMENT.—By the power of life and death vested in courts-martial, the duty of carrying out the extreme sentence of the law devolves upon the naval officer. Happily this is of so rare an occurrence, that few can be conversant with the unattractive detail of the duty ; and from motives of humanity I think it right to explain it. It is a repulsive subject, and I may perhaps be considered guilty of very questionable taste in discussing it ; but I don't object to that, should it happen at any time to tend to the furtherance of the service. The traditionary knot is made with a bight, as for a sheepshank, the end then wound round its own and all parts, passed through the upper bight, which is then hauled down, and a running noose formed. The whip is led through a block on the cap, down through one on the fore yard-arm; the end sheepshanked with a hitch only round the lower bight, but the upper bight seized to the standing part with a slight twine stop. At six feet from the end, below the seizing, a toggle is seized, to cause the drop. The stop carries away on being brought up against the block, the sheepshank fall adrift, and the toggle, with a jerk bringing up against the block, answers the purpose of "belay" to the men on the whip. The execution takes place when and where the commander-in-chief directs, but usually on board the ship in which the crime has been committed. The boats of the fleet form round; the whip is manned by two men from a boat of each ship (a lieutenant from each attending), taken from whatever thwart in the boat that the captain, superintending the duty, thinks fit to direct. The criminal being pinioned, is removed from irons, and brought on deck under a guard; the sentence of the court-martial, and article of war is read—the cap drawn down—the knot adjusted—the gun fired, and the sentence executed.*

---

* In Osler's "Life of Lord Exmouth," among the many instances of his stern energy of character, there is one related in connection with this subject, which I am led to extract, as much for the example

ORDER OF CONDUCTING FUNERALS.—*Of a Lieutenant.*

Band.
100 Marines (firing party)—four abreast.
Relay of Seamen, to carry the Coffin.

Lieutenant.		Lieutenant.
Lieutenant.		Lieutenant.
{ One other W. R. Officer }		{ One other W. R. Officer. }

Of the Ship

Surgeon and Captain (Chief Mourners.)
Boys—Midshipman in charge.
Seamen—   ,,   ,,
Petty Officers—Mate in charge.
Warrant Officers.
Gun-room Officers.
Ward-room Officers.

Of the Squadron { Boats' Crews, attended by Boat Midshipmen. Officers.

Going—Juniors first.   Returning, Seniors.

---

it affords of mental intrepidity in the discharge of duty as for the opportunity it gives me of bringing that matchless biography to the notice of those who are strangers to the record of that great and good man's life.

"Considerate as he was upon all occasions when human life was concerned, and unwilling to resort to punishment, he was always anxious to make it as impressive as possible whenever it became necessary to inflict it. He assisted to try one of the mutineers of the 'Hermione,' whose crime was attended with circumstances of peculiar aggravation,

374

532. DRESSING SHIP.—There are ten numeral flags, twenty-one alphabetical (thirteen square, and eight triangular), and twelve pendants, of which the answering and dinner pendants are to be left out. The ship's number we will assume to be R, union, N, which, with the ship's pendant also, lay on one side, and divide the flags as follows:—

From flying-boom end to fore top-gallant mast-head,	8 pendants, and 7 square flags, alternately.
Thence to main top-gallant mast-head,	4 square & 4 triangular flags, alternately.
Thence to mizen top gallant mast-head,	3 square & 3 triangular flags, alternately.
Thence to peak,	3 square flags.
Thence to boom-end,	5 square flags

From the spanker-boom end hang the ship's pendants, and from the flying-boom end, the number; a lead attached

---

—Captain Pigott having brought him up from a boy, and treated him with much kindness and confidence. His crime was fully proved; and the court being cleared, Sir Edward proposed that sentence should be executed immediately. The circumstances of the case demanded, in his opinion, unusual severity, which might be expected to have a good effect upon the fleet; while there was every reason to conclude, from the prisoner's demeanour before them, that if delay were allowed, he would meet his fate with a hardihood which would destroy the value of the example. The court at first questioned their power to execute without the warrant of the Admiralty, but this was quickly settled by reference to the Act of Parliament. The president then declared that he could not make the order. 'Look here!' said he, giving to Sir Edward his hand, trembling violently, and bathed in a

to each to keep them from flying away.   If the ship's number consist of two square flags, or two triangular flags, with the union, the necessary alteration can be made by substitution, between the main and mizen-masts.

Top-gallant yards are generally not sent down on the evening previous to dressing ship; but, should they be, cross them in the morning at seven bells. . The flying jib and royal halyards are used to trice up by, rove through blocks at the mast-heads, with down-hauls attached; and the flags, in addition to being stopped at the head and tack, are stitched to the halyards amidships.   Reeve them before breakfast, and bend the flags on; and at two min-

---

cold perspiration.   ‘ I see it, and I respect your feelings,’ replied Sir Edward, ‘ but I am sure that such an example is wanted, and I must press the point.’   ‘ Well.’ he replied, ‘ if it be the *unanimous* opinion of the court, it shall be done.’   It was agreed to, and the prisoner was called.   Though sure that he must be condemned, he entered with a bold front ; but when he was informed that he would be executed in one hour, he rolled on the cabin deck in an agony.   ‘ What ! gentlemen,’ he exclaimed, ‘ hang me directly ! will you not allow me a few days—a little time—to make my peace with God ?’ The whole fleet was appalled when the close of the court-martial was announced to them by the signal for execution ; and at the end of the allotted hour, the wretched criminal was brought up to undergo his sentence.

“ The clamour of that false humanity which is one of the most prominent vices of the present day would never influence him.   Little consideration can be claimed for that pretended sense of honour which is sensitive to the degradation of punishnnent, but callous to that of crime.”

376

utes before eight trice up mast-head ensigns, made up, and send aloft the captain of each top and two hands, one of whom, going to the mast-head, stops the tack in when broke; the other, remaining in the top, clears the flags, should they foul,

When dressing in honour of a foreign power, as in the case of salutes, neither custom nor the Queen's Regulations have determined at which mast-head the foreign colours should be displayed. Custom authorizing the fore or main, according to individual opinion, and the regulations only requiring it to be hoisted at "a mast-head," or at "one of the mast-heads;" courtesy would seem to require that the place of honour—the main top-gallant mast-head—should be given to it.

On a shift of wind, or at the turn of the tide if lying in a tideway, send hands aloft together to clear the flags.

533. HER MAJESTY'S BIRTHDAY.—Dress ship, and on life-lines at 8 A.M. Noon, away aloft, lay out and fire the first gun of a royal salute. The salute over, the band plays the national anthem, all present standing with heads uncovered. When finished, three cheers for the Queen; then lay in, down from aloft, and off life-lines. When the ship is illuminated in the evening, lanterns are placed in all the ports, and hung at the yard-arms, mast-heads, &c.

ANCHORING IN A FOREIGN PORT.—After the salute to the flag, of twenty-one guns, the admiral of the port is saluted, and if you think fit, the governor also; but, at the salute to the admiral, the jib is run up or fore topsail loosed; hoisted, or let fall at the first gun; and hauled down, or picked up when over, This indicates a salute to some one afloat, but it is not always observed.

534. HOISTING IN HEAVY WEIGHTS.—A 30-ton gun or mortar.   Lower the main yard to a distance of forty feet from the deck, clap a couple of stout anchor-strops on the lee quarter, cleat them up, and pass trustworthy lashings, *a, a,* through the bights of the strop and round the mast;

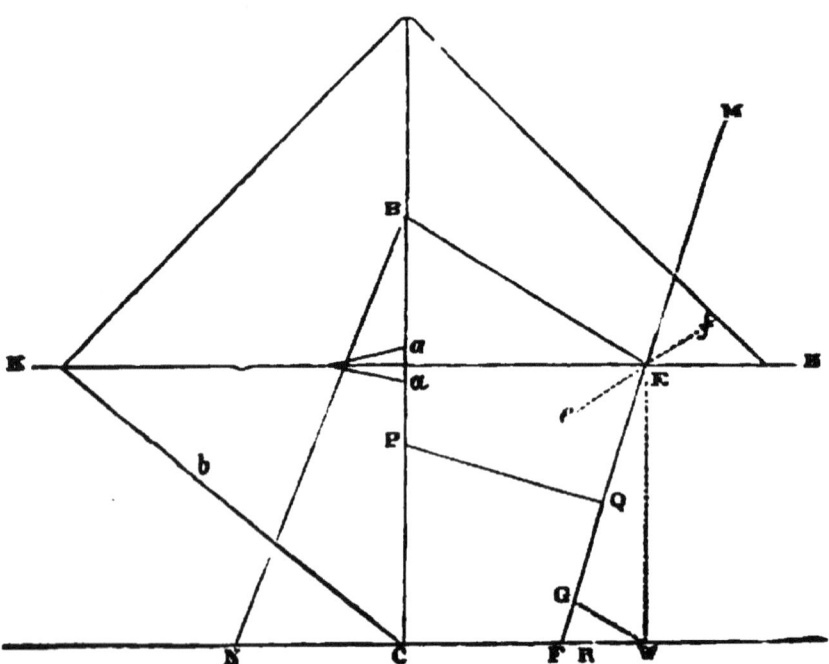

overhaul the lee quarter-tackle, *b,* and hook it to a bolt in the partners.   Hang the yard by up-and-downs from the lower pendants, pass a cross-lashing round yard and mast, and unreeve the jeers.

Derrick.—Get the spare main topmast up, droop it to the proper angle, wedge the heel up and secure it, shore

378

the decks up, and lash the derrick with a cross-lashing to the after side of the main yard,—the lashing passed in the direction *e f.*

Topping lift.—Fish-fall, rove from the opposite side of the deck, through the fish-davit head block at the mast-head.

Derrick-head guys.—Main runners and tackles—forward and aft; runners hitched round derrick-head and yard.

Shore, P. Q.—Mizen gaff. The jaws lashed upon the derrick, and the peak to the mast with a cross-lashing and turns through the peak-halyard bolts.

Belly guys.—Forward and aft. Up-and-down tackles with luffs on their falls; two to be hooked forward, the outside one to be dipped outside the derrick purchase as the stay purchase is hauled on, and the midship one come up when the other is taut.

Derrick-head purchase.—Blocks, treble and fourfold 30-inch purchase blocks. Fall, 9-inch hawser.

Mast-head purchase.—Reeve two top-tackle pendants through the top-blocks, pass the ends up through the hole for the slings on the fore part of the top, and secure them round the eyes of the rigging. Haul the top blocks out to the derrick-head by a fish-fall, rove full; the hauling part being led through a block at the mast-head. Reeve a cat-fall through two cat-blocks for the purchase, trice it up and hook it to the pendants.

The main yard is used to prevent the derrick coming in when the stay purchase is hauled upon; and it also

2 B   379

acts as a cross-piece to the topmast, to prevent the purchase slipping down. It consequently hangs freely, being supported at the yard-arm by the topping-lift; and the trifling strain brought upon it, being horizontal, is thrown upon the quarter and cross-lashings round the mainmast.

To ascertain the strain the gear will have to bear, lay off B C equal to the length of the mast from deck to trestle-trees, minus the drop of the topping-lift block, which will be about 63 feet. Project the main yard, K H, at the calculated height from the deck, = 40 feet. Raise the derrick, F M, at the necessary angle, and position upon the deck, N R. Connect E B N, to represent the topping-lift; and let fall E W, to represent the purchase with the weight attached.

On the line E W lay off E W = 40 tons (weight + resistance in lifting, or 30 + one-third), and draw W G parallel to B E. Then G E will represent the pressure on the derrick in the direction of its length, and G W the tension on the topping-lift E B. Measure G E and G W; and it will be found that the derrick will have to support a strain of 35 tons, and the topping-lift a strain of 12 tons.

To find, now, what the purchases, topping-lift, and derrick are capable of bearing :—

Derrick-head purchase.—Seven parts of 9-inch hawser, minus the allowance for friction, by rule previously given (Art. 32), are capable of *lifting* 73·5 tons.

Mast-head purchase.—Two pendants of 9-inch rope = 39 tons. Fall, six parts of 6-inch = 39 tons.

380

Topping-lift.—Five parts of 5-inch = 23 tons.

To ascertain the strength of the derrick.—*

Least diameter of topmast, 20 inches ...	1·301030
	4
	5.204120
121	9·082785
	4·286905
Tab. No. Norway spars, 5830000... ...	6·765669
	1·052574
EQ, 21 ft. = 252 in. Squared	4·802802
	lbs. 6·249772
112 lbs. in cwt.	2·049218
	cwt. 4·200554
20 cwt. in ton	1·301030
4)793 ... ... tons	2·899524

198 tons = practical strength of derrick.

The whole length of the derrick, EG, is 42 feet; but, as it is securely held amidships by the shore and belly-guys, the distance between the supports is that alone affected by the strain. Without the shore and belly-guys, the derrick, by calculation, would only support a weight of 50 tons. And, as strength varies inversely with the square of the

---

* See page 389 par. 16.

length, $21^2 : 42^2 :: x : 198$.   By this, also, $x = 50$ tons nearly.

Thrown into a tabular form it will be seen that there are means for lifting any possible weight with ease and safety.

Gear.	Capacity for strain : calculated at the minimum strength of materials.	Strain produced.
Derrick-head purchase	{ Fall............73 tons } { (Blocks ......84 ,,) }	40 tons.
Mast-head purchase ...	39 ,,	
Topping-lift	23 ,,	12 ,,
Derrick	198 ,,	36 ,,

To bring the mortar in over the main hatchway, rig a stay derrick of the spare fore topmast, and support it by a topping-lift, belly-guys, and a shore to the mainmast.

Purchase.—Blocks, upper fore and main jeer-blocks, 26-inch and 24-inch treble.   Fall, fore and main jeers, 8 inch and 7½-inch spliced together.

Topping-lift.—A cat-fall, rove through top-tackle blocks.

Mast-head purchase used for hoisting up, is eased in, and becomes a stay purchase.

382

EXPLANATION OF TABLE VII.—"The first column of figures, marked C, contains the mean strength of cohesion on an inch section of the material; the second, marked S, the constant for transverse strains; the third, marked E, the constant for deflections; and the fourth, marked M, the modulus of elasticity.

"1. *To find the absolute strength or force of direct cohesion of beams or rods of given materials*, that is, their absolute resistance to longitudinal tension or strain in lbs. Rule.—*Multiply the area of the transverse section of the rod or beam in inches by the tabular number, in the column marked C, opposite the name of the material, and the product will be the strength or resistance required.* Note. 1.—In practice the weight or strain should not exceed $\frac{1}{3}$ of the absolute strength according to Barlow, or $\frac{1}{4}$ according to Tredgold. Thus, the force which would tear asunder a piece of teak $4\frac{1}{2}$ inches broad and 2 inches thick, is $2 \times 4\frac{1}{2} \times 15000 = 135000$ lbs. Hence a longitudinal strain of more than 45000 lbs. would be unsafe in practice. *Note* 2.—The tenacity of materials of the same kind is proportional to their specific gravity. Hence, a piece of teak whose specific gravity was $\frac{1}{20}$ part less than that of the preceding, would have $\frac{1}{20}$ part less of cohesive power.

"2. When the direction of the straining force does not coincide with the perpendicular to the centre of tenacity or centre of gravity of the transverse section, the Rule is modified as follows : Multiply the tabular number in column C by the breadth and the square of the thickness of the beam, both in inches, and divide the product by the sum of the thickness and 6 times the distance of the line of direction from the centre of the section, in inches ; the quotient will be the absolute strength required, of which take $\frac{1}{3}$ as before, for the practical load. *Note*.—In actual constructions an allowance of $\frac{1}{3}$ of the thickness should be made for the probable deviation of the direction of the stretching force. The absolute strength will then be $\frac{1}{3}$ of that found by the Rule in the preceding article ; and the practical load $\frac{1}{9}$ of the same quantity, or $\frac{1}{12}$ according to Tredgold.

383

" 3. *To find the dimensions of a rod or beam to resist a given longitudinal strain*, that is, to sustain a given weight without fracture in the direction of its fibres. *Rule.—Multiply the tabular number in column* C, *by the number denoting the ratio of the breadth to the thickness, and divide* 9 (*or* 12) *times the given weight in lbs. by the product; the square root of the quotient will be the required thickness in inches, and the thickness multiplied by the number of the ratio will give the breadth required.* Thus, the dimensions of a beam of the strongest English oak to sustain a load of 20 tons in the direction of its fibres, supposing the breadth to be 3 times its thickness is $\sqrt{\{(9 \times 44800) \div (3 \times 15000)\}} = 3$ inches nearly, the thickness required; whence $3 \times 3 = 9$ inches, the breadth required. *Note.*—If the beam be cylindrical, divide 9 times the given weight by ·7854 times the tabular number, and the square root of the quotient will be the diameter.

" 4. *Force of the Transverse Resistance of Materials.*—This force is proportional to the product of the breadth and the square of the depth in rectangular beams (more properly parallelopipedal beams), and to the cube of the diameter in cylindric beams ; but it is in the inverse ratio of the length, modified by the cosine or square of the sectant of the angle of deflection immediately before fracture, and by the manner in which the beam is supported. In ordinary practice, thé consideration of the angle of deflection may be omitted.

" 5. *To find the relative strength or force of resistance of rectangular beams or rods of given materials, to transverse strain or pressure in lbs.* 1. When the beam is *fixed* at one end and *loaded at the other. Rule.—* Multiply the tabular number, in the column marked S, opposite the name of the given material, by the breadth of the beam in inches, and this product by the square of its depth in inches, and divide the result by the length of the beam in inches, the quotient will be the strength or resistance required. 2. When the beam is *fixed* at the one end and *uniformly loaded*, the strength or resistance will be *double* the preceding resistance, which for brevity we shall call the *prime* resistance. 3. When the beam is *supported* at both ends and *loaded in the middle*, the strength will be *four times* the prime resistance. 4. When the

384

beam is *supported* at both ends and *uniformly loaded*, the strength will be *eight times* the prime resistance.   5. When the beam is *fixed* at both ends and *loaded in the middle*, the strength is *six times* the prime resistance.   6. When the beam is *fixed* at both ends, and *uniformly loaded*, the strength is *twelve times* the prime resistance.   7. When the beam is *supported* at both ends and *loaded at a point not in the middle*, the strength is found by multiplying the prime resistance by the square of the length, and dividing the result by the product of the lengths of the segments into which the beam is divided at the point of application of the load.

"6.   In all the preceding cases, it must be remembered that not more than *one-third* of the ultimate strength found by the rule, ought to be depended upon for any permanent construction, according to Barlow, and only *one-fourth* according to Tredgold, who adds that if the beam be not horizontal, the distance between the supports must be the horizontal distance.   As an example, the weight which a beam of Riga fir, 20 feet long, 12 inches broad, and 12 inches deep, supported at both ends, would sustain in the middle, is (1130 × 12 × 144) × 4 ÷ 240 = 32544 lbs. and the practical load is 32544 ÷ 3 = 10848 lbs. or 32544 ÷ 4 = 8136 lbs.

"7. When beams are cylindrical, their resistance to transverse pressure is only two-thirds of that of a square prism of the same thickness.   In the case of a hollow cylinder, the resistance will be found by multiplying the difference of the cubes of the interior and exterior diameter, by 8 times the modulus of elasticity and dividing the product by 9 times the length.   If the hollow part be $\frac{9}{10}$ of the diameter of the cylinder, its strength will be reduced to about $\frac{1}{12}$ more than a $\frac{1}{4}$ of that of the solid cylinder; but if the tube were formed into a solid rod, its strength would be only $\frac{1}{12}$ part of that of the solid cylinder.   A cylinder having half its core hollowed out should be rendered only $\frac{1}{8}$ part weaker, which agrees with an experiment made by Barlow.   We see here the divine process of nature in making the bones of animals hollow, and the imitative ingenuity of man in making cast-metal pillars tubular, thus combining lightness with strength in their structures.

385

"8. The *lateral* or transverse strength of any beam thus depends mainly on the distance and cohesion of the upper and under surfaces. Whatever stiffens the exterior layers contributes greatly to strengthen the whole. A small incision drawn across the under side weakens a bar essentially; while a notch cut near the middle of the upper side will not impair the strength, but if filled up with a harder material will even sensibly augment it. Thus Duhamel found that a bar of willow cut through $\frac{1}{3}$ of its depth, the cut being filled up with a thin slip of hard wood, was thereby rendered $\frac{1}{8}$ part stronger than before. It was even then remarked that the incision could be carried much farther without injuring the strength of the bar.*

"9. *To find the breadth and depth of a beam of given length and material, so that it may, in practice, support a given load*, in the case of prime resistance (art. 5.) *Rule.*—Multiply the given weight in lbs. by the length in inches, and divide this product by 4 times the product of the tabular number in col. S, and the number denoting the ratio of the breadth to the depth; then, the cube root of the quotient will be the required depth in inches, from which the breadth is found as before (art. 3.) In all other cases, the tabular number in col. S must be multiplied by the number denoting the increase of strength or resistance arising from the mode of fixing the beam (art. 5), before the above rule be applied. Thus, the depth of a beam of Scotch fir, 18 feet long, to bear a load of 20 tons at the middle, when supported at both ends, the breadth being half of the depth is $\sqrt{\left\{ (4 \times 44800 \times 216) \div (1140 \times \frac{1}{2} \times 4) \right\}} = 20\cdot4$ inches nearly; whence the breadth is 10·2 inches. When the breadth or depth is given, the calculation is easy, as the rule in art. 5 requires only to be reversed.

"10. *Deflection of Beams under Transverse Strains.*—The deflection of beams under given weights is proportional to the product of the weight and cube of the length directly, and to the product of the breadth and the cube of the depth inversely; whence the elasticity is

---

* Leslie's Natural Philosophy, p. 271.

deduced, being proportional to the deflection. Consequently, beams will be of the same stiffness, when the depth is increased in the same proportion as the length, the breadth remaining the same ; and the deflection of beams arising from their own weight, having their several dimensions proportional, will be as the square of either of their like lineal dimensions. The same will apply to beams loaded throughout proportionally to the dimensions : this ought to be kept constantly in view in the construction of models, on a small scale, of works intended to be executed on a large one.

"11. *To find the Deflection of a Beam:* 1. *When supported at both ends and loaded in the middle.* For brevity's sake, we shall call this the *prime* deflection. *Rule.—Multiply the given weight in lbs. by the cube of the length of the beam in inches, and divide this product by the continuous product of the tabular number, in the column marked* E, *opposite the name of the given material, the breadth, and the cube of the depth, the quotient will be the required deflection in inches.* 2. When the beam is fixed at one end and loaded at the other, multiply the prime deflection by 32. 3. When it is fixed the same, but uniformly loaded, multiply the prime deflection by 12. 4. When it is supported at both ends and uniformly loaded, take $\frac{5}{8}$ of the prime deflection. 5. When it is fixed at both ends and loaded in the middle, take $\frac{2}{3}$ of the prime deflection. 6. When it is fixed the same, but uniformly loaded, take $\frac{5}{12}$ of the prime deflection. Thus, the prime deflection of a beam of pitch pine, 30 feet long, 6 inches broad, and 10 inches deep, supported at both ends, and loaded in the middle with a weight of 1000 lbs. is $(1000 \times 27000 \times 1728) \div (5000000 \times 6 \times 1000) = 1\frac{5}{9}$ inches nearly ; whence the deflection due to other modes of fixing and supporting, may easily be found. *Note.*—If the beam be a cylinder, the deflection will be 1·7 times that of a square beam in similar circumstances.

"12. *To find the weight which will produce a given prime deflection on a beam of given material and dimensions.* *Rule.*—Find the continuous product of the tabular number in col. E, the breadth, the cube of the depth, and the given deflection, and divide this product by the cube of the length; the quotient will be the weight required. Thus, the weight which will produce a deflection of $1\frac{1}{2}$ inch on a wrought iron beam, 20 feet long, 3 inches broad, and 9 inches deep, supported at both ends, and loaded in the middle, is $(91440000 \times 3 \times 729 \times 1\frac{1}{2})$ $\div (8000 \times 1728) = 21699$ lbs. or near 10 tons; whence, the weight for other deflections may easily be found.

"13. *To find the depth requisite for a beam of given material, length and breadth, to bear a given load with a given prime deflection. Rule.*— Divide the given loads in lbs. by the continuous product of the tabular number in col. E, the breadth and deflection, and multiply the cube root of the quotient by the length; the product is the depth required. Thus the depth of a wrought-iron beam, 20 feet long, 3 inches broad, requisite to support a load of 10 tons with a prime deflection of $1\frac{1}{2}$ inch, is $240 \times \sqrt[3]{\left\{ (10 \times 2240) \div 91440000 \times 3 \times 1\frac{1}{2}) \right\}} = 9 \cdot 1$ inches nearly. When the breadth is not given, multiply the given weight by the cube of the length, and divide this product by the product of the tabular number in col. E, and the given deflection, the quotient is the product of the breadth and cube of the depth. Hence, when the beam is to be square, the fourth root of the quotient is the breadth or depth required: and when it is to be cylindric, multiply the quotient by $1 \cdot 7$, and the fourth root of the product will be the diameter.

"14. *The modulus of elasticity* is the measure of the elastic force of any material. It is found by the following proportion: As the portion of the length of a column of the material, which it loses by compression, is to the whole length before compression, so is the force which produced that compression to the modulus of elasticity. Sir John Leslie has shown that the modulus of elasticity is found by dividing 5 times the fourth power of the length of a beam by 32 times the product of its spontaneous depression and the square of its depth. In his work on *Heat*, he observes that a white deal 138 inches long and $\frac{9}{20}$ of an inch deep, suffered a depression of $2\frac{1}{2}$ inches by its own weight; hence $(5 \times 138 \times 138 \times 138 \times 138) \div (32 \times \cdot 45 \times \cdot 45 \times 2 \cdot 5) = 111936000$ inches or 9328000 feet, in round numbers. The

388

umbers in col. M may be found from those in col. E, by multiplying
the latter by 576, and dividing the product by the corresponding
specific gravity.

" 15. *The resistance of Materials to a crushing force*, appears to be
directly proportional to the fourth power of the diameter in cylinders,
or of the side in square prisms, and inversely proportional to the
square of the height.

" 16. *To find the weight which a column of given material will
support before flexure.*—Multiply the tabular number in col. E by
121 times the fourth power of the diameter in inches in cylindric
columns, or ·2056 times the side in inches, in square prismatic
columns, and divide the product by the square of the length in inches,
the quotient is the weight required in lbs. *Note.*—When the base
of the column is rectangular, multiply the tabular number by ·2056
times the area multiplied by the square of its breadth, and divide
as before. Only $\frac{1}{3}$ or $\frac{1}{4}$ of this weight ought to be depended upon
in practice; for when once the column begins to bend, the consequences are inevitable. Thus, the weight under which a pillar of
New England fir would begin to bend, supposing its length 20 feet,
and its diameter 12 inches, is (5967000 × ·121 × 12 × 12 × 12 × 12) ÷
(20 × 20 × 12 × 12) = 259922·52 lbs., or nearly 116 tons, a most enormous
load, according to theory; but 29 tons could only be trusted in practice.

" *The Resistance of Materials to the force of Torsion, or Twisting*, is
directly proportional to the angle of torsion and the fourth power of
the diameter in cylindric shafts, and inversely as their length, according to Sir John Leslie: other writers say, that it is directly proportional
to the cubes of the diameters. According to the Professor's law, the
power of an iron cylinder to resist the torsion of a weight in lbs.
acting at a distance of a foot, is found by dividing 600 times the fourth
power of the diameter by the length. The preceding principle is
employed in the construction of the *Balance of Torsion*, invented by
Coulomb."

535. FOREIGN MEASURES.—As six metres are equal to 19½ feet, there is just water enough for you; and, at high water, as "the rise and fall is about a metre," there would be upwards of three feet to spare.

In the new French charts, the soundings are in *mètres;* but in their old charts, in *brasses.*

536. ASCERTAINING LOCAL DEVIATION OF THE COMPASS. —Lay a kedge out, and swing the ship with *her head* to each point of the compass, observing, as each point comes on, the bearing of some object whose distance—not less than six or eight miles—is such that its angular distance, between the limits of the ship's position while swinging, will not be perceptible.   Note down these bearings, then land with a compass, and ascertain the bearing of the object on shore, when the ship and the distant object are in one. The difference between that and the various bearings taken on board, will give the local deviation for each point of the compass;—east, when the ship's bearings are to the left of the true magnetic bearings; and west, when the contrary is the case.

Example.—Oct. 1, 1856.   Second Bar Pagoda, distant 13 miles, bore from H.M.S. ——, at anchor off Chuenpee, N. 32° 20′ W. with the ship's head south; and N. 23° 5′ W. with her head N.W.   From Anunghoy, with the ship and object in one, the Pagoda bore N. 29° W.   Consequently the deviation of the south point of the compass was 3° 20′ E.; and of the N.W. point, 5° 55′ W.

In a close harbour, where there is no object sufficiently remote for the purpose, it will be necessary to erect a mark on shore, and to land an assistant with a compass to take reciprocal bearings. When ready, you hoist a preconcerted signal, which you dip as the ship is swung on each point of the compass to the mark ashore. The difference between the bearing of the mark from the ship, and the bearing of the ship from the mark, reversed, is the deviation of the compass on board, corresponding to the direction of the ship's head at the time of each observation. If there is any actual difference between the compasses employed, the correction must be made. To ascertain it, land the compasses, and compare the bearings of an object taken with each; but the compasses should not be within twelve feet of each other.

When unable to land, take the bearings of a distant object, with the ship's head round the compass. Assume the true magnetic bearing to be the mean of these; and by comparison ascertain the deviation on each point accordingly.

As the deviation in the northern hemisphere is changed in the southern hemisphere, it will be frequently necessary at sea, if the deviation is great, to determine it afresh as you alter your latitude. You should, therefore, take advantage of light winds, or calm weather, to ascertain the variation of the compass by azimuth observations, with the ship's head in different directions, computing the deviation on the points you have not observed, from those that have been; the rule for which will be found in Inman, art. 308.

391

537. POSITIONS AND DIMENSIONS OF MASTS AND YARDS.—All the information here given is derived from Fincham's "Treatise on Masting Ships," to which the reader is referred for a complete investigation of the subject in all its bearings.

"The common rule for determining the masts and yards by the length and breadth of the vessel, has been admitted by long use, and may be considered equally good with any of the rules at present given as approximations; for the yards must be governed by the length, in order that the sails may have a suitable spread; and the breadth, which determines the length of the masts, that they may have proper support by the spread of the rigging, has the greatest influence on the stability."

In accordance with this principle, Tables IX. to XV. are formed; and though much curtailed, they are sufficient to solve the proposed questions, and to meet any probable case that may occur on service.

The following sketches are also from Fincham.

1. BERMUDA SCHOONER,

2. SLIDING GUNTER.

393

3. SETTEE.

4. LATEEN.

5. THREE STANDING LUGS,

6. CUTTER WITH A STANDING LUG.

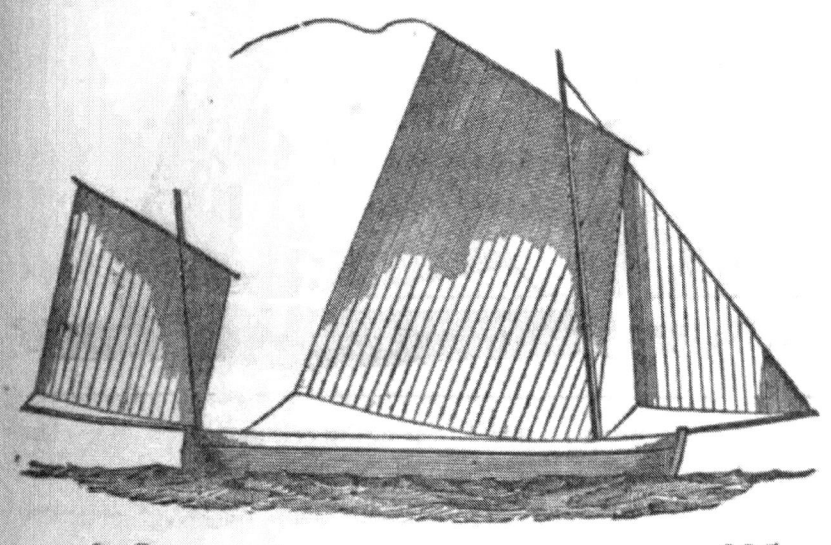

7. THREE SPRITS AND A JIB.

8. CUTTER WITH A DIPPING LUG.*

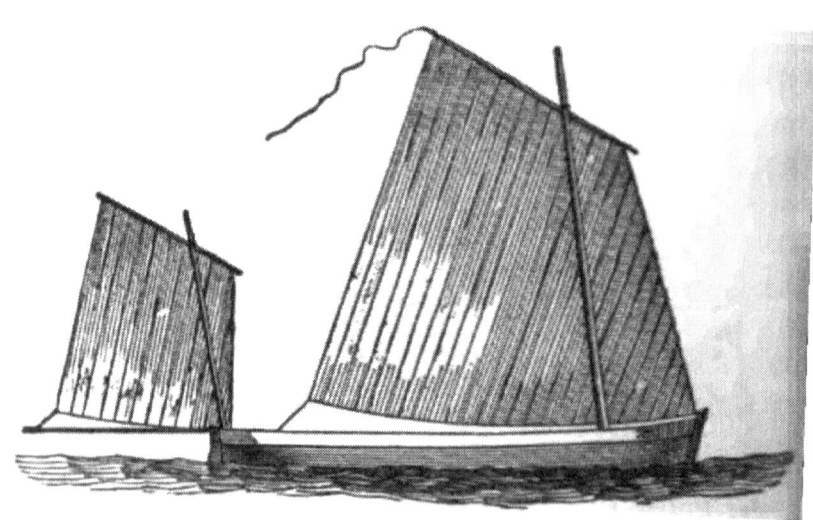

* A cutter's mizen, fitted in the ordinary manner, is not a hand
sail. On shoving off from a ship, it is often a troublesome matter
get the boomkin clamped; the tiller gets jambed, the coxsw[...]

538. HEAVING DOWN.—The following account of the
heaving down of H.M.S. "Formidable," 84 guns, from
the " Nautical Magazine," contains an explanation of the
subject.

The "Formidable" arrived in Malta harbour on the
13th of January, 1843, and received orders to prepare for
heaving down ; the ship was accordingly moored head
and stern, with her bower chains and anchors, off the
careening wharf, and cleared of everything.   Not a pig of
ballast, or a moveable article was left in her, with the exception of the coppers, range, and main-deck tank, which
were all well shored from the ship's side, and otherwise
secured.   As the ship was to be hove down on the starboard side first, the hammock-nettings on that side were
removed, and the partners of fore and mainmasts on upper
and main decks were taken up.

---

bewildered, and a great deal of confusion is occasioned in consequence.   Should you want to keep away suddenly, it is of no avail to
let go the sheet, for, except in a stormy breeze, it will not overhaul.
To remedy this, cut the boomtkin off to within a couple of feet of the
stern, stepping, and clamping it as hitherto.   Provide a boom of the
same spread as the original boomkin, seize the tack of the sail to the
outer end, fit a swivel-bolt to the foremost end, and forelock it to a
band round the mast.   Splice a topping-lift from the mizen mast-
head round the outer end, seize a sheet-block to the boom amidships,
fit another to travel along the boomkin, and reeve the sheet with the
standing part alongside the block on the boom.   On getting the
masts down, top the boom up, unclamp the boomkin, and (without
unreeving the sheet, which is passed round all as a gasket) make the
boom and boomkin up with the mast and sail.

2 C 2

Bulkheads.—The bulkheads were three in number ; two were placed on the main deck—one at each end of the starboard skids, and the third was built across under the break of the poop.   They were constructed in the following manner.   Strong frames were nailed to the beams overhead, and deck ; into these were morticed strong half-round uprights, and against the flat sides of these were placed the planks which went athwartships.   The workmen commenced boarding from top to bottom, which from the sheer of upper deck, left the space to be filled up by the last, or midship plank, in the form of a wedge ; by this means, when the board was driven in, the whole thing was wedged up taut.   The bulkheads were caulked and payed, then shored up behind from the beams, and from cleats nailed to the deck.   All the bulkheads extended from the ship's side to amidships.

Ports.—The lower-deck ports were barred in and caulked ; the scuttles in them well secured, and boarded over outside, then payed with pitch.   The main-deck ports, with the exception of the four midship ones, between the bulkheads, which were left open, were boarded in with two-inch plank, then caulked, and shored up from inside to cleats on the deck.

Outriggers.—Nine to mainmast—five on lower deck, and four on the main deck ; seven to foremast—four on lower deck, and three on main deck.   Those on lower deck were square balks of timber, 2 feet in the square, 40 feet 6 inches long, and were placed in ports as near abreast of the respective masts as possible ; then secured by being

398

well chocked in the ports, the heels butting against comb-ings, bitts, &c. Where there were none, they had a heel-shore from starboard waterway, and were also secured from fetching way or rising, by being well shored in every direction. The main deck outriggers, about 18 inches in the square, and 35 feet long, were placed and secured in the same manner as those on lower deck. All the out-riggers were rounded, shouldered, and cleated for rigging to butt against, at about 18 inches from the outer end.

Outrigger Martingales—were 8-inch rope, fitted with a large thimble at each end, middled and taken with a round turn over the end of the spar, then seized. Those of main deck were pulled up to short chocks in lower-deck ports; those of lower deck, to span shackles driven through ship's side, and forelocked inboard. Starboard scuttles, scuppers, and chain-pump pipe were all plugged up, and boarded over outside; the pigeon-holes only, between main-deck bulk-heads, were filled in and caulked, being the only place where water was allowed to come.

Bilge-pumps.—Of these there were five—two in fore hatchway, two in main, and one in after hatchway. They were stepped in the lower-deck ports for wells, and the lower deck was scuttled abreast the hatchways, close in to starboard waterway, to allow the water to pass up from orlop deck to pumps. Temporary stages were erected in the square of the hatchways, for pumping party to stand on while working.

Masts—Were stripped of everything but lower rigging; the tops and cross-trees being removed, and fished on fore

399

and after sides; the heads of the fishes close up to the trestle-trees, and the heels down to lower deck—the partners on upper and main decks, being away, allowed sufficient space for their passing down. The fishes were woulded in nine places, nine turns in each lashing (3-inch rope), and well wedged up. The masts were stayed perfectly upright, but both main stays were taken on lee side of the foremast, to allow the mast to come well over on port side. The upright shores of mainmast were three in number; the first and largest was a rough 22-inch spar, and went up within 6 inches of the trestle-trees, the head being chamfered out to allow it to rest against the bibs; the second was placed a third lower down; and the last between the head of the second and the deck. They were all secured to the mast by a head-lashing, and had also horizontal shores between them and the mast, of pieces of oak plank, about 2½ inches thick, placed wherever the belly-lashings were passed, and proved an immense support to the mast. Of these horizontal shores and belly-lashings, there were three on the long shore, and one on each of the others. All the heels of the upright shores rested on a thick elm plank laid along the waterways; the deck being well shored underneath.

Preventer Rigging—For mainmast consisted of eight shrouds and one pendant, 13-inch rope, fitted with a long and short leg, and an eye spliced into the end of each. In placing them over the mast-head, the long leg went foremost, as it set up to the foremost lower-deck outrigger; the short one to foremost main-deck out rigger.

Two pair of shrouds were placed first, to form a bolster
400

for the purchase block; then remainder of the shrouds; lastly, the pendant with a lashing-eye. The rigging was pulled up by double 20-inch blocks, double stropped, the bight of the shroud taken through the strop, and toggled. The lower block strop went over the head of the outrigger; and the falls were of 7-inch rope. The foremast was secured precisely the same as the mainmast, excepting that it had but one fish, and that on the after side; seven shrouds of 13-inch rope; two upright, and three horizontal shores, and belly-lashings; and both fore and mainmasts had, when secured, runners and tackles steadied forward to assist the stays. The heels of fore and mainmasts were well shored in the hold on port side. The mizen mast was stripped of everything, the same as the other masts, excepting that the cross-trees were left on; and the only support given to this mast, beyond its own rigging, consisted of the sail-tackles from mast-head pendants, hooked to the weather chains, which took some strain off the rigging.

Setting up Rigging.—The masts were steadied over against the port lower-deck partners, the wedges having been removed; the starboard rigging was then pulled up for a full due, the preventer rigging pulled up with luffs on their own falls, and secured to the toggles. The standing part of the fall went with a running eye over the end of the outrigger, and the preventer rigging was pulled up last.

Mast-head Purchase Blocks.—Main purchase block, 40 inches; main small ditto, 30 inches; fore ditto, 40 inches; all treble sheaved, and treble stropped. The 40-inch blocks were, in the first place, double stropped with 9-inch

401

cable-laid rope, with a long eye to take the turns of the lashing; and they had also a preventer strop of 9-inch rope, long enough to go round the mast-heads, where they were secured with two lashing-eyes. The 30-inch block was double stropped with 8-inch, and with a 9-inch preventer fitted as above. The purchase blocks were lashed at main-mast-head after the first two pair of shrouds were placed; and at the fore, after the first pair of shrouds. As there were two main purchases, the largest was lashed on fore-most quarter of mast-head, and the smaller one on the after quarter, but no shrouds were between them. The lashings were selvagees, 500 new yarns, 30 fathoms long; those for preventer strop were the same size, but not so long, and had been used before. In lashing the blocks, the fore and main runners were used in the following manner :—Supposing the main to be the block to be lashed, the fore runner pendant block was lashed at fore-mast head, and the runner taken to mainmast head; the tackle was hooked up and down to the foremast, and had a tricing-line on upper block from the mast-head, to over-haul the runner after it had been pulled up; the selvagee was middled, and seized to the strop in the eye; one end was passed round the mast-head, through the eye of the strop, then racked to the runner pendant, which was pulled up on deck. When taut enough, and the turn of the lash-ing had been racked, the runner was overhauled by the girtlines and tricing-lines as before mentioned.

Pit Purchase Blocks—were double 40-inch, double stropped with 9-inch rope; the leading blocks 36-inch, single stropped.   The double blocks were stropped on the bars in the pits; the leading blocks had strops long enough to go round one bar, and lash to the other, there being two in each pit.

Capstans.—Three in number, of the same sort as those used at sheers: 20 bars each, six men on each bar.

Tripping Cables—were two in number, one forward and one aft.   A hemp cable, having been chafed when heaving the ship off at Barcelona, was condemned and cut in two, and used for this purpose.   Two purchases of new 9-inch hawsers, through treble 40-inch blocks, were rove.   For the after cable, one block was lashed ashore round the arches at the buildings, on the opposite side of the creek, abreast the careening wharf (creek about 60 fathoms wide), and the other block was clinched to the end of sheet cable, and then hung to a lump to keep it off the bottom.   The other end of that cable was taken under the ship's bottom, and brought up on the starboard side through a starboard upper-deck port, before the after hatchway, then across the deck, and clinched through two ports on the port side. The fore tripping-cable was fitted the same as the after, but came through third port on the forecastle, starboard side, and made fast as before mentioned.   From its leading over the fore chains, they were well shored up, but were burst down from the immense strain on them when the ship was half-way down.

Righting Cables—were fitted the same as the above, but smaller, the stream cable being used instead of sheet. The shore blocks were lashed to bars in the pits, the cables went under the bottom, and were clinched through the port main-deck ports. These were precautionary measures, no strain being ever brought upon them.

Reeving-lines and Falls.—Reeving-lines were new 7-inch rope, about 150 fathoms long. Falls ; fore and main 10½-inch, quite new, hawser-laid rope ; fall for the second main purchase, new 9-inch hawser-laid rope. The 10½-inch was reduced to 9½ inches when unrove. The falls were 140 fathoms long, and then rather short.

When hove down the first time, they found the ship's buttocks hove her stern so high out as to be inconvenient to the workmen ; therefore, before she came down the second time, thirty butts were lashed under the fore chains, which had the desired effect of keeping her keel parallel. She was kept quite free by one of Hearle's engines.

———

In the third vol. of the " Nautical Magazine " there is an account of an accident which happened to H.M.S. " Success," Captain W. Jervoise, by running on a reef of rocks at the entrance of Cockburn Sound, in 1829 ; to which is appended a description of the means employed for heaving her keel out for repair, by means of outriggers from the side.

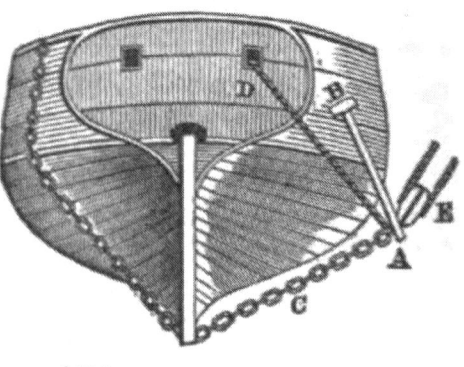

A is the after out-rigger, stepped in a shoe, B, which is bolted to the ship's side, abaft the main chains.

The foremost outrigger is planted abaft the fore chains.

C, the after girder, secured inboard the port side, brought under the keel, and attached to the end of the outrigger.

D, the after guy, the foremost guy being led in through the gangway port.

E, the after purchase block.

"The foremost cap-stan was taken out of the 'Success,' and fitted in the fore hatchway of His Majesty's cruiser," by which vessel the "Success" was hove out.

539. O R C H A R D'S METHOD OF SLINGING SUNKEN VESSELS.—

Fig. 1 shows the position of the sweeps, and vessels employed, before heaving taut. When single sweeps are rove, only one chain is

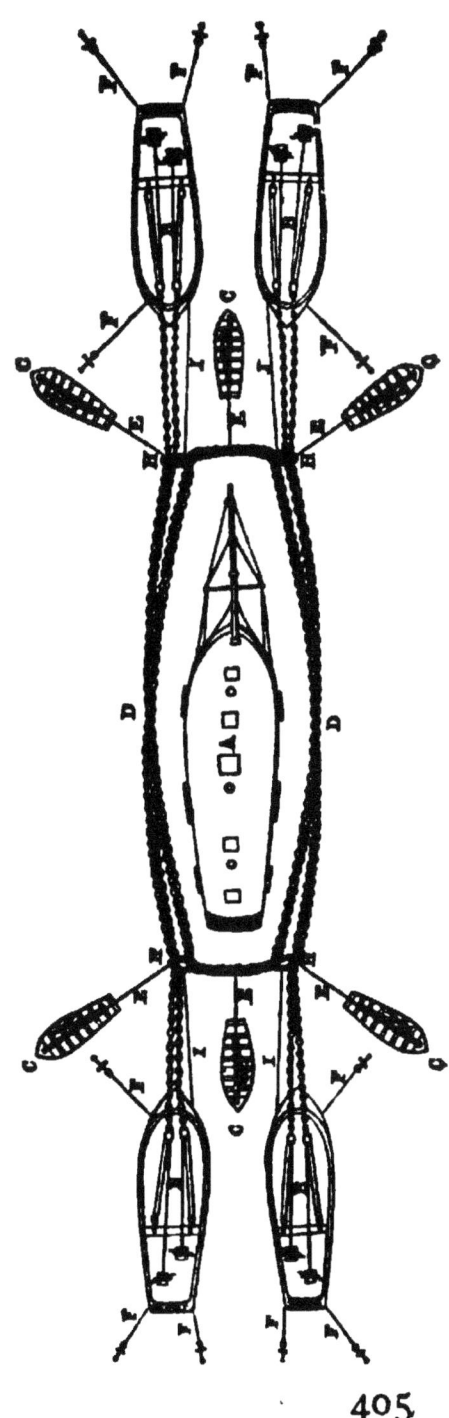

405

Fig. 2 shows the wreck slung and weighed.

rought on board each weighing vessel.   **A.** The wreck.
l. Weighing vessels.   C. Launches, for suspending the
weeps at the proper height.   D. Sweeps.   E. Suspending
opes.   F. Cables and anchors.   H. Jewel rings.   I. Jewel
opes.

540. To calculate a Vessel's Tonnage.—The old
system of measurement is that still employed in the navy,
and is of use only in giving an idea of the relative size of
the ships of *each class;* for as length and breadth alone
enter into the calculation, a razee still retains her original
nominal tonnage, whatever be the reduction in size consequent on the alteration.

The length for tonnage, the breadth, and half the
breadth, multiplied together, and divided by ninety-four,
give the tonnage by what is termed old measurement.
The "length between perpendiculars," is that at the middle
deck of three-deckers, and at the upper deck of all other
rates, from fore part of stem, to after part of stern-post,
and when corrected for the rake of stem and stern-post,
it is called "length of keel for tonnage."   The "breadth
for tonnage," is the extreme beam of the ship (from outside
to outside), with a trifling deduction for the thickness of
the wales in excess of that of the bottom planking.

By the new measurement, a far more accurate estimate is
obtained of a ship's internal capacity; as length, breadth,
and depth are all employed.

The length of the upper deck is divided into six parts,
a, a', and the depth taken at the foremost, aftermost,

407

and midship points of division. These three perpendicular measurements are each intersected at four intermediate points, *b*, *c* which divides them into five equal parts.

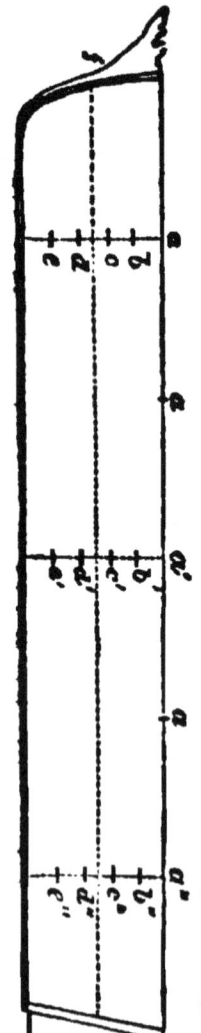

The length for tonnage, *f g*, is the length of the ship from after side of stem to fore side of stern-post, at a height half-way up the midship line of section *a'*.

The depths to be employed are, twice the depth of the midship line of section at *a'*, added to once the depth of the foremost and aftermost sections, at *a* and *a''*.

The breadths used are, at the foremost section *a*, the (internal) breadth of the ship at *b*, added to the breadth at *c*. In the midship section *a'*, three times the breadth at *c'* are added to once the breadth at *c*. In the after section *a''*, once the breadth at *b''* is added to twice the breadth at *c*.

Then, the product of the sum of the depths, into the sum of the breadths, into the length for tonnage, divided by 3500, gives the number of tons for register.

If the vessel has a poop; multiply together the inside length, breadth, and height, divide the product by 92·4, and the quotient will be the number of tons to be added.

To find the real capacity of a vessel, multiply the register tonnage by 92·4, for the contents in cubic feet.

408

Example.

Length at half midship depth ....159·4   Feet.
Depth at foremost division .... 29·66   29·66
  ,,   midship   ,, ... 30·66 × 2 = 61·32
  ,,   aftermost   ,, ...··· 29·08   29·08
                      Sum of depths.................120·06

Foremost division :—

Breadth at one-fifth of the depth ....37·74   37·74
    ,,   four-fifths of the depth...........31·00   31·00
        Midship division :—
Breadth at two-fifths of the depth ....40·00 × 3 = 120·00
    ,,   four-fifths   ,, ...36·08   36·08
     Aftermost division :—
Breadth at one-fifth of the depth............34·58   34·58
    ,,   four-fifths   ,, ...17·50 × 2 = 35·00
                      Sum of the breadth...........294·40

                                                    Feet.

Then, $\dfrac{120·06 \times 294·4 \times 159.4}{3,500} = 1,609$ Mean length of poop 39·0

$\dfrac{39 \times 30 \times 6·5}{92·4} = 82$,,   breadth   ,,   30·0

           1,609   ,,   height   ,,   6·5

   Total register 1,691 tons.   1,691 × 92·4 = 156,248 cubic feet.

541. STOWING BOOMS.—I know of no better plan than the following, for it possesses the great advantage of allowing any one spar to be taken out without disturbing the rest. A and B are iron crutches. A is one of the foremost ones, in which the sterns of the barge and pinnace rest; and B B are the after ones, sufficiently far forward to allow play to the mizen topmast and hand-mast, when they

409

require to be removed.   The bows of the barge and pinnace rest on crutches similar to A, but without the cross-piece.

PORT BOOMS.   STARBOARD BOOMS.

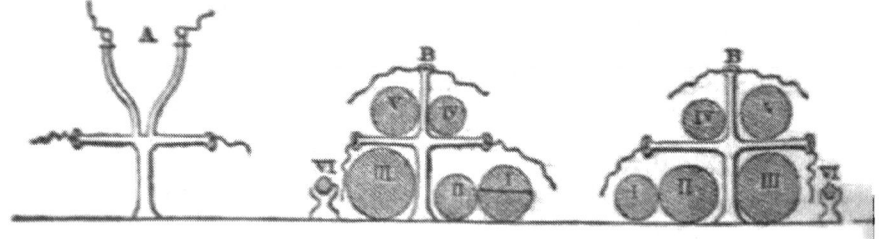

Port Side.	Starboard Side.
I. Fishes.	I. Hand-mast.
II. Hand-mast.	II. Mizen topmast.
III. Fore topmast.	III. Main topmast.
IV. Fore top-gallant mast.	IV. Main top-gallant mast.
V. Jib-boom.	V. Jib-boom.
VI. Fore topsail yard.	VI. Main topsail yard.

The mizen top-gallant mast is stowed on the top of the fishes; the spare fore top-gallant yard alongside the jib-boom on the port side; a top-mast studding-sail boom on each side; and a couple of small spars, stowed where convenient, between the larger ones, comprise the whole of the booms.   In the starboard main chains lies the spare main top-gallant yard, and in the port chains, the mizen topsail yard.

Iron-clad ships are not often supplied with more than one spare jib-boom, topmast, or topsail yard ; small spars for boats' mast, &c., can be stowed in the hammock nettings.

410

542. FIRE ON SHORE—The following disposal of a "fire brigade for landing," was drawn up for a corvette.

On the boats being called away for the above purpose, the pinnace-men will drop their boat under the main yard, ready to receive the engine and field-piece limber carriage; and the midshipman of the boat will see all the wash-deck buckets passed into her by the boat's crew, and will be responsible for their not being lost ashore.

The gunner and his crew will provide a 100-lb. barrel of powder (previously bored and plugged), two port-fires, or a fathom or two of Bickford's fuze in preference, if there is any, and a slow-match; pass them into second cutter; and, on landing, be in readiness to blow up any building that it may be necessary to level, to arrest the progress of the fire.

The boatswain, with forecastle-men and riggers not belonging to boats, provide fire-grapnel, and two hook-ropes; pass them into the second cutter, and, on landing, take charge of them.

The carpenter and his crew, having passed the engine gear into the pinnace, will provide a couple of axes, and go down into the boat.

The sergeant will tell off twelve men into the pinnace, under a corporal to work the engine; and fall in a corporal and eight men on the quarter-deck, in readiness, to receive ball cartridge, and then land in charge of them in the first cutter.

The lieutenant in charge will take the second gig, and be accompanied by the assistant-surgeon with provision for

2 D   411

accidents. and with the bugler to sound the assembly, calling the men together at any particular spot.

All the party are to shift in their old blue clothes, and rig in caps, shoes and stockings. On landing, they v man the drag-ropes, and, with all speed transport the engi and gear to the scene of action.

Mr. ——, will remain in charge of the boats a boat-keepers.

———

If the fire is not very alarming, the right thing to do w probably be seen at a glance; but, should it already ha spread to any great extent, or have caught, by the fallin sparks, &c., at more points than one, with many interve ing buildings, the exertions of your party cannot be effic ently directed unless you have been able to take a surve of the fire from the top of a house which commands view of the whole. From such a position, you can se where a stand must be made to check its progress; and having formed your plan, let nothing divert you from it accomplishment No time should be lost in passing ou furniture, and in tearing down windows, jalousies, do and wooden erections of all kinds; for, by trying to s too much, you risk the loss of all. If you have any scalin ladders, they will be found of the greatest use; and range of the engine may be considerably increased placing your thumb on the nozzle occasionally, that, on withdrawal, the water may escape with greater force.

Wherever there are no organized fire companies, inde sion is always painfully apparent. A plan is no sooner

412

upon that it is abandoned for another which appears more feasible; while the fire, in disadvantageous contrast, steadily pursues its undeviating course. Wherever, therefore, the services of his men are needed, the naval officer should promptly assume the direction of affairs.

543. RUDDERS ARE HUNG—By pintles and gudgeons; the pintles slip into the gudgeons, which are fixed to the stern-post, and are prevented from unshipping by wood-locks.

544. BALANCED RUDDERS.—Owing to the increased size of ships, and the corresponding increase in the dimensions of rudders, immense power is required to efficiently control the helm.

To obviate this the balance rudder has been introduced into several of our new ships, and has, on the whole, been attended with marked success; this rudder instead of hanging to the stern-post by pintles and gudgeons, steps on an extension of the keel and pivots at about one-third of its length from forward; its advantage consists in the pressure of water on the fore part, partially counteracting the pressure of water on the after part, particularly when much helm is given.

Although this form of rudder gives the most satisfactory results in ships under steam ; still, when under sail only, it has been found to retard the ship's way, and act too suddenly in stays ; to meet this, an ingenious improvement has been tried, as shewn in the figure, by which the advantages of a balance rudder are derived when steaming,

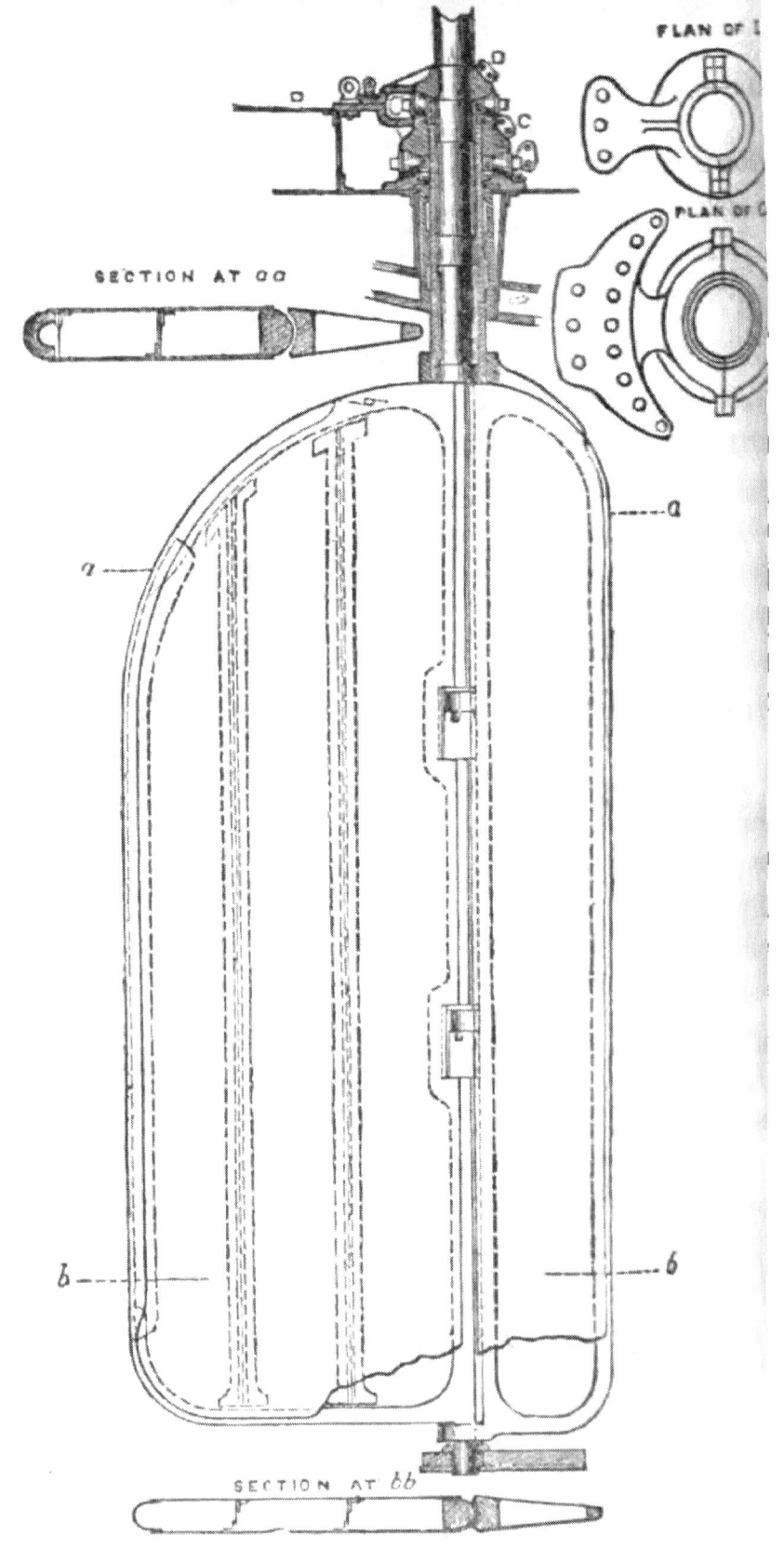

SECTION AT aa

PLAN OF I

PLAN OF C

a

a

b

6

SECTION AT bb

: by simply locking the fore part ; it can if necessary,
uickly converted into an ordinary rudder.

JXILIARY RUDDERS.—Much attention has of late been
ted to the want of auxiliary steering power to be used
he event of a ship's rudder being disabled. An
apt to meet this difficulty has been made in H.M.S.
m ; in this vessel an iron trunk has been built on each
ter before the screw ; a rudder is enclosed in each
ʟ, connected by a chain taken round a steering wheel
ed between the trunks ; when not in use the lower
s of the rudders are flush with the counter, from the
mpanying plate* it will be seen that the effect of turning
wheel, correspondingly raises or lowers the rudders.

15. ACTION OF RUDDER.—The great thing to remember
is, that when a ship is answering her helm it is the
ı being thrown round by the pressure of water on the
ler which alters her course, and that it is the head
ɩh is governed by the stern, and not the stern by the
l; so much is this the case in screw ships able to
a large angle of helm, that if the helm be first put
l over and the engines started ahead, the ship will
. two or three points before gathering way.

s a general rule it may be stated that screw ships turn
ı point one-third before their centre, therefore in avoid-
collision when nearing the danger, steer so that your
ʹ may go clear; having done this, as the point on
ɔh your ship pivots passes, reverse the helm, and by

---

* See next page.

415

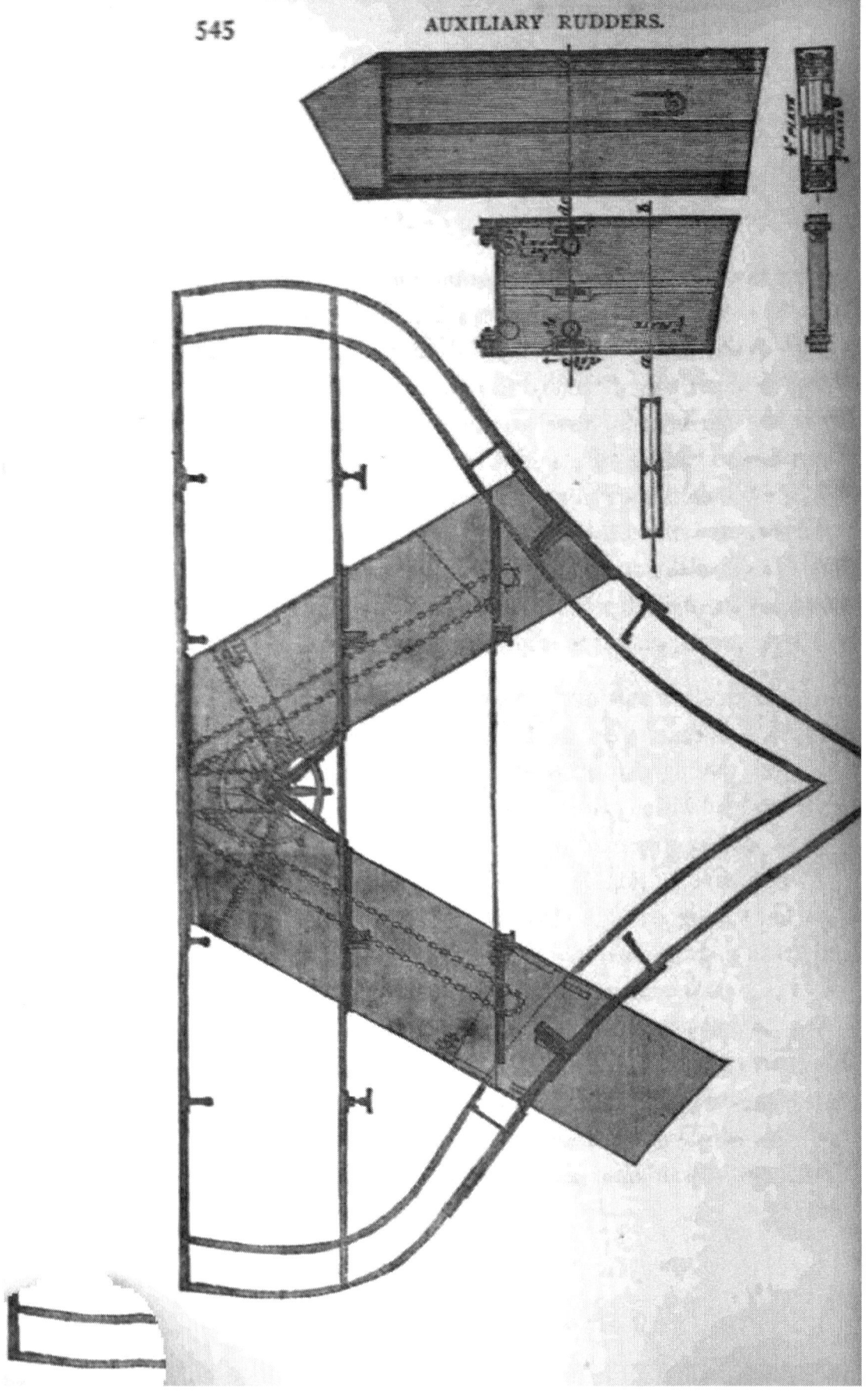

o doing, endeavour to throw your stern clear. The more helm given, the smaller will be the diameter of the circle made; the more speed used with the same helm, the quicker will you turn though describing a larger circle.

546. WEATHER HELM.—The centre of effort of the sails is generally abaft the centre of the vessel, the ship is pressed more against the water, on the lee side; the heel of the ship immerses the lee bow, which tends to throw the ship up in the wind.

That the amount of weather helm carried increases as the wind freshens and the ship heels more, is partly attributable to the oblique angle given to the rudder, causing it to lose much of its effect; the best practical proof may be found in boat sailing; in a steady breeze a boat can be so trimmed that she will carry a very small weather helm, but let the wind become squally, and as she heels to each puff, the small weather helm will be doubled. Weather helm may be diminished by reducing or bracing in the after sails, or by relieving her of any sail that may be pressing the bow, and by trimming more by the stern; but long screw ships will always be found to carry much weather helm when under sail alone.

547. SHIFTING A RUDDER.—In the upper deck, over the rudder-head, are a couple of holes for the reception of the eye-bolts to which the tackles are suspended, which, when the plugs are driven out, are forelocked above the deck. Hook to them the upper blocks of two up-and-downs, unreeve the falls, pay them down through the

417

rudder-well, and reeve them through the lower blocks outside the ship; when rove full, lead them along the deck. Shore the deck up if necessary, and run guns forward to bring her stern sufficiently out of the water to enable you to get at the wood-lock, which you unship. Drive an eye-bolt into the rudder, on each side, to hook the tackles to, sufficiently low down to allow the rudder to be unshipped without bringing the blocks up against the stern. Top the spanker-boom well up, hook a burton from the mizen cap to the boom-end, at which point attach another burton, overhauled down to the water. Haul up a couple of boom-boats under the stern, with their stems forward; lash them together with a spar across the bows, and another over the after thwarts, leaving sufficient space for the rudder to hang between them. Unshackle the rudder-chains, man the tackles, and unship the rudder. Pass the end of a hawser from the boats, between the rudder and sternpost, and drop it down within a few feet of the keel; knot the parts together, and hook the burton to it; then walk back the tackles, and pull up on the burton as it clears the rudder-hole. As soon as the head is clear, pass the other end of the hawser round it, walk back, and hang it to the spar across the bows of the boats; pull up the burton, and hang the lower part of the rudder to the spar across the sterns of the boats; unhook the tackles, and tow the boats ashore.

The new rudder is shipped by the same means, except that the burton is dispensed with, and a heel-rope from the midship lower-deck ports on each side is employed to

418

rouse the ruddder to.   These are fitted with long eyes, and are each passed through a hole in the heel of the rudder before it is launched; a toggle is slipped through the eyes, and lanyards from them are led up to the bolt for the rudder-chains, so that, when the rudder is shipped, the guys can be disengaged.

With the spanker-boom, and a runner and tackle, you may shift a rudder as follows:—Runner rove through a block on spanker-boom, cleated to prevent its slipping forward, down through a hole in the upper deck, and hitched through the tiller-hole.   Tackle led along upper deck. Spanker-boom shored up; and heel of rudder lifted by burton from spanker-boom 'end to a lashing round rudder at water-line.

548. TEMPORARY RUDDER—in accordance with Admiralty Order of 4th January, 1840.

419

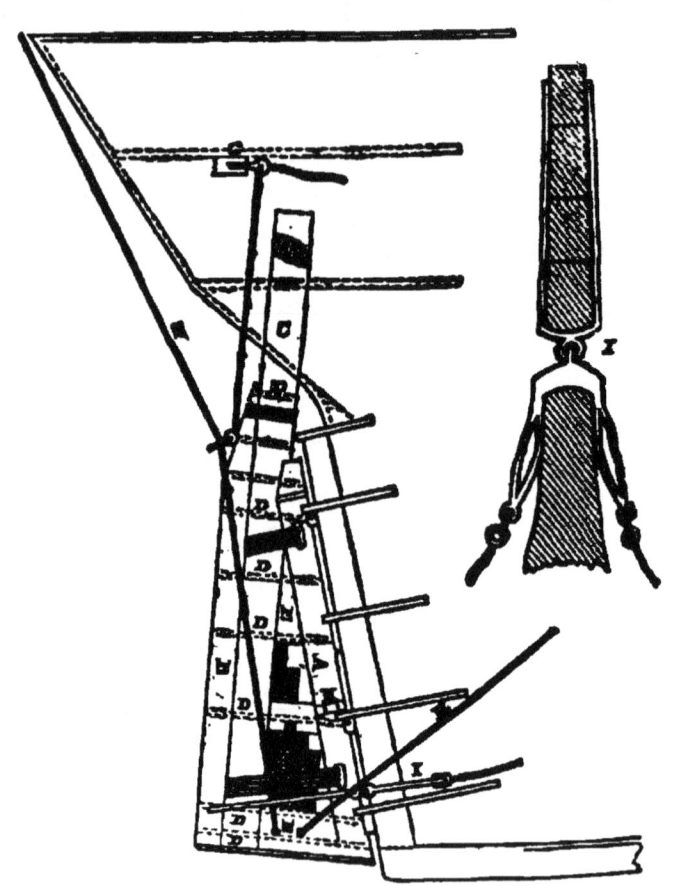

A. A piece of fir, sided one-third less than the stern-post; fitted with iron pintles while in dock, and supplied to each ship.

B. A piece for the back, either provided, or taken from the ship's stores; sided one-half of post, at the heel.

C. Spare topmast, cut off clear of the sheeve-hole.

D. Iron bolts.

E. Chocks.

F. Iron pig ballast.

G. Screw eye-bolt in quarter-deck beam, to be put in when required.

H. Rope-guys (through the heel-chock E), to facilitate the hanging of the rudder.*

I. Gudgeon-brace, fitted to the stern-post while in dock, and supplied to the ship.

K. Lower pintle, to be 4 inches longer than the others.

---

*The guys attached to the gudgeon, I, should be led in through the hawse-holes, hove taut, and secured.

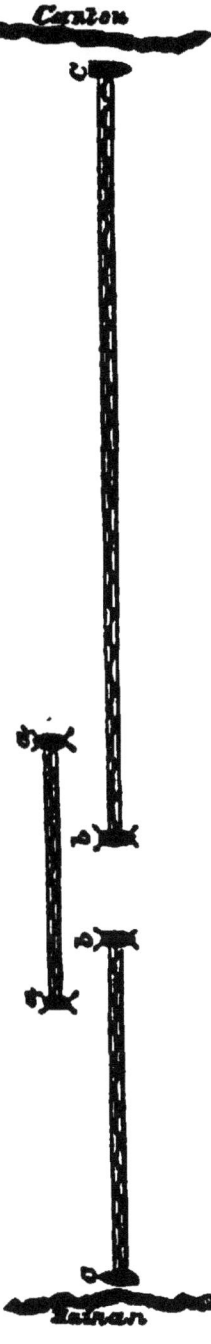

549. FALSE KEEL.—In the event of a ship getting ashore, the false keel will come away and free her, when more than an ordinary strain is brought upon it, and the main keel thereby remains uninjured.

550. PRECAUTIONS AGAINST FIRE-RAFTS.—The following were adopted in the Canton river, 1856-7 :—

Ships off the Factories, moored head and stern, were protected by a boom thrown across the river, above and below the position. The largest boom, above the Factories, was formed of two layers of large spars, lashed together, with a stream chain laid between them, bolted to the spars on alternate sides, and the whole woulded round at intervals.

The spars were not placed so as to lock in throughout, but a small space was left every forty feet or so, to impart flexibility to the boom. At $c\,c$ were two loaded sunken junks. At $b\,b$ two junks moored head and stern, with long 32's mounted forward, and guns' crews on board. At $a\,a$, two junks, to which was attached a small boom to screen the entrance.

421

The ships were fortified with a spar from each bow, meeting, and lashed together at the outer ends, and drooped by a tackle from the jib-boom end. Flying-boom kept in. From these outriggers, spars were continued aft to the gangways, supported by tackles from the lower yard-arms and boomed out by spars from the ship's side, which afforded space and shelter for the boats to lie within.

From the jib-boom end was suspended a fire grapnel, or a small anchor, shackled by a length of small chain to the riding-cable, outside the hawse. This was intended to drop into the fire-vessel, and anchor her by, on the cable being slipped and the ship dropping clear.

Over the stern, an anchor was hung, which, in the event of a fire-vessel becoming fixed to the bows, would, on being let go, and the lower cable slipped, bring the ship up by the stern, and throw the junk off.

As wooden tanks, containing upwards of a ton of powder floating at the water's edge, were occasionally sent down, the fire-booms were kept eased down, and floated on the water, and a guard boat anchored ahead.

To prevent attacks from torpedo boats, guard should be rowed round the ship at night, and one boat anchored some distance ahead of the ship, both having orders to seize any suspected boats by the stern.

551. DESTRUCTION OF BOOMS.—Blow the boom up with a breaker of powder; rouse up the bight of the chain; load with shot a launch's gun; lash the chain across the muzzle; fire, and take advantage of the result. You may

422

even fracture a chain in the same manner with a blank cartridge.

552. MOORING HEAD AND STERN.—The appliances for securing stern cables are usually very insufficient. Some ships are unprovided with either bollards or ring-bolts. When this is the case, having passed the cable out through the bow hawse-hole, and brought it round outside, reeve it in through one stern hawse-pipe, out through the other, and shackle it to its one part, outside, with a slip-stopper.

Let go headmost anchor, veer away, let go stern anchor from the bows, heave in forward, and veer away stern cable to the slip,

553. REPLACING COPPER UNDER WATER.—With reference to this subject, the following copy of a letter has been issued by the Lords Commissioners of the Admiralty.

"BERMUDA YARD, *March* 20, 1844.

"SIR,—In obedience to your directions to report the manner in which I proceeded to replace a defective sheet of copper on the bow of H.M.S. 'Hyacinth,' the same being five feet below the light water-line, I beg leave to state, that on considering what means could be adopted for so doing, short of heaving the vessel out, it occurred to me that the principle of the coffer-dam might be applied to it. I accordingly caused a water-tight case, of three sides and a bottom, to be made ; ascertained the curve of the bow on each side of the defective part, and cut the

423

mouth, or open side of the case, to fit it; and, having lined, or dressed the curved edges with felt, saturated with tallow, and attached ballast to the bottom, the case was suspended by a tackle to the rough tree rail, and lowered until the top was within a few inches of the surface, opposite the defective part, over which it was hauled by means of two hawsers : one passed vertically, from the rough tree rail, under the keel, to the opposite side ; the other horizontally, from the quarter, round the stern, to the opposite side, where both were set taut with tackles. By these means the case was made to fit close to the bottom, where it was further secured by a shore, reaching from the side of the ship to its outer edge, to prevent its rising. The suction-hose of a fire-engine was then placed in the case, and the water contained in it pumped out ; when empty, the shipwright descended, and removed the defective copper, replacing it with a new sheet. The operation, from the time of suspending the case until completed, did not occupy more than twenty minutes.

"If I might be allowed to offer an opinion, I should say that this principle could be applied to the repairs of many defects under water, such as the wing cocks of ships, or the pipes in the bottom of steam-vessels ; and little difficulty could be experienced in this, as every vessel in Her Majesty's service has the means within itself of applying the principle.

"I have the honour to be, &c.
                                "W. MOODY,
                                    "*Foreman of Shipwright.*"

424

"If you have not the requisite drawings on board, the curve of the ship's bottom outside may be approximated from a mould taken from the inside, on either side, and below the injury, up to a short distance above the water-line ; and, unless the case, when hove to, fits very tight, it will be necessary to chinse it in between its edge and the ship's bottom, as you pump out."

554. LIFTING A SHIP'S STERN OVER THE SILL OF A DOCK—with tanks. Rig a stage of large spars astern, lash the foremost end down to the ship at low water, and keep the after end down, and secure it, by shores from the stern and quarter.

Sling the stage by tackles, so that at low water the sur-face may be a few inches below the tops of the tanks, when floated underneath.

To float them under, partially fill them ; then rouse them under, and secure them : as fast as they are placed, pump them out, and watch for the rise of tide.

555. BOATS IN TOW.—Dismount the gun, and place it at the bottom of the boat amidships ; shift the shot-boxes aft, and haul the boat *close up* under the stern—the closer the better. Tow with a hawser from each quarter, to keep her steady, and as a precaution in case one carries away. Reeve one through the shackle in the stem, take a turn round the standing thwart, and let a hand hold on to it, ready to slip in a moment ; take the other also round the thwart, frapping it in slackly to the stem, (for if out on the bow, the boat would steer wildly), and let it be similarly

425

attended. Caution the coxswain to be particularly careful about the steerage; call all out of the boat but these three hands, and see the hawsers parcelled in the nips.

Watch the boat yourself from the steamer, not leaving her for a moment, and acquaint the officer of the watch should the swell of the water rise up to the gunwale, that the steamer's speed may be slackened. If you see the water come over, do not wait till she buries herself, but give the order immediately to let go in the boat.

I had the misfortune once to be implicated in the loss of a pinnace that was towed under, in a calm day, without a ripple on the water; and therefore know that you cannot be too careful.

In towing a light boat, reeve the tow-rope through the ring in the bow, and secure to the bolt in the keel. If secured forward, you run the risk of tearing the bows out of her.

556. MEASURING HEIGHTS.—Pick a couple of sticks, or straws, and bring one to your eye, holding it horizontally. At convenient distance along it, erect the other at right angles, its height being equal to the distance along the horizontal stick from the eye to the point of section. This being done, approach, or recede from the tree in the direction in which the ground is most level, until the top of the trunk is *on* with the top of the stick. Mark the spot; and the distance from where you are standing, to the foot of the tree, is necessarily equal to the height of the tree from the level of your eye, Pace it off, or measure it in sticks'

lengths to be reduced to proper
measurement on your return on
board; add the height of the eye,
and the result will be the height
of the tree.

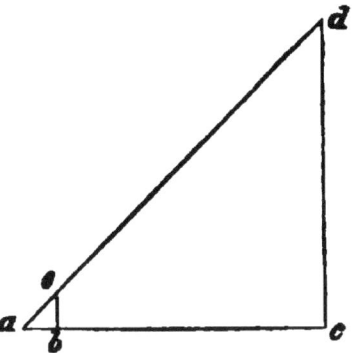

$ab : be :: ac : cd$

$ab \cdot cd = be \cdot ac$

ab, and be, being equal,

$cd = ac.$

If the foot of the tree is at the time inaccessible, bring
the stick as before to your eye, and on it, at any distance,
place a straw vertically; walk back from the tree until the
top of the straw and the top of the tree are in one, and
mark the spot. Then move the straw its own length further
along the stick; walk back until the top of the straw is
again *on* with the top of the tree; and the distance from
this to the former station, plus the height of the eye, is
equivalent to the height of the tree.

bg, and dh being synonymous,

$cd : bg :: ec: ef$

$ef \cdot cd = bg \cdot ce$

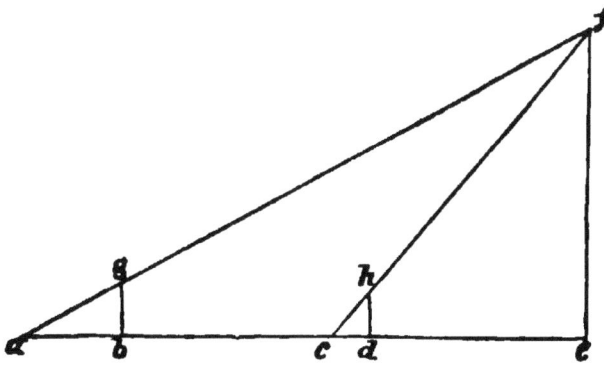

Again,

ab being equal to $cd + bg$

$cd + bg : bg :: ac + ce : ef$

$ef . cd + ef . bg = bg . ac + ef . cd$ ($ef . cd$ being substituted for $bg . ce$)

Then, by subtracting $ef . cd$, and dividing by bg, $ef = ac$.

557. TO ASCERTAIN DISTANCE BY SOUND.—The mean velocity of sound, under ordinary circumstances, is 1,110 feet in a second.   In a breeze this must be corrected in proportion to the velocity and direction of the wind, though this is not generally important, as its utmost velocity is much less than that of sound.   The velocity is not affected by its intensity, as the faintest sound moves as rapidly as the loudest.   One of its greatest conductors is water, on which it can be heard nearly twice as far as upon land.

Multiply the number of seconds which elapse between the flash of a gun and the report by 1,110, and the product will be the distance in feet; which divide by 5,280, for an ordinary English mile; by 6,072 for a geographical mile; and by 6075.6 for a nautical mile.

558. HAWSE-PIPES BROKEN.—Knock them out; place starboard pipe in the port hawse-hole, and port pipe to the starboard one.   Slue them round, to bring the underneath and damaged part uppermost, and drive home.   Cut the inner edge off flush where they overlap.

559. RIDING OUT A GALE.—All other things being equal, the greater the weight of a ship the greater the strain on her cables.

428

The weights should not be too much centralized, for inertia in the extremities serves to keep her from flying round like a teetotum. Neither should they be placed too low, especially if the masts are cut away.

If necessary to cut away the masts, a dangerous alternative in a screw steamer, the mizen-mast had better be left standing.

560. TOWING SPARS.—Tow with the bluff end first, for although it thus takes more force to start it, it yet requires less to maintain it in motion than with the small end foremost. You also tow nearer to the centre of gravity, and in proportion do so with greater ease and steadiness.

When towing anything in a boat, never make the tow-rope fast to the stern-ring, or even reeve it through it, as it strains the boat, and renders steering impossible, except by the oars. When the thwarts will bear it, make a bow-line knot in the end of the tow-rope, and toggle it with a stretcher, laid over the two after thwarts. Then, to steer the boat, lift the tow-rope over towards the quarter to which you wish to turn. When the strain or jerking is heavy, secure the tow-rope to the ring-bolt for the slings in the keel.

561. FLASHING SIGNALS.—This excellent method of signalling, invented by Captain Colomb, R.N., after long and careful trial, has now been generally introduced into the Royal Navy.

Flashing Signals are made by the motion of any single object. In most instances the object is made to appear

and disappear; and in others it is made to change
position, so that one position shall represent the appe
ance, and the other the disappearance of the object. T
symbols are determined by successive appearances a
disappeances at regulated intervals, constantly recurri
after a fixed pause, in a manner precisely similar to tho
of revolving or flashing lights in lighthouses. Signa
made on this principle can therefore be scrutinized
long as may be necessary to make quite sure of the
purport by comparison with the codes, before they a
answered, in the same way as any series of flags hoiste
together in the daytime may be fully examined befor
they are acknowledged.

Every signal—consisting of from one to four numera
signs, with or without a special sign, and representing from
one to four numeral flags with or without a pendant—i
made to recur once in every twenty to thirty seconds; so
that an observer watching a signal for three minutes, may
see it legibly repeated from six to nine times. This speed
is found most suited to general service, and usually the
observation of three repetitions is sufficient to make the
signal understood, without the possibility of mistake.

The appearances of the object are termed "flashes,"
and are of two lengths, termed respectively "short" and
"long" flashes, which are used in combination, to express
the signs required. The long flash is about a second and
a half duration, and the short flash about half a second.
The disappearances of the object are termed intervals,
and are of three lengths. That between the flashes com-

430

osing a figure, is equal in duration to a short flash ; that etween two figures is equal to a long flash ; and that etween any two repetitions of a signal is equal to one-hird of the whole length of the signals, or, from about even to ten seconds. Thus it will be seen that the gibility of the signals depends on the measurement of wo lengths of flashes and three lengths of intervals, or ve elements, and each is of equal importance. At night hese signals are made by the obscuration and exposure f a single light.

The lines opposite each number denote the flashes sed to express it :—

1. __		6. ____	
2. _ _		7. _ ____	
3. _ _ _		8. ____ _	
4. _ _ _ _		9. _ _ ____	
5. _ _ _ _		0. ____ _ _	

Other combinations of flashes are used to take the place f those flags and pendants, that have special significations ssigned to them in flag signals, and are as follows :—

Compass.	____ _ ____
Pendants.	____ _ _ ____
Numeral.	____ _ _ _ _
Special and Repeat.	_ ____ _ _
Horary.	_ _ ____ _

431

Interogative. ▄ ▄ ▄ ▄▄▄

Negative. ▄▄▄ ▄ ▄ ▄

List of Navy. ▄ ▄▄▄ ▄

Alphabetical. ▄▄▄ ▄▄▄

Answer ▄▄▄ ▄ ▄▄▄ ▄ ▄▄▄ ▄ a continuatio
of long and short flashes.

Spelling. ▄ ▄▄▄ ▄▄▄ ▄

Preparative ▄ ▄ ▄ ▄ a continuation of sho
flashes.

Stop ▄▄▄ ▄▄▄ ▄▄▄ a continuation of lon
flashes.

HORARY TABLE.

11	...	...	...	1 P.M.	23	...	...	...	...	1 A.M.
12	...	...	...	2 ,,	24	...	..	...	...	2 ,,
13	...	...	...	3 ,,	25	...	...	...	...	3 ,,
14	...	...	...	4 ,,	26	.	...	...	...	4 ,,
15	...	..	...	5 ,,	27	...	...	..	...	5 ,,
16	...	...	...	6 ,,	28	...	...	..	...	6 ,,
17	...	...	...	7 ,,	29	...	...	...	..	7 ,,
18	...	...	...	8 ,,	30	...	...	...	...	8 ,,
19	...	...	...	9 ,,	31	...	...	...	...	9 ,,
20	...	...	...	10 ,,	32	...	...	...	...	10 ,,
21	...	...	...	11 ,,	33	...	...	...	...	11 ,,
22	...	...	...	12 Midnight.	34	...	...	...	...	12 Noon.

Minutes are denoted by their proper figures. Thus:
Hor. 2135 = 35 minutes past 11 P.M.

Seconds must be made separately.

432

ALPHABETICAL TABLE.

he following alphabet, &c., can be used under circum-
ces when it is not convenient or possible to have
urse to the Signal Book, and forms in itself a perfect
raphic system, necessarily somewhat slow in its
lication, but having the great advantage of requiring
little previous knowledge and practice to work with
rectness.

		A 5 - - - - -		
B 6 —	C 7 - - —	D 8 — -	E 9 - - —	F 10 — - - -
G 11 - -	H 12 — - -	I 13 - - - -	J 14 - - - —	K 15 — - - -
L 16 - —	M 17 — - —	N 18 - —	O 19 - - —	P 20 — - -
Q 21 - - -	R 22 - — -	S 23 - - -	T 24 - - — -	U 25 - - - - —
V 26 - - —	W 27 - - - —	X 28 - - — -	Y 29 - - - —	Z 30 - - - — -

All other lights in the vicinity of a Flashing Signal at night, should be concealed; signals should not be answered until thoroughly comprehended, and no signal should be commenced until the signal preceding it has been finished.

562. TO FIND THE TIME OF DAYLIGHT AND SUNSET. —The morning gun is ordered to be fired at day-break, except when on foreign service, the commander-in-chief on the station shall direct otherwise.

Daybreak, or the commencement of morning twilight, occurs when the sun is 18° below the horizon.

Rule.—Under the latitude put the declination, marking them with their proper names; if they are like, take the difference; if unlike, take the sum: under this, put the constant angle 108°. Take the sum and difference, add together the log. secants of the two first terms (rejecting tens in the index), and the half haversines of the two last. With the sun as a log. haversine, take out the corresponding angle in time, at the top of the page, which will be the time of ending of evening twilight, and which subtracted from twelve hours, will give the beginning of morning twilight, or daybreak—in apparent time.

```
Lat.  22° 17′ N.        Sec. 0·033708
Dec.  15   3  N.        Sec. 0·015158
      ———
       7 14
     108
      ———
     115 14             ½ hav. 4·926591
     100 46             ½ hav. 4·886675
      ———                    ————
      7h. 49m.          Hav. 9·862132
     12   0                  ————
      ———
      4  11    Morning twilight begins.
```

434

RULE FOR FINDING THE TIME OF SUNRISING AND
SUNSETTING.—Add together the log. tangents of latitude
and declination, subtracting ten from the index. The
result will be the log. cosine of an angle in time, which if
the latitude and declination are *unlike*, will be the apparent
time of sunsetting, and subtracted from twelve hours, the
apparent time of sunrising.

If the latitude and declination are *alike*, the angle first
found will be the apparent time of sunrising, and subtracted
from twelve hours, the apparent time of sunsetting.

If mean time (*i. e.* harbour time) is required, the equation
of time must be applied, after the time of sunrising has
been determined from sunsetting, and *vice versâ*.

Lat. ....22° 17' N.		Tang. 9·612561	
Dec. ....15 3 N.		Tang. 9·429566	
	5h. 35m.	Cos. 9·042127	
	12 0		
App. time... 6 25			
Eq. time ... 0 3			
Mean time 6 22 Sunset.			

NAUTICAL SURVEYING.

NAUTICAL SURVEYING.

The word Surveying is often deterring to the young officer as signifying something with which he has, and expects to have, nothing to do. It is intended here to point out and briefly explain the useful work of this kind which can be accomplished with the instruments to be found on board of every man-of-war, and with which every officer should be acquainted, and be competent to perform.

There is Surveying of a more accurate and extended character requiring instruments, means and opportunities, only to be found in surveying ships or organised surveys on coasts : Surveyors are employed on this work, the teaching of which is not contemplated here.

ON THE INSTRUMENTS.

These are necessary;—sextant, artificial horizon, chronometers, hack watch, azimuth compass, box of instruments, parallel rulers (if with graduated edge the better), common horn protractor, and tracing paper, and these are to be found on board every man-of-war; whilst a theodolite, sounding and pocket sextants, a circular or semi-circular brass protractor with vernier, a station pointer, and a three-feet metal standard scale, with bevelled and perfectly straight edge, are valuable in extending and greatly facilitat-

439

ing the performance of the work, and placing it on paper: the use of these latter is strongly recommended to be acquired : a little practice under instruction, or guided by a "Treatise on Mathematical Instruments," would soon make any enquirer acquainted with it.

PREPARATIONS.

These preparations are such as should be made on board every man-of-war before starting on a cruise, whether with a purpose of some surveying work, or merely *as a preparation* for any that may offer; they are especially expected from the Navigating Officer, and therefore he *must* be competent to make them, but they are such as every young officer ought to be equally well acquainted with. The chronometers, most likely three in number, on being brought on board should be placed carefully in a box prepared and divided into compartments, and fixed therein firmly by small pads, bits of buntin or tow, jambed in around them : a place for the *Chronometer box* must be carefully chosen, low and near the centre of the ship is desirable, but access, light, liability to vibration as of machinery, and especially the importance of equal temperature, are all considerations that must determine the spot. The box being fixed and the Chronometers stowed, let them rest a few days, and then ascertain their errors and rates. "Equal altitudes" of the sun is by far the best method, and the practice of taking them is this :—compare the hack watch (a chronometer whose performance is trustworthy for a few hours) with each of the three chronometers and proceed with it at a suitable time. A.M. to the shore: with sextant and artificial horizon observe two or three sets, with intervals, so as to increase the chances of not losing the whole of the corresponding P.M. sights by clouds; return on board and compare again. Compare and return to the shore at the proper time, P.M., and complete the observation, and compare again, on finally returning on board. From this will be deduced the error of each chronometer at noon of that day. Repeat this determination of errors about a week afterwards, and then after each few days, up to the latest convenient day before sailing, and comparing these errors with the number of elapsed days, you get the rates of each chrronometer.

The Chronometer esteemed the best is usually selected as a "Standard," and with it each of the others is compared at the time of winding daily; the comparisons entered in a book, the "Chronometer Journal." To wind at 8 a.m. is most convenient on board a man-of-war; the time, however, is unimportant, regularity, every day the same, is important: turn the Chronometer over from right to left, and hold it firmly there by the left hand; turn the key slowly and steadily, and more cautiously still, as the known last turn comes, until it butts, withdraw the key and turn the Chronometer back with its face upwards; in turning either way, it is liable to slip out of the hand. By the method of equal altitudes, the error of a Chronometer is most correctly obtained, and any error there may be in the sextant used does not affect the result; but it is not always practicable to observe equal altitudes, especially in the cloudy weather of temperate climates; the a.m. sights are often obtained, the p.m. lost; in such a case the errors must be obtained from single altitudes (the a.m. or p.m. sights of equal altitudes can be rendered as single altitudes), but in these cases it must be remembered that those rates only will be trust-worthy, which are deduced from similar observations : thus, the errors obtained by equal altitudes one day, should be compared only with errors obtained by equal altitudes after an interval of days; the errors obtained from a.m. single altitudes, with errors obtained by a.m. single altitudes, after an interval of days; and so p.m. with p.m.

In using a mercurial artificial horizon, wipe any dirt or dust out of the trough, place it nearly in its position towards the sun, and to pour out the mercury, turn the vessel completely over, and do not pour out the whole of it, the scum or tarnished part keeping on the surface, will be each time left behind in the vessel. When half the observations are made, turn the roof, whereby the errors in parallellism of its glasses will be obviated. In hot climates and especially at night, an unaccountable dimness sometimes comes over the observations, which has been found to arise from condensation on the inner surface of the glass roof of the horizon—take it off and wipe it dry when necessary.

An important preparation, and one that has to be repeated, with every material change of geographical position, or of situation of iron on board, is the determination of the deviation of the compass; there are three

442

convenient methods of doing this; first by reciprocal observations, with an assistant on shore; secondly, by bearing of a distant object whose true bearing is known; and thirdly, by bearings of the sun, the apparent time and latitude being known. The first is most suitable in a close harbour, or when cloudy weather prevails; the second is better if there be no reliable assistant, but would involve more work if the true bearing of the distant object and variation of the compass, are not previously known; the object must always be so distant as not to affect the bearing by the swinging of the ship when moored or hove short if at single anchor; and the third is especially used at sea, when of course, the other two methods are impracticable. Tables of "Sun's true bearing completed for intervals of 4 minutes between the parallels of lat. 30° and 60°, inclusive," which give this result by inspection, are supplied to every ship. The practice of the first method will be described.

The "Standard" Compass is the one whose deviation is determined, its position most likely is more available for observing, but the steering binnacle compasses are compared with it at the time of each observation. The Standard Compasses supplied to H.M.'s Ships are faultless in quality and convenience, each has two cards A and J, one heavier than the other; selecting one and noting which it is, examine the pivot and see that the card works freely on its centre; record the kind and distance of the nearest iron, and the distance of the largest masses, for the guidance in comparing any future determination after changes; hoist a flag or other mark, directly over the standard com-

2 F

pass, to be observed from the shore, as the compass ceases to be clearly seen at very short distances. The preparations for swinging her being ready, either by hawsers, to buoys &c. near or kedge, or by steam assistance; the ship moored or hove short if at single anchor ; or underweigh under steam, if intending to put her round underweigh, place the ship's head towards any convenient point of the compass, and hoist an agreed signal to the dip to "stand by"; the assistant having landed the azimuth compass, with legs, previously examined as to its working order, and selecting a spot free from any iron or influences to affect the compass, and where the ship will be plainly visible through her swinging, now begins to observe the flag or mark over the standard of the compass. As the ship's head approaches the desired point and being steadied there, hoist the signal close up, each observer now closely takes the bearing of the other, and records that of the moment when her head is fixed on the desired point, and the signal smartly dipped low : each observer numbers and records each observation, and it is better that each should note the time also by watches compared, for future guidance ; this is repeated with the ship's head on each point of the compass. In this method the bearing observed from the shore is the true magnetic bearing, the bearing from the ship should be exactly its opposite, what it differs is " Deviation."

APPLICATION.

Thus prepared, the ship leaves a port, and in due time reaches another one : the first piece of useful work is to

444

measure the " Meridian distance " of the two. As soon
s possible get equal altitudes, and as before, find errors
ad rates of the Chronometers. The rates determined
éfore starting, and now on arrival are assumed to give
le mean rates of the interval, with which data the
measurement is thus computed, and more clearly explained
y tabulation.

) compute Meridian distance between Stornaway and Thorshaven.

DATES, ETC.	CHRON. A.	CHRON. B,	CHRON. C.
	H. M. S.	H. M. S.	H. M. S.
hors on M. T. Stornaway, zah. G.M.T., 9th Aug., 1868.	Slow 4 17 16	Slow 4 2 2·1	Slow 4 22 39·6
late on leaving Stornaway	Gaining 1·02	Gaining 4·42	Gaining 1.92
late determined on arrival at Thorshaven	Losing ·56	Gaining 2·57	Gaining 1·04
lean Rate	Gaining ·23	Gaining 3·5	Gaining 1·48
terval—8 days	× 8	1 × 8	× 8.
ccumulated Rate	1·84	28	11·84
srors on M. T. Stornaway, zah. G.M.T., 17h.	Slow 4 16 59·8	Slow 4 1 34·1	Slow 4 22 27·8
Srors on M. T. Thorshaven, zah. G.M.T., 17h.	Slow 4 15 27·5	Slow 4 0 3·5	Slow 4 20 .54
	1m. 32·3s. ⎫ 1m. 30·6s. ⎬ 1m. 33·8s. ⎭	1m. 30·6s. Mean 0h. 1m. 32·2s.	1 33·8

By this computation Thorshaven is made 1m. 32·2s. West
of Stornaway: and in this way the longitudes of places
have been, and are, determined by our surveying ships, and
can now be verified, and new places done by any other
men-of-war, only so much less reliably, as the usual numbers of three chronometers is less than theirs. It is not

2 F 2

445

the absolute longitude of any place that is required, only careful measurements of the distances between any number in this way, where it will be seen the longitude of any need not be exactly known: and when by the means found only in an observatory, or the electric telegraph, or other, the absolute longitude of any one place in the whole chain is reliably ascertained, the longitudes of the whole may be assumed to be known for all purposes of geography or navigation. If somewhat greater accuracy would be attempted, the "mean rate" can be reduced by the "method of least squares," whereby a series of determinations of errors being made first at one place and then at the other, the rate is determined at the time of the last of the former and first of the latter, (and not at the time of the middle of each series as in the simple plan,) whereby the interval in which change could take place is lessened, and you have true rates at each end of the measurement, and *the rate* is the soul of the interesting computation of "Meridian distances." The remarks upon rating chronometers, about comparing the results of equal altitudes, a.m. and p.m. sights, with their fellows only, are here of vital importance.

LATITUDE.—The latitude should always be determined as a verification or at lesser known places as original; it will be wanted as an element in finding "time," "error," and "meridian distances." The method employed must depend on the accuracy required or aimed at, time available, and circumstances: a meridian altitude of the sun with sea horizon, or circum-meridian altitudes are better.

446

Both are better still if the altitudes are observed on shore, with artificial horizon: in and near the tropics it is often impossible to observe the sun's m.a. in an artificicial hori-son; the sun being too high the observer's head intercepts it, or the graduation of the sextant is less than double the altitude: this has often been experienced when fixing spots in rivers with no natural horizon; then the moon's m.a. may often be observed, but far better are the meridian altitudes of several stars, some north and some south.

It is recommended to make a practice of observing the index error of the sextant before or after every observation by day (by joining the sun's edges off and on the arc) and recording it: it prevents your ever losing your labour by finding too late, your sextant has been shaken without your knowing it, and gives you confidence in the fixedness of its error: its other adjustments should be frequently looked to.

Variation of the Compass.—Charts of curves of varia-tion, over the whole world, are supplied to H.M.'s Ships, which give it quite near enough for purposes of naviga-gation, but it is a datum which should be independently ascertained on shore at every opportunity, for it is ever varying with time and place. Proceed thus: examine the compass, land with it, select a spot free from the influences of any iron, and from which some distinct and well defined object, distant at least three or four miles, is clearly seen; it may be the sharp top of a mountain, a sudden cleft in a ridge, a perpendicular cliff on the horizon, a white sandy patch, edge of a clump of trees, church spire, or anything

447

else. Set up the compass, and observe the bearing of th object, and if several bearings are taken whilst the bowl i being turned wholly round, a little at each observation, an error in the centreing of the card, is neutralized; mean these for the *magnetic* bearing, which compared with th *true* bearing of the object from that spot is the variation How to determine the *true* bearing, which is needed here and in any attempt at surveying that may be undertaken any where, will be explained. Or if the sea horizon with the rising or setting sun be visible, observe carefully it amplitude and compare with the computed or true on for variation.

Or, when landing for a.m. or p.m. sights, take your com pass to the spot, observe a set of sun's azimuth's, noting times, while an assistant observes the altitudes, mean them, compute the true azimuth, and compare with the observed one for variation. The same observer may also take the altitudes, by taking a set before, and another after his set of azimuthal bearings, and then reducing by proportion to the moment of that bearing. And it is desirable that every observer should practice taking time for himself with all observations—the eye and the ear soon become accustomed and proficient—and after a time it will often be preferred.

To determine a true bearing.—At the spot selected for observing for variation, or, if in a survey, at a convenient station in the triangulation, one end of a base, take the necessary observations as above for computing the sun's true bearing, measuring at the same instant the angular

448

distance between the edge of the sun and a conspicuous object (in a survey, the other end of the base), which should be close to the horizon, in order that the elements may form a quadrantal spherical triangle, and simplify the calculation; if it be above it, another computation is required than the one to be given below; the object need not be the same as observed for variation, and, indeed, had better not be if the latter were a hill-top or something far above the horizon. From the observed find the apparent altitude and reduce the angular distance to the sun's centre, then from log cosine of distance take log cosine of sun's apparent altitude, and the remainder is log cosine of the horizontal angle between the sun and the object, or their difference of bearing; and the sun's true bearing being known; that of one terrestrial object becomes known also from one known spot. If the object observed for variation be high, repeat this measurement between it and the point now determined, by measurement of its altitude and their angular distance: but in practice, the horizontal angle would be observed at once, not of course to the top of the hill, but to the base of a perpendicular from it, which the practised eye would fix at once in the sextant. But at first a plumb line may be held up at some distance from the observer between his eye and the top of the high object, to find out this perpendicular. It is to be understood that an artificial horizon must be used when the natural one is not available in measuring altitudes for this or any other purpose.

If the horizon with the rising or setting sun be visible,

449

the measure of the horizontal angle between the object, if it be not much above the horizon, and the rising and setting sun, applied to the true amplitude, gives at once a true bearing.

The tides.—The tides present so many eccentricities in different places, that very close and long continued observations, and records of these are necessary to ascertain them : but no opportunity should be lost of observing them, and when they are normal it is simple enough. Set up a tide pole, which may be a batten marked, to feet, and sub-divided by lines, and secured to some fixed object, as the piles of a jetty ; or it may need to be driven into the ground independently, in which case it must be closely watched for settling down, whilst the level of some mark on it should be referred to a rock or object on shore, to enable it to be replaced if by accident it should be removed during a series of observations ; or the perpendicular side of a tide-washed rock may be marked if fortunate enough to have one ; the spot selected must be sheltered, yet with free access from the sea, and where the gauge may be conveniently read by night and day, and with its zero below low water at springs. Let it be remembered, that which is principally wanted, is to ascertain the time of high water, at full and change of the moon (commonly called the *establishment*, because that being established, the time of high water on any other day can generally be known), and the rise at springs and at neaps. The observation should be begun by noting the height every half-hour for a complete 24 hours, to ascertain whether at the particular place, there be the usual two tides

450

DIAGRAM Nº 1.

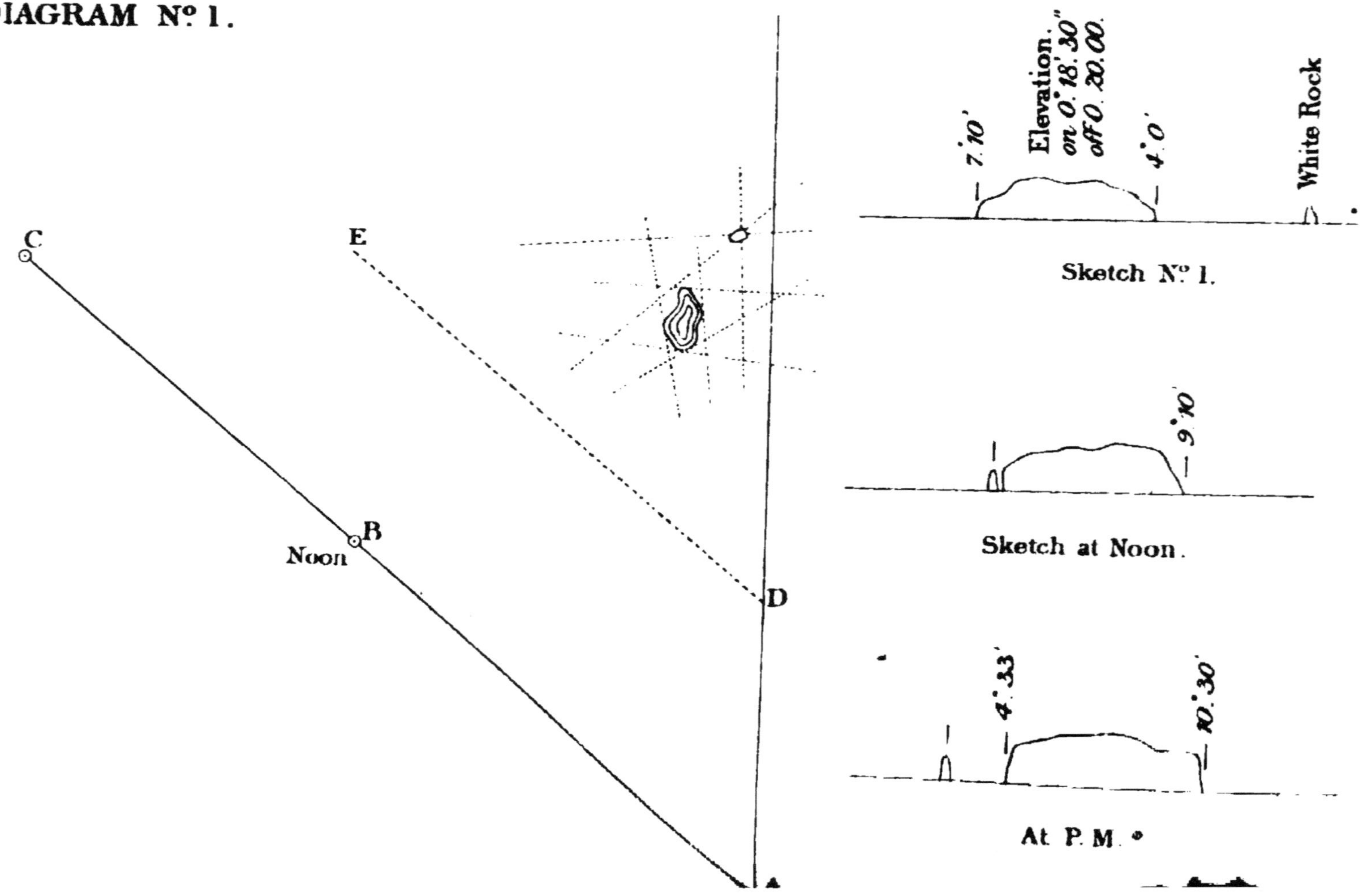

White Rock

Sketch Nº 1.

7.10'

Elevation
on 0.18.30"
of 0.20.00.

4.0'

Sketch at Noon.

9.0'

At P.M.

10.30'

4.33'

C

B
Noon

D

E

in a day, or only one in four, or any other peculiarity; then, if their be nothing unusual, note the time and height at every ten minutes from half-an-hour before to half-an-hour after every high and low water, day and night, and to be complete, this must be continued at least through a lunar month. Let the watch used be set to mean time and the observed times of high and low water should be daily compared with that of the moon's transit, for the tide should follow this transit regularly; and if it be found not to do so, it indicates peculiarity, that there is no proper *establishment*, and that the common method of observing the tides will probably be valueless. Whilst any sounding is going on, the tide gauge should be watched and registered every half-hour, or at any material sudden rise or fall, to enable the soundings to be reduced to the level of *low water springs*, for placing on the chart.

On Passing an Island.—Having lately left a port where the Chronometer was rated, &c., let it be supposed that an island is passed, whose position, extent, and general outline, it is desired to ascertain, whether from it not having been done before, or any other reason.

(See Diagram 1.) Suppose the ship arrived at A, and the time 8·30 a.m., suitable for sights; stop or heave to and observe thus—take the angular distance from the sun, to a conspicuous off-lying rock, to the right (choosing it because it is more easily recognized again, than any other point chosen might be) for its true bearing; observe its bearing by standard, measure with sextant the horizontal angles between white rock and each extreme of the island. Set

451

the patent log and put it over; let the ship proceed on her course if it is not wished to delay at all, otherwise on such a course and rate as would bring her true west of the island at noon. In the diagram she proceeds on her course, N 60° W., by compass; it is essential that the ship be carefully steered; a practised hand would easily make all these observations without stopping the ship, and especially with an assistant observer. At noon, stop, or not, determine the latitude by sun's mer. alt., and the white rock may be supposed to be just coming open of the left visible extreme of the island : observe its bearing by standard (and remember whenever a bearing by standard, is observed the direction of ship's head, at the moment, must be observed also); measure the angle to the right extreme of island, read the patent log, and put it over again. Proceed on the course, the ship steered carefully, and when the sun is suitable for p.m. sights, the island, and rock being still plainly seen, stop (if necessary), take sights, true and compass bearings, and angles as before; haul in and read patent log; and now is collected all the data necessary for fixing the island correctly, supposing there be no current.

If the noon position were in the parallel of the island (the island bearing true East or West), and one position at time of sights either a.m. or p.m., had been on its meridian, (the island true North or South) about D and E, these two would have been enough, and the position of the island would have been determined most favorably; and to arrange this, the distance from the island at which to

452

begin, course of ship, and rate of going must be regulated according to circumstances.

The ship need not be steered on any one course, (though it is better), but her course and distance, by reckoning, must be very carefully determined, from one fixed station to the other (A to B to C) and applied to those positions as fixed by observation, as the best available means of detecting current.

If the water were moderately shallow, and especially if doing this work under steam, whilst stopped at stations A, B, C, a kedge were dropped, and the direction and rate of the current ascertained, the observations &c., would be better made, and the whole task performed with much more exactness. To ascertain the height of the island : from one of the fixed positions observe with a sextant its angle of elevation above the horizon at its base, off and on the arc ; mean these, and with height of eye and its distance from that station (determined afterwards in the plotting), its height is readily calculated.

To put this work on paper.—(See diagram 1.)

Choose the point A, and draw a vertical line through it for the true meridian, and set off from it the true bearing of the white rock ; then from this line as zero set off the angles observed to the extrémes of the island. Having selected a convenient scale, lay off from A position, B and C relative to A, as determined by the astronomical observations, courses and distances made good by reckoning, and the current ascertained from the two. Now set off from B, the bearing of white rock and angle observed

453

to the extreme of the island : the intersection of
lines mark the spot of white rock and the limits of the i
From C lay off again the true bearing of white rod
the angles observed to the extremes of the island,
intersecting the previous lines mark the limits of the
more nearly, and should pass through the point of
section for white rock. If it does not, supposing n
to have been made in any of the observations, it d
current which could not be ascertained, and the in
tions from the two positions estimated to have bee
affected by it should be used only. On the paper n
the true bearing and distance of the white rock from
of the stations, and their lats. and longs. being known
of the white rock is determined, and a small m
Mercator's projection may be made, including it.
compass bearing of white rock having been obs
when its true bearing was taken from A, the variation
deviation being known, you ascertained the whole
error and so were able to observe with it and lay
true bearing of white rock from B.

This operation is often applied conversely and
usefully in navigation, where a ship after a sea cruise, p
ing an island or head-land, well known to be accur
fixed on the chart, the navigator determines in the s
way his position with reference to it, and comparing
with that determined by his chronometers, finds their t
errors and proceeds on his voyage with confidence. A
the same is in daily use when sailing along a coast it
wished to be certain of the distance from any object l

454

DIAGRAM Nº 2.

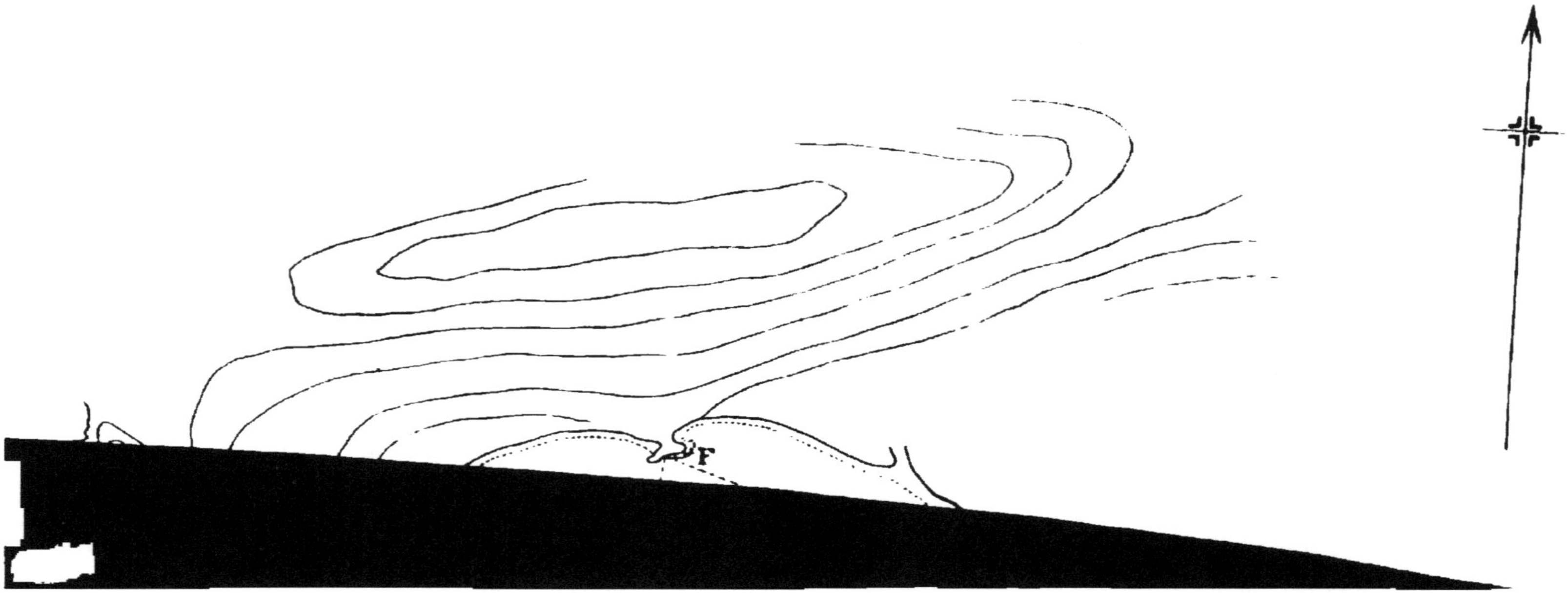

case, upon which further triangles may be constructed with new points within the work. Thus on A B are constructed A D B, and A B E; and on A E is constructed A E F. Set up at each station A B C D E F, a pole with cross boards at right angles at its top, or a white-washed cairn of stones, or other good mark, and measure carefully the horizontal angles of each of the triangles formed at them; and when the three angles of each triangle are added together and make 180°, this part of the work has been done correctly; very often it may be necessary or convenient to calculate a third angle of any triangle, by subtracting the sum of the other two from 180°, without observing it; and sometimes in measuring angles with a sextant, the angle may be beyond the capacity of the instrument; in this case measure two, choosing some conspicuous natural mark between them and add them together.

Now construct this triangulation on the paper; either A C may be assumed any convenient length; and when any one side of the triangulation is by-and-bye measured, the scale will be ascertained and put on the plan; but more formally and better, measure one of the sides (this matter will be treated of after), and from it and the known angles calculate the lengths of all the sides in all the triangles. Then drawing a line for the true meridian of A, set off A C its true length, and on its true bearing, and on it build the triangulation by the sides with a pair of compasses and scale. A triangle is more correctly laid down by its sides than by its angles (in large work this is done by a beam compass).

456

Now each station must be visited, and by lines of intersection, all the various points and objects lying between these stations must be cut in, and the coast line completed by hand and eye as you go round. It may often be necessary to whitewash large stones, or set up poles with a flag or cross boards nailed at right angles at the top, where there may be a long interval without any natural mark. At first it may often be necessary to visit a station more than once, but a very little practice will generally obviate this and curtail the work, in many particulars, in fact, teach the *surveyor* to kill two birds with one stone.

It must be rembered that much may be put in beyond the triangulation, as the seaward side of the bay in the diagram if it be seen from sufficient of the points, but it is generally better to extend the triangulation, so as to include all the proposed work. To sound this bay, and search for shoals, and hidden dangers, and ascertain the nature of the bottom, and so the best parts for anchoring, the better way would be to sound in lines north and south parallel to each other, beginning at the western end, and at such distances apart as the variation of the depths shows to be necessary. To do this, an assistant places two poles in line, north and south, on the north shore, a few hundred yards apart, fixing by angles the spot of one of them, and thus the line is shown across the bay, on which the boat sounds by keeping them in line ; the point on this line is fixed at short intervals by observing from the boat an angle between the line of the poles, and any

457

other station or object fixed on the plan on either side of
the line, making any angle from about 30° to 150° with it.
As the sounding is performed more frequently than it is
necessary to fix, place the intermediate ones proportionally.
Supposing the boat to have left the south shore, and
sounded towards the poles on the north, she reaches that
shore ; the poles are placed on a new line to the eastward
and the boat re-crosses the Bay, with her stern towards
them, and thus backwards and forwards until the east end
of the Bay is reached.

But without this assistance from the shore, sounding
is thus performed ; remembering that the position of a
sounding is fixed by quickly observing two angles between
three objects fixed in the work, that the centre object
should always be the nearest, and that angles from 60° to
90° are best. Starting from one shore note any two conspicuous objects on or nearly on with each other, in the
direction which it is intended to sound, and this direction
must be decided upon by any tide there may be, or in
which the marks will be most favorable. Fix the boat at
starting and sound, pull in the direction, keeping the lead
going and recording the depths and nature of the bottom.
Every now and then, according to the speed of the boat.
fixing afresh, making a tick against the sounding at that
instant, and whenever any important change in the depth
or bottom takes place, until the shore is reached in the
direction determined : fix again there and proceed in a new
direction until the bay has been sounded over, leaving no
considerable unsounded spaces. It will often be necessary
to change the objects for fixing, the time should be re-

458

corded about every half-hour to enable the soundings to be reduced to L.W.S. Any two fixed objects in line or transit with one angle right or left of it makes a fix of great reliability. With three objects in a curve concave to the observer, or the middle object farthest from him, it is always difficult, and sometimes impossible to fix; this must be avoided; but it may sometimes be necessary to use a compass bearing and an angle.

To put these soundings on the plan, first reduce them to L.W.S, and then on a sheet of tracing paper assume a point and lay off three lines, measuring the two angles observed between them, and putting the names or initials of the object on each line; let the lines be long enough, and move the tracing paper about on the plan until the three lines pass through the spots of the respective objects; then, with a needle, prick through the assumed spot on the tracing paper, which is the spot on the plan of the corresponding sounding which was ticked, which introduce reduced. Plot the next ticked sounding in the same way, and then fill in the intervening space by a selection in proportion, of the intervening reduced soundings, and proceed thus through the whole.

The tides having been attended to, a fair copy must now be made, and scale attached; denote latitude and longitude of the observation station, calculated from the meridian distance, and name the last known meridian measured from variation of the compass; time of H.W.F. and C., with rise at springs and neaps, and the standard to which the soundings are reduced, usually and properly to L.W.S., should be appended to the title.

2 G

459

If any sketches, however moderately well executed, can be appended, so much the better, and especially of objects used as marks, or likely to be alluded to in remarks on the place ; and the height of one or more of the principal hills, if there be any, should be ascertained and shewn.

On Measuring a Base.—We have illustrated a base measured by the latitude and longitude, both ends of it being determined astronomically, and alluded to a base measured by a distance run by Patent Log ; now in the case of a plan of a harbour, the best method is to arrange the triangulation, so as to bring one side of any one of the triangles along a sandy beach, or level piece of land, and this being actually and carefully measured, the actual measure of every side in the triangulation is readily calculated by the sines of the angles being proportional to their opposite sides.

Or, since the height of the truck of every man-of-war above its netting and water-line is known, or can easily be found, if in the plan before us, the angle of its elevation be observed from B and from D, the distances B to ship, and D to ship are calculated, and the horizontal angle made at B and D with B D and the ship, or the included angle at the ship, "D ship B," observed; the side B D is easily calculated, and from it again all the other sides in the triangulation.

Again, when the distance to be measured is considerable, extending over a mile, it may be more convenient to measure by sound, though it can scarcely ever be so accurate. Send a boat's gun to C, while you are at A, with the hack watch, between which two stations it is proposed to

460

easure the distance. Now the watch may beat every half-
cond or five times in two seconds—when every beat
quals four-tenths of a second.

Arrange a signal to be displayed at C, ten or fifteen
conds before the firing of the gun; now with your eye
esh, and fixed on C, and your ear and half an eye if you
ive it, left on the watch conveniently held before you,
gin to count aloud the beats, remembering, or an assist-
it noting the beat at the moment of the flash; do not be
sturbed by it, but count aloud steadily, stopping the
oment the report is heard,—you have now the number
beats between the flash and the report, and so the num-
:r of seconds and tenths of seconds: now the flash is
sumed as instantaneous, it took no time to travel, the
port travelled at the rate of 1090 feet in each second,
the thermometer showed 32°); therefore, multiply 1090
the seconds and tenths, adding one foot for every two
grees of the thermometer, above 32° Fah., and you have
e distance A C in feet.

Or to avoid the trouble of landing a gun, the ship her-
lf may fire, and you may make the observations at one
more of the stations, and so work into the triangulation,
in the case of observing the truck's angle of elevation.
ou would of course repeat the firing and measuring until
e similarity of results showed there was no material
ror in the practice.

A River Survey.—If it is wished to make a careful and
mplete survey of some miles of a river, with time to do
in, and supposing its banks and adjacent country to con-
t of hill and plain, all accessible, a base should be

measured and a triangulation carried over it. But if a
boat or steam launch be detached to ascend an unknown
or a not well known river, desiring to make the most of
the run up without delaying, yet intending to devote
several days at least to this work. Starting from a spot at
the mouth, whose latitude and longitude you have ascertained either from the chart or by your own observations,
take the bearing of a point up the river towards which you
will first steer; use a patent log, taking care occasionally to
ascertain the rate of the current down, and allow for it,
and so you have a course and distance to lay down; then
take the bearing of another point, and steer to it in the
same way, and so on through the day, laying down these
courses and distances as you go on, and sketching in, the
intervening rivers banks, *and* sounding as the boat proceeds, and taking angles of any conspicuous objects which
will be fixed by intersection from your different points.
Wherever you may be at a suitable time for a.m. sights
land and take them ; wherever you may be again at noon,
land and ascertain the latitude by sun's meridian, altitude;
take sights again p.m., and whenever you halt at night, ascertain the lat. at least by moon or stars; (you would have
brought at least one chronometer with you); thus with a
series of latitudes and meridian distances, you have a long
chain of fixed points on your paper, which you now fill in
from your rough survey made on the passage. It may need
expansion in one part, and compression in another, or the
opposite, but if you have been careful and paid good
attention to the current, you will be surprised how little
alteration it needs.

462

DIAGRAM Nº 3.

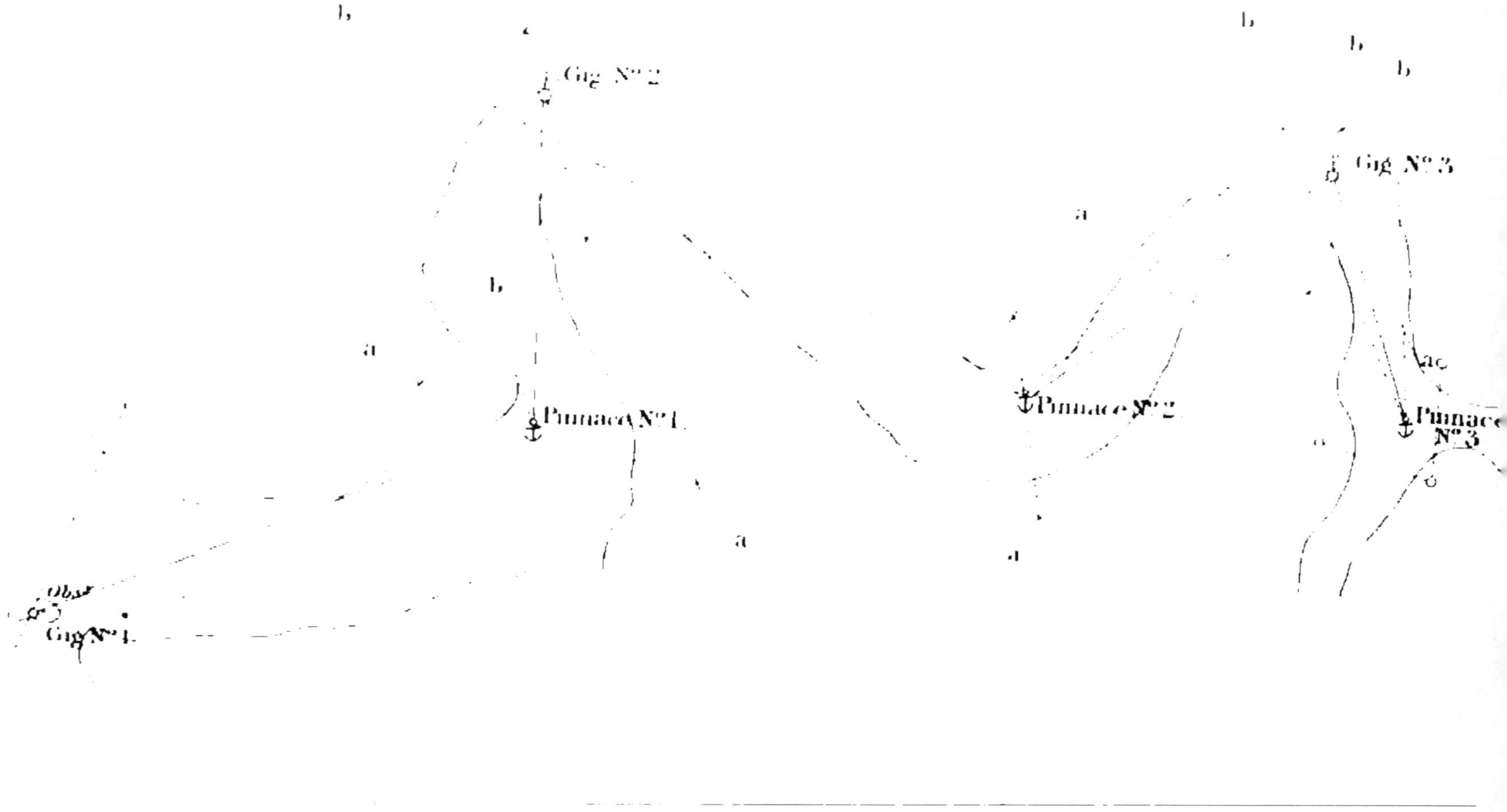

Pinnace Nº 3

Gig Nº 3

Pinnace Nº 2

Gig Nº 2

Pinnace Nº 1

Gig Nº 1

Wherever you may halt for an hour or so, or after
stopping for the night, or before starting in the morning,
you would make a fuller plan of that part of the river,
measuring its breadth, and cutting in all points in sight up-
and-down; measuring a base by running a line along
a piece of level bank, or by sending the boat across the
river from where you are, and observing the altitude of
its mast.

Supposing you finally attain some considerable
distance from the sea, it is more than useful to ascertain
the height above the sea level, by continued registration
of an aneroid barometer and loose thermometer which you
would compare with the mercurial one on board before
leaving, and on your return: and also to determine the
variation of the compass.

Lastly, (see Diagram No. 3.) suppose you have two
boats, but only a day or two to do the most you can in; if
there is a reliable assistant in the second boat, more work
will be done, and it will be better done, but if there be
only yourself, (as is assumed generally in these remarks),
take the gig and send the pinnace to the first point of the
river you wish to fix; she should always sound as she
proceeds up the river; her mast should be stepped, and
perhaps a lighter pole lashed to lengthen it, the top made
conspicuous by cross boards or a signal cone, and the distance carefully measured from this extreme top to the
boat's gunwale. Arrived at the point you have sent her to,
she anchors or is fastened to trees or a rock, as close the
shore as she can. You observe the angle of elevation of her
pole (always off or on) and take the bearing by azimuth com-

463

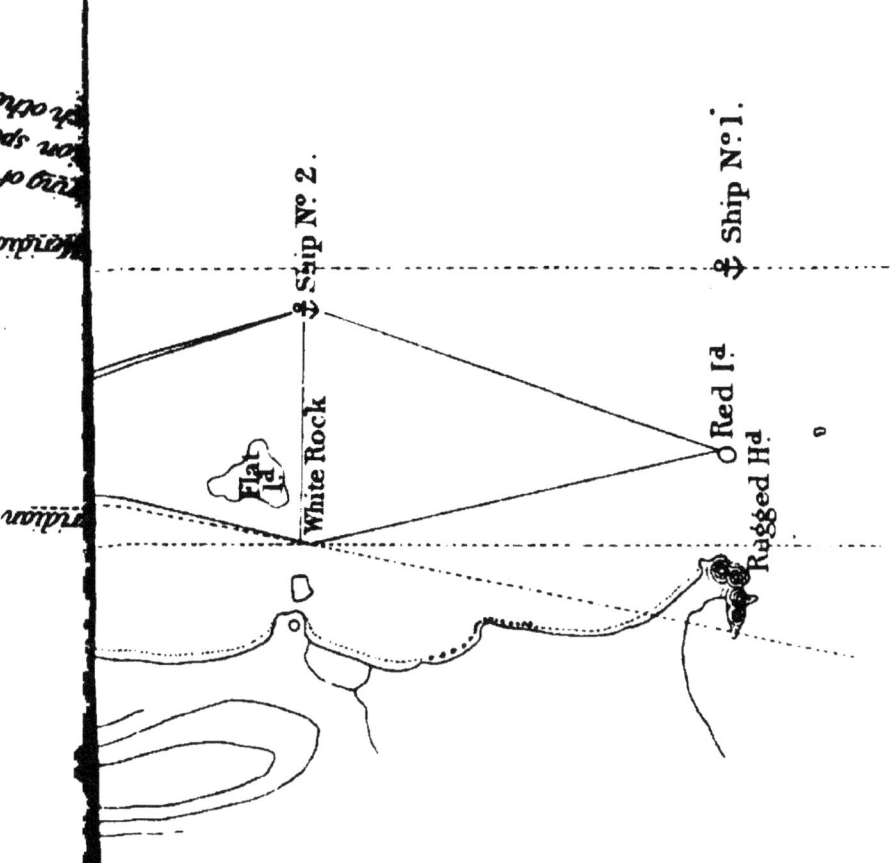

DIAGRAM N° 4.

Ship N° 2.

Ship N° 1.

White Rock

Flat Id.

Red Id.

Rugged Hd.

Griffin & C° Portsea

When time or circumstances forbid your proceeding
ther, it would be of great value to your work to land
th your azimuth compass and take a run to the top of a
ar moderate hill which you have included in your angles,
d from it take a bearing of the ship herself off the mouth or
e mouth, or your first station, or any of the most salient
nds of the river, or hills, or noteworthy objects, any
all of them. There is a point up every river beyond
iich the influence of the sea tide ceases to be felt ; a
ty or two's trip would not probably reach this, but on an
tended trip it should be ascertained.

Nomendature.—In all surveys, but especially in extended
ver surveying, names for villages, islands, hills, distant
iountains, branches of the river, and of the river itself,
:c. (for it varies), will be wanted ; always ascertain if
ossible, and use, the *native names.*

COAST SURVEY.—It is proposed to spend a few days off
piece of coast for the purpose of surveying it to the best
f your ability, supplied only as before with the means an
rdinary man-of-war affords ; let it be supposed that the
hore is inaccessible, the ship is abreast Red Island (see
Diagram No. 4) three or four miles from it, and the time
iuitable for beginning the work. If the wind, weather, and
lepth of water admit, drop a kedge say at position No. 1,
make a rough outline sketch of the coast from Red Island
to Flat Island, and observe the true bearing of any distinct
object, say the peak of Red Island ; take angles between
it and the limits of Rugged head, and of Flat Island, and
to White rock, the point behind it, and to any hill top,
house, rocky point, limits of sandy beach, or every other

465

notable point between Red Island and Flat Island, and
record these angles on your rough sketch ; take angles of
elevation of any hills you intend to introduce on the coast,
and of off-lying islets or islands , let the direction and
force, and changes if any, of the tide, be ascertained whilst
at anchor ; now weigh and steer a steady course to position
No. 2, sounding as you go, though you may not be able
to plot these soundings yet, the objects you may use
having yet to be fixed, and heave the Patent Log over,
until arrived at a position off Flat Island, where all the
coast you have passed is clearly in sight, then drop the
kedge again. Remember with reference to the Patent
Log, that any one drawn from store and used, is not at
once to be depended on ; it may have an instrumental
error, which can only be proved by using it over an
actually ascertained distance ; if it has, it may be corrected, but perhaps it is better to make the proportional
allowance whenever it is used : the same remark applies
to sounding machines, and in both cases " Massey's
Patent" are particularly correct. These excellent
instruments are like first-rate watches—they need regulat-
ing, or their known and constant irregularity allowed for.

Besides your rough outline sketch, you must by this
time have prepared a projection. Assuming a point for
your position, No. 1, lay off from it the various lines of
bearing you observed, and then the course and connected
distance run to position 2. At 2 observe the true bearing
of peak of Red Island, and the angles from it to all the
same points and objects you observed before, and laying
them off, these lines will intersect those from position 1 ;

ıd thus, aided by your sketch, you fill in the coast line
om Red Island to Flat Island. You will fasten at 2;
ıke angles of notable objects to the northward; make a
ketch; observe the tide, &c.; and then proceed to any
osition farther on, say 3, and repeat this work until your
ime or purpose is suited. You have now a map of a
iece of coast line, with all conspicuous objects duly fixed
ıpon it, you can proceed to complete the sounding by
ıanding off and on the land, fixing and sounding. How
ar to stand off must be regulated by many considerations,
whether the shore is steep, and of great depth, or gradually
shallowing; whether the land be higher or lower, and the
ime you have to spare, &c.; but how far to stand in would
be regulated by considerations of safety to the ship;
whether you are in a sailing or steam ship greatly alters
the work of sounding: and finally, you would examine in
a boat the whole shore, standing off and on, sounding
within the limit of your ship work, you would complete
or corroborate the sweep of the bays, and look carefully
for hidden dangers, especially off the projecting points,
whether of mainland, or off-lying islets and islands. At
each of your ships positions at anchor—but certainly, if
possible, at the first and last, you would have made
observations for true bearing, and for lat. and long., and
by connecting the ship's position with the shore, you fix
the limits, and introduce your surveying work between
them. It may not fit exactly; you must decide upon
the greater reliability of your astronomical, or trigonome-
tral data, and amend the work accordingly. For instance,
in this case with the coast, nearly north and south, great

467

value would be given to the determined latitudes, if the observations made for them were satisfactory.

Let it be now supposed that the coast is accessible, landing safe and practicable anywhere, the weather fair, time ample, and qualified assistants on board. Referring to the same diagram the ship being off the coast, near Flat Island, in position No. 2, it is determined on to survey from Rugged Head to the northward.

White rock appears to be a good commanding spot for angles, and it is therefore determined to make it the observatory station. When this point is settled, ship runs out and anchors in position No. 2, which is supposed to be at the distance of three or four miles from White Rock, and in a direction so as to form good angles with the intended extreme objects along the coast, north and south; these are Red Island on one side, and Cone Mount on the other. Sail is shortened, and the ship anchored, or steadied with a kedge.

The surveying boats are two in number, a pinnace and a gig; and the principal requires two careful assistants. If there be but one, he should be left on board the ship; for the correct construction of the triangles, on which the survey is based, entirely depends on the perfect understanding and accord between the principal and this assistant. The work is supposed to commence at 7 a.m.; thus :—

Despatch one assistant in pinnace to Red Island, with directions to show a flag or build a mark there; and prepared to take angles of all objects, and measure a base by sound. The distance between ship and White Rock he will take and register at each gun. After base is measured

468

he will survey and sound the coast between Rugged Head and White Rock, and then return to the ship.

The assistant left on board the ship will take angles between the principal objects and White Rock, from the foremast, at each gun ; then angles to *all* objects that are likely to be in any way useful. True and compass bearings of some conspicuous object should also be taken, as well as angles of elevation of the principal peaks. Here, Red Island is the principal object on one side of White Rock, and Cone Mount on the other ; next in importance is Double Head, then High Mount. As it is intended to carry the survey along the coast to the northward, reconnoitre well with a glass in that direction, and take angles between all remarkable objects and White Rock. Some of them may turn out to be of greater importance than is at first expected.

The principal having left clear directions with his assistant on board the ship, to ensure combined action, proceeds himself to white Rock, with chronometer, sextant, &c. By the time he lands, pinnace may have arrived at Red Island, then he, being ready, will make an agreed signal for the ship to fire, for measuring a base by sound. Ship will answer by hoisting a large flag at the fore, *half-mast ;* when the gun is ready hoist it close up ; and dip to half-mast again, the instant *before* firing. Repeat thus thrice, at intervals of about three minutes, and thus the distances Red Island to ship, and White Rock to ship (No. 2) are obtained. At the time of firing, angles between the principal objects are taken from the ship, and from observatory station at White Rock ; these angles, as well as the inter-

469

vals of time for the base, should be observed and regis tered three several times (once at each gun), to prevent the possibility of mistake. Afterwards take angles to all objects that are likely to be useful in fixing the features of the coast. When all is complete, ship will weigh, stand in, and anchor conveniently near observatory station. Pinnace will sound and survey the coast between Rugged Head and White Rock.

.Each observer should place his angles on an *outline* sketch of the coast, as well as recording them in his angle book.

The Chief, at observatory station, will be fully occupied with observations. He should note the state of the tide directly he lands, and occasionally afterwards, at convenient intervals throughout the day. True bearings should be taken, both a.m. and p.m., if possible. Sets of sights for equal altitudes of the sun, for time, should be taken at short intervals between 8.30 and 10.30 a.m., so as to have every chance of obtaining a sufficient number of corresponding sights in the afternoon; and the circum- meridional altitude of the sun for latitude, and angles, to fill up the spare intervals of time will keep him employed When the ship anchors near observatory station, he can send for the azimuth compass, and take sets of bearings of the true bearing zero point for magnetic variation.

After p.m. sights and true bearing, the Chief returns on board and compares all chronometers; he will then examine the ship's work, and assure himself that it is complete and correct. When pinnace returns, he is fully

470

acquainted with the state of the day's work, and can then determine whether it will be proper to advance on the following day.

An analysis of the day's work shows, that on the common base line between observatory and ship, we have, first in importance, the triangle formed with Cone Mount ; secondly, that formed with Double Head ; and thirdly, the one formed with Red Island ; of which last we have measured all the angles. From this data, the sides of the triangles forming the distances between the observatory station at White Rock, and Cone Mount, Double Head, and Red Island should be *calculated*.

Objects of secondary importance, fixed by lines *from* stations, forming good triangles with such objects, may be *projected*. For example, in the diagram, lines from Red Island and White Rock will fix any object along the coast between these stations.

We will now suppose that the Chief has secured the latitude and longitude of White rock ; true and magnetic bearings of some remarkable object used in the survey ; angles to all points, bluffs, peaks, and other objects likely to be useful ; together with angles of elevation of the principal mountains ; and that the ground round Flat Island has been sounded, and the survey complete from Rugged Head up to the ship's anchorage ; which we will assume to be the first day's work.

At daylight on the following morning, ship weighs, and runs off shore about seven miles (more or less, according to the depth of water, &c.), then in to five miles, and out again ; fixing by angles at each alteration of the course,

471

and carrying a zigzag line of soundings between those limits, along the coast for about ten miles, to position No. 3, where she should anchor by 2 or 3 p.m., and get ready for measuring a base by sound.

Pinnace also proceeds to sound along the coast, making a zigzag line between two and five miles from the shore, returning to the ship by sunset.

The officers in charge of the sounding, on board both ship and pinnace, will frequently be called on to exercise their tact and forethought in the choice of objects to fix their positions by. It may be taken for granted that most of the remarkable objects *on* the coast line, and *all* outlying rocks and islands, will be fixed by the Chief when he comes along; but it should be remembered, that he may not be able to see anything *within* the coast line, from the view in that direction being interrupted by trees, and therefore hills and other objects remarkable from the sea may be shut out from him altogether. When the ship finds any difficulty in fixing, she should go direct to her arranged next position, and anchor, thus making a good mark for pinnace to fix by.

The Chief, in gig, proceeds first to the point within White Rock, for angles to lay in the coast line by; afterwards take up a station in depth of the bay, between it and Double Head, then at the outer point of Double Head. She would carry a line of soundings along the coast, between each of her stations, and if there be time, run a mile or so off shore occasionally. By the time gig has finished as far as Double Head, the ship will probably be anchored in position No. 33; if so, Chief will take the

472

angle between her and Cone Mount, from Double Head station; and should there be any rocks extending from Cone Mount Point, take an angle to one, for a station. One or more stations between Double Head and Cone Point, according to circumstances, will be necessary. They will probably be fixed by the objects—Double Head, ship and Cone Mount; but if possible, return angles should be obtained to them from either Double Head or ship. The Chief should therefore always endeavour to take up his stations, for laying in coast line, on remarkable points or rocks. In such cases a little whitewash will be found very useful to mark the stations, in the direction it is particularly wished they should be seen from.

On arriving at Cone Point station, gig will show signal for measuring base by sound. Ship fires three guns as before, and again angles are taken to objects on each side. Here Double Head is the object on one side, and Pinnacle Mount on the other; take also the angle between Cone Mount and gig's station at the point. From the ship, this angle being so small will be best observed by a reference of both objects to some well-defined point, forming a considerable angle right or left, and taking the difference between them: this method is recommended when measuring a side angle with a sextant.

The Chief will, of course, take angles to *all* objects, and a true bearing of some point, before leaving the station, and wind up by bringing a line of soundings off to the ship. The assistant on board the ship has obtained all the necessary angles at the time of measuring the base,

473

and arranged them properly on a sketch of the coast. He ought also at each position to obtain true and compass bearings of some important object, and angles of elevation to all the principal peaks.

In the case here illustrated, we will suppose that both Chief and assistant have fixed on Pinnacle Peak as the northern point for angles. To the southward, Double Head is the object; and as the positions of Double Head and Cone Mount were fixed from our stations of yesterday (White Rock, and No. 2 ship), we now have an opportunity of checking the first day's work. White Rock is not in sight, or it would, of course, have been used in preference to Double Head.

The survey being complete up to the ship's position, No. 3, and objects to northward fixed for the morrow's work, the ship can be got ready to weigh at daylight.

Next day's operations are carried on in the same manner. Ship anchors in position No. 4, off Pinnacle Point, and Chief takes up his station for measuring base on the point itself. When all the observations have been taken, he reconnoitres the bay to the northward of him, and judging from appearances that it will require a close examination, he signals to ship, on which ship weighs again and enters the bay, accompanied by pinnace.

We have now surveyed upwards of twenty miles of coast from our last observation spot, and as we have determined to make a separate plan of the bay on a large scale, we will bring our coast survey to a close, and obtain sights for latitude, longitude, &c., at Pinnacle Point station, and proceed as illustrated under " Harbour Survey."

474

On reference to the ship's position, No. 4 on the diagram, it will be seen that Cone Mount is the southern point of our main triangle in that direction; consequently we have a check on the distance between Cone and Pinnacle Mounts obtained yesterday. On checking the distances along the coast, by the different bases measured by sound, they are found to agree, and numerous true bearings corroborative of each other, have kept the work correct in azimuth.

PLOTTING.

To plot this work, mark a spot in a convenient position for the south observatory station, and draw a vertical line through it, for the true meridian. Set off the true bearing lines of direction to Red Island station, Double Head, Cone Mount, and ship; on which lines fix the positions of those points according to their mean distances. Next, place Cone Point station by Double Head and Cone Mount, and when this station is satisfactorily fixed, lay off ship at No. 3, and Pinnacle Mount, using the mean of the distance obtained from the ship's positions, Nos. 3 and 4. If Pinnacle Mount be seen from the point, fix the station here, as at Cone Point; and from it, the ship at No. 4. As it is often difficult to fix a station on a point, without a line of direction from some position already fixed, the surveyor ought to provide for it in his progress along the coast, by anticipation. Thus, at observatory station, he should take an angle to a remarkable rock or object on the extreme point of Double Head. At the point of Double Head take some object on the point off Cone

2 H   475

Mount for a station, and should there be several remarkable rocks, take them all.

If stations on the summits of Double Head and Cone Mount were taken up, there would be, generally, no occasion for the stations on the outer points.

When the main triangles are plotted from calculation, the minor points, and coast line, may be projected.

To test the work, draw the true meridians in pencil through the two observation spots at White Rock and Pinnacle Point; then draw a line through the two stations, and take off the course and distance from one to the other. With the observed latitude and longitude calculate the same. They should agree exactly; though, provided the courses or bearings agree, a difference in the distance is not material, as it is nearly certain to be regular throughout; and the survey will be graduated, and its scale determined from the astronomical positions.

Should the coast surveyed run nearly north and south, as in the case before us, and the difference of longitude by projection and observation not agree, it may be advisable, in order to keep the work correct in azimuth, to disregard the second longitude by observation; and assuming that projected to be correct, graduate from it, and the difference of latitude by observation. This can only be done when the Chief feels confidence in the correctness of his true bearings; it is therefore absolutely necessary that he should be exact and expert in taking them. On an irregular coast survey, such as the one here treated of, true bearings should be observed from the shore and from the ship twice a day in each position.

476

Constructing a Chart.—There are several methods, each f which may be more desirable under varying circum- tances. In low latitudes a mercator projection may well e used in plotting a survey ; a more invariably useful one is that of the plane spherical principle, that is with the meridians inclined to each other, representing nearly the atural appearance of the earth's surface, and which is escribed, and an example given in the Admiralty Manual, ages 58 and 59, which is on board every man-of-war. ut in the case of an exact piece of triangulation in a omplete survey with astronomical and geoditical data, it plotted as on a plane, and reduced for any adoption by killed draughtsmen.

TO FIND THE HEIGHT OF MOUNTAINS.

In surveying work this problem is used not only to scertain the height of a mountain absolutely, but that of ne station above or below another ; and in this way a hain of elevation accompanies a triangulation, verified ow and then by the actual measurement of the height of ny one conveniently near the sea, above the main sea vel. It is a calculation of great nicety when the accuracy f geodesy is attempted, arising from the spheroidal figure f the earth, and the varying and subtle curvatures for fraction. As a part of such surveying work as we have een describing, it is comparatively simple : observe the ngle of elevation off and on, and with the known distance roceed thus.

2 H 2

For curvature, take one-half of the distance, and subtract one-eleventh of the distance for refraction. To this add the observed angle of elevation, subtract the true dip, and the result will be the true angle of elevation. Then add together log. of the distance, tang. of angle of elevation and log. of the number of feet in a mile; the result will be the log. of the height in feet.

To find the true dip.—To the constant log. 6·49057 add half the log. of the height of the eye in feet, and the sum will be the log. tang. of the true dip. If the angle of elevation be taken on shore with a level, reduce it to the mean tide level.

Example.—Mount Etna was seen at 57 miles distance, and subtended an angle of 1° 30′ 0″ with the horizon, the height of the eye was 20 feet; required the height of the mountain.

Distance.........57′			57..... ....1·755875	
			tan. of elev. .....8·499300	
½..................	28	30″	60756 ....3·783576	
¹⁄₁₁	5	11		
Observed angle	23	19	Height = } ....4·038751	
of elevation	1° 30	0	10934 ft. }	
	1 53	19		
True dip......	4	46	Const. log. ......6·49057	
			½ log. 20...........0·65051	
True angle of	1 48	73		
elevation			tan. true dip =4′ 46″ .. 7·14108	

To ascertain the Height of a Station above or below another, proceed thus:—To constant log. 7·9933, add the

478

log of distance, take out natural number, which, divided by 2, gives curvature. $\frac{1}{12}$th of first natural number is refraction; always take the difference, adding to an elevation, subtracting to a depression, then take out the log tangent (sine small arcs) of corrected elevation or depression, and add to it the log of distance, which gives the difference of height.

Each height as it is worked should be numbered, so that should any question arise as to the accuracy of the work, it can be easily looked up.

After ascertaining in this way the height of a mountain from a ship at sea, and an opportunity offering for visiting its summit, a verification can usefully be obtained by "Barometrical Measurement"; an aneroid compared with standard and carried to the top as spoken of in "River Survey," would inform you of the amount of confidence to be placed on this method, when it may be the only available means on future occasions.

Having now pointed out and endeavoured to explain how much valuable work of a surveying character can be accomplished by means of the instruments found on board every man-of-war, it is desired to impress upon every young officer, that he should be able to perform the same ; and certainly no navigating officer can be held to know his work thoroughly, who is unequal to this amount of surveying : its application is continually of the greatest value in his work of navigation and pilotage, it facilitates the ascertaining of a ship's true position, of the requisition of land, of currrents, &c., and is invaluable in imparting confidence.

Trust nothing to memory ; let your angles and notes be copious, for from them you must draw up your remarks and explanations, called " Sailing Directions," which add greatly to the value of a piece of work ; and after a very little practice, briefer and less formal methods, and labour saving variations will develope themselves, which will add a charm to the work, and will often lead an officer to the acquirement of a knowledge of exact surveying, which it has not been pretended to treat of here.

PART III.

———

TABLES.

TABLE I.*

FOR ASCERTAINING THE STRENGTH OF HEMPEN CABLES.

Size in Inches.	No. of Yarns.	Weight in lbs. of 100 Fathoms.	Breaking Strain in Tons.			
			Maximum.	Minimum.	Mean.	Weakest ‡
26	3528	14112	122·2	105·9	111·6	101·5
25½	3393	13572	117·5	101·9	107·3	97·6
†25	3267	13068	113·0	98·0	103·2	93·8
24½	3122	12488	114·4	94·4	102·5	90·1
24	3006	12024	115·7	91·0	101·9	86·5
23½	2880	11520	117·0	87·6	101·3	82·9
23	2763	11052	118·3	84·2	100·7	79·4
†22½	2646	10584	119·5	81·0	100·1	76·0
22	2529	10116	111·4	77·9	95·0	72·6
21½	2412	9648	103·5	74·9	90·1	69·4
21	2304	9216	95·8	72·0	85·3	66·2
†20½	2196	8784	88·3	69·2	80·6	63·1
20	2088	8352	81·0	66·5	76·1	60·0
19½	1980	7920	76·7	62·1	71·3	57·1
19	1881	7524	72·6	57·9	66·6	54·2
18½	1782	7128	68·6	53·8	62·1	51·4
18	1692	6768	64·7	49·8	57·7	48·6
†17½	1587	6353	61·0	46·0	53·4	45·0
17	1512	6048	57·3	44·9	51·0	43·4
16½	1422	5688	53·9	43·8	48·7	40·8
16	1332	5328	50·5	42·8	46·5	38·4
15½	1251	5004	47·3	41·9	44·3	36·0
†15	1170	4716	44·2	41·0	42·3	33·7
14½	1098	4392	41·6	38·4	39·9	31·5
14	1026	4104	39·1	36·0	37·6	29·4
13½	954	3816	36·7	33·6	35·4	27·3
13	882	3528	34·4	31·3	33·3	25·3
†12½	810	3240	32·2	29·2	31·3	23·4
12	756	3024	29·8	26·6	28·6	21·6
11½	693	2772	27·6	24·2	26·1	19·8
11	630	2520	25·5	21.8	23·7	18·1
10½	576	2304	23·4	19·6	21·4	16·5
†10	522	2088	21·5	17·5	19·2	15·0
9½	468	1872	19·0	15·7	17·1	13·5
9	432	1728	16·7	14·0	15·2	12·1
8½	396	1584	14·6	12·4	13·4	10·8
8	315	1260	12·6	10·9	11·7	9·6
†7½	288	1152	10·7	9·5	10·2	8·4
7	252	1008	9·3	8·2	8·8	7·3
6½	216	864	8·1	7·0	7·5	6·3
6	189	756	7·0	5·8	6·3	5·4
5½	162	648	5·9	4·8	5·3	4·5
†5	135	540	5·0	3·9	4·3	3·7
4½	108	432	4·0	3·1	3·4	3·0
4	90	360	3·2	2·5	2·7	2·4
3½	69	276	2·4	1·9	2·1	1·8
3	54	216	1·8	1·4	1·5	1·3

* Tables I. to IV. are from Tinmouth. The lines marked thus † contain the
lations. The right hand column ‡ has been calculated from the weakest of all
caution necessary. 482

TABLE II.

For ascertaining the Strength of Chain Cables.

Size in Inches.	Testing Strain. in Tons.	Weight in lbs. of 100 Fathoms.	Breaking Strain in Tons.			
			Maximum.	Minimum.	Mean.	Weakest. ‡
2¼	91⅛	27216	130·3	121·8	125·9	107·4
2⅛	81¼	24276	116·2	108·6	112·3	95·8
† 2	72	21504	103·0	96·25	99·5	—
† 1⅞	63¼	18900	99·0	88·0	92·8	—
† 1¾	55⅛	16464	85.25	65·0	74·1	65·0
1⅝	47½	14196	75·0	59·5	66·5	56·0
† 1½	40½	12096	65·5	54·5	59.5	—
1⅜	34	10164	53·6	44·4	48·5	40·1
1¼	28½	8400	42·8	35·3	38·5	33·1
† 1⅛	22¾	6804	33·0	27·0	29·5	26·0
† 1	18	5376	27·25	22·0	24·3	21·2
† ⅞	13¾	4116	22·5	20·3	21·1	16·2
† ¾	10⅛	3024	15·0	12·5	13·5	11·9
11/16	8½	2541	12·3	10·8	11·4	10·0
† ⅝	7	2100	9·87	9·37	9.5	8·2
9/16	5½	1701	—	—	—	—
½	4½	1344	6·3	5·9	6·0	5·3

results of actual experiments, and the intermediate lines those derived from calcu-
the experiments, and may be serviceable where risk is apprehended, and great

TABLE III.

For ascertaining the Strength of Hawser-laid Rope.

Size.	No. of Yarns.	Weight in lbs. of 100 Fathoms.	Strain in Tons.		
			Maximum.	Minimum.	Mean.
† 12	1173	2940	45·5	35·0	40·0
11½	1077	..	41·7	32·0	36·7
11	987	..	38·2	29·3	33·6
10½	900	..	34·9	26·7	30·7
10	816	2136	31·7	24·2	27·9
9½	738	..	28·6	21·8	25·2
9	660	1712	25·7	19·6	22·6
8½	591	..	23·0	17·5	20·2
8	522	1379	20·4	15·5	18·0
7½	459	..	18·0	13·6	15·8
7	399	..	15·8	11·8	13·8
6¼	345	..	13·7	10·2	12·0
† 6	294	834	11·7	8·7	10·3
5½	249	712	9·8	7·3	8·7
5	204	..	8·2	6·1	7·2
4½	168	413	6·7	5·0	5·9
4	132	..	5·3	4·0	4·7
3½	102	..	4·1	3·2	3·7
3	75	203	3·1	2·4	2·8
2¼	54	..	2·2	1·8	2·1
2	33	..	1·5	1·3	1·4
† 1¾	27	..	1·28	1·13	1·23
† 1½	21	..	·90	·86	·88
† 1¼	15	..	·60	·53	·56
† 1	12	..	·58	·46	·51
† ¾	9	..	·51	·42	·46
† ½	6	..	·28	·28	·28

† The lines thus marked contain the results of actual experiments,

TABLE IV.

…r ascertaining the Strength of round-linked Crane Chain.

…Size.	Weight in lbs. of 100 Fathoms.	Strain in Tons.			
		Maximum.	Minimum.	Mean.	Testing Strength.
† 1 5/8	15569	75·0	68·0	73·0	31·6
1 1/2	..	64·0	58·2	62·3	27·0
1 7/16	..	59·0	53·8	67·4	24·7
1 3/8	..	54·2	49·6	52·8	22·6
1 5/16	..	49·7	45·5	81·4	20·6
1 1/4	..	45·3	41·7	44·1	18·8
1 3/16	..	41·2	38·0	40·1	17·0
1 1/8	7481	37·3	34·5	36·3	15·3
1 1/16	..	33·6	31·2	32·7	13·6
1	6490	30·1	28·1	29·3	12·0
15/16	5600	26·8	25·2	26·1	10·5
7/8	4500	23·7	22·5	23·1	9·1
† 13/16	4000	20·9	20·0	20·4	7·9
3/4	3449	17·8	16·6	17·3	6·8
11/16	2900	14·9	13·5	14·6	5·6
5/8	2538	12·3	10·8	12·0	4·6
9/16	2001	10·0	8·7	9·7	3·8
1/2	1583	7·9	6·9	7·7	3·0
7/16	1060	6·0	5·2	5·9	2·3
3/8	827	4·4	3·8	4·3	1·6
5/16	581	3·0	2·7	3·0	1·1
1/4	392	1·9	1·7	1·9	·75
3/16	..	1·1	·97	1·0	·42

…nd the intermediate lines those derived from calculation.

TABLE V.

Showing the Strength of Wire-rope.

Circumference.	Weight of one fathom	Breakg. Strain.
Inches.	lbs.	Tons.
1	1	2
1⅛	1½	3
1⅜	2	4
1⅝	2½	5
1⅞	3	6
2	3½	7
2⅛	4	8
2¼	4½	9
2⅜	5	10
2½	5½	11
2⅝	6	12
2¾	6½	13
2⅞	7	14
3	7½	15
3⅛	8	16
3¼	8½	17
3⅜	9	18
3½	10	20
3⅝	11	22
3¾	12	24
3⅞	13	26
4	14	28
4½	18	33
5	22	38

TABLE VI.*

Showing the Strength of Blocks

Single Blocks:	Capacity for Strain.
Inches.	Tons.
6	1⅛
7	1¼
8	1½
9	1⅞
10	2⅜
11	3¼
12	4⅛
13	5¼
14	5⅞
15	6⅛
16	7¾
17	8½
18	9½
19	10¾
20	11⅝
21	12⅛
22	13⅞
23	14⅛
24	16⅛
25	18
26	20⅛
27	22
28	24

A common thin block reeves a rope one-third the length of the block.
A clump block, half the length.
A thin block, one-fifth.
A fiddle block, one-sixth.

The stropping of a single block is one-third the size of the block. For instance, the stropping of a 6-inch block is of 2-inch rope: of a 15-in. block 5-inch rope, &c.

Double blocks require double strops; and threefold blocks, either a double strop of larger rope, or a single preventer strop in addition to the double one.

Although a single block has the same sized pin as a double or a treble block, it must not be inferred that a single block will sustain an equal strain with a treble block. A treble block is in fact three blocks in one; and the weight being distributed between them renders it capable of sustaining three times the weight of a single block of corresponding size.

* Bushell's "Rigger's Guide."
(A valuable little book.)

TABLE VII.*

MATERIALS.	C.	S.	E.	M.
WOODS.	lbs.			
†Ash	17000	2026	6580000	4988000
Beech	11500	1560	5417000	4457000
Deal, Christiana	11000	1550	6350000	5378000
—— Memel	11000	1730	6420000	6268000
‡ Elm	5780	1030	2803000	3007000
Fir, New England ...	12000	1100	5967000	6249000
—— Riga	12600	1130	5314000	4080000
—— Mar Forest......	12000	1140	3400000	2797000
Mahogany	8000			
Norway spars	12000	1470	5830000	5789000
Oak, English { from	9000	1200	3490000	2872000
{ to...	15000	2260	7000000	4702000
—— Adriatic	14000	1380	3880000	2257000
—— African	14400	2000	9500000	5583000
—— Canadian........	12000	1760	8950000	5674000
‡Poon	14000	2200	6760000	6488000
Pine, Pitch	10500	1630	5000000	4364000
—— Red	10000	1340	7360000	6423000
‡Teak	15000	2460	9660000	7417000
IRON.				
Iron, cast ... { from	16300			
{ to ...	36000	8100	69120000	5530000 §
—— Malleable	60000	9000	91440000	6770000
—— Wire	80000			

* From the "Mechanics' Pocket Guide."   † Of English growth.

‡ East Indies.   § Mean of English and Foreign.

The application of this Table at the end of Art. 536.

TABLE VIII.

SPECIFIC GRAVITY AND WEIGHT OF MATERIALS.

Species.	Specific Gravity.	Weight of 1 cub. ft. lbs.	Weight of 1 cub. in. oz.
Water, distilled	1·000	62·5	0·579
—— from the Baltic	1·015	63·75	
—— Mediterranean	1·029	64·38	
—— Dead Sea	1·240	77·5	
Brass, cast	8·396	524·8	4·859
Copper, cast	8·788	549·3	5·086
—— sheet	8·915	557·2	5·159
Gold, pure, hammered	19·362	1210·1	11·205
—— standard	17·647	1102·9	10·213
Gun metal	8·784	549·0	5·083
Iron, wrought	7·786	486·6	4·506
—— cast	7·352	459·5	4·255
Lead, cast	11·352	709·5	6·569
Mercury, fluid	13·568	848·0	7·852
Platinum, pure, hammered	20·336	1271·0	11·767
Silver, pure, hammered	10·511	656·9	6·083
—— standard	10·534	658·4	6·096
Steel, tempered	7·818	488·6	4·524
Tin, cast	7·291	455·7	4·244
Zinc, cast	7·190	449·4	4·161
Coal, mean of sorts	1·270	79·4	0·735
Granite ditto	2·698	168·6	1·561
Limestone, ditto	2·945	184·1	1·705
Marble ditto	2·720	170·0	1·574
Ash, and Dantzic Oak	0·760	47·8	0·440
Beech	0·700	43·8	0·405

Species.	Specific Gravity.	Weight of 1 cub. ft. lbs.	Weight of 1 cub. in. oz.
Cork	0·240	15·0	0·139
Deal, Christiana	0·681	42·5	0·394
—— Memel	0·590	36·9	0·341
Elm and Larch	0·540	33·8	0·313
Fir, New England	0·550	34·4	0·318
—— Riga and Maple	0·750	46·9	0·434
—— Mar Forest	0·700	43·8	0·405
Lignum Vitæ	1·333	83·3	0·771
Mahogany	0·637	39·8	0·369
Norway Spars	0·580	36·3	0·336
Oak, English	0·900	56·3	0·521
—— African	0·980	61·3	0·567
—— Adriatic	0·990	61·9	0·573
—— Pine, Pitch, and Red	0·660	41·3	0·382
Poon and Hazel	0·600	37·5	0·347
Teak and Plum Tree	0·750	46·9	0·434
* Atmospheric Air	1·000	0·075	0·0007
Hydrogen Gas	0·069	0·006	0·0001
Oxygen Gas	1·111	0·090	0·0008
Alcohol, absolute	0·797	49·8	0·461
—— highly rectified	0·829	51·8	0·480
Beer, mean of sorts	1·028	64·3	0·595
Whale Oil	0·923	57·7	0·534
Olive Oil	0·915	57·2	0·530
Gunpowder, shaken	0·932	58·3	0·539
Wine, Port	0·997	62·3	0·577

* Water is used as the standard of comparison of solids and liquids, and atmospheric air as the standard for gases.

TABLE IX.*

SHOWING THE POSITIONS OF THE MASTS, SAILS, &C., OF
SHIPS AND BRIGS.

Species of Mast and Gear.	Known Quantities, etc,	Proportions in Terms of known Quantities.	
		Frigate.	Brig.
Fore-mast before the middle of the length of the waterline, taken from fore part of stem to after part of stern-post	Length of water-line .. ×	·37	·331
Main-mast abaft ditto	Length of water-line .. ×	·062	·147
Mizen-mast abaft ditto	Length of water-line .. ×	·341	—
Rake of fore-mast	In 12 feet	2-in.	3-in.
——— main-mast	In 12 feet	6-in.	10-in.
——— mizen-mast	In 12 feet	10-in.	—
Stive of bowsprit	In 12 feet	63-in.	51-in.
Main-mast below water-line	Breadth .. .. ×	·3	·245
Fore-mast below water-line	Breadth .. .. ×	·25	·2
Mizen-mast below water-line ..	Breadth .. .. ×	·06	—
Bowsprit housed from fore part of stem	Breadth .. .. ×	·46	·5
Centre of effort before the middle of the water-line	Length of water-line .. ×	·059	·026
Height of centre of effort	Breadth .. .. ×	1·56	1·5
Area of sail	Area of load water section ×	3·14	3·74
Moments of sail	Area of load water section ×	160·0	175·8
Difference of draught of water, excess aft	Length of water-line .. ×	·005	·035
Relation of moment of sails before the middle to the moment aft	Fore to the after as 1 to	·69	·83
Length on deck	.... Feet	113·75	
Breadth extreme	.... Feet	31·83	

* Tables IX. to XV. are from Fincham.

PROPORTION OF MASTS AND YARDS.

TABLE X.

Species of Mast and Gear.	Known Quantities.		Proportions in Terms of known Quantities.	
			Frigate.	Brig.
M... ...	Breadth	×	1·04	1·03
...	Hounded length	×	·733	·733
F...	Mainmast hounded	×	·91	·875
...	Hounded length	×	1·33	·733
Mainmast ...	Mainmast hounded	×	·75	—
...	Hounded length	×	1·50	—
M... ...	Breadth	×	1·13	1·13
... hounded	Hounded length	×	·56	·535
F... hounded	Main-topmast hounded	×	·91	·93
... hounded	Hounded length	×	1·56	1·535
M...	Main-topmast hounded	×	·77	—
... hounded	Hounded length	×	1·56	—
Main topgallant-mast hounded	Breadth	×	·61	·73
... pole	Hounded length	×	·75	·75
F... topgallant-mast hounded	Main-topgallant-mast hounded	×	·5	·5
... yard	Hounded length	×	·75	·75
M... topgallant-mast hounded	Main-topgallant-mast hounded	×	·75	—
... pole	Hounded length	×	·75	—
F...	Foremast hounded	×	·7	·733
...	Bowsprit	×	·733	·73
Bowsprit ...	Jibboom	×	1·1	1·22
Mainyard ...	Length	×	·553	·542
Main-topsail yard	Mainyard	×	·74	—
Main-topsail yard	Main-topsail-yard for ships Mainyard for brigs	×	·61	·400
Main ... yard	Main-topgallant yard	×	·7	·...
F...	Mainyard	×	·873	·900
F... topsail yard	Main-topsail-yard	×	·...	1·...
F... gallant yard	Main-topgallant yard	×	·55	·...
F... royal yard	Fore-topgallant-yard for ships Main-royal-yard for brigs	×	·7	1·...
C... yard	Main-topsail-yard	×	1·0	—
M... ... yard	Ditto	×	·65	—
M... ... yard	Main-topgallant-yard	×	·53	—
M... ... yard	Mizzen-topgallant-yard	×	·7	—
S... yard	Fore-topsail-yard	×	1·0	1·0
Driver ... boom	Length	×	·5·5	·5...
G...	Driver-boom	×	·54	·5...
B...	Gaff	×	·3	·3
M...	Ditto	×	·5	·5
S...	Mainyard	×	·5	·5

* The "hounding" is the whole length of the mast, exclusive of the head.

TABLE XI.

) CALCULATE THE LARGEST, OR GIVEN DIAMETERS* OF THE SPARS OF SHIPS AND BRIGS.

SPECIES.	PROPORTIONATE DIAMETER.
'ore and mainmasts	One inch for every three feet of the length.
Mizen-masts	Two-thirds of the diameter of the mainmast.
Topmasts	One inch to every three feet in length.
Top-gallant-masts	One inch to every three feet in length.
Bowsprits	The same diameter as the mainmast.
'ore and main-yards	Seven-tenths of an inch to every three feet in length.
Topsail, cross-jack, and spritsail-yards	Five-eighths of an inch to every three feet in length.
Top-gallant-yards	Six-tenths of an inch to every three feet in length.
Royal yards	Three-fifths of an inch to every three feet in length.
Studding-sail-yards and Studding-sail booms......	One inch to every five feet in length.
Jib-booms.....................	Seven-eighths of an inch to every three feet in length.
Flying-jib-booms............	One inch to every six feet in length.
Driver-booms	The same diameter as the main-top-sail-yard.
Gaffs........	Two-thirds of an inch to every three feet in length.

In *standing masts,* this is at the partners or decks ; in masts of three-deck ships, e given diameter is at the middle deck ; and in all the other ships, at the upper highest wedging deck.
In *topmasts,* and *top-gallant-masts,* the given diameter is at the caps, or at the ads of the mast below, to which they are affixed. In *bowsprit,* it is at the bed ; cept in those of cutters, where it is generally one-third from the inner end. In *rds,* it is at the slings or middle ; in *jib-booms,* at the bowsprit-cap, or at one-ird from the inner end ; in *driver or main booms,* at one-third from the after end, at the taffrail or sheet ; in *studding-sail booms, top and top-gallant,* at e-third from each end, between which they are parallel ; and in *swing or lower udding-sail booms,* at one-third from the outer end.

TABLE XII.

THE PROPORTION WHICH EACH PART OF A MAST OR YARD BEARS TO ITS OVERALL DIAMETER

Spars	Heel	Quarters		First fourth	Upper fourth	Diam. Masthead, top of ...
Lower masts						
Topmast						
Top-gallant-masts						
Yards						
Bowsprit						
Jib-boom						
Driver-boom						
Gaff						

TABLE XIII.

Proportional Dimensions of Tops, Caps, and Cross-trees.

Species.	Length.	Breadth or Width.	Depth or Thickness.
Tops	$\frac{3}{4}$ the breadth at fore cross-tree	At fore cross-tree, $\frac{1}{3}$ the whole length of the topmast. After part $\frac{2}{5}$ the length of the topmast.	
Trestle-trees	Length of the top fore-and-aft, or $\frac{3}{8}$ the whole length of the topmast	Two-thirds of the depth	$1\frac{3}{4}$ of an inch to every foot in length.
Fore cross-tree ..	[illegible] of the breadth of the top at the fore part of the square hole	Same as that of the trestle-trees	$\frac{3}{5}$ of their breadth.
After cross-tree ..	[illegible] of the top at the after part		
Lower cap	Wood left before the round hole is $\frac{3}{8}$ the depth of the cap. Wood abaft the square hole the depth of the cap	Two diameters of the topmast, and one inch	One inch less than the diameter of the topmast.
Bowsprit cap ..	Five diameters of the jib-boom	Twice the diameter of jib-boom	$\frac{3}{8}$ diameter of jib-boom.
Topmast cap	In the same proportion to the top-gallant mast, as lower cap is to topmast.		
Trestle-trees	Seven-twelfths of the lower trestle-trees.		
Cross-trees	After horn, $\frac{3}{8}$ of the lower after cross-tree. Foremost horn, $\frac{2}{3}$ of the after one.	The breadth of the trestle-trees	$\frac{4}{5}$ of the breadth.

TABLE XIV.

PROPORTIONS FOR THE SPARS OF SCHOONERS AND CUTTERS.

Length. Breadth. Length. Breadth.

Schooner, Three Masts .. 78·7-ft. 21·6-ft.   BermudaSch..95·0-ft. 24·7-ft.

Ditto, Brig forward .. 110·6 ,, 25·6 ,,   Cutter, Yacht 63·1 ,, 19·2 ,,

Ditto, Common ...... 90·0 ,, 24·0 ,,   Rev. Cruiser 63·7 ,, 22·1 ,,

	Proportions in Terms of known Quantities.					
	SCHOONERS.				CUTTERS.	
	Three Masts.	Brig forward.	Common.	Bermuda.	Yacht.	Revenue Cruiser.
Main-mast hounded	2·78	3·11	2·61	2·75	3·34	2·63
── headed	·1	·13	·12	·13	·2	·20
Fore-mast hounded	·95	·734	·92	·97	—	—
── headed	·1	·193	·12	·13	—	—
Mizen-mast hounded	·74	—	—	—	—	—
── headed	·1	—	—	—	—	—
Main-top-mast hounded	·25	1·1	·83	1·0	2·305	1·77
── pole	·31	·43	·5	·5	·26	·3
Fore-top-mast hounded	·92	1·08	1·0	·9	—	—
── headed	·31	·156	·5	·5	—	—
Mizen-top-mast hounded	·9	—	—	—	—	—
Fore-top-gallant-mast hounded	·24	—	—	—	—	—
── pole	—	—	—	—	—	—
Bowsprit	—	·77	—	—	—	—
Foremast, in schooners / Length, in cutters	·35	·55	·49	·43	·825	·8
Fore-yard	·3	·575	·37²	·48	—	—
Fore-topsail-yard / Ditto	·7	·738	·71	·71	—	—
Fore-top-gallant-yard / Fore-royal-yard	·46	·874	·458	·85	—	—

Square-sail-yard	Length	×	·607	·75	·77	·75	·7	·7
Main-topsail-yard	Square-sail-yard	×		·48	·5	·78		·51
Main-top-gallant-yard	Ditto ditto	×	·226	·386	·7	·66	·936	·92
Main-boom	Length	×		·386	·53	·44	·627	·68
Main-gaff	Boom	×			·73			
Fore-gaff	Main-gaff	×	1·06	1·0		1·0		
Mizen-gaff	Ditto	×	·9					
Mizen or Driver-boom	Length	×	·39					
Jib-boom	Bowsprit	×	·97	1·21	·87	1·3		
Flying jib-broom before jib-boom	Jib-boom	×	·4	·4				
Swinging-boom	Fore-yard	×	·5	·68				·352
Ringtail-boom	Length	×	·21		·4	·37	·562	·51
Square-sail-boom	Ditto	×	·22				·464	·25
Gaff-topsail-yard	Gaff	×					·25	
Main-mast from the middle	Length of water-line	×	abaft.	abaft			before.	before.
			·033	·11	·046	·108	·112	·13
Fore-mast before ditto	Ditto ditto	×	·295	·3	·338	·279		
Mizen-mast abaft ditto	Ditto ditto	×	·366					
Main-mast to rake	In 12 feet	:	27 in.	33 in.	24 in.	24 in.	12 in.	14¾ in.
Fore-mast ditto	Ditto	:	24 ,,	28 ,,	15 ,,	16 ,,		
Mizen-mast ditto	Ditto	:	30 ,,					
Bowsprit to stive	Ditto	×	22 ,,	36 ,,	34 ,,	24 ,,	7½ ,,	18 ,,
Main-mast below load-water-line	Breadth	×	·227	·26	·26	·31	·31	·272
Fore-mast ditto ditto		×	·17	·22	·22	·27		
Mizen-mast ditto ditto		×	·232					
Centre of effort from the middle of the length of the water-line	Length on water-line	×	abaft.	abaft.			abaft.	abaft.
			·0065	·0163	·02	·023	0·395	·0167
Height of the centre of effort above the load-water-line	Breadth	×	1·539	1·72	1·5	1·5	1·5	1·27
Area of sails	Area of load-water section	×	4·944	4·59	3·63	3·54	3·2	3·56
Moment of sails	Breadth of load-water section	×	164·4	204·0	138·0	128·6	89·1	97·7
Bowsprit housed from the fore part of the stem	Breadth	:	·32	·35	·46	·448	·62	·65
Difference of draught of water, excess aft		:	36 in.	24 in.	12 in.	24 in.	54 in.	65 in.

495

TABLE XV.

PROPORTIONATE DIMENSIONS (MAXIMUM), FOR MASTING BOATS.

Length............32 feet.
Breadth ....8·5 feet.

Species of Mast.	Known Quantities.		Fig. 1	Fig. 2	Fig. 3	Fig. 4	Fig. 5	Fig. 6	Fig. 7	Fig. 8
Main-mast hounded ..	Breadth of boat .. ::	×	3·1	2·46	2·15	1·76	2·7		2·7	
.........pole ..	Main-mast hounded ..	×	·15							
Fore-mast hounded ..	Main-mast, figs. 1, 2, 3, 4, 5, 7, Breadth, figs. 6 and 8 ..	×	·92	·9	·8	·98	·9	3·08	·9	3·08
.........pole ..	Fore-mast hounded ..	×	·15							
Mizen-mast ..	Main-mast, figs. 1, 2, 3, 4, 5, 7, Fore-mast, figs. 6 and 8 ..	×		·54	·43	·67	·6	·6	·6	·6
Main-yard ..	Length of boat .. ::	×			·83	1·06	·4			
Fore-yard ..	Main-yard, figs. 1, 2, 3, 4, 5, 7, Length, figs. 6 and 8 ..	×			·95	·9	·9	·4	·9	·5
Mizen-yard ..	Main-yard, figs. 1, 2, 3, 4, 5, 7, Fore-yard, figs. 6 and 8 ..	×			·36	·53	·7	·87	·9	·76
Main-sprit, or slide ..	Main-mast .. ::	×		1·o						
Fore-sprit, or slide ..	Fore-mast .. :	×		1·o						
Mizen-sprit, or slide ..	Mizen-mast ..	×		1·o						

496

Spar	Reference		C1	C2	C3	C4	C5	C6	C7	C8
Main-gaff	Length of boat	×	·26							·45
Fore-gaff	Main-gaff	×	·92							·44
Main-boom	Length of boat	×	·6							
Boomkin	Ditto ditto	×					·43	·45	·43	
Outrigger	Ditto ditto	×		·34	·380	·25	·4	·45	·44	
Bowsprit	Ditto ditto	×	·43	·43		·343	·44	·42		
Main-mast from the middle	Ditto ditto	×	before ·031	·056	abaft ·037	before ·018	before ·066	·359	before ·066	
Fore-mast before ditto	Ditto ditto	×	·343	·343	·312	·37	·33		·33	·359
Fore-mast to rake	Aft in a foot	:	2 in.	·1		forward 3½ in.	·1	2 in.	·1	1 in.
Main-mast ditto	Ditto ditto	:	4 ··	·2			·2		·2	
Mizen-mast ditto	As the transom	:								
Diameter of masts	One inch to	:	4'5	4'0	3'6	3'6	4'4	4'4	4'4	4'4
........yards	Ditto	:			5'0	5'0	5'0	5'0		5'0
........booms	Ditto	:	5'5							
........gaffs	Ditto	:	3'2							
........bowsprits	Ditto	:	2'5	2'5			2'5	2'5	2'5	2'5
........outriggers	Ditto	:		3'0	3'0	3'0	3'0	3'0	3'0	3'0
........sprits	Ditto	:							9'0	
........slides	Ditto	:		5'4						
........boomkins	Ditto	:			2'4	2'4				

Feet in length.

497

TABLE XVI.

NUMBER OF HEMPEN CABLES AND HAWSERS ON BOARD.

Line-of-battle Ship.	Iron Clad—" Prince Consort" Class.	Corvette—"Volage" Class.	Corvette—"Dido" Class.
Stream Cable 14½ inch.	Stream Cable 14½ inch.	Stream Cable 13½ inch.	
CABLETS.	CABLETS.	CABLETS.	
3 .... 9 inch	1 .... 12 inch	1 .... 9 inch.	1 .... 8 inch.
1 .... 7½ ,,	2 .... 9 ,,	1 .... 7 ,,	1 .... 7 ,,
1 .... 6 ,,	1 .... 8 ,,	1 .... 6 ,,	1 .... 6½ ,,
1 .... 4½ ,,	1 .... 7½ ,,	1 .... 5 ,,	1 .... 5½ ,,
	1 .... 6 ,,	1 .... 4 ,,	1 .... 5 ,,
	1 .... 4½ ,,		1 .... 4½ ,,
			1 .... 3½ ,,

This Table is intended to give a general idea of the number and size of hawsers supplied to different ships, and as part answer to Question 122; one commonly given at a Seamanship Examination, the correct solution however can be best obtained on board.

TABLE XVII.

I.—TIME.

60 Seconds	1 minute.
60 Minutes	1 hour.
24 Hours..	1 mean solar day.
7 Days	1 week.
28 Days	1 lunar month.
12 Calendar months (365 days).......................	1 civil year.
365 Days, 5 hours, 48 minutes, 47·6352 seconds...	1 solar year.

Note.—As the ordinary civil year consists of but 365 days, instead of nearly 365¼ days, an additional day is added to the month of February in every fourth, or leap-year, which is a compensation that originated with Julius Cæsar. Leap-year is found by dividing the year, or the two *last* numbers of the year, by 4; the remainder shows the number of years that it is after leap-year, or leap-year, simply, if without a remainder. As, however, the astronomical year is not quite 365¼ days, the intercalation is too great to the amount of 3 days, 2½ hours, in 400 years; and to correct this error, it was provided by Pope Gregory XIII., in 1582, that the first year of every century should not be considered leap-year, as it would be in the Julian calendar, unless the two *first* numbers of the year are divisible by 4. Thus, 1800 was an ordinary year, and so will be the year 1900; but A.D. 2000 will be a leap-year. By this reduction the error is contracted to an excess of one day in 3546 years. The Gregorian, or new style, was not adopted in England until 1751, when 11 days were omitted to effect the requisite reformation in the calendar. The Russians still adhere to the old style.

II.—MONEY.

4 Farthings	1 penny, *d.* (*denarius*).
12 Pence...	1 shilling, *s.* (*solidus*).

499

20 Shillings .... 1 pound, £. (*libra.*)

21 Shillings ....·...................... 1 guinea.

Note.—A sovereigh weighs .... 5 dwts. 3 ⁝⁝⁝ gr. Troy.
Half-sovereign .... 2 „ 13 ⁝⁝⁝ „
Crown.................... 18 dwts. 4 ₁ gr. Troy.
Half-crown ....: 9 „ 2 ₁ „
Shilling .... 3 „ 15 ₁ „
Sixpence.................... 1 „ 19 ₁ „
Fourpenny piece .... 1 „ 5 ₁ „
Threepenny piece .... 0 „ 21 ₁ „

In estimating the fineness of gold it is supposed to be divided into 24 parts, called carats, and its purity is expressed by the number of those parts of pure gold that the mass contains. Thus, gold 24 carats fine is pure gold. Jewellers' gold, of 18 carats fine (which is the lowest degree stamped), contains six parts, or one-fourth of the material of alloy. The standard gold coinage is 22 carats fine ; the remaining 2 carats, or one-twelfth, being an alloy of silver and copper, to render the coin harder and more durable. From a ℔. Troy of this metal are coined 46 ₃₈ sovereigns = £46 14s. 6d.

Standard silver, for silver coins, contains 37 parts in 40 of pure silver, and 3 parts alloy. A ℔ Troy of this metal consists of 11 oz. 2 dwts. of pure silver, and 18 dwts. of copper, which is coined into 66 shillings.

From a ℔. avoirdupois of copper are coined 24 pence.

A sovereign passes for its full value if it reaches the weight of 5 dwts. 2¾ gr., for gold coins are allowed by law to pass under their full weight, in consequence of their unavoidable loss by wear. Silver coins are not a legal tender for more than 40s. nor are copper for more than 12d.

III.—DIVISION OF THE CIRCLE.

60 Seconds .... 1 minute
60 Minutes .... 1 degree.
360 Degrees .... 1 circumference.

500

Note.—A great circle on the earth's surface, which is about 24,869 miles in circumference, produces a degree 69·08 miles in length ; and the sixtieth part of this constitutes a geographical or nautical mile, which is thus about 1·15 of a land mile. The length of a degree of longitude, on a parallel of latitude, is found by subtracting the log. secant of the latitude from the log. of 60′.

4 Minutes of time = 1 degree of longitude.

15 Degrees   = 1 hour.

IV.—WEIGHTS.
TROY.

24 Grains........................ 1 pennyweight.

20 Dwts........................... 1 ounce.

12 Oz. .... 1 pound.

Used for the precious metals, and in philosophical experiments.

Diamonds and other precious stones are weighed by carats of 3¼ grains. 151½ carats are equal to an ounce Troy.

Note.—By Act of Parliament (5 Geo. IV., c. 74), it was enjoined that the standard of *weight* for the kindom should henceforward be the *imperial pound Troy* of 5760 grains ; and that, in case the standard should be lost or injured, it might be recovered from the knowledge of the fact, that a cubic inch of distilled water, at a temperature of 62° Fahrenheit, and when the barometer is 30 in., weighs 252·458 of these grains.

AVOIRDUPOIS.

27·34375 Troy grains.............. 1 dram.

16 Drs............................ 1 ounce.

16 Oz. .... 1 pound.

14 Lbs............................ 1 stone.

28 Lbs............................ 1 quarter.

4 Qrs.. .... 1 hundredweight.

20 Cwt............................ 1 ton.

Used for all ordinary goods.

Note.—By the before-mentioned Act it is provided that the lb. avoirdupois shall consist of 7000 grains Troy.

501

APOTHECARIES.

20 Grains.............	1 scruple.
3 Sc.	1 drachm.
8 Drs.	1 ounce.
12 Oz.	1 pound.

By this weight apothecaries compound their medicines, but drugs are bought and sold by avoirdupois weight.

Note.—The gr., oz., and lb. are the same as in Troy weight.

480 Minims, or drops = 1 fluid ounce
20 Ounces = 1 pint.
8 Pints = 1 gallon.
8750 Grains of distilled water = 1 imperial pint.
437.5 Ditto ditto = 1 imperial fluid ounce.

V.—MEASURES.

WINE MEASURE.

4 Gills.............................	1 pint.
2 Pts.	1 quart.
4 Qts.	1 gallon.
10 Galls.	1 anker.
18 Galls...........................	1 runlet.
42 Galls......	1 tierce.
63 Galls...........................	1 hogshead.
84 Galls......	1 puncheon.
126 Galls..........................	1 pipe.
252 Galls..........................	1 tun.

ALE MEASURE.

4 Gills.............................	1 pint.
2 Pts.	1 quart.
4 Qts.	1 gallon.
9 Galls.	1 firkin.
18 Galls.	1 kilderkin.
36 Galls.	1 barrel.
54 Galls.	1 hogshead.

72 Galls.	....	1 puncheon.
108 Galls.	....	1 butt.

Note.—In the above measures the imperial gallon, containing 277·2738 cubic inches, is designated. The old ale gallon contained 282 cubic inches, and the old wine gallon 231 cubic inches ; hence—

$$\left. \begin{array}{l} \text{Old ale gallon} \quad \times \; 1\cdot01704 \\ \text{Old wine gallon} \times 0\cdot83311 \end{array} \right\} = \text{imperial gallon.}$$

By the Act before cited, the imperial gallon was made the standard *of capacity* for both dry and wet goods, and was described as containing 10 lbs. avoirdupois of distilled water, weighed in air, at a temperature of 62° Fahrenheit, with the barometer at 30 inches.

DRY MEASURE.

2 Imperial gallons	....	1 peck.
4 Pecks	....	1 bushel.
8 Bushels	....	1 quarter.
32 Bushels	....	1 chaldron.
40 Bushels	....	1 wey, or load.
8 Bushels	....	1 last.

Note.—The Winchester bushel contained 2150·42 cubic inches, and the imperial bushel contains 2218·192 cubic inches ; hence, Winchester bushel × 0·969447 = imperial bushel.

MEASURE OF LENGTH.

12 Lines..	... .	1 inch.
12 Inches	....	1 foot.
3 Feet	....	1 yard.
5½ Yards	....	1 pole (rod, or perch.
40 Poles	....	1 furlong.
8 Furlongs (1760 yards)	....	1 mile.
2240 Yards	....	1 Irish mile.
14 English miles	.........................11 Irish miles.
6076 Feet	....	1 geog. or nautical mile.
3 Miles	....	1 league.

Note.—The imperial yard is the standard of *length*. This yard is divided into 3 feet, and each foot into 12 inches ; and its length is fixed by comparing it with that of a pendulum, vibrating seconds. *in vacuo*, in the latitude of London, at the level of the sea, the length of which is 39·13929 inches (or thirty-sixths) of this yard. The yard may be otherwise defined as the length of a pendulum which oscillates, *in vacuo*, in the latitude of London, at the level of the sea, 90088 times in a a mean solar day.

MEASURE OF SURFACE, OR SQUACE MEASURE.

144	Square inches	1 square foot,
9	Square feet	1 square yard.
30¼	Square yards....................	1 square pole.
40	Square poles....................	1 square rood.
4	Roods (4840 square yards) ...	1 statute acre.
640	Acres	1 square mile.
6084	Square yards....................	1 Scotch acre.
7840	Square yards	1 Irish, or plantation acre.
113·0972	Square inches	1 circular foot.
183·346	Circular inches	1 square foot.

Note.—A circular foot is a circle whose diameter is one foot.

SUPERFICIAL MEASURE FOR LAND.

62·7264	Square inches	1 square link.
10000	Square links	1 square chain.
10	Square chains........	1 acre.

MEASURE OF SOLIDITY, OR CUBIC MEASURE.

1728	Cubic inches	⎫
2200	Cylindrical inches, nearly...	⎬ 1 cubic foot.
3300	Spherical inches, ,,	⎪
6600	Conical inches ,.	⎭
27	Cubic feet..........	1 cubic yard.
1357·17	Cubic inches...........	1 cylindric foot.
904·78	Cubic inches....................	1 spherical foot.
459·39	Cubic inches....................	1 conical foot.

Note.—A cubic inch is a cube 1 inch square ; a cylindric inch is a cylinder 1 inch long, and 1 inch in diameter ; a spherical inch is a

here 1 inch in diameter ; and a conical inch is a cone 1 inch in
length, and 1 inch in diameter at the base.

VI.—MISCELLANEOUS.

3 Inches	1 palm.
4 Inches	1 hand.
9 Inches	1 span.
18 Inches	1 cubit.
5 Feet	1 pace.
6 Feet	1 fathom.
120 Fathoms (strictly 126½ fathoms)	1 cable's length.
8 Cables' length	1 nautical mile.
600 Square feet of inch boards..................	1 load.
40 Cubic feet of round timber ....}	
50 Cubic feet of hewn timber ....}	1 ton, or load.
1000 Billets, or ....}	
8 Cubic feet, or ....}	1 cord of wood.
10 Cwt. ....}	
108 Cubic feet	1 stack of wood.
630 Lbs., or ....}	
6 Ft. × 6 ft. × 2 ft. ....}	1 fathom of wood.
84 Lbs.	1 bushel of coals.
2 Cwt.	1 sack of coals.
10 Sacks (42 in. by 30 in.)	1 ton of coals.
40 Cubic feet	1 ton of shipping.
120 Deals or nails	1 hundred.
6 Stone of new hay ....}	
9 Stone of old hay ....}	1 cubic yard.
36 Lbs. of straw ....}	
56 Lbs. of old hay ....}	1 truss.
36 Trusses	1 load.
8 Lbs. of meat or fish	1 stone.
56 Lbs. of butter	1 firkin.
250 Lbs. of hops, Kentish ....}	
112 Lbs. of hops, Surrey and Sussex......}	1 pocket.

505

236 Gallons sweet oil .... }
252 Gallons fish................... ....} 1 ton.

24 Sheets of paper .... 1 quire.

20 Quires .... 1 ream.

VII.—WATER AND PROVISIONS.

WATER.

1 Ton = 35·84 cubic feet—224 galls. (210 galls. Victualling Yard).

1 Cwt. = 1·8 cubic feet—11·2 galls.

1 Gallon = 277·2738 cubic in.—10 lbs. avoirdupois—7000 gr. Troy.

1 Cubic foot = 997·137 oz. avoir. temp. 62°—62·5 lbs.—6·25 galls.

1 Cubic inch = 252·458 grains avoirdupois, temp. 62°.

1 Cylindric foot = 49·1 lbs.

1 Cylindric inch = ·02842 lbs.

CONTENTS OF CASKS.

Leager	164 gallons.
Butt	110 ,,
Puncheon	72 ,,
Hogshead	54 ,,
Barrel	36 ,,
Half-hogshead	25 ,,
Kilderkin	18 ,,

TANKS.

No.	Galls.	Length. ft. in.	Breadth. ft. in.	Depth. ft. in.	
1	600	4 1	4 1	6 1	Whole.
2	500	4 1	4 1	5 1	,,
3	400	4 1	4 1	4 1	,,
4	200	4 1	2 1	4 1	Half.
5	200	4 1	4 1	2 1	,,
6	193	4 1	4 1	2 1	,, (corner off).
7	200	3 3	3 3	3 3	,,

506

8 ...	100 ...	3	3 ...	1	8 ...	3	3 ...	Quarter.
9 ...	100 ...	3	3 ...	3	3 ...	1	9 ...	,,
10 ...	375 ...	4	1 ...	4	1 ...	4	1 ...	Bilge.
11 ...	264 ...	4	1 ...	3	7 ...	4	1 ...	,,
12 ...	110 ...	3	3 ...	2	7 ...	2 10 ...	,,

BALLAST.

Runs 7, 18, 20, and 40 to a ton. There are two sizes of 20, one being shorter and thicker than the other.

PROVISIONS.

Biscuit ....Bags .... 112 lbs.

Rum —
- Puncheon .... 72 gallons.
- Hogshead .. .. 54 ,,
- Barrel .... 36 ,,
- Half-hogshead .... 25 ,,
- Kilderkin .... 18 ,,
- Small Cask .... 12 ,,

Salt Beef —
- Tierce... .... 38 8-lb. pieces.
- Barrel .... 26 ,,

Salt Pork —
- Tierce .... 80 4-lb. pieces.
- Barrel .... 52 ,,

Flour —
- Barrel .... 336 lbs.
- Half-hogshead .... 250 ,,

Suet —
- Half-hogshead .... 168 ,,
- Small Cask .... 70 ,,
- Ditto .... 56 ,,

Raisins —
- Barrel .... 336 ,,
- Half-hogshead .... 224 ,,
- Small Cask..................... 112 ,,

Peas —
- Barrel .... 5 bushls = 40 galls.
- Half-hogshead .... 3½ ,, = 28 galls.

Oatmeal —
- Barrel .... 7½ ,,
- Half-hogshead .... 5½ ,, = 44 galls.
- Small cask .... 2½ ,,
- Ditto 2

2 K

Sugar	Barrel	392 lbs.	
	Half-hogshead	280	,,
	Ditto	112	,,
Chocolate	Half-hogshead	108	,,
	Small cask	55	,,
Tea	Chest	83	,,
	Half-chest	36	,,
Vinegar	Puncheon	72 gallons	
	Hogshead	54	,,
	Barrel	36	,,
	Half-hogshead	25	,,
	Kilderkin	18	,,
	Small cask	12	,,
Tobacco	Barrel	150 lbs.	
	Half-hogshead	90	,,
Soap	Half-hogshead	120	,,
	Barrel	250	,,

TABLE XIX.

FOREIGN WEIGHTS AND MEASURES.

———

FRENCH.

The French standard mètre is the unit of *length*. It is defined as the ten-millionth part of the arc of the meridian included between the pole and the equator.

The are, equal to one square décamètre, is the unit of *surface*.

The stère, equal to one cubic mètre, is the unit of *solidity*.

The litre, equal to one cubic décimètre, is the unit of *capacity*.

The gramme, equal to one cubic centimètre of distilled water, at a temperature of 39° Fahrenheit, is the unit of *weight*.

By the centesimal division of the circle, the circumference is divided into 400 degrees, a degree into 100 minutes, and a minute into 100 seconds; consequently—

508

    1 centesimal degree = 54   sexagesimal minutes.

    1 centesimal minute ,, 32·4   sexagesimal seconds.

    1 centesimal second ,, ·324 sexagesimal second.

In the French decimal system, the prefix to the terms in the ascending scale is taken from the Greek numerals *deka, hekaton, fioi,* and *murias ;* and in the descending scale from the Latin numerals *decem, centum, mille ;* hence—

Deca signifies ten times ; and *deci,* a tenth part.

Hecto signifies a hundred times ; and *centi,* a hundredth part.

Kilo signifies a thousand times ; and *milli,* a thousandth part.

Myria signifies ten thousand times.

Thus, knowing the value of the unit of each measure, the equivalant of the other terms employed is at once obtained by shifting the decimal place.   For instance,—

Mètre = 39·37079 inches.   Myriamètre = 393707·9 inches, or ·2138 miles.   Millimètre = 0·03937 inches.   16 Kilomètres = 10 miles, nearly.

Are = 119·60333 square yards.   Hectare = 11960·33 squars yards, x 2·4711 acres.   Centiare = 1·1960 square yards.

Stère = 35·31658 cubic feet.   Hectostère = 3531·66 cubic feet, or 130·8 cubic yards.   Millstère = ·0353 cubic feet, or 61·0273 cubic in.

Litre = 1·76077 pints.   Myrialitre = 17688 pints, or 2211 gallons. Millilitre = ·00177 pint.   Hectolitre = 22 gallons, nearly.

Gramme = 15·434 grains.   Myriagramme = 154340 grains, or 22·0486 lbs. avoirdupois.   Milligramme = ·0154 grain.

In addition to the various intermediate parts of the above—

    1 Quinral = 220·485 lbs. avoirdupois.

    1 Millier, or bar = 2204·85 lbs. avoirdupois.

    1 Livre usuelle = 16 ounces = 1·10243 lbs. avoirdupois.

    1 Once usuelle = 8 gros = 31·25 grammes.

    1 Toise usuelle = 6 pieds = 6·56180 English feet.

    1 Aune usuelle = 3·93708 English feet.

    1 Boisseau usuelle = 2·75 imperial gallons

2 K 2

MEASURES OF LENGTH USED IN FOREIGN CHARTS.

FRENCH.

Pied and toise, as above.

Brasse, or fathom = 5·329 feet.

But in recent Charts the Mètre is invariably used, and the following Table will be of service.

Conversion of Mètres into English feet and fathoms.

1 Mètre	= 3·2809 Eng. feet	= 0·5468 Eng. fath.			
2 ,,	= 6·5618 ,,	= 1·0936 ,,			
3 ,,	= 9·8427 ,,	= 1·6404 ,,			
4 ,,	= 13·1236 ,,	= 2·1873 ,,			
5 ,,	= 16·4045 ,,	= 2·7341 ,,			
6 ,,	= 19·6854 ,,	= 3·2809 ,,			
7 ,,	= 22·9663 ,,	= 3·8277 ,,			
8 ,,	= 26·2472 ,,	= 4·3745 ,,			
9 ,,	= 29·5281 ,,	= 4·9214 ,,			

By removing the decimal point as required, this Table admits of extensive application :—thus 375 mètres = 984·27 + 229·66 + 16·40 = 1230·33 feet,—or 164·04 + 38·28 + 2·73 = 205·05 fathoms.

1851·852 mètres = 1 nautical mile; and 5·5555 kilomètres = 1 sea league.

RUSSIAN.

Russian foot is equal to .... 1·145 English feet.

Sashine .... 6·9995 ,,

Arshine .... 2·33317 ,,

Verst .... 0·66287 mile.

The Russians now adopt a *Sea* Sashine = 1 English fathom, consisting of 6 feet, each of the same length as the English foot.

SPANISH.

Spanish foot (pié) is equal to .... 0·9142 English feet.

Braza .... 5·485 ,,

Vara .... 2·74252 ,,

510

WEIGHTS AND MEASURES.

The Spanish Hydrographic Office is now using the Metro, equivalent to the French Mètre, in their Sailing Directions and Nautical Notices.

DANISH.

Danish foot (fod) is equal to   ... . 1·0297 English feet
Favn .... 6·1783   ,,
Mile .... 4·68 English miles.

DUTCH.

Dutch Palm (= 1 French Décimètre) is equal to 0.32809 English feet. Also, the Dutch Elle = 1 Mètre ; and 1 Elle = 10 Palmer = 100 Duimen.

SWEDISH AND NORWEGIAN.

Swedish foot (fot) is equal to .... 0·9741 English feet.
Norwegian foot (fod) is equal to .... 1·0294   ,,

PRUSSIA.

Rhineland foot (fuss) is equal to .... 1·0297 English feet.

MISCELLANEOUS CONTESTS.

Diurnal acceleration of the stars   .... = 3m. 55s. 9093.
Sidereal day .... ,, 23h. 56m. 4·09s.
Sidereal revolution of the earth .... ,, 365·2564 days.
Equatorial radius of the earth   .... ,, 20923600 feet.
Polar   ditto   ditto   .... ,, 20853657 ,,
Circumference of the earth at equator .... ,, 24900 statute miles.
Length of 1° of the meridian at the equator ...... ,, 362755·6 feet.
  ,,   ,,   in lat. 45° .... ,, 364609·4 ,,
  ,,   ,,   at the pole .... ,, 366479·0 ,,
1′ of longitude at the equator .... ,, 365233·7 ,,
  ,,   in lat. 45° .... ,, 258698·4 ,,
  ,,   in lat. 60° .... ,, 183083·3 ,,
Paris is 0h. 9m. 20·63s or 2° 20′ 9″·45 E. of Greenwich.

TABLE XX.

SIMPLE DATA FOR ORDINARY CALCULATIONS.

CIRCLES.

1. The circle contains a greater area than any other plane figure bounded by an equal perimeter, or outline.

2. Circumference = 3·1415926 of diameter.

3. Diameter = 0·31831 of circumference.

4. Areas of circles are to each other as the squares of their diameters

5. Area = $\begin{cases} \text{square of diameter} \quad \times \ \cdot 7854 \\ \text{square of circumference} \times \ \cdot 07958. \end{cases}$

6. Diameter = square root of area × 1·12837.

7. Diameter of a circle of equal area = side of a square × 1·128.

8. Side of a square of equal area = diameter × ·8862.

9. Area of the space contained between two concentric circles = sum of the diameters, × difference of the diameters, × ·7854.

TRIANGLES.

Right-angled Plane Triangles.

Two sides, or one side and an angle (exclusive of the right-angle), being given, to find the remaining parts :—

1. $\dfrac{P}{H} = \sin.$; $\dfrac{P}{B} = \tan.$; $\dfrac{H}{B} = \sec.$, consequently.

$\dfrac{H}{P} = \mathrm{cosec.}$; $\dfrac{B}{P} = \mathrm{cotan.}$; $\dfrac{B}{H} = \cos.$; $P = H \times \sin.$; $H = \dfrac{P}{\sin.}$, &c.

$H^2 = P^2 + B^2$; or $H = \sqrt{P^2 + B^2}$;

$B = \sqrt{(H+P) \times (H-P)}$; $P \sqrt{(H+B) \times (H-B)}.$

Oblique-angled Plane Triangles.

The angles being denoted by capital letters, and their opposite sides by the same letters in italics.

When two sides and an opposite angle, or two angles and a side, are given :—

512

2. $a : b :: \sin. A : \sin. B.$

Two sides and the included angle given, to find the remainder :—

3. $\text{Tan. } \dfrac{A-B}{2} = \dfrac{a-b}{a+b}. \text{ Cot. } \dfrac{C}{2}$; then,

$$\dfrac{A+B}{2} + \dfrac{A-B}{2} = \text{angle opposite greater side, and}$$

$$\dfrac{A+B}{2} - \dfrac{A-B}{2} = \qquad ,, \qquad \text{less}$$

or

$$\dfrac{a+b}{a-b} = \dfrac{\text{Tan. } \frac{1}{2}(A+B)}{\text{Tan. } \frac{1}{2}(A-B)}$$

4. Three sides given, to find the angles :—

Let s = sum of the sides, then

$$\text{Cos. } \dfrac{A}{2} = \sqrt{\dfrac{\frac{s}{2}\left(\frac{s}{2} - a\right)}{bc}} \text{ or Cos. } A = \dfrac{b_2 + c^2 - a_2}{2bc}$$

5. Area of a triangle $= \dfrac{\text{base} \times \text{height}}{2}$

6. Area $= \sin. A \times \dfrac{bc}{2}$; or $\dfrac{\sin. A \times ab}{2}$

SQUARES.

1. Area = square of one side.
2. Area of a parallelogram = length × perpendicular breadth.
3. Side of a square = square root of area.
4. Diagonal $= \sqrt{\text{side}^2 \times 2.}$

SPHERES.

1. Surface = diameter × circumference.
2. Surface = square of diameter × 3·1416.
3. Diameter $= \sqrt[3]{\dfrac{\text{contents}}{·5236}}$

4. Contents = cube of diameter × ·5236.
5. Contents in imperial gallons = cube of diameter × 3·263 if in feet, or by ·001888 if in inches.

513

CYLINDERS.

1. Surface = length × circumference.
2. Solidity = length × area of base.
3. Contents, in imperial gallons = square of diameter × length, × 4.895 if in feet, or by ·002832 if in inches.

CONES.

1. Surface = $\dfrac{\text{slant height} \times \text{circumference of base}}{2}$

2. Solidity = $\dfrac{\text{perpendicular height} \times \text{area of base}}{3}$

OF AN ELLIPSE, OR OVAL.

1. Circumference = half sum of the two diameters × 3·1416.
2. Area = major axis × minor axis × ·7854.

CUBES, OR PARALLELOPIPEDS.

1. Solidity = length × breadth × depth.

THE WEDGE.

1. Solidity = (twice length of base + length of edge) × breadth of base × perpendicular height from base ÷ 6.

GRAVITY.

Let T = time, in seconds, that a body is in falling ; V, the velocity in feet, acquired in that time ; and S, the space, in feet, fallen through. Then, the time being known,

1. $S = t^2 \times 16\frac{1}{12}$; $V = t \times 32\frac{1}{6}$; also,

2. $S = \dfrac{v^2}{64\frac{1}{3}}$; $V = 2\sqrt{s \times 16\frac{1}{12}}$; $T = \sqrt{\dfrac{s}{16\frac{1}{12}}}$, or, $\dfrac{v}{32\frac{1}{6}}$

514

PROPORTION.

1. If $a : b :: b : c$, then $ac = b^2$, and $a : c :: a^2 : b^2$.

2. If $a : b :: c : d$, or $\dfrac{a}{b} = \dfrac{c}{d}$, then $a : c :: b : d$,

   or, $a + b : a \bullet b :: c + d : c \bullet d$; and $ad = bc$.

3. If $a : b :: c : d$, and $e : f :: g : h$; then $ae : bf ::: cg : dh$.

MISCELLANEOUS.

1. Square inches   × ˙007 = square feet.

2. Cubic inches   × ˙00058 = cubic feet.

3. Ditto ditto   × ˙003607 = imperial gallon nearly.

4. Ditto feet   × 6˙232 = imperial gallon nearly.

5. Avoirdupois lbs.   × ˙00893 = cwts.

6. Ditto   do   × ˙00045 = tons.

515

APPENDIX.

BRIEF

INSTRUCTIONS

FOR OFFICERS OF THE

MERCHANT SERVICE.

By W. H. ROSSER,

Author of the "Self Instructor in Navigation." The "Stars—how to know them, and how to use them." "Foreign Exchanges." "The Pacific Islands," &c., &c.

BRIEF INSTRUCTIONS FOR OFFICERS OF THE MERCHANT SERVICE.

MASTER'S NAME ON SHIP'S CERTIFICATE OF REGISTRY.—On being appointed by the owner to the command of a vessel, you must forthwith see your name put on the Ship's Certificate of Registry as Master: in any port of the United Kingdom this will be done at the Custom-house, and the "Merchant Shipping Act" (with which every Ship-master ought to be provided) will give you information as to the persons who are deemed Registrars in the Colonies and elsewhere. It is unnecessary to give the form of this Certificate here, as it is supplied in the "Act;" it is a parchment document which the master must retain and have at hand for production when required, as for instance at the Custom-house on the vessel arriving at a Port, on leaving Port, &c., and it is to be used only for the lawful navigation of the ship.

It should be borne in mind that the owners of a ship have always the power of superseding the master (provided he is not part owner) at any time they please; and the master upon being so superseded, is bound to deliver up the ship's certificate of registry to his successor,—the penalty of improperly retaining it being £100. Should

519

the master be superseded without good cause, he has his remedy against the owners for any loss or damage accruing to him.

CHARTER-PARTY.—The Charter-party is a contract "by which an entire ship, or some principal part thereof, is let to a merchant for the conveyance of goods, on a determined voyage to one or more places." It is not required to be drawn up in any precise form of words ; this depends on the circumstances and character of the voyage, for as there are generally peculiar regulations and customs attached to special trades, so there must be a corresponding diversity in the form and terms of the Charter-party; thus, it must be so framed and worded as to suit the wishes and intentions of the parties concerned, and the trade in which the vessel is about to be employed. Such being the case, most mercantile firms have their own printed form of Charter-party, with blank spaces for the details relating to the trade for which the ship is hired. Nevertheless, it may be stated that the main features of this document have not varied for years past, for the most important questions involved in it refer to the risks and responsibilities of parties arising out of the usual perils of the sea, compensation for delays, alterations of the agreement, &c.; and it may be noted that the printed part is of as great weight as the written part.

The substance of a Charter-party is as follows :—The owners (or his agent, or the master) covenant to provide a ship, strong, staunch, and in every respect seaworthy; well and sufficiently found in sails, sailyards, anchors, cables,

ropes, &c., and other instruments, tackle, apparel, furniture, provisions, &c., needful and necessary for such a
ship, and for the given voyage, together with an able
master, and a sufficient compliment of seamen ;—binding
themselves also that the cargo shall be delivered *(the act
of God, the Queen's enemies, and all and every other dangers
and accidents of the seas, rivers, and navigation, of whatever
nature and kind soever, during the said voyage, always
excepted)* in like good condition as when shipped, and with
as much speed as may be, at the place of discharge agreed
upon : it fixes the terms on which the cargo is to be carried,
the number of lay-days allowed for loading, and the
amount for demurrage, and the merchant or charterer
stipulates to comply with the payment promised for freight,
and on demurrage, according to the terms of the contract:
and both owner and charterer bind themselves in penalties
for non-performance of the covenants, articles and agree-
ments, in the Charter-party. It is signed by the contracting
parties in the presence of a witness, who also puts his
signature to it ; but when charterer and owner (or master)
sign at different times, a witness is required to each signature. In terms of the Stamp Act, to be a legal document,
it must be stamped.

Letters altering a charter are liable to the same stamp
duty as the Charter-party.

A charterer may load the ship with his own goods, or
with those of other parties ; or he may underlet the vessel
to another party provided no clause in the Charter-party
prohibits him so doing

521

As nearly all the rights and liabilities of both the merchant and shipowner respecting the carriage of cargo, depend on the stipulations contained in the Charter-party, and as both parties are bound by the terms of the contract they thereby enter into, care should be taken that it contains no provisions which are unusual, or which may be prejudicial to the rights of the parties.

When a ship is chartered by the "month," calendar months are understood, and the master must accept any kind of cargo which is not injurious to the ship, and to any quantity within its carrying capacity, *unless* special provisions in the Charter-party restrict this right.

If the ship is chartered for a lump sum, the draught of water should be specified in the Charter-party to prevent over loading.

In chartering, do not allow the charterer to sign as agent unless you approve of his principal ; nor agree that he shall not be liable for any delay in loading ; nor that his responsibility shall cease when the cargo is on board ; nor that the ship shall discharge in turn (unless according to the custom of the Port) ; nor that the master shall sign bills of lading at any rate of freight as presented and without qualification.

The ship must be properly dunnaged, according to the usages of the trade in which she is employed, or according to the nature of the cargo : and the goods must be stowed in the most approved method, so as to prevent damage.

For the purposes of loading and discharging the ship,

522

tate whether the *lay-days* are "running days" or "working days," according to the intention. Also be particular about the number of days and the amount to be paid *on demurrage*.

Lay days commence from the day when the ship is in her place of discharge (as per Charter-party), or as near thereto as she can safely get. The place of discharge is determined by the custom of the Port and the usage of the trade in which the vessel is engaged.

When no *lay days* are specified, the length of time for loading and unloading must be determined by the nature of the cargo, or the number of days usually allowed at the Port. To be valid, the custom or usage of the Port must be a legal one.

If the owner or master is bound to provide ballast, he may put in heavy merchandise, provided that it occupies no more space than ballast would do, and is not injurious to the cargo.

If it is intended that the deck load is to be entirely at merchants' risk, let it be so stated in the Charter-party, otherwise the shipowner must bear his share of the loss, in general average, if it is jettisoned, and he cannot recover the amount from the under-writers.

As soon as the vessel has taken in the full complement of cargo, and all things necessary are arranged, as clearing at the Custom house, payment of Port charges, &c., the voyage must be forthwith commenced, *weather* permitting.

The master must not take on board any contraband goods, or have in his possession any false or colourable

2 L

papers whereby the ship and cargo are rendered liable to seizure; but he must obtain all papers and documents which are necessary to protect the ship and cargo in all the countries to which he is trading.

By the terms of the Charter-party, not to be held liable for injuries arising from "the act of God, and the Queen's enemies, &c.," the master or owner is not responsible for damage arising from the sea, winds, &c., unless such injury or damage be the result of negligence or imprudence.

When the Charter-party names a full and complete cargo, the master must take on board as much as he can, *with safety*, and without injury to the ship; and the freighter is obliged to furnish the same, either of his own goods, or the goods of others.

The Charter-party should stipulate for a *full* cargo, if that is intended, otherwise the charterer will only be liable to pay on the quantity of goods which he ships, unless he has agreed to pay at the rate of so much per ton of the ship's capacity.

If any clause of the Charter-party is ambiguous, the interpretation should be liberal; or if the Charter-party is silent in respect to any point, the usage of the trade in which the ship is employed must be adopted.

No master should consent to vary the terms of the Charter-party, or alter his voyage, without the greatest caution, and then only with the charterer himself or his agent, having his written consent, which written consent ought to be given up to the master before making the alteration, otherwise the charterer will be discharged from the con-

525

tract, and the owner liable to an action for breach of contract. If there be a telegraph, it would be better for the master to refer to his owner for instructions.

If the Charter-party is entered into by the master, then he must be sued by the charterer in case of any dispute, unless the master, in signing, expressly states that he signs only as agent for the owner.

If, by the terms of a Charter-party, the ship has to proceed to a given Port, the merchant covenanting to furnish a cargo there, and on arrival the contracting party, or his agent, is unwilling or unable to furnish a cargo, the master should, on the expiration of the lay-days allowed by charter, protest against the merchant for non-fulfilment of the Charter-party, and he is then at liberty to return in ballast, and has a right to the full freight. *The better plan*, however, is to take the best homeward freight he can get, and claim the deficiency of freight from the merchant. It is not necessary to wait the demurrage days unless required so to do by the merchant or his agent. A prohibition by the government of the country to export the proposed articles of cargo, neither disolves the contract, nor excuses the non-performance of it. Send the protest home to the owners.

If a consignee refuses, and persists in his refusal, to receive cargo within a reasonable time, the master had better, after consulting with and entering a protest before the Consul, sell the cargo for what it will fetch, and proceed on the Charter-party for the balance of freight, if any.

If while loading it becomes an admitted fact that the

charterer is a bankrupt, the ship can repudiate the Charter, unless guaranteed by the bankrupt's assignees personally. An owner cannot be *compelled* to complete the Charter, and come for payment as one of the creditors. If, however, the ship has got sufficient goods on board to cover freight, demurrage, &c., and has a lien expressly given on the cargo to cover the same, the ship had better sail to her destination, and so deliver the cargo as to insure payment of such charges.

Depth of water at discharging or loading port, according to draught of ship.—This is a very important thing for a master to ascertain before the terms of the Charter-party are settled and signed, as a vessel may have to wait for a spring-tide to enter and depart ; or the port may be a barred harbour, and she may have to discharge and load partly in the roads, and partly in the river or docks,—or she may, from her draught, not be able to enter the harbour at all, and thus have to load and discharge in the roads ; in any case, unless, according to circumstances, such provisions as—"so near as she may safely get," "lighten and load at merchant's expense," or other equivalent words are introduced into the Charter-party ; the expenses entailed on the ship may be very considerable, and, in fact, a loss. Only in the case where it is the regular custom of the port to lighten the ship before she gets to her final berth, will the merchant be bound to do it

Form of Notice to be given after the Lay-days and Demur-rage-days are expired, and a full Cargo has not been supplied :—

527

To Messrs.————

As the Lay-days for loading my ship———— pired on————last; and as, according to the Charter- rty, you have not yet supplied a full Cargo, I hereby quire that you will forthwith inform me whether it is ur intention to supply any more Cargo.

Also, take notice, that unless the remainder of the Cargo supplied before————next, I shall, at the expiration that time, proceed on my voyage with the quantity of argo you have supplied to the said ship, and you will e held liable for Dead-freight and Damages for not sup- lying a full Cargo, according to Charter.

Dated this————day of————18——

A. B.,

Master of the————

Form of Notice to be given after the Lay-days and Demur- age-days are expired, and no Cargo has been supplied :—

To Messrs.————

I hereby give you notice that the Lay-days for loading my ship————expired on————last, and as you have not yet supplied any Cargo, I require you forthwith to commence to load the said ship, according to the Charter-party. Should you neglect to do so, I shall, after————next, hold myself at liberty to depart in ballast or re-charter the ship, according to circumstances, and you will be held responsible for all loss and damages

528

which may be sustained by the owners of the said ship in consequence of your having neglected to load her.

Dated——day of——18—

A. B.,

Master of the——

N.B.—Keep copies of these Notices or enter them in the Log Book.

A BILL OF LADING is a *formal receipt* signed by the master of the ship in his capacity of carrier, whereby he acknowledges that he has received the goods specified on board his ship, and binds himself (under certain conditions) to deliver them, in the condition received, at the place, and to the person named in the bill, or to his assigns, on his or their paying him the stipulated freight, If there is no charter-party, then the Bills of Lading will be evidence of the contract, and of the shipment of the goods.

The usual form of a Bill of Lading is as follows :—

X Y, No. 1 a 12.   N.B.—Shipped in good order and well conditioned, by D.E., Merchant, in and upon the good ship—— whereof A. B. is master, now in—— and bound for——, the goods following, viz.,——marked and numbered as *per* margin, to be delivered in the like good order and condition at—— aforesaid, (*the act of God, the Queen's enemies, fire, and all and every other dangers and accidents of the seas, rivers, and navigation, of whatever nature and kind soever, excepted)* unto the said D.E. or his assigns, he or they paying for the said goods at the rate of——— per ton freight, with primage and average accustomed. In witness whereof, I, the said master of the said ship, have affirmed to three bills of lading, of this tenor and date; any one of which bills being accomplished, the other two are to be void.

London, this——day of—— 18—.

A. B.——, Master.

Never be induced to sign Bills of Lading before the goods are on board, or without the mate's receipts being given up or cancelled, or without first carefully reading them over and comparing one with the other; not only see that they are alike, and that the quantity of goods and rate of freight are correct, but that nothing is inserted contrary to the fact on the Charter-party if there be one.

Do not sign Bills of Lading for a less freight than what is stated in the Charter-party, but say—"Freight, demurrage, and *all other conditions* as per Charter," for the consignee of the cargo is ordinarily only liable to carry out the requirements named in the Bill of Lading, as he does not necessarily know the terms of the Charter-party.

Insert the *correct* number of days consumed in loading, on the margin of the Bill of Lading.

Interest and insurance on money advanced, and address commission paid at port of loading, ought to be endorsed on the Bills of Lading. This is a receipt which the receivers of the cargo cannot dispute.

According to circumstances and the state in which goods are shipped, qualify your risk by adding—"quantity and quality unknown," or "weight and quantity unknown," or "weight and contents unknown," or "number and contents unknown." If the master suspects the contents of cases, &c. are damaged, he can demand to see them, but he is not justified in opening a case unless the shipper or his agent is present. The master should, however, give the shipper notice in writing, and if he fails to replace such damaged goods with sound, say—"shipped in a damaged condition," or "shipped in an improper condition."

With liquid goods you may add—"not accountable for leakage," or with brittle goods—"not accountable for breakage"; but here you are only protected so far as the leakage or breakage arises from accidental causes, not when such damage arises from negligence or want of care.

Enter deck load at shipper's or charterer's risk, even if provided for in Charter, or otherwise.

If the shipper refuse to allow the qualifications stated above, or the insertion of any words the master considers

531

ought to be inserted on the bill of lading, sign **under protest,** thus :—

" Signed under protest,"

A. B., Master.

Bills of Lading, when there is no Charter-party, should **say**—" Consignee paying freight, demurrage, and all other **charges**"; also, "goods to be taken from alongside at **Consignee's** expense and risk."

In England it is customary in the case of ships loading **general** cargoes for abroad, to sign Bills of Lading for **freight** paid in advance, but not to receive it for a month **or** six weeks after the sailing of the vessel : in this case, **say**—"nevertheless the owners to have a lien on the **goods** for freight until paid."

Three Bills of Lading should be stamped ; one for the **shipper,** another for the consignee, and the third for the **master's** use and guidance in delivering cargo ; but a *copy* requires no stamp. A master is not bound to sign a **Bill** of Lading unless it is properly stamped, as it cannot **be** stamped afterwards. In England the penalty for **signing** an unstamped bill of lading is £50.

A master of a ship, on signing Bills of Lading, ought **clearly** to understand he is only required to give a receipt **for** the cargo ; not to enter into a second agreement ; **hence** the necessity of referring to the Charter-party in the **Bill** of Lading for " freight and conditions "—the Bill of **Lading** being the last document signed.

A master has no right to insert any new conditions in

532

the Bills of Lading, and the charterer is justified in such a case in detaining the ship until the bills are duly signed. Also, if the charterer, after the expiration of the lay-days, detains the ship by not presenting proper Bills of Lading for the master's signature, the charterer will be liable to pay demurrage for such detention.

Refuse to sign Bills of Lading binding you to go to any other place or places of discharge than the place or places covenanted for in the Charter-party. If you cannot get proper Bills of Lading after waiting a reasonable time, protest, and sail without them, or sign them under protest as to the contents objected to.

A master must sign the necessary ship and cargo papers, in whatever language they are, but he is not bound to sign a document he does not understand; therefore, before signing foreign Bills of Lading, &c., it is his duty to have them explained by his Consul, or a Notary Public, as some of them omit the usual exceptions, "the act of God; the Queen's enemies, &c. (*see* above), and have objectionable clauses in them. Where they cannot be translated, add—"freight and all other conditions as per Charter-party; and anything contrary thereto to be void."

After signing one set of Bills of Lading, do not sign another set unless those previously signed are given back to you to be destroyed; you might otherwise find yourself liable to deliver goods to the holders of both sets.

Every indorsee of a Bill of Lading to whom property in in the goods passes by the indorsement is now liable to the shipowner, and the shipowner is liable to him in case

533

of any breach of contract. An indorsee, however, who indorses it again to another party, does not remain liable after indorsing it away.

Deliver the cargo to no one unless he produce one of the Bills on Lading which you have previously signed, properly endorsed.

A Bill of Lading may be negociated by simple indorsement and delivery, which will carry a right to the goods.

LAY-DAYS.—This is the term applied to the number of days specified in the Charter-party for loading and discharging a vessel.

As a general rule, *i.e.*, in the absence of a custom of the Port, or a stipulation to the contrary, "lay-days" mean "running days," and include Sundays and fixed holidays ; one exception being where the ship has reported too late for the Merchant to begin discharging in fair time on Saturday, in which case the Merchant would be entitled to begin to count his "lay-days" from the following Monday, or first *working* day, which the late reporting of the ship on Saturday gives him the advantage of ; the ship's days would then run on as *running* days—the succeeding Sundays and holidays counting as "days" against the Merchant. Also, in most Continental ports, according to usage, holidays count as Sundays, in which case the Merchant would not recognize a notice given on such a day, and the ship's time would only count from the day after the holiday. In London, however, by the custom of the port, "days" are held to mean "working days," unless otherwise specified.

534

"Lay-days, Sundays excepted," mean "working days;" Sundays not counting as days.

"Running lay-days" mean every day to count, viz: working days, Sundays, and holidays.

"Lay-days," subject to the exceptions stated above, are to be construed to count as "running lay-days."

In calculating a ship's "days," part of a day is reckoned as a whole day; thus, though discharging did not commence until 2 h. or 3 h. P.M., that day would count against the Merchant.

Lay-days for discharging cargo commence the day after the vessel is entered at the Custom House, and after her arrival at the usual place of discharge in the port; but she must be *ready* to discharge her cargo before the days begin to count; and if some particular place in the port is specified in the Charter, they do not commence until that place is reached. If a vessel can get over a bar at spring-tide, and afterwards discharge afloat, she must wait for the springs, and the lay-days will not commence until she is in her place of discharge.

If a vessel is, according to her Charter, always to lay afloat, and has arrived within the limits of her port of discharge, or as near thereto as she can *safely* get, and has to be lightened to reach her final discharging berth, the days, day, or part of a day consumed in towing up to, or otherwise reaching that final place, would count in the lay-days.

Also, if the clauses of the Charter-party stipulate, "calling at C——for orders, which are to be given in——

hours, or lay-days commence," and "——days at Port of delivery for unloading," then the lay-days commence at C——after the expiration of the given hours allowed for receiving orders, and they may be deducted from the days allowed for unloading.

" Regular turn " is explained and governed by the usage of the Port ; and a vessel's lay-days in this case commence when her turn comes.

" Usual dispatch " is held to mean the usual dispatch of persons who have a cargo in readiness ; and " reasonable time," if there is no usage of the port to decide the question, means a reasonable time under *ordinary* circumstances.

If a vessel is duly loaded within the time named as lay-days, and she is ready for sea, the Charterer has no power to detain her.

Form of Notice that Ship is ready to Load :—

To Messrs.————

Take Notice that my vessel the————is now lying at ————, and is now ready to receive her cargo.   The Lay-days, according to Charter-party, commenced————, and will exipre on————; after which time the vessel will be on Demurrage.

Dated this——day of————18—.

A. B., Master of the————

536

ON DEMURRAGE.

Form of Notice that Ship is ready to Unload.

To Messrs.———

Take Notice that my vessel the———arrived here ———, and is now ready to unload. The Lay-days for discharging the cargo will expire on———, and after that date you will be liable, per Charter-party to pay Demurrage at the rate of £———per day. If the discharge of the cargo is commenced before you pay the Freight, I will reserve my right to detain a sufficient portion of the cargo until said Freight is paid.

Dated this———day of———18—.

A. B., Master of the———.

N.B.—Do not forget to keep copies of these notices, and a memorandum of the date on which they were delivered.

DEMURRAGE. If a vessel is detained, either in loading or unloading, for a longer term than the number of days stated in the Charter-party, or on the Bills of Lading, the Shipowner is entitled to *Demurrage*, the rate of which, *per day*, is also stipulated for in the Charter-party.

Demurrage can only be claimed for detention at the port of loading, and at the port of discharge. It should also be claimed day by day as it arises, and on Saturday for Sunday, for *all* days count on demurrage, even if the Charter-party specifies that the Lay-days are to be working

537

days only. Further, if no notice has been served on the **Merchant** for Demurrage, the claim resolves itself into **one** of undue detention, which must be proved, and is outside the Charter-party.

A ship-owner has no lien on the cargo for Demurrage, **unless** that is a stipulation in the Charter-party or Bills of Lading.

If a Charter-party provides for a certain number of days *on demurrage*, at a given rate per day, and the vessel is detained longer than the time specified, then, for the additional term, the ship-owner is not restricted to the amount of demurrage named in the Charter-party; but the only way to secure a claim on an increased scale, is to give ample notice that if the vessel is detained beyond the days named *on demurrage*, an increased rate per day will be charged as compensation for the detention.

If lay-days are not mentioned in the Charter-party or Bill of Lading, the vessel must be loaded or unloaded with reasonable dispatch; and if demurrage is supposed to accrue, it must be regulated by the custom of the Port, by the decision of arbitrators, or by a jury, as to what, under the circumstances, would be a fair and reasonable time for loading or discharging.

The owner is the proper party to sue in a demurrage case.

Form of Notice that Ship is on Demurrage :—(Loading.)

To Messrs.————

Take notice that the lay-days for loading my vessel,

538

the————expired on————and since that time she has been, and is still on demurrage, for the payment of which you and all concerned will be held liable.

Dated this————day of————18—

A. B., Master of the————

Form of Notice that Ship is on Demurrage :—(Discharging.)

To Messrs.————

Take notice that the lay-days for discharging the cargo in my vessel the————, have expired, and that she is now on demurrage, for the payment of which you and all concerned will be held liable.

Also take notice, that if you neglect forthwith to discharge the said cargo, you and all concerned will be held liable for all expenses of storing the same, should it become necessary to do so.

Dated this————day of————18—

A. B., Master of the————

N.B.—Do not forget to keep copies of these notices, and a memorandum of the date of delivery.

CARGO AND ITS STOWAGE.—Owners and Masters are considered in law in the same situation as common carriers, and it cannot be too clearly understood that the payment

580

of freight very much depends on the care bestowed on the cargo. All due precautions must therefore be taken to receive and stow cargoes in good order, so that the goods may be delivered in the like good order and condition (the act of God, dangers of the seas, &c., excepted).

Owners have often had large sums to pay for damage to cargo, arising from the following causes, which with ordinary care might have been prevented :—runs not being clear; dunnage not being good and sufficient; ship not being properly matted out; pump well, mast cases, bulkheads, shifting boards, and chain locker not being substantial and secure; neglected air ports, by which cargo reaches the pumps and chokes them; leaky ports; covering of hatchways and coating of masts being insufficient or imperfect; inattention to pumps; improper stowage; cutting timber or deals, and breaking open packages (for stowage) beyond what is provided for by the Charter, by the usages of the trade, or without the written consent of the charterer or shipper; deck load being carried over a perishable cargo; rats, mice, and other vermin.

The law holds the shipowner liable for the safe custody of the goods when properly and legally received on board in good order, and for the "delivery" to parties producing the Bills of Lading.

Goods are not unfrequently sent alongside in a damaged state, and letters of indemnity given to the master by the shippers for signing in good order and condition; this is nothing more or less than conniving at fraud. Fine goods are often damaged in the ship's hold by lumpers, if per-

2 M

mitted to use cotton-hooks in handling bales. All goods must be received on board according to the custom of the port where the cargo is to be taken in, and the same custom will regulate the responsibility of the master and owner.

Before taking in Cargo, see that the limbers are clear; the hold well swept; examine the mast cases, pump well, and chain trunks; and have the dunnage properly laid.

The parts that require the most dunnage are the bilges, pump well, masts, in the wake of the chain plates, scuppers, hooks and transoms; in the 'tween decks lay the dunnage athwartships.

During the voyage attend the pumps carefully, and enter in each day's log,—"pumps carefully attended."

Stow cases with the mark and number uppermost.

Stow bales on their flats, mark and number uppermost; except wing bales, which stow on their edges.

Stow oil, resin, pitch, tar, &c., in the fore peak.

Stow casks bung up and bilge free; the ground tier on beds, and put quoins on top of the beds at each side; the next tier in the cantlines of the ground tier, and put quoins under the quarters at each side; chock them off in the wings with dunnage wood between the quarters of the casks and the wings. If you have but a hundred or so casks, stow them in the fore hold.

Stow acid, vitriol, &c., on deck, ready to throw overboard, if necessary.

For an entire cargo of iron, rig a platform about a foot higher than the keelson; then lay it grating fashion from

541

he after part of the fore hatch to the fore part of the after hatch, keeping the bars an inch or two apart; carry it over into the wings right up both sides, taking care to have bars along the sides to keep the chafe off the skin; bring it up from the ends in a slant towards the main hatch; secure it by tomming it off from the beams, with planks under the toms.

A part cargo of iron stow fore-and-aft from the after part of the fore hatch to the fore part of the after hatch, until level with the keelson; then grating-fashion, and bring it up square at the ends.

All dead weight as iron, copper, lead, and other metals, used to stiffen the ship, should be stowed in the bottom, from the after part of the fore-hatch to the fore part of the after-hatch.

Stow a heavy piece of machinery in the centre of the main hold.

To stow a cargo of copper ore.—A good substantial platform should be built above the keelson, and a trunk-way formed by building strong bulkheads in the wings, well shored and cleated from the sides; by this means you keep the dead weight in the body of the ship, rising it, and rendering the ship easier in a sea-way. N.B.—If materials for building a trunk-way are not available, good strong casks (the head-staves perpendicular) will make a good substitute; the ground tier forming the platform, and winging up with casks at the sides.

To stow guano.—The hold and limbers having been prepared, dunnage as high as the keelson, and three or

2 M 2   542

four inches in the sides ; the masts, pump well, &c. being well cased round and matted ; then sew bags together and line the ship throughout, nailing the bags to the sides where necessary, being careful to see all listing pieces and air-holes are filled in. N.B.—Ships are found with sufficient bags and twine by the shipper.

Or, build a platform as high as the keelson ; then partially fill bags with guano, so that when stowed, the bottoms of the half-filled bags shall lay over the mouths of each other ; line the lower hold in this manner, then fill in with guano in bulk. By this plan you save time and twine, but the former method is preferable. N.B.—The ship to be balked at the ends by filled bags.

To stow a cargo of tea.—Dunnage the ship with good *dry* stone ballast even with the upper part of the keelson, or higher, according to the vessel's stability and the heights of chests you can stow under the lower deck beams ; level the ballast and round it down towards the wings to give it the same curve as the deck and beams ; also throw up sufficient ballast fore and aft in both wings to chock off the three lower tiers. The ballast should then be covered with *thin dry* boards, and the ground tier stowed, keeping the lower corners of the wing chests from 14 to 16 inches from the bilges ; then fill in the wings with ballast, levelled and covered with dry boards : now stow the second or riding tier, keeping the lower corners of the wing chests 10 or 12 inches from the sides, and chock off by filling in the wings with small ballast ; stow the third tier, keeping the lower corners of the wing chests 4 inches from the

543

sides, filling and chocking off with ballast. When the third tier is stowed it should be a perfect level, fore and aft, with a gradual droop towards the wings, according to the curve of the beams. Above this tier dunnage the sides from 3 to 4 inches, up to the lower beams—in the 'tween decks 1 to 2 inches of dry dunnage laid athwartships—sides the same. The pump well, chain locker, masts, &c. should be *well* dunnaged. N.B.—With a tea cargo great care should be used in selecting dry hard stone or shingle; the same remark applies to the dunnage.

The following instructions for stowage of various cargoes are according to Lloyds' rules :—

HEMP, FLAX, WOOL, and COTTON, should be dunnaged 9 inches on the floors, and to the *upper part* of the *bilge,* the wing bales of the second tier kept 6 inches off the side at the lower corner, and 2½ inches at the sides. Sand or damp gravel ballast to be covered with boards. *Sharp-bottom ships one-third less dunnage in floors and bilges.* Avoid Horn Shavings as dunnage from Calcutta.

All CORN, WHEAT, RICE, PEAS, BEANS, &c., when in bulk, to be stowed on a good high platform, or dunnage wood, of not less than 10 inches, and in the bilges 14 inches dunnage; the pumps and masts cased, to have strong bulkheads, good shifting boards, with feeders and ventilators, and to have no admixture of other goods. Flat-floored, wall-sided ships should be fitted with bilge pumps. On no consideration must the stanchions under the beams be removed.

OIL, WINE, SPIRITS, BEER, MOLASSES, TAR, &c., to be stowed bung up ; to have good *cross beds* at the quarters, (*and not to trust to hanging beds*), to be well chocked with wood, and allowed to stow three heights of pipes or butts, four heights of puncheons, and six heights of hogsheads or half-puncheons. All moist goods and liquids, such as SALTED HIDES, Bales of BACON, BUTTER, LARD, GREASE, CASTOR OIL, &c., should not be stowed too near " dry goods," whose nature is to absorb moisture. Ship-owners have often to pay heavy damages for leakage in casks of Molasses, arising from stowing too many heights without an intervening platform or 'twixt decks. From Bengal, goods also are frequently damaged by Castor Oil.

TEA, and FLOUR in barrels ; FLAX, CLOVER, and LIN-SEED, or RICE in tierces ; COFFEE and COCOA in bags, should always have 9 inches at least, of good dunnage in the bottom, and 14 inches to the upper part of the bilges, with 2 ½ inches at the sides ; allowed to stow six heights of tierces and eight heights of barrels. All ships above 600 tons should have 'twixt decks or platforms laid for these cargoes, to ease the pressure—caulked 'twixt decks should have scuppers in the sides, and 2 ½ inches of dunnage laid athwart ship, and not fore-and-aft ways, when in bags or sacks ; and when in boxes or casks not less than 1 inch. RICE from Calcutta is not unfrequently damaged by indigo, for want of care in stowing.

Entire cargoes of SUGAR, SALTPETRE, and GUANO, in bags, must have the dunnage carefully attended to, as laid down for other goods. TIMBER ships are better without 'twixt

545

decks if loading all timber or deals. Brown sugar to be **kept** separate from white sugar, and both kept from direct **contact** with Saltpetre.

POT and PEARL ASHES, TOBACCO, BARK, INDIGO, **MADDERS**, GUM, &c., whether in casks, cases, or bales, **to be** dunnaged in the bottom, and to the upper part of **the** bilges, at *least* 9 inches, and 2½ inches at the sides.

MISCELLANEOUS GOODS, such as boxes of CHEESE, **kegs** and tubs of LARD, or other small or slight-made **packages**, not intended for broken stowage, should be **stowed** by themselves, and dunnaged as other goods.

Barrels of PROVISIONS, and TALLOW Casks, allowed to stow six heights. All METALS should be stowed under, **and** separated from goods liable to be damaged by **contact**.

All MANUFACTURED GOODS, also DRY HIDES, Bales of SILK, or other valuable articles, should have 2½ inches of dunnage against the side, to preserve a water-course. Bundles of SHEET IRON, RODS, pigs of COPPER or IRON, or any rough hard substance, should not be allowed to come in contact with bales or bags, or any soft packages liable to be chafed. When mats can be procured they should be used at the sides for Silk, Tea, &c.

TAR, TURPENTINE, RESIN, &c., to have flat beds of wood under the quarters, of an inch thick, and allowed to stow six heights.

Very frequent and serious loss falls on merchants on the upper part of cargoes, particularly in vessels that bring wheat, corn, tobacco, oil cake, &c., arising from

546

vapour damage imbibed by wheat, flour, and other goods stowed in the same vessel with turpentine, or other strong scented articles : the shippers are to blame for such negligence, for not making due inquiry before shipping.

Ships laden with full cargoes of coal, bound round Cape Horn, or Cape of Good Hope, to be provided with approved ventilators as a preventive against ignition.

No vessel bound on any over-sea voyage, should on any account be loaded beyond that point of immersion which will present a clear side out of water, when upright, of three inches to every foot depth of hold, measured amidships, from the height of the deck at the side, to the water. In stowing, 42 cubic feet measurement make a ton.

STOWAGE OF GRAIN CARGOES FROM CANADA AND THE UNITED STATES.—No ship exceeding 400 tons register can be entirely loaded with grain in bulk; and all exceeding 400 tons register may take two-thirds of the cargo grain in bulk, and one-third in bags, or rolling freight instead thereof. In the latter case, the grain in bulk should be stowed six inches, but not more above the beams, to allow for settling.

When ships take wheat, corn, &c., in bulk, it must be stowed in sections or "bins" (not to contain more than 12,000 bushels each), to be lined with thoroughly seasoned boards, grain tight, not less than 10 inches from the flat of the floor, and from 14 to 16 inches in the bilges, graduated to the sides, which must be clapboard lined to the deck. Care must be taken to preserve a water-course under the lining. Good shifting boards, secured to the stanchions,

547

extending at least six feet downwards and fitted tight to the deck. The stanchions not to be removed, but firmly secured. No loose grain to be stowed in the extreme ends, and no admixture of other goods. Pumps and masts cased and covered with mats or canvas, made thoroughly grain-tight, with sufficient space in the well to admit the passage of a man to the heels of the pumps, and access had to the same by means of a man-hole from the deck, or by a clear passage from the 'tween decks aft. Mats to be used for covering knees, keelson, and stanchions, if required, but not for lining or covering the sides.

Grain, when stowed in bags, must be dunnaged not less than 10 inches on the floor, 14 to 16 inches in the bilges, 3 inches on sides up to the deck; between decks the dunnage must be laid thwart ships, at least 2 inches from the deck. Shifting plank extending at least 4 feet from deck beams downwards, secured to stanchions. The dunnage in the hold must be entirely covered with boards and sails, or mats, grain-tight.

All bulk or loose grain must be taken in bins prepared for that purpose.

For dunnaging deals are preferable to anything else. They should be laid fore and aft about 3 inches apart, the second tier over the spaces of the first tier, the third tier over the spaces of the second, and so on. Staves or other materials generally used for dunnage to be placed so as to give free course for the water to reach the pumps. The dunnage should be raised from 10 to 12 inches from the floor, and in the bilges from 14 to 16 inches, according to

548

the build of the ship, and the discretion of the Inspector. Flat-floored, wall-sided ships should be fitted with bilge pumps.

The studs for the bulkheads should be made of three-inch deals, placed about two feet apart, and firmly secured at the top and bottom, and properly braced and cleated on the lining and to the beams (or deck), to resist the pressure of the grain.

The studs for the bulkheads forward, and after bulkheads for ships not exceeding 10 feet depth of hold, must be 4 by 6 inches in size, and of one entire piece; of a greater depth than 16 feet, they must be 4 by 8 inches. They must be set 20 inches apart from centre to centre, firmly secured at the top and bottom, and properly braced and cleated on the ceiling and deck, to resist the pressure of the grain.

The sides above the turn of the bilge must be lined on 1 inch battens after the manner of clap-boarding.

Shifting planks 2 inches thick must extend to the deck on each side of the stanchions, fitted tight under and between the beams and carlines, and extending not less than 6 feet downwards; care must be taken that the stanchions are well secured at both ends. In no case can single boards be substituted for plank, and the shifting-boards must be shored from sides, midway between the stanchions.

Materials for bins must be perfectly seasoned; un-seasoned lumber must not be used where it will come in contact with the grain. Water-tanks, whether of wood or

549

iron, must be cased with wood to prevent damage from sweat or leakage. And all ships with grain in bulk ought to have feeders and ventilators.

It must be seen that the grain is well trimmed up between the beams, and the space between the beams completely filled.

When ships are chartered, the draught of water should be limited, and provision made for loading under inspection.

The load-draught must be regulated by the depth of the hold, allowing three inches to every foot depth of hold, measured from lowest line of sheer of deck amidships to the water, when upright. Ships having an additional deck put on after construction, the depth of hold to be measured from original deck.

Ships loading grain complying strictly with the above rules, lined and loaded under the supervision of the surveyor appointed by Lloyds' agent, will be entitled to a certificate to that effect.

Caution.—Never stow any part of the cargo, nor put any stores in the space allotted to the crew, as each man can claim one shilling per day for the whole time that the crew space is so occupied.

FREIGHT is the sum which the merchant pays for the safe conveyance of cargo, or for the use of the ship; it is payable according to the terms of the Charter-party.

Do not make the freight payable two months, or any time *after* the delivery of cargo, but either "during the delivery," or "on delivery." When bills are to be given, have them good and approved bills, and not charterer's

550

acceptance. When foreign money is to be paid, make it "at current rate of exchange."

When an advance of freight is to be paid, make it payable on signing Bills of Lading, and not on the sailing of the ship.

If it has been necessary to abandon the vessel, freight will be earned by conveying the goods to their destination by the best means which circumstances will admit of.

Freight cannot be claimed on damaged cargo sold at an intermediate port; hence, it is always better to put it into the best condition possible, and bring it on.

If the freight is calculated by time, it begins to run from the period of the ship's breaking ground, and commencing her voyage.

The owner has a lien on the cargo for freight, but none on goods conveyed for dead freight.

A ship having been fully chartered to the charterers, the master has no right to fill his cabin for his own or his owner's benefit, so as to receive "extra" freight as against charterers; the latter may claim compensation on showing loss. The master's is a permissive custom rather than a right.

If goods have increased in bulk (as in the case of grain), freight must be calculated on the quantity put on board; if there has been a decrease (as in the case of molasses, &c.,) it must be calculated on the quantity delivered.

Where a lump sum has to be paid for freight, and a part of the cargo only is delivered in consequence of some accident, a proportionate sum will be payable.

551

Though the cargo be so much damaged when the ship arrives at the port of destination as not to be worth the freight, the merchant cannot avoid payment of the freight by abandoning the cargo to the ship-owner, from whatever cause the damage may have arisen.

"Right and true delivery," means delivery of the right quantity, although the quality may be damaged.

Where the amount of freight named in the Bills of Lading differs from that named in the Charter-party, the master can only claim from the consignee the amount named in the Bills of Lading, and the lien on the cargo is only for that amount: the balance must be claimed from Charterer.

The master can detain for the freight any part of the cargo consigned to the same person: also, in case the cargo is damaged, or where there is short delivery, he can hold it till the whole freight due on the quantity delivered is paid.

PROTESTS AND SURVEYS.—It is always safe and judicious, even when no damage to cargo is apprehended, to note a protest, "against wind and weather," within 24 hours after the ship's arrival at her port; if need be, this protest can then be extended according to the exigencies of the case. A protest is made before a Notary Public; if there is no such person, then before a British Consul, a magistrate, or the collector of customs. Keep a copy of the noting, and have it signed as a "true copy."

A ship having received damage, or having touched the ground during the voyage to her port of loading, ought to

552

be surveyed, and a certificate of her sea-worthiness, in duplicate, obtained before taking on board cargo.

If it is found necessary to put into an intermediate port for repairs, the master must have a certificate of survey on the damage received, and the ship's sea-worthiness before leaving. If the cargo be a perishable one, and there is reason to think it is damaged, it will be necessary to have a survey on it, and obtain a certificate that it is, or has been, put into proper condition for the passage to the port of destination.

If in consequence of bad weather there is reason to suppose the cargo has been damaged, before opening hatches at the port of discharge, get two shipmasters (as surveyors) to inspect them, and obtain from them a certificate of survey (in duplicate), stating that the hatches have been well parcelled and battened down; the same surveyors can also inspect the damaged packages of cargo, and certify as to whether they were properly dunnaged and stowed, giving a certificate respecting them.

Under any circumstances let the surveyors, when a certificate of survey is necessary, be two shipmasters, or a shipmaster and a merchant uninterested in the cargo.

A certificate of survey, specifying that the hatches were properly battened down, and the cargo sufficiently dunnaged and generally well stowed, but that the goods were damaged by sea water, prevents a claim being made on the ship for the amount of damage.

When you proceed to extend your protest, take with you to the Notary the certificates of survey and the log

553

book, and leave them with him till the claims are settled : be careful that whatever statements you make are correct.

The owner should have a copy of the certificate of survey, and also of the protest, transmitted to him by post ; the other the master keeps *for his own use.*

CALLING FOR ORDERS.—When you call at one port for orders to discharge or load at another, ask for your orders in *writing*, and take care of them, as they will be useful in case of dispute.

AN INVOICE for shipping purposes is an account of goods sold or consigned, containing a description of the goods, with their marks and numbers ; their prime cost ; and charges, which include freight, insurance, entry bond duty, dock charges, lighterage, &c.

A COCKET is a Custom-house warrant, given on the entry of goods for exportation, in evidence of their having paid duty, or being duty free.

MANIFEST.—This is a document made from the Bills of Lading, dated and signed by the master at the place of lading. It sets forth the ship's name ; Port of registry ; registered tonnage ; master's name ; a specific account and description of *all* goods on board, with the marks and numbers thereon ; the names of the shippers and consignees ; the place or places where the goods have been received on board, and the place or places for which they are respectively destined ; and in fact, *full particulars* relating to the ship, the cargo, the crew, and the passengers, if any.

It must be handed over to the Custom-house authorities

554

on the arrival of the ship at the port of destination ; and must also be ready to be produced at any intermediate port the ship puts into. In many places goods on board and not in the manifest are not only liable to confiscation, but the master is subjected to a heavy penalty for the omission ; and no such ambiguous term as "merchandise" is admitted.

ENTRY INWARDS AND CLEARANCE OUTWARDS.—The master must immediately on reaching his port of destination see that his vessel is *entered inwards* at the Custom-house, and take with him the manifest and all the necessary papers for that purpose. So, on his departure he must likewise have his *clearance outwards.*

BILL OF HEALTH.—Every ship on leaving port should be furnished by the sanitary authority with a bill of health, which should be countersigned by a Consul of the country to which she is bound, otherwise she is liable to unnecessary delay and detention in quarantine ; a similar bill should be obtained at intermediate ports belonging to different countries.

BOTTOMRY AND RESPONDENTIA. — Bottomry is the mortgaging of a ship, when, in a foreign port, the master cannot obtain money on his own, or his owner's credit ; it is a bond whereby the ship is pledged as security for the repayment of money borrowed to repair the ship, and so complete the voyage ; the money advanced, together with the premium or interest, becomes repayable on the ship terminating the voyage successfully,—the vessel as well as the borrower being then liable for the money lent.

555

If the ship is lost, the lender loses the money; and since he has to sustain the hazard of the voyage, he is allowed a greater interest or premium than the usual rate acknowledged by law.

If on a voyage, two or more bottomry bonds be entered into, the last is payable first, since they take precedence in the reverse order of the bonds being taken up.

Money borrowed on bottomry must be obtained by advertisement, and the lowest offer (of interest) accepted.

The seamen's wages must be paid before the bottomry bond.

If money is necessary and it cannot be obtained on bottomry, the cargo may be pledged : this is *respondentia*, and is subject to the same laws as bottomry.

If money cannot be obtained on bottomry or on respondentia, the master may sell a part of the cargo.

AVERAGE, in the law of shipping, is generally applied to the loss occasioned by any sacrifice made to insure the safety of a ship and cargo; it is usually settled by an "average adjuster."

PORT CHARGES are generally taken to include pilotage, towage, harbour and hospital dues, &c., and whatever charges of a similiar description are customary at any given port.

SHIPPING AND DISCHARGING CREW,—SHIP'S ARTICLES OF AGREEMENT,—VICTUALLING SCALE.—A few days before the ship is ready for sea, attend at the Shipping Office and state your requirements as regards hands, &c.; you will there be furnished with all the necessary preliminary papers, and the seamen will, in due course, be procured for you, and desired to attend on the day you propose to *sign Articles*. These Articles of Agreement state the character of the voyage, and fix the *status* of each of the crew, the rates of wages, the scale of victualling, &c. On the given day, and at the given time, the Articles of Agreement, the Victualling Scale, and the Regulations for maintaining discipline (sanctioned by the Board of Trade) are read to the crew, the Deputy Superintendent seeing that they understand what has been read. and, if necessary, explaining it to them. The master first signs his name in full to the Agreement and Duplicate, and fixes the day and hour the crew are to be on board, which is duly entered on the Agreement: the crew then sign in rotation: the Deputy-Superintendent then attests the execution of the Agreement, and previous to dismissing the crew informs them when they are to be on board. When all the arrangements are completed, and all the necessary papers signed and attested, the master will receive from the Deputy-Superintendent the Ship's papers, together with the Certificates, Indentures and Discharges of the crew, and all requisite forms : also the Clearance Certificate to be produced to the Collector and Comptroller of Customs.

When about to sail, nail a copy of the Victualling Scale in the forecastle, where it can be seen by the crew: also muster the crew to ascertain if all are on board : if any are missing. ship others in their place; when the Pilot leaves give him a copy of the Articles to take to the owners, with a list of the deserters and their substitutes.

557

Similarly, the crew must be discharged at a Shipping Office on the completion of the voyage, and "an account of wages must (under a penalty not exceeding £5) be filled up and delivered to each member of the crew, at least 24 hours before he is paid off, and no deduction will be allowed unless duly inserted." On the given day for paying off, "Discharges" being ready for delivery, the crew must muster at the Office; the master will first sign the "Release," and as the men are paid off, they will sign it also in rotation, each receiving from the Deputy Superintendent his discharge. You will also have to give an account of the wages and effects of all deceased seamen.

If the crew or any portion of them are to be discharged abroad, and there is no Shipping Office, it must be done before the Consul.

Every seaman has a lien on the ship for his wages.

There is no *authorized* VICTUALLING SCALE; whatever the crew agrees to, they must abide by, but the articles as proposed must be served out in the proper quantities, else they are entitled to compensation; the following scale was promulgated by the Committee of the General Ship-owner's Society in 1844.

Days of the week	Bread	Salt Beef	Salt Pork	Flour	Rice	Peas	Tea	Sugar	Mustard	Water	Vinegar	Per Act Parliament Lemon or Lime Juice	Sugar for Lime Juice
		lb.	lb.	lb.		pt.	oz.	oz.		qt.	pt.	oz.	oz.
SUNDAY ...	As much as they can eat without waste.	1½		½	1 lb. per week.	...	⅛	2	To be considered as an extra, and issued at the discretion of the Master.	3	½	½	½
MONDAY ...		...	1¼			⅓	⅛	...		3	...	½	½
TUESDAY ...		1½		½			⅛	...		3	...	½	½
WEDNESDAY ...			1¼			⅓	⅛	...		3	...	½	½
THURSDAY ...		1½		½			⅛	...		3	...	½	½
FRIDAY ...			1¼			⅓	⅛	...		3	...	½	½
SATURDAY ...		1½		½		...	⅛	...		3	...	½	½
SUNDAY ...			1¼			⅓	⅛	2		3	½	½	½
MONDAY ...		1½		½			⅛	...		3	...	½	½
TUESDAY ...		...	1¼			⅓	⅛	...		3	...	½	½
WEDNESDAY ...		1½		½			⅛	...		3	...	½	½
THURSDAY ...			1¼			⅓	⅛	...		3	...	½	½
FRIDAY ...		1½		½			⅛	...		3	...	½	½
SATURDAY ...		...	1¼			⅓	⅛	...		3	...	½	½
Totals for 14 days		[illegible]	[illegible]	[illegible]		[illegible]	[illegible]	[illegible]		42	1	7	7

When bread is allowanced out, it must be 1 lb. per man per day.

SUBSTITUTES.—1 oz. of coffee or cocoa or chocolate for ¼ oz. of Tea.

Molasses for Sugar ; the quantity to be one-half more.

1 lb. potatoes or yams to be considered equal to ½ lb. flour or rice, or ¼ pint peas.

When *fresh meat* is issued, the proportion to be 2 lb. per man per day, in lieu of salt meat, flour, rice and peas.

The allowance of small stores being considered as an equivalent for spirits, spirits are only to be issued under particular circumstances at the discretion of the master.

Caution respecting *Lime Juice :*—By the Merchant Shipping Act, 7 & 8 Vict. c. 112, s. 18,—Lime or lemon juice, sugar, and vinegar, are to be served out to the crew, whenever they shall have been consuming salt provisions for *ten days*. The lime or lemon juice and sugar daily, after the rate of half an ounce of each per day, and the vinegar weekly, at the rate of half a pint per week to each person, so long as the consumption of salt provisions be continued.

SHIP'S LOG-BOOK.—The ship's log-book kept and written up daily by the chief-mate, and signed by the master, should receive more attention than is ordinarily bestowed upon it, for it is impossible to say at what time it may be required as evidence in a court of law ; besides which, the remarks in it are the foundation of the master's protest, and consequently they should be strictly correct. The remarks should describe most particularly the wind and weather, and the effect on the ship as regards any accidents that may arise therefrom,—the amount of damage sustained and the cause to which it may justly be attributed, as far as can be ascertained at the time ; the latitude and longitude ; the hour of occurrence ; the attention given to the pumps, and to the lead-line, &c. All interlineations and erasures should be avoided ; and if any correction is necessary while writing it, make it by drawing the pen through the error.

It is also requisite that the log-book should be properly written up by the time the ship arrives at the Port of destination, ready to be produced when asked for, as in

560

case of damage to ship or cargo, serious difficulties may otherwise be experienced in the settlement of average.

These requirements are especially necessary; for in many foreign Ports, the Notary Public, on receiving the log-book, may examine any two of the crew privately and separately on the statements therein, before receiving the master's protest; and again, in some Ports it is required by the authorities that the ship's officers, on arrival, should sign the page where the writing ends, for the purpose of preventing any subsequent additions.

A master is allowed to use any form of log-book he prefers.

THE OFFICIAL LOG-BOOK of the voyage for certain special entries, must also, by the Merchant Shipping Act, be kept by every ship master, who is further required, within 48 hours after the ship's arrival at her final Port of destination in the United Kingdom, or upon the discharge of the crew, whichever happens first, to deliver it to the Shipping master, before whom the crew is discharged. Full and ample instructions will be found in the first pages of that book, for filling up all the various entries; it is unnecessary, therefore, to give them here in detail, beyond stating that they relate to the name of the ship and official number; name of the master; the voyage; a list of the crew, stating the conduct, character, and qualification of each man; a list of the passengers; an entry of all offences, convictions, punishment, fines, illness or injuries, medical treatment, deaths, births, and marriages, wages of seamen entering the Royal Navy, wages and sale

561

of the effects of any seaman who may die during the voyage, collisions, and the circumstances under which the same have occurred.

N.B.—Neglect to comply with the requirements specified entails a penalty, and ignorance is not held to be a justifiable plea for such negligence.

It may, however, be incidentally noticed that special attention must be given to make particular and correct *entries of wages and effects of deceased seamen;* and when a man commits an offence, no deduction from his wages on that account can be made unless there is an entry of the date, ship's position, and charge made against him ; the entry having been made, then read the charge to the man in the presence of the mate or a witness, stating in writing that you have so read it ; sign it, and let the mate sign as witness ; call upon the man for his defence, and if he make any, write it under the offence ; then sign again as before.

BLANK FORMS

OF THE

PRINCIPAL PROBLEMS

IN

NAUTICAL ASTRONOMY;

ACCOMPANIED WITH BRIEF EXPLANATORY REMARKS.

BLANK FORMS OF THE PRINCIPAL PROBLEMS
IN NAUTICAL ASTRONOMY.

Given Ship Date and Long. to find Greenwich Date.

	D.	H.	M.	S.	
M. T. at Ship	...	...	...	...	
Long. in Time		...	...	..	add if W., sub. if E.
M. T. at Green.	..	...	...	...	

Given Greenwich Date and Long. to find Ship Date.

	D.	H.	M.	S.	
Green. Date M. T.	...	...	...	...	
Long. in Time		...	...	...	sub. if W., add if E.
M. T. at Ship	...	...	...	...	

To convert Civil into Astronomical Time :—If the Time is P.M., the Civil and Astronomical Dates are alike ; but if the Civil Time is A.M., add 12 to the hours and diminish the day by 1.

To correct Sun's Declination :—Diff. in 1h. × No. of hours, &c. since that noon.

To correct Equation of Time:—Diff. in 1h. × No. of hours, &c. since that noon.

To correct Chronometer:—Daily rate × No. of days = Accumulated rate.

For Polar Distance:—If Lat. and Decl. are of same name, sub. Decl. from 90° ; if of different names add 90° to the Decl.

N. A. in the following pages stands for Nautical Almanac.

566

To correct Sun's Obs. Alt., &c.

	°	′	″
Sun's Obs. Alt. ...	...	...	
Ind. Er + or	—	...	...

... ...

| (Eye) Dip | — | ... | ... |

... ...

| Ref. in Alt. | — | ... | ... |

... ...

| Semid (N.A.) + | ... | ... |
| Par. in Alt. | + | ... |

Sun's True Alt. ... ... (N. or S.)

sub. from   90

for Zen. Dist. ... ... (S. or N.)

To correct Star's Obs. Alt., &c.

	°	′	″
*Obs. Alt. ...	...	...	
Ind. Er. + or —	...	...

... ...

| Dip. — | ... | ... |

... ...

| Ref. — | . | ... |

.s True Alt. ... ... (S. or N.)

sub. from 90

for Zen. Dist. ... ... (N. or S.)

Zen. Dist. is always of the same name as observer; N. when he is N. of the object; S. when he is S. of the object.

.

Latitude from a Meridian Altitude of the Sun above the Pole.

	D	H	M	S
App. T. at Ship ..	o	o	o	
Long. in T.		...	...	...
Gr. Date, App. T. ..	...	...	...

	°	′	″
Sun's Decl. (N.A. p I.) ...	...	...	
Cor. for Gr. Date		...	...
Corrected Decl.	...	...	...

```
                                    o    ,    ,,
Obs.  Alt.  Sun's l. l.    ...  ...  ...
            Dip            —    ...  ...
                           _____
                           ...  ...  ...
     Ref.  in Alt.         —    ...  ...
                           _____
                           ...  ...  ...
     Semid.  (N.A.)        +    ...  ...
     Par.  in Alt.              +    ...
                           _____
     True Alt.  Sun's cent.  ...  ...  ...  (N. or S.)
                           90
                           _____
     Sun's  Zen.  Dist.    ...  ...  ...  (S. or N.)  ⎧ add if both
            Decl.          ...  ...  ...  (S. or N.)  ⎪ are N., or
                           _____               ⎨ both    S.,
     Latitude (see below)  ...  ...  ...              ⎪ otherwise
                           _____               ⎪ take  their
                                                     ⎩ difference.
```

The Lat. is S. if both Zen. Dist. and Decl. are S., or N. if both are N. ; but of the same name as the greater when one is N., and the other S. ; also if Decl. is o Zen. Dist. is the Lat.

Lat. from Mer. Alt. of Moon above the Pole. •

```
                              H    M                                    o    ,    ,,
Mer. pass. at Gr. (N.A.) ...  ...      Moon's Decl. (N.A.) ... ... ...
    Cor. for Long.            ...      Cor. for min. of Gr. D.    ...  ...
                           _____                              _____
Mer. pass. at Ship       ...  ...          Cor. Decl.    ...  ...  ...
    Long. in Time        ...  ...                               _____
    Gr. Date, M. T.      ...  ...
                           _____
                           ,    ,,                                   ,    ,,
Moon's semid. (N.A.)   ...  ...        Moon's Hor. Par. (N.A.) ...  ...
Cor.     + or –             ...            Cor.  + or –             ...
                           _____                             _____
                           ...  ...                            ...   ...
Augmentation            +   ...          Red. for Lat.         —    ...
                           _____                             _____
Moon's cor. Semid.      ...  ...        Moon's red. Hor. Par.  ...  ...
                           _____                             _____
```

	°	'	"
Moon's obs. Alt.	...	...	...
Dip.	− ...	...	

	..	...	...
Aug. Semid.		...	...	+ for l.l., − for u. L

	...	...	..
Par. in Alt. − Ref. = Cor. of Alt.	+	...	...
True Alt., Moon's cent.	...	...	... (N. or S.)
	90	...	...
Zen. Dist.	...	...	... (S. or N.)
Decl.	...	...	... (S. or N.)
Latitude	...	...	...

add if both are N., or both S., otherwise take their difference.

To name the Lat., *see* Lat. by Sun. p. 568.

Lat. by Mer. Alt. of Star above Pole.

	°	'	"
Star's obs. Alt.	...	...	...
Dip	− ...	...	
	...	...	...
Ref.	− ...	...	
Star's true Alt.	...	...	... (N. or S.)
	90		
Zen. Dist.	...	...	... S. or N.
Star's Decl. (N.A.)	...	...	... S. or N.
Lat.	...	...	... (*see* Lat. by Sun p. 568.)

Lat. by Sun near the Meridian.

	D.	H.	M.	S.
Time by Watch .	...	..	...	
Error + or —			...	...
Approx. T. at Ship .	...	...	...	
Diff. Long. made			...	... (+if E.,—if W.)
App. T. at Ship .	...	...	...	
Long. in time	...	...	...	
Gr. Date, App. T .	...	...	...	

	°	'	"
Sun's Decl. (N. A. p. 1)	...	...	...
Cor. for Gr. Date		...	...
Cor. Decl.	...	...	...

From the observed Alt. obtain the True Alt. as before.

	M	s		Constant Log. 0·301030	
Time from Noon	...	...		Log Hour ∠ *	......
	°	′			
Lat. by D. R.	...	...		cos.	......
Decl.	...	...		cos.	......
† Mer. Zen. Dist.	...	...		cosec.	......
		′	″		
Reduction	+ ...	...		sin.	......
True Alt.	...	...	...		
Red. Alt.	...	...	...	(N. or S.)	
	90				
Mer. Zen. Dist.	...	...	...	(S. or N.)	
Decl.	...	...	...	(S. or N.)	
Lat.	...	...	...	(*see* Mer. Alt., p. 568.)	

* Or, Log. sine square of Raper.

† For Mer. Zen. Dist., take sum of Lat. and Decl. when they have different names ; if they have the same name take their difference.

Longitude by Chronometer from Alt. of Sun.

	D.	H.	M.	S.	
Time by Chron.	...	...	...	...	
Orig. Error + or −			...	...	add if slow, sub. if fast.
	...	...	...	...	
Rate × elapsed time			...	...	add if losing, sub. if gaining.
Green. Date, M.T.	...	...	...	...	

	°	′	″				M	S
Sun's Decl. (N.A. p. II.)	...	...	...	Equat. T. (N.A. p. II.)				
Cor. for Gr. Date	...	...		Cor. for Gr. Date			...	
Corrected Decl.	...	...	...	Correct Eq. T.			—	...
Polar Dist.	...	...	...					

	°	′	″
Sun's obs. Alt. L.L.	...	...	...
Dip.	—	...	...
	...	...	...
Ref. in Alt.	—	...	...
	...	...	...
Semid.	+	...	...
Par. in Alt.		+	...
True Alt.	...	...	...
Lat.	...	...	...
Pol. Dist.	...	...	...
Sum.	...	...	...
½ sum.	...	...	...
½ sum—Alt.	...	...	...

sec.   . ...
cosec.   . ...

cos.   . ...

sin.   . ...

	D.	H.	M.	S.
† If P.M., App. T. Ship	...	...	...	...
Eq. T.			...	...
M. T. at Ship	...	...	...	...
Gr. Date, M. T.	...	...	...	...

log. of hour ∠ . ...*

+ or − (see N. A. p. I.)

} diff.

Long. in T.   ... ... = ... W. if Gr. T.

is best; but E.

if Gr. T. is least.

* Or, Log. sine square of Raper.

† If A.M. obs., sub. the hour angle from 24 h. before you apply the Equation of Time.

571

	D	H	M	S		H	M	S
Time by Chron.	.	...	...	...	Star's R.A. (N.A.)	...	...	...

						°	′	″
Orig. Er. (+ or −)			...	...	Star's Decl.	...	...	...
	.	...	...	...		90		
Accum. rate (+ or −)			...	...	· Pol. Dist.	...	...	..
Gr. Date, M.T.	.	...	...	...				

	H.	M.	S.		°	′	″
Sidereal Time } (N.A. p. II) }	...	...	...	Stars' obs. Alt.	...	...	...
Acceleration } for Gr. Date }		...	...	Dip. — ...	...	...	
Mn. Sun's R.A.	...	...	...		...	...	...

				Ref. — ...		...	...
Star's True Alt.	...	...	...				
Lat.	...	...	...	sec.	.	...	
Pol. Dist.	...	...	...	cosec .		...	..
sum.	...	...	...				
⅓ sum.	...	...	...	cos.	.	...	
½ sum − Alt.	...	...	...	sin.	.	...	

* Star's W. mer. dist	...	...	..	Log. of hour ∠	.	...	
Star's R.A.	...	...	...	(add)			
R.A. of Mer.	...	...	...				
Mean Sun's R.A.	...	...	...	(sub. borrowing 24h. if necessary. .

Ship' Date, M.T. .	.	...	...	...	} diff.
Gr. Date, M.T.	.	...	...	...	

					°	′	″
Long. in Time	...	...	...	=	...	...	...

* If the star is E of the meridian, subtract its mer. dist. or hour angle from 24h. before adding its R.A.

	D	H	M	S				
App. T. at Ship .	...	...	...		Sun's decl. (N.A. p. I.)	...	...	...
Long. in time		...	...	...	Cor. for Gr. Date		...	...
Gr. Date, App. T.	...	...	...		Cor. decl.		...	...	...

	o	'	"		
Decl.	...	...	...	sine	. ...
Lat.	...	...	...	secant	. ...

} sum.

* True Amp. (E. or W.)   ...   .   (N. or S.) sine . ...

Mag. Amp.   ...   .

† Variation   ...   .   (E. or W.)

* Name the true amp. E when rising, W when setting, towards N. or S, according to Decl.

† If amplitudes are both N. or both S., take their diff.; if one is N. and the other S., take their sum for the variation; also, the variation is E. if true amp. is to right, but W. if to left of magnetic amplitude.

	D	H	M	S				
M.T. at Ship	...	...	...	...	Obs. Alt. Sun's l.l.	...	...	...
Long. in T.		...	...	...	Dip	—	...	...
Green. Date, M.T.	...	...	...	...		...	...	...
					Ref.	—	...	...

	o	'	"				
Decl. (N.A. p. II.)	...	...	...		...	...	...
Cor. for Gr. Date		...	...	Semid.	+	...	...
Cor. Decl.	...	...	...	Par.	+	...	
Pol. Dist.	...	...	...	Tr. Alt.	...	...	...

573

	°	′	″		
Tr. Alt.	...	...	...	sec.	....
Lat.	...	...	...	sec.	....
Pol. Dist.	...	...	...		
Sum	...	...	...		
½ Sum.	...	...	...	cos.	....
½ Sum ⌐ Pol. Dist.	...	...	...	cos.	....
				2).........	

	°	′	″	
½ Azimuth	...	...	...	sin. . ...

			2	If Tr. Az. and Obs. Az. are
Tr. Azimuth	...	...	...	both N. or both S., their
Obs. Azimuth	...	...	...	Diff. is the Var.; if one
				is E. and the other W.,
Variation	...	...	...	take their sum.

N.B.—The Tr. Az. is reckoned from N. in S. Lat., and from S. in N. Lat; towards E. when Alt. is increasing, but towards W. when Alt. is decreasing. Also, when one Az. is N. and the other S., subtract Tr. Az. from 180°.

The Var. is E. if Tr. Az. is to the right, but W. if Tr. Az. is to the left of magnetic Az.

This form is equally applicable to a Star Azimuth.

Lat. by Mer. Alt. below the Pole.

To true Alt. of object's centre add its Polar Dist.

N.B. When *above* the pole, the object rises until on the meridian; when *below* the pole, it descends until on the meridian.

Form to compute Lat. by Double Alt.

½ Elaps. T.   sin. . ...

Pol. Dist.   sin. . ...   cos. . ...
                                 ────────────

Arc. A.   sin. . ...   sec. . ...   cosec. . ...
           ────────────   ────────────

             ° ′ ″

Arc. B.   ... ...   cos. . ...
                          ────────────

Arc. A.   sec. . ...
½ sum. Alt.   sin. . ...   cos. . ...
½ diff. Alts.   cos. . ...   sin. . ...
                                         ────────────

Arc. C.   sec. . ...   sin. . ...
                     ────────────

Arc. D.   ... ...   cos. . ...

Arc. E.   ... ...   cos. . ...
Arc. C.   cos. . ...
                          ────────────

Approx. Lat.   ... ...   sin. . ...
                ────────────   ────────────

Arc. B. is of the same affection as the Pol. Dist.

Take arc D from arc B, for arc E., except in Tropical Latitudes, where if Lat. and Decl. are of same name, and Lat. less than Decl., take sum of B and D. for E.

─────────────

To compute an Altitude.

           ° ′ ″

Object's Hor. Ang.   ... ...   cos. . ...

Lat.   ... ...   cot. . ... sin. . ...
                       ────────────

Arc. I   ... ...   tan. . ... sec. . ...
Pol. Dist.   ... ...
              ────────────

*Arc. II.   ... ...   cos. . ...
                                         ────────────

True Alt.   ... ...   sin. . ...
                                         ────────────

*Arc. II. is the diff. of Arc. I. and Pol. Dist., unless the object's hour angle is more than 6h. or 90°, in which case take their sum.

575

	°	′	″		
Sun (or Star's) App. Alt.	...	...	...	sec.	....
Moon's App. Alt.	...	...	...	sec.	....
App. Dist.	...	...	...		
Sum.	...	...	...		
½ sum.	...	...	...	cos.	....
App. Dist. ⌢ ½ sum = Diff.	...	...	...	cos.	....
Sun (or Star's) True Alt.	...	...	...	cos.	....
Moon's True Alt.	...	...	...	cos.	....
Sum of True Alts.	...	...	...	2)	....
½ **sum** of True Alts. = Arc. I	...	...	...		
Arc. II	...	...	...	sin.	....
(Arcs. I and II) Sum.	...	...	...	cos.	.........}
,, Diff.	...	...	...	cos.	.........} sum.
				2)	... .

	°	′	″		
½ True Dist.	...	...	..	sin.	. ...
			2		
True Dist.	...	...	...		

576

INDEX.

2 P

TABLES.

GRIFFIN & CO., PRINTERS, 2, THE HARD, PORTSEA.

MILITARY SCIENCE AND HISTORY.

OUR IRON-CLAD SHIPS; their QUALITIES PERFORMANCES, and COST, with Chapters on TURRET SHIPS, IRON-CLAD RAMS, &c. By E. J. REED, C.B. With Illustrations. 8vo. 12s.

SHIP-BUILDING IN IRON AND STEEL; a PRACTICAL TREATISE giving full details of CONSTRUCTION, PROCESSES OF MANUFACTURE and BUILDING ARRANGEMENTS; with Results and Experiments on Iron and Steel, and on the Strength and Water-tightness of riveted work. By E. J. REED, C.B. With Plans and Woodcuts. 8vo. 30s.

A TREATISE ON NAVAL GUNNERY. By GEN. SIR HOWARD DOUGLAS, Bart. *Fifth Edition.* Plates. 8vo. 21s.

THE PRINCIPLES AND CONSTRUCTION OF MILITARY BRIDGES AND THE PASSAGE OF RIVERS IN MILITARY OPERATIONS. By SIR HOWARD DOUGLAS. *Third Edition.* Plates. 8vo. 21s.

THE ROYAL ENGINEER AND THE ROYAL ESTABLISHMENTS AT WOOLWICH AND CHATHAM. By SIR F. B. HEAD, Bart. With Illustrations. 8vo. 12s.

THE METALLURGY OF LEAD, including DESILVERIZATION and CUPELLATION. By JOHN PERCY, M.D., F.R.S. With Illustrations. 8vo.

IRON AND STEEL; their Elasticity, Extensibility, and Tensile Strength. By KNUT STYFFE. Translated from the Swedish by C. SANDBERG. With Preface by Dr. PERCY. With Plates. 8vo. 12s.

MODERN WARFARE AS INFLUENCED BY MODERN ARTILLERY. By COL. P. L. MACDOUGALL. With Plans. Post 8vo. 10s. 6d.

A NAVAL AND MILITARY DICTIONARY OF TECHNICAL TERMS—FRENCH AND ENGLISH,—ENGLISH AND FRENCH. By COL. BURN, R.A. *Fourth Edition.* Crown 8vo. 15s.

INSTRUCTIONS IN PRACTICAL SURVEYING, TOPOGRAPHICAL PLAN DRAWING, and on sketching ground without instruments. By G. D. BURR. *Fourth Edition.* With Woodcuts. Post 8vo. 6s.

JOHN MURRAY, Albemarle Street.

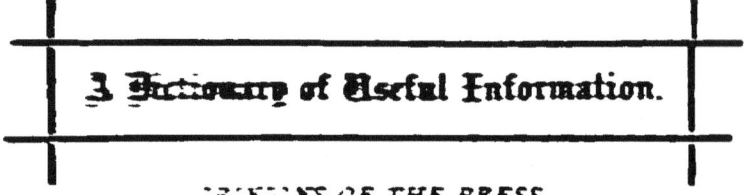

WORKS PUBLISHED BY JAMES IMRAY AND SON,

MINORIES AND TOWER HILL, LONDON, E.

A SELF-INSTRUCTOR IN NAVIGATION AND NAUTICAL ASTRONOMY for the Local Marine Board Examinations, and for use at Sea. Second Edition, enlarged and improved—with numerous Woodcuts, Chart, and Coloured Diagrams. By W. H. ROSSER. Price 7s. 6d.

NAUTICAL, LOGARITHMIC, AND ASTRONOMICAL TABLES, to accompany the "SELF INSTRUCTOR in NAVIGATION, &c." For use at Sea, and for Navigation Schools. Third Edition. By W. H. ROSSER. Price 4s.

THE STARS.—HOW TO KNOW THEM, AND HOW TO USE THEM; with numerous Problems, Diagrams, and four large Maps of the Stars. By W. H. ROSSER. Price 7s. 6d.

THE LIGHTS AND TIDES OF THE WORLD, WITH NOTICES ON THE VARIATION, DIP, &c., OF THE MAGNETIC NEEDLE; Charts, and numerous Illustrations. By James F. IMRAY, F.R.G.S., and W. H. ROSSER. Price 6s.

STEAM AND THE STEAM ENGINE, FOR CAPTAINS AND MATES; with Illustrations. By S. M. SAXBY, R.N. Price 1s.

THE MERCANTILE MARINE MAGAZINE AND RECORD OF THE ROYAL NAVAL RESERVE. This is an important work for the Officers of both the Royal Navy and Merchant Service, as by its aid they can Correct their Charts and Sailing Directions. *Published Monthly.* Price 6d. Vols. I to XVII, bound in cloth, 7s. 6d. each. Back numbers may also be obtained.

OUTLINE CHART OF THE WORLD, for marking off a Ship' Track, and showing the Variation of the Compass. Price 12s.

NOTES on the NORTH ATLANTIC, 1s. 6d. On the SOUTH ATLANTIC, 1s. On the INDIAN OCEAN and CHINA SEA, 2s. 6d On the PACIFIC OCEAN. By W. H. ROSSER. Price 3s. 6d.

These Notes are a Synopsis of the Physical Geography and Meteorology of the Oceans to which they relate; describing the Winds, Weather, Currents, &c., together with general remarks on Making Passages.

FOREIGN EXCHANGES for all parts of the World. By W. H. ROSSER. Price 5s.

Just Published.—Price 5s. 6d.

RAVERSE TABLE;

WITH SIMPLE AND BRIEF METHOD OF

)RRECTING COMPASS COURSES.

By R. A. EDWIN, COMMANDER, R.N.

present method of Correcting Compass Courses.by considering whether the
se to be Corrected is to the Right or Left of either North or South, involves
necessity of applying the *same* correction different ways to points and degrees,
e same half of the Compass; thus, a correction of, say 10° East, is *Additive*
N. & E. Course; but it is *Subtractive* from a S. & E. one, and though sub-
ive to the S. & E., it is *Additive* to the S. & W.; and again is *Subtractive* to
rses between N. & W.

By using the degrees of the Compass from 0° to 360°, this intricacy is avoided,
no matter what Course may be steered, the simple ADDITION or SUBTRACTION
ie requisite corrections is all that is necessary to find the True Course.

By this method of Correcting Compass Courses it is *unnecessary* to consider
ther the Course to be Corrected is to the Right or Left of either North or South.

The Correction of any number of Courses will be performed with greater
racy, and in less time than by the present method.

OPINIONS OF THE PRESS.

From the Shipping Gazette, Jan. 14. 1871.—"Lieut. R. A. Edwin, R.N., while serving on board
Majesty's ship *Falcon*, devised, and successfully used, a set of rules for Correcting Compass
ses. These he has published under the title of "Traverse Table." Following an explanation
use of the rules, 300 tables are appended to assist Navigators. Instead of following the
ent plan of correcting compasses by considering whether the course to be corrected is to the
it or Left of either North or South, the author shows how to avoid these complications by
g the degrees of the compass from 0 deg. to 360 deg. By this method, no matter what course
be steered, the mere addition or subtraction of the requisite corrections is all that is needed
id the true course. Each page of the Traverse Table contains five miles, and every opening
s quarter compass points. The Navigator has but to turn to the book to find the number of
'ees corresponding with any course and distance. The author's system is familiarly illustrated
few extracts of daily work from his log of the *Falcon*. The volume will, no doubt, be appre-
:d by those who are interested in working a ship's true course."

From the Nautical Magazine, March, 1871.—"To those who require to make use of a
verse Table we heartily commend Lieut. Edwin's painstaking compilation of calculations.
endless columns of figures represent a great deal of work, and the apparent correctness and
ibility of the calculations are really worthy of the confidence of nautical men."

PORTSMOUTH: GRIFFIN & Co., 2, THE HARD.
(PUBLISHERS TO H. R. H. THE DUKE OF EDINBURGH.)
LONDON:

SIMPKIN, MARSHALL & Co.; E. & F. N. SPON, CHARING CROSS;
IMRAY & SON, MINORIES; PHILIP & SON, LIVEPOOL.

1871.

FOURTH EDITION, IN I VOL., 8vo.,

With 330 Illustrations and 4 pages of Colored Flags, Signals &c., handsomely bound in cloth, price 21s.,

SEAMANSHIP.

BY CAPT. G. S. NARES, R.N.,

Late of H.M. Training Ships, "Boscawen" and "Britannia."

THIS work, which is Illustrated by 330 highly finished and carefully executed wood Engravings, is the most complete book ever published on the subject, and has been written with a view to supply the great want in the Royal Navy and Mercantile Marine, of a thoroughly valuable and authentic book of information on all points of Practical Seamanship.

PRINCIPAL CONTENTS.

Names of the principal parts of a Ship—Masts, Sails Yards, &c.,—Knots and Splices—Fittings of Standing Rigging—Rigging of Masts—Yards and Bowsprit—Fittings of Tackles—Setting up Rigging—Tanks, Ballast, and Provisions—Rule of Road and Vessels Lights—Sea Terms—Managing Sails—Boat Sailing—Stowage of Anchors and Cables—To Unmoor and Proceed to Sea—Mechanical Powers—Manœuvring—To Tack Ship—Trimming Sails—Making and Shortening Sail—Ropes and Spars carried away—Instructions on the Management of Boats in a Surf, &c., &c.

EXTRACT FROM PREFACE.—"Engines and machinery, liable to many accidents, may fail at any moment, and their is no greater fallacy than to suppose that ships can be navigated on long voyages without masts and sails, or safely commanded by officers who have not a sound knowledge of Seamanship."

PORTSEA:—GRIFFIN & CO.,

Booksellers & Publishers to Her Majesty and H.R.H. the Duke of Edinburgh.

LONDON:—LONGMANS, GREEN, & CO.

Second Edition—Price 3s. 6d.

THE MANUAL OF THE

HYDROMETER;

taining its History, Philosophy, Mode of Graduating Scale, Application to
:hnical and General Purposes : with Rules, Worked Examples, and Complete
)les. Chapters on the EFFECTS OF SURFACE CONDENSERS ; the Cause of
YDATION AND DEPOSITIONS IN MARINE BOILERS, its Prevention and Cure ;
PRIMING ; MANAGEMENT OF BOILERS AND SUPERHEATERS.

y LIONEL SWIFT, Inspector of Machinery Afloat, Royal Navy.

OPINIONS OF THE PRESS.

From the Shipping and Mercantile Gazette.—"The second edition of the
.all volume on the Hydrometer, or Salinometer, by Mr. Lionel Swift, R.N.,
spector of Steam Machinery, has just been published. Although called a
Manual of the Hydrometer," it gives a practical history of the instrument, and
e mode of graduating scales, with rules and examples, essays on surface con-
·vsers, the cause of oxydation and the depositions in marine boilers and their
evention and cure, and other information of a kindred character. The author
ices the introduction of the hydrometer to its original inventor, Hypatia, the
ughter of Theon, a mathematician, of Alexandria. From its ancient form he
ices it down to the patents of the present day, and, having described the
rdrometers now in use, he enters fully into the specific gravities of sea-water,
id shows what its component parts are formed of. Tables for finding the amount
· brine are appended. The causes and prevention of boiler priming and oxyda-
n and the management of boilers and superheaters, will be found of considerable
terest to Engineers and all those who are interested in the safe and economical
orking of steam engines."

From the Army and Navy Gazette.—"To this, the second edition of this
ractically useful work, the author has added some additional chapters in reference
the high importance and economy of surface condensers, the value of scum
)llectors, and the views of the *modus* of calcareous depositions in marine boilers.
'hese are subjects of very interesting inquiry, and have been treated in the clear
nd simple manner which has been already manifested by Mr. Swift in his accurate
escription of the history and philosophy of the hydrometer."

PORTSMOUTH : GRIFFIN & Co., 2, THE HARD.
(PUBLISHERS TO H. R. H. THE DUKE OF EDINBURGH.)
LONDON :
SIMPKIN, MARSHALL & Co.: E. & F. N. SPON, CHARING CROSS;
IMRAY & SON, MINORIES; PHILIP & SON, LIVERPOOL.
1871.

Lightning Source UK Ltd.
Milton Keynes UK
UKHW051554230421
382502UK00006B/1149

9 781248 076880